# McKINLEY STATION

## PEOPLE OF THE PIONEER PARK

McKINLEY PARK'S FIRST FAMILY : HARRY, LOUISE and EUGENE KARSTENS

# McKINLEY STATION

## PEOPLE OF THE PIONEER PARK

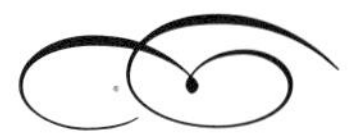

TOM WALKER

Library of Congress
Control Number 2009922788

ISBN 978-1-57510-145-3

FIRST PRINTING February 2009

PRINTED IN CANADA BY FRIESENS, ALTONA, MANITOBA

COVER ART BY HEATHER KARSTENS
www.heathersportraitshoppe.com

FRONTISPIECE BY MATT UNTERBERGER

COVER AND BOOK DESIGN BY ARROW GRAPHICS

PUBLISHED BY
Pictorial Histories Publishing Company, Inc.
713 South Third Street West, Missoula, Montana 59801
phone (406) 549-8488, fax (406) 728-9280
email phpc@montana.com
www.pictorialhistoriespublishing.com

# CONTENTS

I am especially indebted to Gene Karstens and Ken Karstens of the Karstens Library, for access to the writings and photos of Henry P. Karstens. Their help made this book come together with greater accuracy.

Nan Eagleson and Megan Holloway gave able research assistance. Ann Lowery transcribed some oral histories. Mike Brown, of the BLM, provided vital research data. Candy Waugaman offered the use of her photographic collection and suggestions for further enquiry. My long-time friend and author, Jim Rearden, detailed market hunting activities and made available to me his collection of taped interviews with Frank Glaser. Historians Terrence Cole, Ann Kain, and Frank Norris commented on parts of the manuscript. Karen Erickson volunteered her research skills. Dr Steven Rogers volunteered to do research at the National Archives in College Park, Maryland, and uncovered some interesting items. Lisa Frederic and John Hewitt reviewed a draft manuscript. Ginger Wadsworth, Hal Evarts' granddaughter, provided a copy of Evarts' biography. Bruce Baldwyn and Kathryn Davis provided information on Ynez Mexia. Archivist Polly Darnell of Vermont's Shelburne Museum, the repository of a Charles Sheldon collection, assisted me with photographs. Earl Plumb, Ralph Beistline, and Alice Morino graciously supplied photographs for the book. Stanton Patty and Michael Carey offered valuable research tips.

Bill Nancarrow, the park's first full-time naturalist, gave generously of his time. Both he and his wife, Ree, offered unflagging encouragement. Denali National Park's Cultural Resource Specialist, Jane Bryant, provided research assistance and photographs, and waded through the original rough draft offering numerous vital suggestions. I am grateful for her continuing support, friendship, and help. My daughter Mary Anne edited the final manuscript with a critical eye and attention to detail.

Any mistakes made in this work are entirely those of the author's.

# PROLOGUE

During two lengthy forays into what he called "The Wilderness of Denali" naturalist Charles Sheldon conceived the idea of creating a national park to protect the region's abundant wildlife, primarily the golden-horned, all-white Dall sheep.

In the winter of 1907–08, Sheldon witnessed the grisly work of market hunters, who were shooting hundreds of sheep and caribou to sell in Interior Alaska's meat-hungry, gold rush towns and camps. He knew that if they were not reined in, the commercial hunters would wipe out the herds living along the north slope of the Alaska Range. Later, Sheldon feared that the planned construction of the Alaska Railroad would spur unlimited market hunting. To America's fledgling conservationists, railroads were synonymous with wildlife destruction. Enter the railroad—gone the wildlife; gone the frontier.

Together with Belmore Browne, a climber and artist, Sheldon promoted the park idea and worked tirelessly to have it established. These two men were well-connected members of numerous East Coast sportsmen's clubs and conservation groups. Even with the backing of Theodore Roosevelt, one of Sheldon's friends and allies, it took years for the park proposal to reach the U.S. Congress. On February 24, 1917, President Woodrow Wilson signed into law an act establishing Mt. McKinley National Park.

For four long years, the park was a park in name only. In 1921, the Government finally appropriated funds to hire rangers to enforce regulations designed to halt the wildlife slaughter. The first ranger would meet a hostile reception. Alaskans of that era viewed conservation as a dangerous fad, and an impediment to the exploitation of the territory's natural resources. Many viewed the park as infringing on their "inalienable rights" to hunt, trap, and mine wherever, and whenever, they wanted. The residents of the Kantishna Mining District and the Riley Creek railroad boom camp were typical Alaskans, hardened by the northern wilderness and the challenges of the implacable weather. Some of them were World War I returnees, others veterans of the 1898 Klondike gold rush, and still others were desperados running from former lives and involvements. Many of them would not back down from a fight. Whoever took on the task of carving a national park out of this wilderness, needed courage and an indomitable force of will. Charles Sheldon knew just the man for the job.

This is the story of the park's first superintendent, Henry P. "Harry" Karstens, and his struggle to create Alaska's first national park.

# 1

# The First Superintendent

Henry P. "Harry" Karstens walked the railroad right of way to the south bluff of Riley Creek and looked down. Across the creek the broad clearing for the future railroad trestle stretched before him. On the far bluff he saw the roof of a large building under construction. Downstream to his right, on the north bank, he saw a cluster of cabins, tents, and several men and horses. Below and immediately to his left, on the south bank of the creek, was another jumble of cabins, tents, and shacks. He saw a team of horses pulling a wagon and heard the crack of a whip and the curses of teamsters. The breeze carried the shouts of men wrestling timbers and the ring of axes.

This was not the first pioneer camp Karstens had seen, he'd lived in other northern boom towns including Dawson City during that town's tumultuous heyday. He knew what life was like here. Sprinkled among the honest, hard-working citizens were gamblers, bootleggers, prostitutes and a few genuine desperados, all bent on grabbing as much of the workers' money as they could get. He knew that as the summer of 1921 progressed, the camp would expand as work gangs poured in for bridge construction and track laying. Although he had seen it all before, this time was different. Now he was a U.S. Government agent attempting to establish the rule of law in nearby Mt. McKinley National Park, a truly daunting challenge.

Hearing the crunch of gravel, Karstens turned slightly and acknowledged his traveling partner, Woodbury "Wood" Abbey, the General Land Office engineer assigned to survey the park's boundaries. Karstens waited while Abbey took in the scene. He then caught Abbey's eye and nodded. *No backing down now. Time for hard work. Time to meet the challenge.*

Nearly four long years had passed since an act of Congress had established Mt. McKinley National Park and in all that time not a dollar had bent spent on park staffing. The park was a park in name only. Illegal hunting and trapping continued within its boundaries. Commercial hunters provided railroad construction crews with game meat. Territorial game wardens, who had nominal responsibility for park protection, were few and for the most part ineffective against widespread poaching. Park advocates knew the dangers of unregulated hunting, knew that a ranger force was the park's number one priority. Getting the money to fund a force had taken critical time and effort.

The long funding delay was not mere negligence; the country was in upheaval. World War I, the 1920 influenza pandemic, the "Red Scare of 1919–20" with riots and bombings on the East Coast, had been more pressing concerns. Under-funded national parks in the states pushed Mt. McKinley National Park's needs to the back burner. In 1917 an initial appropriation to protect park wildlife, submitted by Interior Secretary Franklin D. Lane, was rejected. Attempts to secure funding for the park evaporated in the heated days of the Great War.

The Armistice and the general demobilization of American forces freed a vast labor pool. Returning veterans, coupled with increased government funding, helped accelerate construction of the Alaska Railroad then being built from Seward to Fairbanks. The influx of workers also reinvigorated regional mining, including a new mineral strike in the heart of the park at Copper Mountain.

In 1920, park advocates, alarmed by reports of a surge in poaching, again pushed for money to establish a ranger force to protect the park. Speaking before the U.S. House Appropriations Committee, Charles Sheldon, who had championed the park's establishment, testified that "since the park was created it has received no protection. Market hunting has continued, railroad construction has brought numerous people into the region, the game has been slaughtered recklessly." Other influential advocates, including Edward W. Nelson, head of the U.S. Biological Survey, termed the poaching situation "a looming wildlife crisis" and called for immediate funding. In response, Congress passed a bill that included funds to field a ranger force beginning July 1, the start of the 1921 fiscal year.[1]

The park's first superintendent would need courage and indomitable will. For Charles Sheldon, the choice was clear. From the outset he had lobbied for Harry Karstens. "I want Harry Karstens appointed the warden if he'll take it. He was there with me in 1906 and 1907–08 and later pulled Hudson Stuck to the top of McKinley. He is honest and will take pride in the work and knows the country better than others."[2]

Harry Karstens had superlative Alaska credentials. In 1897 he'd scaled the Chilkoot Pass and floated down the Yukon River to Dawson City, arriving just before freeze-up. He then explored for gold in both the Klondike and central Alaska. As a dog-sledding mail carrier he was honored far and wide for his toughness and daring. He accompanied Sheldon into the Toklat River country— those trips inspiring the park idea. Karstens had hauled freight, including fortunes in gold, via dogteam and river launch. In 1913, he led the first successful ascent of 20,320' Mt. McKinley and enjoyed a widespread reputation for honesty, fearlessness, and absolute competence.

Sheldon had made his choice early and had never wavered. "When Mr. Sheldon was north on his second trip," Karstens recalled, "he asked me if I would take the job of managing the Reserve if it got passed. Each year he would write advising me that it would surely be passed this year. In 1917, it was made a park but no appropriation was made, then again each year we were sure to get the money."[3]

Sheldon made it clear that patronage had nothing to do with his support for Karstens. "I have recommended you, not because you are my friend," he wrote, "but because I believe you are the best man for the job."[4]

Karstens was but one of several candidates for park superintendent. In December 27, 1918, Kantishna Mining District resident Steven Foster, a trapper and former game warden, wrote to Stephen T. Mather, Director of the fledgling National Park Service (NPS), and asked for appointment to "wardenship of the park." Sheldon dismissed as nonsense Foster's claims that as a territorial game warden he had "cleaned up the poachers" in the Minchumina area. At one time Foster and his partner, Nels Henderson, intended to extend their Lake Minchumina fur farm and trading post activities to include big game guiding. Foster boasted to Archdeacon Hudson Stuck that he was cutting a 13-foot-wide trail with well-equipped cabins to Mount Foraker and had plans for a great resort for wealthy Eastern sportsmen. But, according to Stuck, this "incessant talker, full of schemes and plans . . . did not have the contacts to pull it off." Both men also knew that Foster had illegally poisoned fur animals, hardly a good resume for park ranger.[5]

Despite what his critics thought, Foster appears to have been a zealous and successful game warden. Poaching was out of control in the Nenana area and south of it. An editorial in *The Nenana News* called for the appointment of a local resident to fill the position of game warden ". . . where he will be in easy reach of the hunting grounds south of town. It is a matter of common knowledge in Nenana that the slaughter of moose, caribou and sheep goes on

STEPHEN FOSTER COLLECTION, #69-92-568, ARCHIVES, UNIVERSITY OF ALASKA, FAIRBANKS

*Stephen Foster, a trapper and former Territorial game warden, applied for the position of Superintendent of Mt. McKinley National Park.*

continuously in the nearby hills in open defiance of the law. The men who are killing off the game at all seasons of the year, to feed packs of idle dogs are not in danger of molestation now."[6]

The editorial stated the blunt facts. Poaching was widespread, the park boundaries meaningless. One winter two trappers—Hanson and Parker—returned to Nenana with a "large bunch of furs" from exploits that took them "to the very base of Mt. McKinley." They returned to town because the fur animals were beginning to "thin out." The next winter "well known hunters" Tom Savage and August Waunch headed to the upper Toklat River for "Dall sheep and other game." In one early case, Warden R.S. McDonald hauled three hunters, Harry Lucke, Henry Knight, and Henry Burns before the Commissioner for killing too many Dall sheep. Lucke and Knight were fined $15 each and Burns $1, with the meat forfeited.[7]

With support from Nenana residents, Foster was appointed territorial game warden on March 1, 1918, and set right to work. A month after assuming his position he brought John Scharle to trial for buying and possessing illegal moose meat. Scharle was fined $1 and court costs. Next he brought in Arno Reinhold for shooting a moose out of season. Again the fine was $1 and costs.

Local judges and juries were often reluctant to convict and penalize game law violators. Undaunted, Foster tried again, arresting Paul Popovich for market hunting. This arrest resulted in a respectable $100 in fine and costs. In the winter of 1919, Foster made a 1388-mile dogsled journey to the Kuskokwim headwaters, via Lake Minchumina and the Kantishna. In the town of McGrath alone, Foster presented 14 poaching cases that resulted in convictions, an incredible success due to a sympathetic U.S. Commissioner. It was the tip of the iceberg. "Several cases of violation of the game laws were discovered in the Kantishna country, but owing to the fact that there was no commissioner in that district, the violators were not prosecuted. No less than 74 quarters of caribou and the carcasses of a dozen cow moose were found in one cache . . ."[8]

That same autumn miners returning from the Kantishna complained of a "scarcity of game, especially moose." They blamed over-hunting by Alaska Natives, handy scapegoats for the miners' own wanton shooting. That year Herman Kessler, trapping on the Toklat River, caught 17 wolverines, an astonishing catch. (A few detractors speculated on the possible use of poison.) He claimed that wolverines were responsible for the killing of large numbers of Dall sheep, "even worse than wolves."[9]

The next summer Foster took a gasoline launch up the Kantishna River for a surprise visit to the Kantishna and Minchumina camps. Again, as he had the previous winter, he found people hunting out of season. Later that summer, in Fairbanks, the burly Foster got into a brief, but losing, fistfight with Deputy U.S. Marshall James A. Hagan over testimony in an illegal fur shipment case. In mid-winter, Foster arrested Dick Kessler for shooting 21 caribou on the Toklat River, which netted a $100 fine.

Although Foster, during his almost three years as game warden, failed to eradicate poaching, he accomplished much more than either his predecessor or his replacement, James Burrows. Since his comings and goings were duly printed in *The Nenana News*, an alert to local hunters, Foster's success was genuine.

Some Alaskans promoted pioneer saloonkeeper William "Big Bill" McPhee, then 71, for park superintendent. McPhee told people that he was planning to hold the superintendent's "job for 35 years, after which he intends to retire . . ." A few influential miners held McPhee in high regard because he had grubstaked many of them, a few striking it rich. "Even Bill's worst enemy—if he has any—will not say that the old-timer . . . ever refused to help a sourdough in need," read one editorial. Everyone knew "Grizzly Bill" including Judge James A. Wickersham who considered him a friend and at least paid lip service to his appointment. The six-foot, 200-pound, McPhee arrived in Juneau on June 21, 1886, a dozen years ahead of the great Klondike stampede. He had grown up in Nova Scotia and claimed extensive experience in quartz mining in California and Nevada before coming to Alaska. In Juneau he built an "opera house," which foundered for lack of customers. Then he moved on to Fortymile, where he ran a saloon. In the spring of 1897, just as the Klondike stampede accelerated, McPhee and his partners opened the *Pioneer Saloon* in Dawson and soon made a fortune in liquor and gambling. In the winter of 1898–99, Dawson's Front Street went up in flames taking the *Pioneer* with it, burying the gold and mail stored behind the bar in charred rubble. McPhee was said to have rushed into the fire, not to save the gold, but to rescue his mounted moose head.[10]

He next stampeded to Nome, where he was elected mayor in 1901. He moved to Fairbanks after the 1903 strike and bought or controlled claims on the Chena River and Bonanza Creek. In the great Fairbanks fire of 1906, McPhee's *Washington Saloon* burned to the ground. Clarence Berry, a millionaire mine owner, who McPhee had grubstaked in the Yukon, paid for the rebuilding. In time, McPhee lost yet another saloon to fire. His bet in 1910 with another saloonkeeper sent four Glen Creek miners up Mt. McKinley in a summit bid. "Bill McPhee has mushed, toiled, prospected, mined, labored, and loafed through the long cold winters and the short hot summers, at all times looking to secure a homestake for himself," read an editorial on his twenty-eighth year in the North, "but never forgetful of the needs of his friends or the more unfortunate pioneers of the country."[11]

No doubt McPhee saw the park and its future tourist trade as a new type of gold mine. McPhee had always been one to sense a looming opportunity. In the 1920s, McPhee held several mining claims in the Kantishna and was often headed up river on the first spring steamer run.[12]

Harry Karstens responded to Charles Sheldon's enquiry about McPhee candidly. Using the Marxist-style rhetoric common to miners of the era, Karstens called McPhee "an exploiter of the people," and pointed to his saloons as proof of McPhee's nature. Despite all of McPhee's positive press there were many miners and mine laborers that remembered, perhaps bitterly, that McPhee had made his livelihood by "mining the miners," causing some of them to drink into insolvency.[13]

A more formidable candidate for park superintendent, backed by Territorial Governor Thomas Riggs, was W.B. Reaburn, brother of topographer D.L. Reaburn. Both brothers had extensive Alaskan experience, including D.L.'s trip with Alfred Hulse Brooks to the base of Mt. McKinley in 1902. From 1915 to 1919, D.L. served as superintendent of Mt. Rainier National Park and in 1920 assumed the same position at Grand Canyon. W.B. Reaburn came to Alaska

HENRY P. KARSTENS COLLECTION, #596, KARSTENS LIBRARY

*Renowned as a premier guide and dog musher, Harry Karstens also had been a partner in Whitely-Karstens, a firm dealing in mining transactions. Here in front of their Fairbanks office in 1910 are (l-r) unknown, Henry Wier, Frank Coombs, H.P. Parkins (in Wolverine coat,) Harry Karstens, Frank Whitely, and unknown.*

in 1906 as a member of Riggs' U.S. Alaska–Canada boundary survey. Beginning in 1914, he worked for the Alaska Engineering Commission (AEC) the agency then surveying potential railroad routes, and later charged with building the railroad. Once actual railroad construction began, he was named AEC's superintendent of river transportation overseeing the movement of tons of supplies to Nenana. By all accounts W.B. was a highly regarded member of the Nenana community. Karstens described Reaburn as a fine man and hoped that if he himself did not the get job that Reaburn would.

National Park Service Director Mather liked to appoint government employees, or military men, rather than locals, to the positions of park superintendent but the fear of nepotism charges ultimately doomed W.B. Reaburn's candidacy.

Despite the heady support of influential people, by 1920, Harry Karstens had grown ambivalent about becoming the first park warden. The pragmatic man knew well the difficulties he'd face. Newly established federal reserves and game laws infuriated Alaskans. Outsiders were seen as sentimental, know-nothing idealists meddling in territorial affairs. The first park representative would have his hands full establishing his presence and the rule of law. "I am not so anxious for that position," he wrote Charles Sheldon, "it's a waiting game and I am a poor politician."[14]

A letter that Karstens sent Sheldon in 1920 almost derailed his chance for the job. "Just received a letter from Fred Houselman [sic] the Swiss on little Moose Creek," Karstens wrote, " . . . he says, our happy hunting ground is gone, a lot of those engineers and assistants of the Alaska Railroad have been in there and just about cleaned up the game, or driven them out, if they don't get a warden in there soon there won't be any need of one, you see it is not very far from the railroad to the Toklat, and the Kantishna is booming and a lot of people going in their [sic]."[15]

Sheldon passed along Karstens comments to Mather. A government enquiry flashed back to Alaska, enraging railroad officials. The ill will from this one letter would cause Karstens much grief and cloud his early tenure as park superintendent. Within a few weeks "Chief Engineer Frederick Browne of the AEC sent for me, he said I was the complaintant [sic] against the engineers of the railroad." Browne would not accept Karstens protestations and demanded he write the Interior Department and Browne's boss, AEC Chairman Frederick Mears, denying the charges against the railroad. Karstens bristled, "I told him I would not do it until I had seen Houselman [sic]."[16]

Karstens soon learned that the U.S. Marshall's Office in Fairbanks was filing complaints about individuals citing "H. P. Karstens complantent [sic] regarding slaughtering game."[17]

" . . . then the next word comes from the Kantishna. John See [a respected veteran of the 1905 Kantishna stampede] came out and told me they had a big meeting in there and condemned me for putting the warden on them."[18]

"You can judge how I stood with the people of interior," Karstens later wrote Sheldon, "I don't mind personally, would fight them to a finish, but I had to make a living for the wife and youngster." (Eugene Henry Karstens, the couple's only child, was born in Nenana a few minutes after midnight on May 1, 1917, the first white male to be born there.)[19]

The AEC's Browne informed Karstens that the source of the trouble was the letter he'd written Sheldon. "Well, I got mine. The [Interior] Secretarie's [sic] office went after the AEC Chairman . . . and he went after . . . Browne . . . and he came after me."[20]

If miffed at Sheldon, Karstens barely let on. "It isn't what you did," he wrote Sheldon, "it is the way they used it in there." In retrospect, Karstens believed that Browne's complaint against him fizzled because "Browne's own son has been hunting in those hills," near and possibly in the new park.[21]

Although Karstens had told the truth, and had not been the complainant, he was viewed as a turncoat by many of his old acquaintances. Alaska then, as it remains, is one vast small town with almost nothing kept secret, where grudges were nursed, and cliques formed over minor differences.

As the year 1920 lurched to its end, Karstens and his wife Frieda Louise decided to leave Alaska for good. Alaska was changing rapidly and the long-promised park job appeared illusory. Both recognized that dogteam freighting was doomed. When completed the Alaska Railroad would rob freight and passengers from both mushers and riverboats. By one account as soon as the railroad commenced regular operations, freight rates would drop from $350 a ton to $25. Karstens had tried to keep pace with the times and modified his transportation services to meet demand. In 1917, he had inaugurated automobile service between Fairbanks and Nenana, then booming from railroad construction. The first trip was a complete disaster. He punctured a tire, fixed it, and continued on only to have the vehicle completely break down. He sent his three passengers and car back to Fairbanks on the train. Two weeks later he made the first successful round trip. The following spring he christened the *Princess May*, a "fast and commodious" launch, and announced an every-other-day schedule of runs to Nenana. In mid-summer he and Frank Burgess established an automobile transport service from Fairbanks to Valdez via the Richardson Highway. Karstens' intimate knowledge of the route paid off; he made the inaugural return trip in an unheard of *two days*. The new business initially proved lucrative enough that Karstens turned down several requests to guide wealthy hunters. By the end of 1920, however, several companies were competing with the Karstens–Burgess Autostage for passengers and the company's receipts plunged. " . . . believe me it was some hard time to do a little better than break even during last summer," he wrote Sheldon. He predicted that his stage line would soon end. "I think this will be my last summer on the trail . . . for every one will travel via the railroad after this coming summer." When Karstens saw the first planes taking off from Fairbanks bound for remote villages and camps he knew the old way of life was gone forever.[22]

Repercussions from the poaching letter partially motivated Karstens to leave Alaska. "You know how Alaskans feel regarding where and when they shall kill game and they resent any one interfering with their pleasure, I think different on the matter and they know it," Karstens wrote. "That is the principal reason why I came out this winter to see if I couldent [sic] locate some where else and start new."[23]

HENRY P. KARSTENS COLLECTION, #877, KARSTENS LIBRARY

*In the years immediately preceding his appointment as park superintendent, Harry Karstens operated automobile stage lines transporting passengers and freight throughout Interior Alaska. Here he is about to embark on a journey down the Richardson Highway.*

Louise and Eugene Karstens left Alaska in September 1920, with Harry staying on until December to take advantage of the end–of–season passenger and freight business. A short time after reuniting in San Diego, where Karstens' mother lived, Harry and Louise were shocked to learn that the park job might soon materialize. They'd left Alaska in the rigors of mid-winter and moved over 3,000 miles only to learn that, under Sheldon's prodding, the selection process for superintendent had moved forward. Arno B. Cammerer, Mather's assistant, soon interviewed Karstens in Lemon Grove, California. Other interviews in Los Angeles and San Francisco were almost pro forma. "Karstens has been strongly recommended to me by a number of men who are much interested in the park, and I have gone so far as to tentatively approve this selection," Mather wrote Governor Riggs.[24]

As his appointment neared, Karstens expressed his resolve to enforce the law despite the local opposition. He acknowledged the personal risks and the naiveté of some of his supporters. "I understand Dr. [Edward W.] Nelson to say there would be no politicks [sic] mixed up in this position," he wrote Sheldon, ". . . if I go in there as warden I don't want any axe hanging over my head for I will go through with it right to the letter of the law which won't make friends with the people there."[25]

Mather made his decision. "There is no question in my mind about Karstens being the man for the place," Mather wrote, "and I wish it might be possible for me to arrange for his immediate appointment." Federal money would not become available until the start of the fiscal year.[26]

Park supporters were pleased with Karstens' appointment. "This will be a fine thing to do and trust Karstens appointment will definitely settle the efforts to put an incompetent man in McKinley Park," Nelson wrote Sheldon. (Although a few locals, including trapper Alex Mitchell, had applied to Governor Riggs for appointment, the "incompetent" referred to was likely Bill McPhee.) [27]

After his appointment, Karstens immediately wrote Sheldon, then in Mexico. "I don't know how to thank you Sheldon for all you have done for me, but will do my best to live up to your expectations."[28]

"I . . . received a nice letter from Mr. Mather regarding my acceptance and wether [sic] I would go in and take charge of the Park April first," Karstens told Sheldon, "He said he thought he could get sufficient funds from friends of the park service to pay my salary and expenses from April first to July first the beginning of the fiscal year, I wrote him I would go in for that time for just expenses and no salary to help get the park established."[29]

On April 12, 1921, Harry Karstens was appointed Chief Ranger–at–large with an annual token salary of $10. Sheldon's friend Major W.C. Gotshall, a wealthy New Yorker, donated $200 to get Karstens into the field, Mather added his personal check of $100. As an interim step, park headquarters would be located in Nenana, 60 miles from the park. Karstens also was given charge of Glacier Bay and Katmai National Monuments, neither of which were funded or staffed.[30]

The actual establishment of the park on February 26, 1917 had gotten very little press in Alaska. The legislation set aside "a vast tract of land in Alaska which some day will be recognized as America's greatest scenic attraction," one paper reported. All anyone seemed to know was that 2,200–square miles had been set aside, the boundaries vague or misinterpreted by most people. Protection of park wildlife was supposed to be the responsibility of the small force of territorial game wardens. Local boosters saw Fairbanks, or Nenana, depending on their allegiances, as its main supply center. "Surely, the incomparable scenery, wildlife, and mines declared to be among the richest . . . in the world . . ." would bring a flood of tourists and dollars. [31]

Others were not so sanguine. Local trappers, miners, and prospectors were outraged. "With the formal withdrawal of the land for the Mt. McKinley National Park no one will be allowed to take land . . . or to kill any wild

HENRY P. KARSTENS COLLECTION, #667, KARSTENS LIBRARY

*Prior to his appointment as superintendent of Mt. McKinley National Park, Harry Karstens was living in California. En route north, he teamed up in Seattle with Woodbury Abbey who was assigned to survey the park boundaries. The Alaska Railroad was unfinished in 1921 and the men rode pack horses from the end of steel at Hurricane Gulch to McKinley Station.*

game on the reservation," raged one editorial. Some people believed that Lake Minchumina was included in the park, while in reality it was far outside its boundaries. But what inflamed passions most was the pervasive Alaskan antipathy for anything that blocked or prevented resource development. Alaskans believed that parks and reserves were the work of Eastern sportsmen and do-gooders uncaring of the Alaska way of life and only looking out for their own self-interests.[32]

In mid-March 1921, Kantishna pioneer Joe Dalton, returning from a trip Outside, broke the news that Karstens had been appointed superintendent. He also reported that the park boundaries would be surveyed and for the first time the complete park regulations distributed in Alaska.* The regulations were published locally in mid-August.[33]

Karstens had planned to leave for Alaska in early March but a maritime strike impeded northbound sailings. Karstens, with Wood Abbey and his

*One park rule read: "All refuse resulting from camping, should be burned or hidden where it will not be offensive to the eye. It is only a matter of a few minutes to gather your tin cans, paper, etc., and drop them into a nearby creek, where they will be washed away."

crew, finally left Seattle on May 17. Nine days later they landed in Seward and boarded the train to the boomtown of Anchorage. On June 1, they caught the northbound train. At the Hurricane Gulch bridge construction camp they unloaded the horses for the trip over the long rail gap that stretched to Healy on the north side of the Alaska Range. On June 6 the pack train reached Riley Creek but they did not linger. Two days later, in Healy, Karstens caught the train to Nenana.[34]

When he stepped down from the train in Nenana on June 8, little more than five months after leaving, he was immediately surrounded by friends and familiar faces. Word quickly spread that the "well known old-timer" was the new park ranger and that he would hire "sourdough Alaskans" to fill positions as they opened up. "Slaughtering of game would not be tolerated," Karstens announced in a long newspaper interview. He must have laughed loud and long when he heard that just two weeks earlier Bill McPhee had gone to the Kantishna where "he intends to camp close to McKinley National Park until he receives his appointment as boss of the government reservation."[35]

The arrival of Harry Karstens and Wood Abbey was heralded in *The Nenana News* by an unusually prescient editorial. "Of great importance to Interior Alaska is the arrival of Harry P. Karstens, newly-appointed superintendent of Mt. McKinley National Park, who has come to assume his duties; and Woodbury Abbey, who was sent from Washington to direct the . . . survey of the boundaries of the park. Their coming marks the beginning of a new epoch in the history of Interior Alaska, for they are here to blaze the trails for the thousands of tourists who are even now awaiting an invitation to visit . . . one of the world's greatest scenic wonders.

"In the meantime," the editorial continued, "Alaskans can help the work along by co-operating in every way possible with the park management—by observance of the park regulations, assistance in the preservation of game within the boundaries of the park, and in such other ways as will help speed the development . . . ."[36]

This positive show of much-needed support contained one false note. It gave the impression that Karstens and Abbey were a team. They were not. Each worked for a different Interior Department bureau and had completely different agendas. Wood Abbey's job was well defined —survey and mark the park boundaries. He had done such work countless times and had a trusted and experienced crew. Harry Karstens was alone and had only the $300 donation to work with. He had to select and develop a headquarters site and patrol a vast wilderness tract between three communities on the park's periphery—

Kantishna in the west, and the Riley Creek and Healy railroad camps in the east—an enormous task for even an experienced crew but a Herculean task for one man.

As a federal employee, Karstens was given the use of an office in the AEC office building in bustling Nenana, a place he had seen sprout up almost overnight. In 1916, the AEC's Northern Division established its headquarters at Nenana on the south bank of the Tanana River just upstream of its confluence with the Nenana River. Here, where the railroad would cross the broad, muddy river, a city developed on a town site surveyed over James Duke's 1901 trading post and homestead. Several buildings in the abandoned town of Chena were torn down and shipped to Nenana to be reassembled. The AEC installed telephone and water lines and built a power plant, huge warehouse, three-story office building, barn, commissary, nine mess halls, and sundry other buildings including a two-story hospital. The government soon auctioned off 349 lots. A livelier place in Alaska in the spring of 1921 would have been hard to find.[37]

Even though Karstens visited Nenana frequently that year, his AEC office got little, if any, use. Karstens' first priority was to purchase park supplies. Although he bought supplies from both the AEC commissary and Fairbanks merchants, *Coghill's Store* in Nenana became a major park supplier. Pioneer merchant William Coghill supplied the park with comestibles, hardwood and *babiche* for sleds and snowshoes, tons of dried salmon, and hardware.[38]

Karstens stowed his dunnage in his office, purchased supplies, and wired reports to Washington. He soon returned to Healy with a mountain of gear, horse feed and tack for himself and the survey party. He spent the next two weeks with the surveyors as they worked out the park's north boundary. This foray provided an excellent opportunity for him to learn the park line, patrol for poachers and locate nearby hunting and trapping camps. The survey crew was short of horses so Karstens covered much of the difficult terrain on foot, a severe limitation. He spoke with two trappers and to their dismay explained that the park trapping ban would now be enforced.

When he returned to Healy after two weeks in the bush with Abbey, Karstens heard that his old friend Patrick J. Lynch at Riley Creek had a horse for sale. Lynch was an experienced teamster and wrangler, said to be good to his horses. Karstens set out at once on the ten-mile hike south through the Nenana Canyon railroad construction zone.

Patrick J. Lynch, 62, a Pennsylvanian and veteran of the 1898 Klondike stampede, and other strikes, staked his homestead in 1920 on land straddling Riley Creek upstream from its confluence with Maurice (later Hines) Creek. He

HENRY P. KARSTENS COLLECTION, #E1011, KARSTENS LIBRARY

*At right, is Maurice Morino's original Roadhouse at Riley Creek as it looked in July 1921. Under construction at the upper left is Morino's new hotel on the edge of the railroad right-of-way.*

began construction of his roadhouse that November and applied for an 80-acre homestead on February 10, 1921. Although Maurice Morino already operated a roadhouse a short distance downstream, Lynch knew that business would boom with bridge construction. It was a common practice during the railroad construction years for entrepreneurs to establish roadhouses and businesses near construction camps. Bootleggers, "sharpies," and painted ladies operated among the many legal businesses. Altogether, three roadhouses operated on Riley Creek during the peak of trestle construction.

Lynch's Roadhouse consisted of a 24-horse barn, a warehouse, blacksmith shop, bunk house, "Ladies Cabin," and mess house. Lynch had spent lavishly on "fancy parlor furniture" and by mid-1921 his roadhouse was called "the palace of the trail." Since the middle of February, when the AEC's telegraph and telephone line reached Riley Creek from the coast, Lynch also boasted of "modern communications to all points." For almost a year Lynch did a roaring business with his facilities in constant use by the AEC.[39]

After a careful appraisal, Karstens bought Lynch's horse, "Old Pat", for $100, an exorbitant sum for the cash-strapped ranger. "Old Pat" was 30 years old but fit and very smart. He routinely threw his shoes and not even the AEC blacksmith could shoe him properly and not be called back within a few days. Karstens spent just one night at Riley Creek and left early the next morning for Healy.

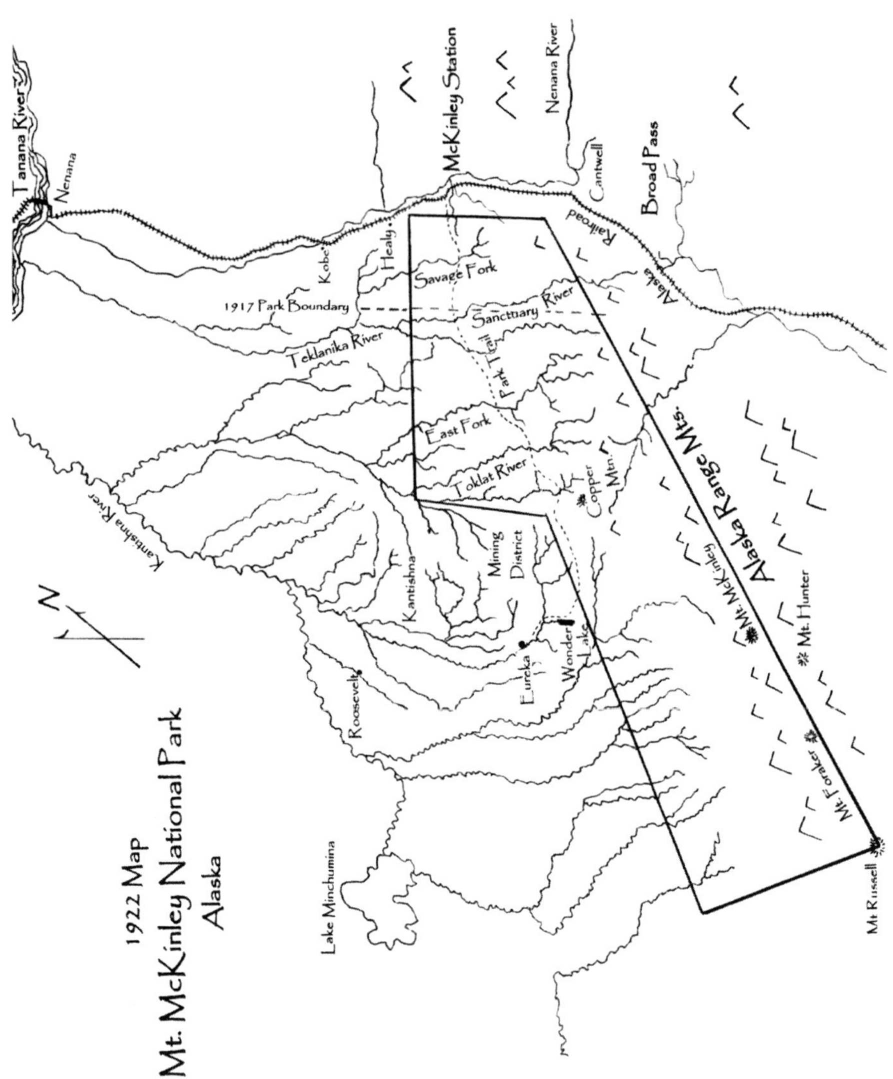
1922 Map
Mt. McKinley National Park
Alaska
N
Tanana River
Nenana
McKinley Station
Nenana River
Cantwell
Broad Pass
Alaska
Railroad
Kobe
Healy
Savage Fork
1917 Park Boundary
Sanctuary River
Teklanika River
Park Trail
East Fork
Toklat River
Copper Mtn.
Alaska Range Mts.
Kantishna River
Kantishna
Mining District
Mt. McKinley
Mt. Hunter
Wonder Lake
Eureka
Roosevelt
Mt. Foraker
Lake Minchumina
Mt Russell

On June 30, at 2 a.m., when the riverboat *Alaska* blew its whistle and docked at Nenana, Karstens was there to meet his family, and he soon had them settled into the *Cooney Hotel.* It had been a long trip for Louise and little Eugene. First they had driven from Lemon Grove, California, to Seattle, where they caught the steamship *S.S. Northwestern.* From Skagway, they caught the train to Whitehorse where they then boarded the sternwheeler bound for Nenana. The day after Karstens was reunited with his family, he officially became Mt. McKinley Park's first superintendent, with an inaugural budget of $8000.

Now that his family was finally reunited, and safely ensconced in familiar surroundings, Karstens was soon making reconnaissance trips to the park. At times, he apologized to Director Mather for being gone from his Nenana base camp for such long periods. Louise needed no such apology; she was used to fending for herself and dutifully supported her harried husband.

Karstens, working out of Healy, had seen enough by early July to select Riley Creek as his choice for the park's first headquarters site. The low pass at the head of Maurice Creek offered a natural and easy route west to the park boundary, then located near Sanctuary River. Karstens would have preferred to build on the flat bluff on the north side of the creek, near the site of the future depot, but Maurice Morino had homesteaded the parcel and was hard at work on a new hotel there. Consequently, Karstens reported to Mather that "I have selected a sunny and sheltered spot on Riley Creek for my Home Camp and Office near the railroad . . . it is sheltered from the winter storms and handy to water."[40]

After a long patrol through the park to the Kantishna and Copper Mountain mining camps, Karstens began clearing land on the northwest bank of Riley Creek directly across from Lynch's Roadhouse. In typical fashion he worked long, bone-wearying days clearing and burning brush and cutting logs for a cabin, with "Old Pat" dragging in the heaviest timbers. Karstens lived in a wall tent as the weather turned cold making the backbreaking labor even more arduous.

Harry Karstens was indefatigable, inured to long hours and the vagaries of working alone. Self-reliance and persistence in the face of adversity were the legacy of his pioneer trail experiences.

Marcus Tyler, the park's first ranger, came to work on November first, and by the end of the month, the two men had built a cabin of salvaged lumber. The small cabin had three rooms, a sod roof, slab floor, small windows and a wood stove.[41]

Camp Riley was booming with activity when Louise and Eugene Karstens arrived on December 7. "It was 15 below zero the day I arrived," Louise Karstens recalled. "Our cabin was not finished so we lived in a tent. It took a whole day to make the journey from Nenana to McKinley Park [via the train] . . . When we arrived at the park we were all loaded on a double ender with one horse on one end and a couple of men on the other end as we had to go down a steep hill. It was very dark and I guess the old horse must have stumbled over a stump for we all rolled off the sled and half way down the hill before we stopped . . . We all got on the double ender again and our next stop was Lynch's roadhouse where we all stayed overnight . . . We next moved into a tent. Mr. Karstens was busy working on our cabin and finally it was finished and we moved in. It was much warmer than the tent."[42]

Louise and Eugene lived in the "Ladies Cabin" at Lynch's Roadhouse for a few days before moving into the tent across the creek. Almost at once Harry took his four-year-old son to the partially-frozen creek and warned him of its substantial dangers and those posed by the neighboring construction camp, the horses and dogs, and the surrounding wilderness. His wife was only one of three married women known to be at Riley Creek then, and likely the only one with a small child. How this beautiful young woman viewed her situation is unknown but she must have experienced moments of trepidation. First, the move to California and then back again and now life in this hardscrabble work camp. Sometimes late at night, alone, listening to the comings and goings of unknown men and the occasional bursts of drunken laughter and shouts, she must have thought, *What has Harry gotten us into this time?* If Harry ever doubted the wisdom of bringing his family to this rough and tumble camp, he never let on.

By mid-December, Karstens had a home, office, and shelter for his livestock, but was again working alone. While lifting a log, Ranger Tyler had suffered a severe inguinal hernia which forced him to resign. Karstens soon began to assemble and train sled dogs for the tough park patrols to come. During the brief Christmas respite, Karstens must have paused to consider the booming camp across the creek and local community. Already federal marshals were making frequent visits to the camp searching for bootleggers, quelling disturbances, and making arrests. Likely, Karstens knew that he'd moved his family into the heart of a volatile, perhaps dangerous situation. With the New Year fast approaching, Karstens was finally in place to begin the tumultuous job of protecting the park.

# 2

# THE WILDERNESS RAILROAD

"THE PHARAOHS OF EGYPT, in building the pyramids, faced no greater difficulties and hardships than did the railroad construction crews working along the Nenana River canyon . . ." intoned AEC engineer E.J. Cronin.[1]

Engineer Cronin can be forgiven his hyperbole because he voiced the sentiments of many who worked on the Riley Creek—Healy River segment of the 470-mile railroad route. Sheer canyon walls funnel the silty Nenana River through a narrow gorge. Early prospectors and explorers declared the whitewater un-navigable and life-threatening and often forged an extensive eastward detour around it. Water volume rises dramatically after every rain with the pounding waters threatening to wash away the rock itself. Soggy hillsides loose thunderous rockslides that spill into the surging river. The explorers who located the rail route, viewed the river's standing waves and powerful hydraulics and then annotated their maps with words like "dangerous" and "hazardous." The surveyors who laid out the route clung at times to the cliffs with ropes. During railroad construction the gorge saw grisly death and dismemberment.

The human loss here was inevitable, a tragic part of the cost of building this vital rail link. For years the lack of dependable year-around transportation had hindered development of Interior Alaska's resources. The Alaska Railway Act of 1914, written by Alaska's non-voting Delegate James Wickersham, authorized President Woodrow Wilson to construct a rail line that would link Fairbanks to a tidewater port. In response Wilson established the Alaska Engineering Commission (AEC) and appointed W.C. Edes, as chair along with two members, Thomas Riggs, Jr., and Frederick Mears. Wilson gave the men instructions to locate a suitable route for the railroad. The AEC opened offices in Seattle on

May 22, 1914, and dispatched its first field crews four days later. Supply points were established and two routes, Cordova to Fairbanks, and Seward to Fairbanks, were investigated. Fieldwork was completed by mid-October, and on April 10, 1915, President Wilson selected the Seward to Fairbanks route. Here was the year-around corridor that would connect Interior with an ice-free port. The line would run close to the edge of Mt. McKinley National Park, creating a host of opportunities and conflicts,

Engineers chose Seward, Ship Creek (which became Anchorage), and Nenana as construction and supply centers. They split the project into two divisions, Northern and Southern, with labor gangs working from the north and the south, toward one another. Funding and manpower peaked prior to World War I, which diverted funds and drained the territorial labor force. Due to the war and an influenza epidemic, the railroad took longer than anticipated to complete and cost on average about $125,000 per mile. The ten-mile segment from Riley Creek to Healy cost $2.5 million, or twice the average. When finished, the cost of the railroad topped $60 million, almost seven times what the United States had paid Russia for Alaska in 1867.[2]

To carve out the rail bed along the Nenana gorge, the AEC set up several camps for its engineers and workers, including Camp Riley (Mile 348), Engineer Camp (Mile 350), and Kestly Camp (Mile 356). (All mileages are rail distances from Seward, Milepost 0.) The AEC's headquarters for construction of this segment was located at Camp Healy (Mile 358) on the west bank of the Nenana River near its confluence with the Healy River.

"A construction camp on rather a large scale is being built at . . . Mile 358 at the foot of the Nenana Canyon . . . Suitable quarters for construction men, engineers and supervisory forces are being built . . . Six station gangs have entered into contracts for moving the several heavy rock cuts along the line and more gangs will be put to work as soon as arrangements can be made to properly provide for them," reported the chief engineer.[3]

Like all Alaskan boom towns Camp Healy, also called Canyon City and later renamed Healy, seemed to sprout overnight and included AEC's general store, office buildings, two mess houses, bunkhouses, a temporary depot, stable, residences, and power plant. Several private businesses, including the Singleton Hotel and offices of the Healy River Coal Corporation were also located here. Businesses of a more disreputable nature flourished on the outskirts of the main camp. Kestly Camp at the canyon mouth, which was the site of an emergency hospital manned by a surgeon and his assistant, housed and fed engineers and rock workers. Engineer Camp supported cooks, blacksmiths, surveyors, teamsters, powder men, and rock men driving the three tunnels in the gorge. Workers lived in crowded, partitioned bunkhouses called "muzzleloaders."

On a flat bluff at Mile 352, called "Riverside," Clara Allred, a Tanana Valley pioneer and longtime Nenana business woman, operated a roadhouse. Allred bought James Trainor's small Canyon Roadhouse in January 1920. In April, she hired Charles Bergman to replace it with a larger one more able to meet demand. The Allred Roadhouse fare of fresh-baked bread, pies, and seasonal vegetables attracted both travelers and workers seeking home-cooked meals. A variety of hangers-on, including a group of market hunters, camped near her famed garden. In May, 1921, Allred, suffering from an illness that would kill her a few weeks later, sold out to Mr. and Mrs. Jack Barker, who changed the roadhouse name back to Canyon Roadhouse.

STEPHEN FOSTER COLLECTION, #69-92-622, ARCHIVES, UNIVERSITY OF ALASKA, FAIRBANKS

*During railroad construction, Clara Allred ran a roadhouse at "Riverside" (Mile 352) in the Nenana canyon, serving rock workers, teamsters, and market hunters.*

In addition to these main camps, smaller tent camps sprouted near various work sites. These six-to-eight man camps were often comprised of a single ethnic group, entirely due to the hiring preferences of the contractor. One camp consisted of Swedish émigrés, another of Russians. Many of these were "White Russians," loyal monarchists who had fought for the Tsar before fleeing the Bolsheviks' reign of terror. By one account the Russians hurled themselves at the dangerous rock work "like an assault on Lenin himself."[4]

Rock workers began setting up camp along the Nenana canyon in December 1918. Blasting posed significant danger and Interior newspapers carried warnings to mushers to use extreme caution when traversing the river ice in the construction zone. The work needed to carve out the rail bed and to excavate three tunnels from the sheer cliffs was inherently dangerous, made more so by the changing weather and incessant winds, which workers called "Healy Hurricanes."

Powder men used multiple shots of high explosives to carve out long sections of line. First, laborers excavated a "coyote hole" in the rock cliff and then packed it with a charge, often in excess of seven *tons* of both dynamite and black powder. The record shot contained *thirteen* tons. Some blasts far exceeded expectations; others fizzled. Much of the powder used during the war years was manufactured prior to 1913 and unreliable. Much of this "20% Giant dynamite" was "defective, worthless, and dangerous," lamented Chief Engineer Frederick D. Browne. "Premature detonations" were a much–feared possibility. After 1920, AEC's contractors successfully obtained quantities of TNT (trinitrololuol) an explosive developed during the war. "TNT is much safer to handle," Browne reported, "now most injuries with blasting is human error or carelessness."[5]

Browne's words proved prophetic. One summer day, AEC timekeeper Dick Healey, 20, crept into position to take a photograph of a pending blast. Three times, the powder men warned him back from the danger zone. Circumventing their advice, he picked out what he thought was a safe place from which to view the explosion. He wound his Kodak and waited. He heard the warning whistle and the cry *"Fire in the hole!"* A tremendous explosion jolted the cliff and hurtled tons of rock across the river and down the slope mangling and burying Healey.[6]

At least one other worker was blasted to bits and many others seriously wounded by flying rock. One worker catapulted from the cliffs into the rushing river 200 feet below and disappeared forever.

In late March 1920, the worldwide Spanish Influenza epidemic struck the

Interior, devastating Nenana. Fairbanks battled the illness for almost two years. The Cooney Hotel and the Southern Hotel were converted to hospitals. In April, the influenza struck the field camps bringing construction to a standstill. Remedies were rudimentary and often ineffective. One treatment consisted of laxative bromoquinine, Campbell's soup and bed rest. Some people used illegal moonshine as a preventative. Mortality rates zoomed upward, decimating whole Native villages. "Wooden boxes [rather than coffins] could not be built fast enough. Several bodies were put in a single box," one man recalled. In all 75, people died in Nenana, including 11 AEC employees, 8 contractors, 14 town residents, and 42 Alaska Natives. When the epidemic abated in the fall, construction accelerated with renewed emphasis on driving the tunnels. Because of the epidemic, the year ended with a 100-mile gap in the track reaching from Healy to the Susitna River crossing.[7]

Just as park advocates had feared, the arrival of the railroad construction workers exacted a terrible toll on park wildlife, the boundary just 18 miles west of the rail line. Market hunting had been a fact of northern life since the earliest gold rushes of the 1880s. Hunters shot moose, caribou, and sheep, and sold the meat in the boom towns. Demand far exceeded supply and some local animal populations were wiped out. Prior to railroad construction the major Interior communities — Tanana, Nenana, and Fairbanks — were a long, hard trip from the Mt. McKinley drainages. Even so, market hunters routinely made the dogteam journey ferrying tons of meat to eager buyers. Despite the Alaska Game Law of 1912, which outlawed market hunting, it continued for years afterward. Rail workers needed meat and without a local beef source, the AEC exploited a loophole in the law, contracting to supply their mess tents with game meat. For years the canyon where the track was being laid was called the "Sheep Canyon" because of the numerous Dall sheep living on its windswept cliffs and bluffs. Hunters quickly blasted these herds into oblivion.

The railroad's pioneer trail was completed in December 1918, when the clearing crews working from north and south linked up in Broad Pass at Summit Roadhouse. A month earlier, when the trailblazers reached Riley Creek, they intersected an old hunting trail that led west over an easy mountain pass to the park. As wildlife populations near the work camps were shot out, market hunters quickly exploited the old trail and pushed westward, establishing hunting camps on Jenny Creek, Savage River, and even inside the park boundary at Sanctuary River.

The Broad Pass Trail quickly saw heavy use. "A good, well-defined trail now leads from Lignite Creek to Talkeetna town [and the northernmost reach of track]," said a reporter, "and there is no danger of a traveler getting lost, as has happened before..." Some southbound travelers from Fairbanks chose the pioneer trail over the usual Richardson Highway route to the coast. By early 1920, improvements in the trail allowed four-horse teams towing heavy loads to pull right up to Maurice Morino's roadhouse, which he had re-named Park Gate Roadhouse. An ever-growing number of people now had access to this formerly isolated spot. Morino, like other area roadhouse operators, bought large quantities of game meat to serve his expanding clientele.[8]

Even as Harry Karstens shouldered his position as park superintendent, intense hunting had been going on in the Nenana canyon for over two years. The imminent completion of the railroad would not end the threat. The development of new towns made possible by the railroad, expanded the challenges he faced.

The last tunnel in the Nenana Canyon was completed in March 1921. With its completion, Colonel Mears, now AEC Chairman, expressed hope of closing the gap in the rail line by year's end. By late August, the canyon work was complete except for the bridge over Sheep Creek, Mile 352.5. In early November, with the bridge in, track-layers reached the north bluff of Riley Creek and stopped in front of Morino's newly-built Mt. McKinley Park Hotel.* [9]

In the south, following completion of the Hurricane Gulch Bridge on August 8, the "steel gang" headed north and reached the south bluff of Riley Creek at 3:00 pm on November 19. Now the only break in the tracks from Seward to Nenana was the bridge itself.

Preliminary work on the bridge had begun before freeze-up. By the time the track layers from the south had arrived, the north approach to the viaduct—a wooden trestle 400 feet long and 60 feet high—was complete. Just prior to Christmas Eve, 1921, workers finished the concrete piers and abutments for the support of the viaduct itself. By then, twenty-four rail cars loaded with 600 tons of steel were on their way north, accompanied by specialized workers and engineers.

Camp Riley boomed as heavy supplies and additional workers arrived by train. In less than a year the camp had swelled from an initial force of 14, mostly surveyors and teamsters, to over 120 workers. Every possible accommodation at Camp Riley was full; newly arrived workers shuttled back and forth to Lagoon, a work camp at Mile 344. Back in October, aware of the hazardous nature of the work ahead, the AEC had shifted surgeon T.O. Lake and his emergency

---

*Contractors *Anderson Bros. & Nerland* of Nenana raced to finish the interior in time for the grand opening meal to be served on Thanksgiving Day.

HENRY P. KARSTENS COLLECTION, #2203, KARSTENS LIBRARY

*In October 1921, the railroad construction camp on the south bank of Riley Creek began to expand in anticipation of trestle construction. At the far end of the clearing is Lynch's Roadhouse. The site chosen for park headquarters is on the far right of the wagon bridge.*

HENRY P. KARSTENS COLLECTION, #2204, KARSTENS LIBRARY

*By December 19, 1921, the work camp had developed to include a hospital, works shops, and living quarters. By the end of the month the clearing overflowed with tents, barns, and shacks of trestle workers. To the right of the bridge is the newly built park headquarters cabin.*

RILEY CREEK RESTAURANT

OPEN FOR BUSINESS DAY AND NIGHT

Meals at All Hours

BREAD and PASTRY JACK J. DONNELLY

THE NENANA DAILY NEWS, DECEMBER 13, 1921

For Sale----

Very Cheap

Riley Creek Restaurant

Inquire on Premises

Jack Donnelly

THE NENANA DAILY NEWS, FEBRUARY 22, 1922

*Five weeks after Jack Donnelly opened his restaurant at Riley Creek, he closed it for good. Construction of the Alaska Railroad was typical of Alaska's boom and bust cycle.*

WILLIAM N. BEACH PHOTOGRAPH, COURTESY OF BAYLES MAULDIN

*During railroad construction, Lynch's Roadhouse, the "palace of the trail," hosted travelers and construction workers. A year after completion of the Riley Creek trestle it became part of the McKinley Park headquarters complex*

hospital from Kestly Camp to Camp Riley. Within days the first causality arrived, a man with a crushed leg.[10]

The Riley Creek Bridge, manufactured in Pennsylvania by the Phoenix Bridge Company and shipped north via the Panama Canal, would be the only large steel structure erected by AEC crews; the American Bridge Company built the others. "The steel bridge over Riley Creek was technically of viaduct construction, consisting of seven steel towers decked with 30-foot and 60-foot steel plate girders," the engineers explained. When finished, the creek crossing would measure 900 feet in length.

The project had its share of less tragic mishaps. One afternoon, with the temperature well below zero, a tractor followed by a team of four-horses pulling a wagonload of gravel tried to cross the frozen creek. The tractor made the crossing safely, but the wagon broke through. The horses made it out but the wagon sank. "Sunday the AEC lost a perfectly good wagon and load of gravel," wrote a reporter. "It isn't lost exactly, they know where it is but eight feet of water cover it . . ."[11]

In the first week of January 1922, despite blizzards, sub-zero cold, and limited daylight hours, workers under the direction of bridge engineer F.H. Chapin installed the first steel bent. Less than a month later, a steam crane

ALASKA RAILROAD COLLECTION, T208, ANCHORAGE MUSEUM AT RASMUSON CENTER

*In early 1921, the gap in the railroad line extended over a hundred miles. Teamsters and dog mushers gathered from all over Alaska to support construction, hauling everything from passengers to small railroad engines. The work engine seen here, called a "Dinky," was sledded up the frozen Nenana River to Riley Creek.*

crossed the bridge from south to north. A few days later, a celebratory excursion train left Seward for Nenana, arriving on February 5, the first through train from the coast. The bunting-bedecked engine pulling passenger cars, a dining car, and the observation car *Nenana,* arrived only a half-hour late. Despite a -30°F wind chill, "about the biggest crowd ever gathered together in Nenana," greeted the train with blaring steam whistles and raucous cheers. After spring break-up, rail traffic moved on to Fairbanks via a ferry across the Tanana River. (It wasn't until 1923, that workers completed the 701-foot single span bridge over the Tanana, then the second longest in the United States.)[12]

In the autumn of 1921, as railroad construction in the Nenana canyon wound down and the focus shifted to Riley Creek, several businesses, legal and otherwise, opened near Morino's old roadhouse downstream of the trestle. Jack Donnelly, who previously had cooked in an AEC canyon camp, ran a small restaurant. Next door, Mary Thompson started a trading post and bunkhouse. Ely Bannich operated the *McKinley Park Cigar Store* and Al Garthorfner ran a barbershop. (In that era "cigar store" was sometimes a euphemism for a contact point for prostitution and the sale of liquor.) Other businesses, including a laundry, dog livery, and bakery, catered to the workers.

The demographics of the camp were typical of Alaska—an array of immigrants, war veterans, pioneer stampeders, prospectors looking for a grubstake, career laborers, and skilled craftsmen. Few, if any, were Alaska Natives and most were male, perhaps numbering 25 or more men for every one woman.

Illegal diversions, such as gambling, prostitution, and liquor sales, flourished openly. A territorial law passed in 1915, outlawed prostitution, and the 1917, "Bone Dry Law" banned all alcohol manufacture, distribution, and consumption, a much tougher law than the National Prohibition Act of 1919. The latter, known as the Volstead Act, banned liquor throughout the United States and ushered in the tumult of the "Roaring Twenties." In Alaska, federal authorities pursued bootleggers and moonshiners a full two years before Prohibition roiled the nation.

These "sin laws" generated countless scofflaws. With the expansion of Camp Riley, federal marshals and "liquor cops" descended in swift raids on makers and sellers of homebrew (homemade beer) and *hootch* whiskey. Other miscreants fell in the dragnets. In early January 1922, Deputy U.S. Marshals arrested Ora Bradley for "setting up and keeping a house of ill-fame for the purposes of prostitution and lewdness." A Nenana judge found Bradley guilty and fined her $50 plus costs, a total of $190. Unable to pay the full fine, Bradley was jailed in Fairbanks for one day per each dollar owed. Her Riley Creek competitors, undaunted by her arrest and incarceration, stayed busy.[13]

Search warrants executed for alcohol offenses often came up empty. The telegraph line was not secure and suspects were often warned of the imminent arrival of Deputy U.S. Marshall James A. Hagan in sufficient time to hide their liquor. A search warrant executed on Mary Thompson's business and home, which she shared with Jack Cronin, a cook, turned up empty. "No liquor found." A search of Michael Joseph Sullivan's cabins at Mile 345 and 346, based on a complaint of liquor sales, also turned up nothing. Hagan's search in Healy for Harry Lucke's *hootch* still drew a blank.[14]

In the earliest recorded liquor case for the area, Deputy Hagan arrested John Bernard for possession of one bottle of *hootch*. Bernard was found guilty and fined. Two years later the two men would again meet, but in deadly circumstances.[15]

In the spring of 1922, Deputy Hagan, and U.S. Marshall G.B. Stevens, raided Ely Bannich's cigar store and seized 34 bottles of homebrew. Bannich was hauled off in handcuffs.

Morino also caught Hagan's notice. On February 12, 1921, Hagan arrested Morino for possession and intent to sell homebrew. The case was heard in a Fairbanks courtroom overflowing with Morino's friends and supporters. A summary dismissal set off a raucous celebration. In June, Hagan, acting on a warrant, searched the Park Gate Roadhouse and outbuildings. "No liquor or manufacturing apparatus found." Seven months later Hagan, on a tip from

Harry Karstens, arrested Morino in his new hotel and seized six bottles of homebrew. The U.S. Commissioner also dismissed this case.[16]

Superintendent Karstens was not operating outside of his jurisdiction when he reported Morino. Under the Volstead Act, territorial game wardens and rangers were required to enforce the law. As a sworn law officer Karstens could not ignore Morino's violation committed in his presence. He did his duty but in so doing earned Morino's enmity.

In his first few months at Riley Creek, Karstens had left distillers pretty much alone; he had enough to do. Over time, as the ranger staff increased, federal authorities pressured him to track down large producers. No doubt the park's premier woodsmen—Karstens, and later, rangers Grant Pearson and Fritz Nyberg—could have tracked down the outlaws if they'd really tried.

While Karstens seemed ambivalent, federal marshals were not. In June 1922, Deputy Hagan raided a still on Riley Creek and arrested Joseph Gagnon and John Fern, both of whom were hauled before Commissioner John J. Donovan in Healy and each fined $500 and costs. Deputies destroyed two hundred gallons of mash, twenty gallons of liquor, and brewing equipment.[17]

The following January, Hagan arrested Eli *"Bill the Turk"* Radovich, the old market-hunter, at his still, west of John Carlson's roadhouse near Cantwell. Radovich pled guilty to two counts of intent to "sell and distribute." To elude the deputies, moonshiners moved their big stills further into the wilderness.[18]

Deputy James A. Hagan, and Henry E. Seneff, a territorial liquor enforcement officer, were tough, vigorous men who would become regular, and dreaded, visitors to Riley Creek. As one authority once wrote, "You can't catch bootleggers with Sunday school teachers."[19]

With the completion of the viaduct, Camp Riley quickly emptied and soon resembled an abandoned gold camp, one day vibrant and booming, and the next, vacant and derelict. Jack Donnelly, 48, seemed to grasp the nature of boom camps better than others perhaps because he'd seen it all before. He had immigrated to the Yukon from Ireland in 1894, and had followed the stampedes to Council City, Eagle, Nome, Iditarod, Otter Creek, and Manley Hot Springs. He opened his restaurant in December 1921, put it up for sale five weeks later, and, with no buyers, closed the door for good in March.

Others seemed incapable of understanding what the boom meant and what the railroad would mean to the Alaska way of life. Roadhouses were built at Healy, Riverside, Riley Creek, Bighorn (Mile 335), Cantwell, and Broad Pass. Passenger trains would bypass, and doom, almost all of them.

The rise and fall of Camp Riley, and other railroad camps, was absolutely

FREDERICK MEARS COLLECTION, #84-75-155, ARCHIVES, UNIVERSITY OF ALASKA, FAIRBANKS

*In early February 1922, a power crane was the first piece of rolling stock to cross the Riley Creek viaduct. The first through train from Seward arrived in Nenana on a frigid February 5, and was welcomed by a tumultuous crowd.*

typical of Alaska's boom and bust cycle, which began during the gold rush era and has repeated itself through modern times, with the construction of the Trans-Alaska Pipeline in the early 1970s as a prime example.

Instead of the local population completely withering away a more permanent community began to develop. Small numbers of men found work with the railroad, the park, the roadhouse, and eventually the concessionaire. Prospectors and miners wintered here, the community becoming an entrepot for the Kantishna and Copper Mountain developments. Trappers and dog mushers summered locally and sought services and supplies year around. Hunters kept a base; a fur rancher established himself downstream of the bridge; and Morino's bluff-top hotel provided meals and lodging for locals and transients alike. When the Alaska Road Commission began hiring summer workers to build a road through the park, a few bootleggers, prostitutes, and at least one gambler settled downstream of the viaduct, locally known as "the hole." And, like most hamlets, there seemed to be a number of people who did nothing more than just hang out and drink.

But what to call the permanent community? *Riley? McKinley Station? McKinley Park?* In the summer of 1922, the post office ruled that henceforth the official postal name would be *Riley*, "for the reason that there is another post office named 'McKinley,'" and hired Rufus H. Nichols as the first postmaster. By September, the government reversed itself, and applied the official name, McKinley Park.* Now both the post office and railroad station bore the same name, yet most locals referred to their community as McKinley Station.[20]

Once the line was operational, railroad managers scheduled two trains a week, one northbound and one southbound, freight and passengers traveling together. In the park's early years, Karstens had to meet the train at all hours and unload everything from groceries, dog food, and horse feed, to building supplies, coal and firewood. One spring day he off-loaded two tons of oats by himself. Louise and Eugene sometimes pitched in as best they could.

These entries in Karstens' reports vividly describe the vicissitudes of reliance on the train:

- "Too cold [minus 45] to take horses out but hauled a load of coal from railroad station to headquarters with dogs."
- "Warm and little snow. Trains delayed by snow and snow slides near Anchorage."
- "Received supplies from Healy last night. Obliged to sit up nearly all night waiting for arrival of freight train, running on irregular schedule."
- "Spent six hours in cold at railroad waiting for freight train which had perishable freight for us."
- Two days before Christmas one year, three tons of hay arrived on the night train and were thrown out in a jumble next to the tracks. Fritz Nyberg helped Karstens haul it, and a load of coal, to the cabins.
- On the day before Thanksgiving one year, Maurice Morino called Karstens to tell him the train had dumped off his perishables and left them sitting in the snow. "The perishables were badly nipped by the [-10°F] frost," Karstens said.[21]

If the winter train schedule proved vexing, the summer one mystified Karstens entirely. "One incomprehensible feature," he reported, "[is that despite] Mt McKinley National Park [being] the most advertised point on the route, the southbound passenger train passes here at 1:15 a.m., and the northbound at 2.40 a.m." This schedule obviously hindered tourism, the very thing the railroad hoped to encourage.[22]

---

*The mining camp at Valdez Creek about 40 miles east of Cantwell was called Mount McKinley until 1922, when it was renamed Denali.

The Alaska Railroad, despite capricious scheduling, served as a lifeline to the park and was an essential partner in its future economic and physical development. On a more basic level, the railroad enabled families to make a home at McKinley Park.

Superintendent Karstens found himself in an awkward position with the railroad. He now had to deal with, and was somewhat dependent on, the very people he'd enraged earlier by passing on Hauselmann's charges of illegal hunting. Karstens attributed his trouble with AEC's Mears and Browne to lingering resentment over the poaching charge. That letter was "reason No.1 [for the conflict]. Browne and Mears have held that against me ever since," he explained to Sheldon.[23]

Karstens found Mears to be especially inflexible. When Mears thought he was right, he could be tough and uncompromising. Mears was used to issuing orders, not building consensus with functionaries of new agencies like the park service. During World War I, he had commanded the 31st Engineers, and received the Distinguished Service Medal and the French Legion of Honor. After the war, this seasoned railroad man had returned to Alaska with orders to complete the Alaska Railroad. It took an indomitable personality and force of will to overcome the remaining obstacles and forge the railroad to completion.[24]

In September 1921, Karstens took the train to Anchorage to confer with Mears. The Colonel expressed a deep interest in Riley Creek and assured Karstens that the railroad soon would establish both a station and railroad siding on the bluff near Morino's new hotel. Mears expressed interest in the park and the development of the Riley Creek area as its natural entrance. He supported Karstens' choice for his headquarters but pointed out that Morino's homestead rights would be honored, even though Morino had just recently filed his homestead application.[25]

Mears' support for Morino's homestead claim, even though it straddled the railroad and blocked Karstens development options, was easily explained. Mears and Morino, the recalcitrant Riley Creek pioneer, were old friends. Prior to Karstens' arrival in the spring, Morino had guided Mears on a bear hunt, the Colonel killing three. Morino also guided Colonel and Mrs. Mears on a successful caribou hunt. On another hunt both men were injured in an accident. After Mears stitched up a wound in his own leg he then shouldered Morino and carried him to safety. During various confrontations with Karstens, Morino could count on the staunch support of his old hunting buddy.[26]

Trying to stretch his limited funds as far as possible, Karstens asked Colonel Mears about a loan or transfer of household and office equipment that the AEC

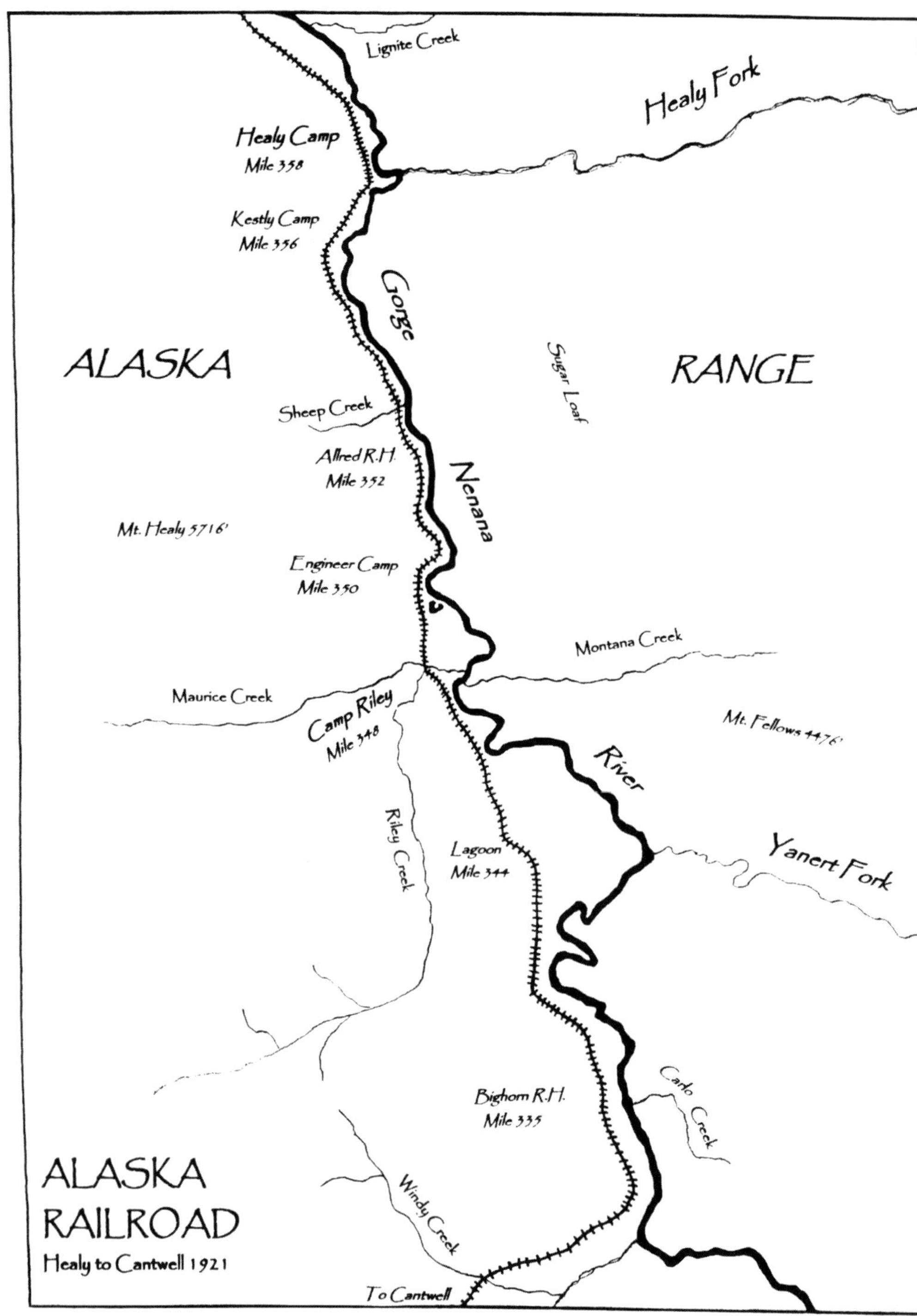
Lignite Creek
Healy Fork
Healy Camp
Mile 358
Kestly Camp
Mile 356
Gorge
ALASKA
Sugar Loaf
RANGE
Sheep Creek
Allred R.H.
Mile 352
Nenana
Mt. Healy 5716'
Engineer Camp
Mile 350
Montana Creek
Maurice Creek
Camp Riley
Mile 348
Mt. Fellows 4476'
River
Riley Creek
Lagoon
Mile 344
Yanert Fork
Carlo Creek
Bighorn R.H.
Mile 335
Windy Creek
To Cantwell
ALASKA
RAILROAD
Healy to Cantwell 1921

no longer needed. Mears was amenable and gave him a letter to pass on to his Northern Division Chief Frederick Browne—who also had been involved in the poaching flap—authorizing transfer of the requested equipment.

At this meeting Karstens and Mears discussed another concern weighing on the new superintendent. That autumn Browne had told the press that "the first and most important" railroad branch line constructed after main line completion should be a branch line via Maurice Creek to Kantishna. In short, he advocated a rail spur through the heart of the park. The news elated miners but flabbergasted park advocates. Although no record exists of the discussion between Mears and Karstens, the proposal dropped from sight.[27]

From Karstens' perspective, the meeting had gone well. Perhaps trying to mend fences a little, Karstens wrote Sheldon that "Colonel [Mears] is a good Sportsman and Railroad man, you would have many things in common," and added, "[but] . . . I don't cringe to him [Mears] and say, yes sir."[28]

As with many of his dealings with the AEC, this simple loan request degenerated into bureaucratic posturing. The AEC's auditor determined that a simple transfer was not possible because the AEC was independent of normal channels and that the park would have to pay for the equipment.[29]

Sorting out the various claims on Pat Lynch's property where Karstens wanted to build his headquarters was an even more vexing issue for Karstens. In January 1922, Karstens had hired Lewis A. Powless, a Kantishna miner, to replace the injured Ranger Tyler. Together the two men had continued to develop park headquarters in the northwest corner of Lynch's homestead. Following completion of the viaduct in February and abandonment of the labor camp, Lynch had closed his roadhouse and moved to Healy, lured by a new construction boom there. The railroad was building a spur line up the Healy River to the developing coal mines and by mid-summer, Lynch's new hotel at Suntrana was almost complete.

When Lynch verbally agreed to abandon his 80-acre claim, Karstens applied for its withdrawal from public entry and its designation for park use. Unknown to him, in July, Ranger Powless had bought Lynch's three cabins, barn, and out-buildings for $1. "Ranger Powless told me he had bought Pat Lynch's homestead & R.H, which to me puts him in a rather peculiar position as a Gov. employee," he wrote in his personal diary. What Powless was up to is a matter of conjecture.[30]

That autumn Karstens learned that the AEC intended to sell the railroad camp buildings that Karstens was using. He immediately caught the train to Anchorage to discuss their transfer to the park. Mears hesitated at first because

COURTESY OF DENISE ABBEY

*Over the course of two years, Woodbury Abbey surveyed the boundaries of Mt. McKinley National Park. Afterward he moved to McKinley Station hoping to procure the park tourist concession.*

# 3

# Woodbury Abbey, Park Surveyor

As the brittle sun cooked up over the distant peaks at 3:30 a.m., the survey crew kicked out of their blankets and crawled from their meager shelters. One-by-one they gathered around their tiny fire of willow twigs to wait for the tea water to boil. A few of the men shivered in the biting wind but did not complain because it kept the legions of ravenous mosquitoes at bay. Because their pack train had once again failed to arrive with much needed supplies, breakfast was the same as it had been for a week: boiled caribou, skillet bread, and weak tea. The park boundary they were surveying followed a high mountain ridge and they needed to complete their work early in the day before the mid-afternoon thermals birthed volleys of thunder, lightning, and torrential rain. So began a typical late June day on the crest line west of the Sanctuary River.

Surveying Alaska's first national park was a challenge even for this experienced crew. Hazards included sudden storms, temperature extremes, river crossings, mosquitoes, bears, and accidents. Reliable communication was impossible. Supplies and equipment came many miles by packhorse, backpack, and later, by dogsled. If the men ran short of food or supplies, they made do or without. At least they had permission to shoot sheep and caribou in the park for meat. The crew boss, "Wood" Abbey, labored and suffered right along with his men.

When J.P. Walker, chief of government surveys for Alaska, looked for someone to oversee the survey of Mt. McKinley National Park, he didn't have far to look. Woodbury Abbey, Cadastral Engineer for the General Land Office (GLO), forerunner of the Bureau of Land Management, was the ideal man for the job. Abbey was well acquainted with wilderness survey work. In 1913, he had surveyed near Idaho's Craters of the Moon and the next year worked along Arizona's Gila River. The GLO sent him to Alaska in 1915 to survey the Lignite coalfields. He spent the next two summers surveying eastward along the Alaska Range, proving his ability to work under harsh conditions. After finishing the survey of the coal fields he surveyed the agricultural land south of Nenana and completed a "shipping survey" downstream of the town. He then spent two years surveying public lands along Goldstream Creek and on both sides of the Tanana River, from upstream of the village of Nenana to its confluence with the Wood River. He wintered in Juneau in 1919, serving as acting supervisor of Alaska surveys. The next spring he and his family returned to Nenana and further work near Lignite. At the end of the 1920 field season, Abbey hired Harry Karstens to drive the Abbey family down the Richardson Highway to Valdez for the trip Outside.

Despite an Eastern prep-school education and a civil engineering degree from Princeton, Abbey fit right into frontier Alaska. When Abbey came north in 1917, he brought his expectant wife, Beatrice, and daughter, Denise, 7, to Nenana where they lived in a house rafted downstream from the crumbling boom town of Chena. Denise attended the new Franklin K. Lane School there and Beatrice volunteered at the hospital and for the Red Cross. An athlete, and former competitive swimmer and football player, Wood Abbey played on the local baseball team. The couple's second child, Woodbury "Bud" Abbey Jr., was born in the new railroad hospital. In 1918, Abbey was elected Deputy Grand Arctic Chief of the Arctic Brotherhood (AB), Nenana Chapter. (The AB was a fraternal organization established in the Klondike to protect stampeder rights. Abbey's election was a prestigious honor for a relative *Cheechako.**) Abbey and his wife had become popular and accepted members of the Nenana community.

Despite his privileged East Coast upbringing, Woodbury Abbey could have been considered a second generation Alaskan. His father, Captain Charles Abbey, was renowned along the Alaska coast. Captain Abbey came to Alaska in 1886, as commander of the revenue cutter *Thomas Corwin* patrolling the Aleutian and Pribilof Islands. The next year, Abbey, enforcing the ban on all fur seal and sea otter hunting, captured seven illegal foreign-flagged sealing ships.

Woodbury Abbey, born January 10, 1884, in Portland, Maine, grew up listening to tales of his father's maritime and Alaskan adventures. He was named in honor of his father's favorite vessel, the cutter *Woodbury,* based in Portland.

Unlike many federal employees, Abbey knew the character of Alaska and

---

**Cheechako,* pronounced *chee-chaw-ko,* is the northern term for "tenderfoot," or "greenhorn," or newcomer to the north.

its people, and knew the sacrifices needed to succeed there. While Abbey was in the field, Beatrice and her children fended for themselves. Reading, and outings to the Nenana movie theatre, "which ran the same movies over and over again," were family favorites. In her latter years Denise recalled that the advertisements for the films read: "This movie was shown here a short-time hence. Don't fail to miss it."[1]

After the 1918 field season, the Abbeys narrowly avoided catastrophe. In early October, the Abbey family, along with Abbey's survey crew, caught a steamer bound for Whitehorse where they would catch the Yukon and White Pass Railroad to Skagway. The lack of an experienced river pilot resulted in numerous groundings and false starts. Near the international border the steamer was halted by a crossing of the Fortymile caribou herd, an estimated 5,000 animals blocking the river.

"We had great difficulty navigating among the swimming animals. For three hours at least we were steaming upstream among them," a passenger reported. "The barge in front of the steamer plowed down some of them, but they seemed to bob up from beneath afterward. The crew got ropes and lassoed a dozen, and dragged them aboard and slew them, and we had the finest of fresh caribou cutlets and roasts. The captain would not allow anyone to kill any more, as he deemed it would be wanton destruction to take more than we could use." The usual eleven-day upstream journey on the Yukon River to Whitehorse took 19 days, just barely beating freeze-up.[2]

The Abbey entourage found Skagway mobbed with people headed Outside for the winter, or for military service. Nonetheless, when Bud Abbey, just a year old, suddenly took ill, his alarmed parents decided to stopover in the port town even if it meant missing the last direct boat south. On a blustery October evening, Abbey bid farewell to his crew as they boarded the *S.S. Princess Sophia* for the outbound voyage. Two days later, the vessel sank with the loss of 353 lives, including five of Abbey's crew and a host of Alaska and Yukon pioneers, including Walter Harper, the first man to reach the summit of Mt. McKinley.

The GLO secured funding for the Mt. McKinley National Park survey in 1920, with the work scheduled for the following year. The survey was seen as "the first step to the establishing of a protectorate over . . . the fountainhead of the Big Game herds of Alaska." Land office engineers estimated that the 250-mile long boundary survey would take just one field season but based on his experience Abbey knew that to be an unrealistic expectation, especially given that he had received the survey assignment too late in the year for an early spring start. A maritime strike further complicated logistics and planning.[3]

Harry Karstens rendezvoused with Abbey in Seattle in May 1921. He had been instructed to rely on Abbey for advice on how to obtain, record, and spend government funds. The voyage on the *S.S. Northwestern* provided minimal time for such training. A command of proper accounting procedures would remain a huge gap in the first superintendent's skills set and the cause of future bureaucratic conflicts.

In March, 1921 the land office advertised for a contractor to supply 15 horses and equipment but no one stepped forward as most teamsters and wranglers were working on the railroad project. Consequently, after reaching Anchorage, Abbey purchased seven horses from the AEC and necessary tack and outfit from local suppliers. On June first, Abbey and Karstens, along with a small crew that Abbey had brought with him from Outside, loaded their dunnage and horses and boarded the northbound train. In part, Karstens had teemed up with Abbey out of sheer necessity. When the Karstens family left Fairbanks in mid-winter they had taken with them what possessions they could and sold the rest. Consequently on the return trip, Karstens was burdened with mounds of baggage, supplies, and essentials needed to reestablish a home and base of operations. Back in Alaska he needed Abbey and his horses to help transport his dunnage across the 55-mile-long gap in the rail line. As it turned out, the

COURTESY OF DENISE ABBEY

*In 1922, the Alaska Road Commission blazed a trail from McKinley Station to Kantishna and set up shelter tents at 15-mile intervals. Woodbury Abbey and his mule "Jack" stopped at the Stony Creek camp.*

men had to hire a freighter to transport their dunnage over the gap to Healy, delaying the start of fieldwork for both men.

Nenana residents warmly welcomed Abbey on his return but he remained in town only long enough to purchase additional supplies and put three of his crew—Bob Toussaint, Bill Wallace, and Joe Cox—to work overhauling the survey equipment he had stored there. He explained his summer plans to a reporter. "[The main camp] will be established on the East Fork of the Toklat, the actual survey commencing from the initial monument which will be established on the summit of a hill lying between the forks of the Toklat, approximately 50 miles west of Healy." From there, he said, the survey party would work west to Kantishna. Once that portion of the line was located and marked they would turn around and head east from the starting point to complete the northern boundary.[4]

He further explained how the park boundary would be marked. "No attempt will be made to place monuments over the more southerly end of the line, where mostly mountains and glaciers exist," he said, "[but] a portion of the north, east, and a portion of the west boundary . . . will be thoroughly monumented in order that the park rangers, tourists, hunters, and mining prospectors may readily discern the park limits."[5]

Given the rugged terrain and weather the survey would require long hours and strenuous labor. In addition to building rock cairns to outline the boundary, the crew would also post 400 paraffin-coated all-weather warning signs printed with a succinct quotation of park hunting laws. The signs had been paid for and provided by the American Game Protective and Propagation Association, the Boone and Crockett Club, and the Campfire Club of America, the original park advocates.[6]

The area to be surveyed was not unknown territory. The previous year, H.M. Eakin and William Foran of the Alaska Geological Survey carried on the mapping of the Kantishna district as begun by Stephen R. Capps. Abbey benefited from their work.[7]

First reports from "Woodbury Abbey and his survey crew of [12] hardy mountaineers" described "mosquitoes in great numbers . . . and the weather of late . . . rather wet." Hampered by difficult terrain and weather the work progressed slowly. Despite the yeoman efforts of head packer Joe Cox, supplies and spike camps were hard to move and slow to reach needed points. A reporter for *The Nenana News* accompanied the survey crew and filed occasional reports.[8]

As the survey progressed toward the Kantishna mines, Abbey met with miners worried about the placement of the boundary. "Numerous inquiries have been made . . . as to whether Lake Minchumina, also known as the Big Lake, would be included within limits of the park," read one news account. "Several people also have told [Abbey] that they have been informed that it was the intent of the Department of Interior to enlarge the park to cover the entire Kantishna district, and he desires to state that all the above hearsay matter is entirely wrong. The Sutherland Bill [then before the U.S. Congress] merely enlarges the park on the eastern end, extending it to the 149th meridian to include the headwaters of the Sanctuary River and Windy Creek, the natural habitat and breeding grounds of the mountain sheep herds . . . the rest of the park boundaries will remain unchanged."[9]

By late-summer it was clear that a second—perhaps even third—field season was needed to complete the survey. The eastern boundary could not be surveyed until after passage, or failure, of the Sutherland bill. In early September, Abbey finished marking the northern boundary to a mountain top on the 149th Meridian, just four miles from Healy. If park expansion won approval, this point would become the northwestern corner of the park perimeter.*

At the conclusion of the field season the entire crew was feted at a party and dance at Nenana's *Cooney Hotel*, hosted by Louise Karstens and friends. "A rollicking time was enjoyed by all . . ." The next day, the survey crew dispersed, Bob Toussaint accompanying the Abbey family on the southbound train. En route Outside, Abbey and Toussaint spent October surveying the mines near Knik, on Cook Inlet. Both men would return to the park in 1922 to complete the survey.[10]

Not surprisingly, it was Charles Sheldon who provided the push for park expansion. The original park boundaries that he had suggested in 1916 had been changed, in part, for political considerations. In the spring of 1921, with the survey about to commence and Karstens en route north, he lobbied for the adjustment of the eastern boundary to achieve maximum wildlife protection. After consultations with Sheldon and the park service, Dan Sutherland, Alaska's Delegate to Congress, introduced the expansion bill into the House of Representatives in May.

The Sutherland Bill called for expansion of the park eastward to the 149th meridian and the adjustment of the southern boundary to meet it with the intent "the protection of caribou and Dall sheep breeding grounds." Abbey's field observations provided expansion advocates with vital information. "If action can be obtained to make the east boundary on the one hundred and forty ninth meridian this will include extensive breeding ground of big horn [Dall] sheep now outside

*The park's original 1917, boundary ran just east of the Sanctuary River, and crosses today's park road at approximately Mile 18.

of the park and originally intended to be contained therein," he wired Washington. "The land to be included . . . is over rugged mountains where there are no settlers or commercial timber or development of any kind and will bring the northeast corner of the park closest to the Government railroad and will therefore be much better for administrative work . . . If the boundary is run as originally delineated this area wherein game breeds will be entirely outside the park and easily accessible to hunters from the towns along the railroad."[11]

Colonel Frederick Mears also recommended extension of the park, but with a different boundary. "In my judgment, the Park Service will make a mistake if they do not at once take measures to extend the eastern boundary of the park to the Railroad," he said. "It will be appreciated that it will be much less difficult to police the Park area and protect the game if the eastern boundary line extends to a physical line such as the track of the Government Railroad. It will be at once known that no shooting of game is permissible west of the railroad line."[12]

George A. Parks, then head of the GLO's Field Division, and later Alaska's Territorial Governor, opposed Mears' suggestion. "The proposed addition between the railroad and the present eastern boundary of the park contains no game of any kind other than birds." he said. According to Parks, this premier sheep and caribou habitat, contained only *ravens and ptarmigan!*[13]

Objections by Utah's Senator William Henry King, a Democrat running for reelection, delayed passage by several months. Foreshadowing future Alaskan conflicts, King objected to passage because he believed that an extension would preclude all future mining and prospecting within the park, except on existing claims. Alaskan newspapers printed the bill in its entirety, editorializing that the act "absolutely prohibits all future prospecting and . . . future development one of the most promising of the Interior's mineral store-houses."[14]

On January 30, 1922, President Warren G. Harding signed the act, adding 445 square miles to the park for a total of 2,645 square miles. The eastern boundary moved from just east of the Sanctuary River to the 149th meridian, a point about four miles west of the Nenana River. Just as Abbey had earlier stated, nothing in the expansion bill prohibited prospecting.

The expansion succeeded in protecting important habitat, but in the process made Karstens' job all the harder. McKinley Station residents resented the new park regulations, with one of them especially galling. "Persons who render themselves obnoxious by disorderly conduct or bad behavior shall be subjected to the punishment hereinafter prescribed for the violation of the foregoing regulations and may be summarily removed from the park by the superintendent and not allowed to return without permission in writing from the Director of the National Park Service or the superintendent of the park." Who exactly was going to define obnoxious or "bad behavior," they asked? Harry Karstens? To make matters even worse the park expansion put local residents' favorite hunting area off limits. With the stroke of a pen Karstens had gone from heroic old-timer to symbol of the much loathed federal government.[15]

When Abbey returned to Alaska in June 1922, to finish the park survey, he brought his family with him. The previous autumn, Beatrice and children had settled in to their new home on the East Coast, fully expecting to be there for years to come, yet here they were back in frontier Alaska. At McKinley Station the Abbeys moved into a cabin behind Lynch's abandoned roadhouse. Life in rough-and-tumble Alaska had changed the city-raised Beatrice Abbey. She had become a crack shot with rifle and pistol, and expert with a woodstove. She picked berries, helped butcher game, and enjoyed frontier life. Beatrice settled in with her family and got re-acquainted with her neighbors, especially Louise Karstens.

Abbey quickly began the survey to locate and mark the new eastern boundary. Even in summer heat, Abbey and his veteran team labored in head nets, heavy long-sleeved shirts and gloves, all necessitated by an extraordinary plague of mosquitoes. Abbey hired horse packer J.E. Van Kirk, and his partner Bert Thorson, to support the survey work. With the railroad all but completed, and work scarce, Van Kirk agreed to transport the surveyors and their gear west and to provide regular re-supply. In mid-June Van Kirk lead his pack strings through the park to establish the surveyors' base camp on the McKinley River.

On July 12, with the eastern boundary surveyed, Abbey, his family, and crew left McKinley Station following the "mountain route" into the park. Van Kirk led the pack string up Maurice Creek and through the low divide. Some men followed afoot, others rode. Wood and Beatrice Abbey walked; both children rode a placid horse named *Chicken*. A new hire, Frank "Pix" Wood, the younger brother of Karstens' old friend, banker Richard Wood, walked with them. "Pix," described as "one of the most popular young men who ever came North," hired on out of health concerns. In the horrific fighting in the Argonne in 1918, the greatest American battle of World War I, Wood had nearly died in a poison gas attack. He was one of the 95,756 wounded Americans, with nearly 27,000 others killed in action. Back home in San Francisco his damaged lungs began to fail. In Alaska, he sought relief from his misery in outdoor work and fresh air. When he applied for work Abbey promptly hired him. The vigorous endeavor seemed to revive him.[16]

On the first night, the party camped on Savage River. Riding up Igloo Creek a day later they saw the "igloo," a teepee-like pole shelter that gave the creek its name. Further west, their trail led below Polychrome bluffs. Encamped below the multi-colored cliffs they stoked their cook stoves with coal taken from an exposed seam. Dinner was canned yams, bacon, and soup from bullion cubes. Breakfast was canned yams and bacon. Their menu regularly featured "canned yams . . . for we were never without them for some unknown reason."[17]

At times, the incessant bugs made the journey west torture for both humans and horses. The entourage made camp each night in canvas tents with sewn-in floors that offered some break from the insects. "The mosquitoes were so thick we camped on the gravel bars in mid-river to take advantage of every little breeze," Abbey recalled.[18]

On July 17, the party reached Copper Mountain, the scene of a mineral strike. The Abbeys stayed in a miner's cabin "overflowing with picks, shovels, sacks of flour, ore and canned goods, and stacks of everything else possible." They spent the next day trapped indoors by a raging blizzard. When they departed two days later they left behind a generous supply of canned yams as a partial thank you.[19]

The next day, they arrived at base camp on Big Timber, a large stand of spruce on the north bank of the McKinley River not far from Wonder Lake. "Old Glory," flying from a spruce pole, greeted them. After the nearly 80-mile trek, the weary hikers happily dropped their packs. Beatrice Abbey arrived nearly barefoot, her hiking shoes disintegrated. This cluster of tents pitched next to the main trail from the Kantishna to McKinley Station would be home for the next five weeks. That night Wood Abbey carved all their names on the ceremonial gate posts which marked the park boundary.[20]

The survey party was soon welcomed by Alex Mitchell, who lived in a cabin upstream of the survey camp. Prior to the arrival of Superintendent Karstens, this site had been his main trapping camp. He was renowned for treating guests like "new-found prodigal sons," entertaining them with pies, copious amounts of *hootch*, and lengthy recitations from Robert Burns's poetry. "The Bard of the Kantishna" presented the Abbey family with one of his trademarks, a fresh-baked blueberry pie.[21]

Over the course of the next few weeks, while the surveyors were in the field, Beatrice and the children entertained several passersby. One couple, Mr. and Mrs. Jack Hamilton, accompanied by their daughter, age 9, offered them the use of their cabin at Eureka. Game warden Jim Burrows visited camp several times promising on each occasion to teach Beatrice to mush dogs the following winter. Joe and Fannie Quigley stopped on their trips back and forth to their

Copper Mountain claims. Prospector Willard J. "Wild Bill" Shannon, and his wife, Anna, stopped en route to their Slippery Creek claims.

The infrequent visitors broke the routine of camp life, which had its challenges. The bugs were especially bothersome. Denise once counted over 100 mosquito bites on her legs alone. Besides the pestering bugs, and wet weather, Van Kirk failed to materialize with the camp re-supply. Despite being a patient man, used to the vagaries of northern life, Wood Abbey repeatedly asked his wife aloud, "*Where on earth is Van Kirk?*"[22]

By late summer the camp began to run low on critical staples and horse feed. Fortunately, government hunter Ed Moore ranged wide afield to keep the camp larder filled with meat. Once he shot a caribou 10 miles from camp. While he was packing it in, a herd came right through base camp but no one had a gun. The onset of cool autumn weather finally ended the mosquito season and hastened the ripening of berries. Beatrice and her children picked blueberries and cranberries by the quart. Blueberry cobblers and pancakes were a welcome addition to their menu.

Besides weather, insects, and dwindling supplies, Abbey also dealt with personnel conflicts. An on-going feud with another crew member drove Moore to camp by himself a short distance from base camp. Bert, the cook, abruptly quit and set out alone to hike back to the railroad. With none of the basic supplies, he'd had enough of trying to feed the ravenous crew. After he left, Beatrice did all the cooking.

Life at Big Timber was not entirely unpleasant. The antics of porcupines, mew gulls, ptarmigan, and arctic ground squirrels entertained the children. The mountains changed constantly in the shifting light with Mt. McKinley as a limitless source of wonder. Regularly someone in the survey camp would arise between 1:00 and 3:00 a.m. to enjoy unobstructed views of the mountain they called "Old Mac." In late August the tundra turned crimson and gold and the days filled with the sounds of passing sandhill cranes. As the nights grew cold and the first frosts edged the river, the stars and northern lights again sparkled above the snowy mountains. Throughout her long and varied life Denise Abbey described the camp location as "magical, offering a superlative view of Denali."[23]

From base camp they witnessed an amazing spectacle. One day a large herd of animals appeared on the plain nearby. "*Caribou!*" someone yelled. Then they saw people and dogs walking in and behind the slow-moving herd. "*Reindeer! Hundreds of them!*" Wood shouted.

Herders were driving almost 1,500 reindeer from Goodnews Bay on the Bering Sea to Broad Pass, a distance of almost 1200 miles. The drive had begun the previous October when Earl Forrest and five Yup'ik Eskimos started the reindeer north toward Akiak on the Kuskokwim River. In mid-winter, Ben Mozee, a well-known reindeer man, accompanied by several Samis (Laplanders) skied into the reindeer camp near Akiak to expedite the long drive. Using skis, snowshoes, and reindeer dogs, the men drove the herd northwest on New Year's Day. The indefatigable Mozee sometimes pushed fifty or more miles ahead of the herd in order to find the best route and forage. The going was often slow, necessitated by breaks for grazing and rest. Between Takotna and McGrath the herd, traveling single-file in Mozee's ski-trail, picked up speed to about 15 miles per day.[24]

In McGrath, Mozee hired two locals to guide them along the north side of the Alaska Range to Broad Pass. Instead, these inept guides led the herd toward Rainy Pass, the absolute wrong way to go. Mozee soon fired the guides and back-tracked toward McGrath. Clear of the mountains he swung the herd east toward the park. In May, the drive paused for fawning in the foothills along the Tonzona River, just shy of the park's southern boundary.

These half-wild reindeer were not easy to drive. They wandered, stampeded, escaped, died in accidents, or, on occasion, were killed by wolves. Native caribou sometimes mixed with the herd or led others astray. Mozee, a brilliant herder, would lasso bull caribou that intermingled with the herd and tied them to trees until the reindeer had moved on. Such heroics, however, did not prevent intermingling and production of hybrid offspring. The successful fawning season on the Tonzona compensated for the losses sustained. The drive resumed in mid-July.

The Yup'ik herders that stopped at the survey camp spoke no English but were able to express their need for salt. Abbey shared his meager supply. One of the white herders that came later that day explained the purpose of the drive. He said the government intended to establish a commercial herd near Cantwell, a place with good forage and near railroad access for shipment of meat and hides.[25]

Although the herders had been told to stay out of the park, the herd passed straight through, crossing the Toklat, Teklanika, Sanctuary, and Savage Rivers. They reached the Nenana River on August 7, 1922, having taken 280 days from Goodnews Bay to Broad Pass.* The drive began with 1437 reindeer but because of fawning and caribou additions perhaps as many as 1600 reindeer reached the grazing grounds.[26]

---

*In 1924, Louis Jensen, a professional butcher, attempted to market Cantwell reindeer. He built corrals, a slaughterhouse, and loading chutes and sent 20 carefully prepared carcasses to Seattle. Nothing came of his experiment to develop a viable market. During its six years, the Cantwell herd—which ranged as far east as Monahan Flats—failed to make a profit, with numerous animals lost to faulty herding practices, wandering caribou, and wolf predation. Herders abandoned the remnants of the 2,000-head Cantwell herd in 1928, freeing the animals to wander and join the indigenous caribou. A few were shipped to the college in Fairbanks. To this day people report seeing unusually small or strangely colored caribou in the vicinity of Monahan Flats.

The lack of supplies sorely hampered the survey work. With their grub getting low, and no sign of Van Kirk, Abbey sent "Pix" Wood to McKinley Station to expedite a re-supply. En route, Wood encountered men riding and packing a string of horses that he recognized as Van Kirk's. Instead it was William N. Beach's hunting party passing through to regions west of the park boundary. Without advising anyone, Van Kirk had sold his horses and tack to Beach and quit the business! Beach was dismayed to learn that Van Kirk had contracted to re-supply the survey party then reneged in the worst possible way. Wood continued on to McKinley Station to see if he could find another packer to carry supplies to camp.

Beach promised "Pix" he would speak with Abbey and to "at least explain our innocence over the mix-up over [the surveyors'] grub." The survey crew "rather enthusiastically" cheered the arrival of the pack train but quieted when they heard the news. Beach gave them what supplies he could spare, later saying that "Wood Abbey, had certainly been handed plenty of misery and was putting up a game fight."[27]

Abbey and Beatrice discussed a change in plans. The sobering news relayed by Beach promised to delay completion of the survey. Once again, weather and logistics had taken its toll. Abbey would be forced to work into early winter to finish the survey, leaving base camp for the duration. Surveying the line to Mt. Russell would be difficult. Beatrice and her children, ages 12 and 5, could not stay alone. With winter fast approaching they needed better shelter and companionship. The vacant Hamilton cabin in the Eureka mining camp seemed the best option. Abbey warned his wife that while he completed the survey she would be on her own for almost three months. "Well, I guess I'll have to learn to shoot the .30/40 Krag then, won't I?" she replied.[28]

On Labor Day 1922, the Abbeys left Big Timber for the last time, their mule, "John Henry McNutt," or "Jack," carrying their belongings. They overnighted at Polly's Roadhouse at the outlet of Wonder Lake, then outside the park boundary. Owners John and Paula Liebau Anderson had stopped at camp earlier in the summer. Polly had sent them a loaf of bread which turned out to be rock hard and inedible. It was so indestructible that it became the camp baseball, getting batted around with great vigor. Although William Beach described Polly's fare as "befitting royalty," young Denise said "[Polly's] efforts were generally fatal to the food she handled and to her boarders."[29]

The log roadhouse was well-crafted, warm and inviting. Its furnishings, made of caribou antlers, were works of art, but "poked you when you sat down," Denise Abbey remembered. That night the Abbeys settled in for a pleasant

JOHN E. ANDERSON COLLECTION, COURTESY OF JAY HATHAWAY

*With the Alaska Range looming in the distance, Paula Liebau Anderson homesteaded at the outlet to Wonder Lake where she, and her husband John, operated a fur farm and roadhouse famed for its view of Mt. McKinley.*

COURTESY OF DENISE ABBEY

*Paula Anderson welcomes a member of Woodbury Abbey's survey crew to her roadhouse.*

conversation and the first sleep indoors in seven weeks. Before drifting off to sleep they listened to the Anderson's tales of gold strikes and prospectors. They learned that John, in his search for gold, had mushed dogs in the winter of 1918, from the Chulitna River over a 3500' high pass through the Alaska Range cordillera to Kantishna where he staked several claims. Anderson and Polly, who owned claims on Glacier Creek, teamed up to homestead at the outlet of Wonder Lake. They prospected in summers; trapped in winters. They kept two teams of sled dogs and also raised mink and fox for their furs. Polly showed off her weather observations and explained how she counted and collected birds for the U.S. Biological Survey.[30]*

When the Abbeys left the roadhouse the next day they stopped to view the 5' high dam at the lake outlet which channeled water into a hand-dug ditch that carried water to a hydraulic mining operation near the confluence of Moose and Eureka Creeks.

That afternoon Wood Abbey helped his family settle into the Hamiltons' comfortable and well-stocked, two-room cabin in Eureka. Abbey had met many local people during the previous summer's survey. One of them, John "Shorty" Graygen, offered to check in from time to time and help Beatrice with heavy

*Edward P. Shannon also staked 160 acres on Wonder Lake, south and west of the outlet, but held no title at the time of the 1932 park extension.

chores. The next morning, with his wife and family safely ensconced in Eureka, Wood Abbey hurried to rejoin the survey crew. As autumn turned into winter, Beatrice and her children settled into life in Eureka, population 12, a pioneer camp left from the stampede of 1905. Due to low water and frost, the Kantishna mining season ended on September 12 and they watched the "clean-up" of 625 ounces of gold worth $10,000. (The equivalent of $531,250 in 2008.)

On occasion Beatrice welcomed Graygen's help but she liked to do her own chores. "She usually chose to saw and chop her own wood, haul her own water in kerosene can 'buckets' from the water hole, and take care of the house and my brother and me," Denise said. She also did not neglect her children's education. She taught them using the correspondence materials from the Calvert School that the Hamiltons' daughter had left behind. For entertainment Beatrice read and re-read the three novels in the cabin. The children played and skated on the frozen ditch that carried water from Wonder Lake. She practiced her shooting and soon killed some ptarmigan for the pot. They visited with local miners, among them Joe and Fannie Quigley and Jim Burrows.[31]

Fannie Quigley often invited the family over for dinner. The first time she laid out a feast of roast caribou, mashed dried potatoes, canned corn on the cob, and peach short cake with whipped evaporated milk. The children at first were taken aback by Fannie's booming voice and profanity, but her genuine affection erased their misgivings. "Mother often warned us about Fannie's salty language and told us to go home whenever she worked with her dogs, because it got worse," Denise said. Beatrice soon learned that even though Paula Anderson and Fannie Quigley were the only two women in hundreds of square miles, they despised each other. Fannie called Anderson a "lady of the evening." Beatrice had found Polly to be friendly and polite, but her rough-hewn neighbor described those traits as "uppity."[32]

Meanwhile, the survey was progressing slowly. In October, to avoid a third field season, Abbey hiked well over a hundred miles from the south boundary to the railroad to make a quick trip to Fairbanks for much needed supplies. In Fairbanks he arranged for mushers to haul food and winter clothing to the distant camp.

Pausing in Nenana on his way back, he announced his plan to quit government service and build a string of first class tourist accommodations in the park, pending approval of his recently submitted application for the park concession. Due to his contacts with wealthy Easterners he felt capable of drawing an extensive clientele. In fact, Abbey was so certain of his ability to attract guests that he predicted that he could bring at "least fifty visitors next summer."[33]

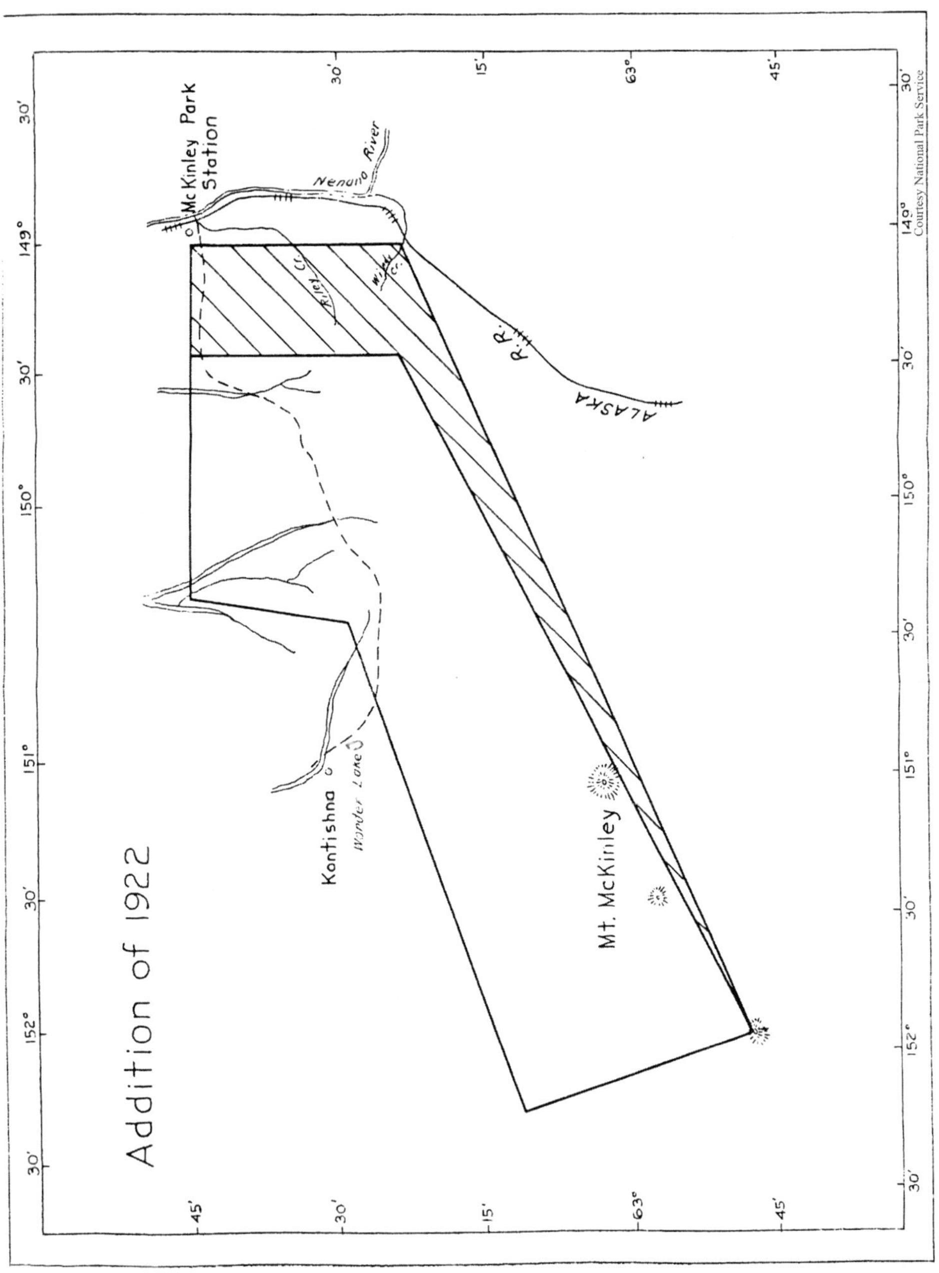


Courtesy National Park Service

He said he "planned to build several substantial log structures at convenient location distances, and to furnish them in a manner . . . equal in appointment to a good hotel in the States [and investing $100,000.] The buildings would be large enough to be able to accommodate a party of considerable size and there would be a stable in connection with each hotel as well as dog kennels." He added that it would be necessary to maintain a stable of pack and saddle horses for the convenience of park visitors. What Beatrice thought of this plan, if she was even aware of it, is unknown.[34]

Finally, in the dark, frigid days of late November, the arduous boundary survey was complete and Abbey joined his exhausted crew on the long trek to McKinley Station. For years, he had wanted to quit surveying and pursue a career as a mining engineer. With the park survey finished, he was free to pursue other interests, including the park concession. When he shipped out his mapmaking logbooks and charts, he included his resignation.

After tying up loose ends, Abbey returned to Kantishna. During the first week of December the family packed for the four-day dogsled trip to the railroad via Knight's Roadhouse. In preparation, Beatrice baked bread, and loaded the grub box with salt pork, ham, caribou steaks, pre-cooked beans, coffee, dried

GEORGE PARKS COLLECTION, #240-587, ALASKA STATE LIBRARY

*In 1922, a sudden late-autumn storm caught the unprepared survey crew on the park's far western boundary. Woodbury Abbey walked over 90 miles to the railroad to procure needed clothing and supplies to finish the survey before winter.*

foods, and some canned goods. Bedrolls were made up and personal items packed. Early on December 12, 1922, the thermometer reading -30°F, the Abbeys said good bye to friends and left Eureka in the pre-dawn darkness. Jim Burrows drove eight dogs, carrying Beatrice and Bud in his sled. Shorty Graygen drove four dogs with Denise riding in the basket. Lars Nelson drove 22 dogs, pulling two heavily-loaded sleds, with Abbey on the gee pole of the leading sled. Al Wigand, family friend and veteran of the survey, walked behind the teams. The expedition headed out on the old winter trail, spending the first night in Diamond, one of the abandoned stampede towns about 25 miles from Eureka. That night, miner Billy Taylor, regaled his visitors with the story of his Mt. McKinley climb, and how he helped carry a spruce pole to the north summit. Taylor said that he and the Glen Creek boys climbed the peak "because that mountain was more ours than it belonged to those *Cheechakos* and outsiders who were making such a to-do about it."[35]

The next day the party pushed on for 20 more miles, over-nighting in an old cabin converted to a horse barn. A similar run the next day took them to Knight's Roadhouse on the Toklat River, an important trail stop built in 1909. Like many roadhouses, Knight's was not designed for privacy and because the place was packed with travelers and government trail workers, blankets were strung around the stove for the privacy of the two females.

The last day on the trail dawned clear and cold, -40°F, with dense pockets of ice fog. The trail was fast and hard-packed. Wigand had to run most of the way just to keep up. Late at night, under a sea of stars and hints of aurora, they pulled into Duyck's Roadhouse near the railroad stop at Kobe, near present-day Clear. In the early morning hours, they walked the half-mile to the "train station," an old, poorly-heated boxcar lit by kerosene lamps. As usual, the train arrived late but the Abbeys reached Nenana that day, in plenty of time to prepare for the holidays. On January 11 1923, the Abbey family returned to McKinley Station, this time to make a home and tackle new adventures.

# 4

# Up and Running

Harry Karstens took the four-in-hand and with a loud *Hee-Yah!* snapped the reins along the horses' backs. The team surged forward against the traces, shoulders and legs straining, hooves cutting the sand, but once again the team could not budge the wagon mired in the gravel of Maurice Creek. With a curse, Karstens dropped the reins and climbed down from the buckboard to pat and calm the horses with soft words.

Olaus Murie, mud-splattered and drenched, walked up from behind the wagon where he had been pushing and clapped Karstens on the shoulder. Time to break out the shovels, pry bars, and jack. Less than a mile from headquarters they were stuck again on the creek bed pioneer trail.

One of Superintendent Harry Karstens first public announcements in 1921 had been a call for the construction of a park road to be opened "as speedily as possible." Building a headquarters and home initially took precedence over everything else but by the spring of 1922, after a long cold winter of settling in and a few preliminary patrols, Karstens turned his attention to building a pioneer road, the first step in opening the park to tourism.[1]

On June 23, Ranger Lou Powless and Karstens rode their horses up Maurice Creek to the open pass near the head of Jenny Creek. The steep, sparsely forested hillsides on the south side of the creek forced them to follow the streambed itself. Occasionally they wove into the dense spruce forest that covered the gently inclining north flank of the drainage. There they led their horses through timber, dense willow and alder thickets, and across muskeg, terrain ill-suited for easy road building.[2]

The arduous going was nothing new to either of them. Overland travel in Alaska is always difficult and challenging. Much northern ground is unstable, saturated, and covered with grass tussocks or dense vegetation. Consequently, waterways in the pioneer era, served as Alaskan "roads" used by boats in summer, dog teams in winter. One trip through the drainage convinced Harry Karstens that the only practical route for the road, barring a huge infusion of cash and labor, was directly up the creek bed, a winter route previously used by miners and hunters heading west. Over several long, hot, buggy days, the two rangers blazed the first eight miles of a summer trail to the pass. Progress was slow and difficult, the mosquitoes intolerable.

Olaus J. Murie, a biologist and "fur warden" working for the U.S. Biological Survey, had arrived at Riley Creek on July 3, to begin a project to capture caribou to cross-breed with imported reindeer. Two days later, Murie, Karstens, and Powless, assisted by prospector Joe Clark and his partner, began work on a wagon road from headquarters to the Savage Fork. With axes they hacked at the brush and trees and used spruce poles to pry boulders out of the way. Their wagon, loaded with Murie's supplies, continually bogged down in the sand or when crossing the boulder-strewn creek.[3]

The men spent five brutal, back-breaking days cutting a pioneer wagon road. After they finally reached the Savage Fork, the prospectors went on to Kantishna and Karstens helped Murie build a cache for his supplies. Together, they spent several days scouting the surrounding country. Near the headwaters of the river, Murie chose a site for his capture corral. "Caribou are plentiful on upper Savage," Murie wrote in his journal. "There are long slopes with fine feed, a good caribou range. Here is where they evidently range in summer. [Karstens and I] found a narrow pass between Savage and Sanctuary thru [sic] which the caribou have worn a well beaten trail. Here we decided is a good place to capture caribou."[4]

Murie made a fine impression on Karstens. Responding to Sheldon's enquiry about the slim, blond, blue-eyed biologist, Karstens wrote: "Mr. Murie is an excellent fellow, devoted to his work, and particularly to Dr. Nelson, whom he considers one of the best ever. He is conservative and not given to idle gossip, in fact he is too interested in his own work to spare the time. Murie holds to his convictions and cannot be turned from them by politicians or any one else when he knows he is right . . . " Others described Murie as gentle, pleasant and agreeable but with "steel within." Like other great turn-of-the-century naturalists, Murie illustrated his field notes with detailed sketches that Karstens admired greatly.[5]

On July 16, Karstens and Murie, with just three horses pulling their wagon, returned to headquarters. "Very rough and rocky road up Morris [sic] Creek but could be made a fair wagon road at small expense," Karstens wrote.[6]

Three weeks later, after a trip to Fairbanks, Murie returned to McKinley Station with a six-man crew to build the capture corral. First, however, they needed a better road and they got right to work. Murie's construction and capture crew consisted of R.A. Perkins, C.T. Cunningham, Sam Ivey, Frank Glaser, and Jule and Ted Loftus, all eager and hard workers. With a route already marked and cleared they made good time to the pass and moved on to Savage where they began clearing a trail to the head of the river. A week later Dan T. Kennedy used his wagon and team to haul Murie's gear up river over the partial corduroy wagon road the crew was "swamping out."[7]

At the tail end of summer Karstens reported construction of the road to his superiors. "Our pioneer road into Savage River, though rough, is serving a good purpose," he wrote. "O. J. Murie, Assistant Biologist, is operating 2 teams of horses, hauling in 1400 pounds to the team, to his camp on the head of the Savage River, where he is building a corral to capture young bull caribou."[8]

The lengthy battle to get even minimal funding for the park made it obvious to Karstens that further funding for a road and infrastructure would not be available soon. It wasn't until 1924 that the Interior Department announced adequate funding for road construction. In the meantime, despite periodic flooding, the pioneer road that Karstens and Murie had built would have to do.

Construction of territorial roads and trails was the province of the Alaska

WOODBURY ABBEY COLLECTION, #95-114-68, ARCHIVES, UNIVERSITY OF ALASKA, FAIRBANKS

*Frequent summer floods on Riley Creek, like this one in 1922, washed out the wagon bridge and smashed giant boulders into the footings of the railroad trestle. This flood threatened park headquarters, Lynch's old roadhouse, and the remaining AEC structures.*

CHARLES PORTER COLLECTION, #796-11F-68, NATIONAL ARCHIVES AND RECORD ADMINISTRATION

*Here, Harry Karstens drives a wagon up the pioneer road along Maurice (Hines) Creek while guiding representatives of the Bureau of Reclamation on an extend trip into the park. The pioneer road was Karstens attempt to open an access route to the park.*

Road Commission (ARC), a unit within the War Department, locally commanded by Colonel James Gordon Steese, an old Alaska hand. Steese, a West Point graduate, first came to Alaska in 1913, assigned to an expedition ordered to test military trucks in roadless terrain. Coming just prior to World War I, when most militaries were still relying on horse transport, this feasibility test was of exceptional importance. During World War I, Steese was promoted to the rank of brevet Brigadier General. After the Armistice, he returned to Alaska as an advisory engineer for the AEC.

As early as 1921, Colonel Steese had pushed for a park road that would benefit both Kantishna tourists and miners. Following the war the Kantishna Mining District was booming, and well-respected miners, like Joe Dalton and Billy Taylor, were pushing for a road, one they hoped would finally allow full development of the Kantishna and Copper Mountain mineral discoveries. "They have a Commissioner and a monthly mail service in there now and are working hard for a road through the park to tap their country," Karstens explained. "...they have succeeded in having a survey made last summer from the railroad through the upper passes to Eureka Creek so it will serve the park as well as an outlet for their minerals."[9]

In 1922, the Secretary of the Interior, Albert B. Fall, requested $360,000 in three annual appropriations to build "32 miles of [park] road suitable for a moderate amount of automobile travel and 60 miles of winter trail doubling as a summer horse trail." When Karstens outlined the plan to the public, it met with immediate approval. "With the increasing tourist travel . . . to this section of Alaska, resulting from the [near] completion of the government railroad, there is a large demand for a road into the park," said one editorial.[10]

By the time Secretary Fall submitted his funding request, the route through the park to the Kantishna had already been selected. Major John Gotwals, ARC Vice-Chairman, ordered Hawley Sterling, a former railroad construction supervisor, to do a reconnaissance of two routes to the Kantishna Mining District. One route, the "lowland route," left the railroad at the Lignite mining camp and cut across country to Eureka Creek. The "mountain route" led from Riley Creek through the heart of the park to Wonder Lake. The task to determine which route was best was a perfect fit for the energetic Sterling, a civil engineer with a decade of Alaska experience.

In early August 1920, Sterling, with a packer and two mules, left Nenana on a two-month-long exploration. On their return, Sterling reported that the Lignite to Kantishna route would be the best year-round route and the favorite of "many people whose business took them into the Kantishna." However, due to multiple river crossings and miles of muskeg swamps, he added, "this route offers more difficulties from an engineering point of view and higher costs than does the Riley Creek, or upper route." He described the mountain route from Riley Creek to be the best summer route, "one less costly for road construction."[11]

In early May, 1921, Sterling returned to the park with Dick McLean and transit man Arnold Nordale to survey the highland route west from Riley Creek. It took them over a month to reach the mining camp of Eureka, their route roughly following a preliminary scouting trip that Major John Gotwals had made during the winter of 1920–21. Sterling soon quit ARC in order to develop his interests in several Kantishna claims.

Karstens initially enjoyed smoother sailing with the ARC than he had with the railroad management. His inflammatory letter concerning illegal hunting in the park did not tar the ARC brass and they had no axes to grind. "Colonel Steese and Gotwals are very well disposed toward the park, and, I believe, to me," he said, "and I anticipate a new era of co-operation. . . . They both seem willing to assist me as much as they can, and are very friendly, which is all I could possibly ask."[12]

In July 1922, ARC crews began brushing out and marking the 86-mile Mt. McKinley Park Trail to the Kantishna, in part following the old hunting trail.

HENRY P. KARSTENS COLLECTION, #1012, KARSTENS LIBRARY

*Training a good dog team was one of Harry Karstens' first priorities. Early in 1923, next to the headquarters cabin, he lined up his team with Rowdy in lead.*

In open areas, they set up wooden tripods to mark the route and erected eight shelter tents with mileage signboards at each. By autumn, a few wagons had managed to lurch over this winter trail cut through the timber on the bluffs above Maurice Creek, but heavy rains rendered it impassable and it was forsaken in favor of Karstens' route on the creek bottom.

As the ARC crews worked west, the government reindeer herd arrived at the head of Jenny Creek. Hearing the news, Karstens walked up to view the resting herd and confer with Murie. Murie and Karstens agreed that the reindeer presented a threat to caribou by disease transmission and genetic contamination. Once the herd moved onto the railroad tracks south of McKinley Station, Karstens issued orders to shoot any reindeer found in the park.[13]

Scattered reindeer turned up in all parts of the park. A prospector saw an all-white one on Brooker Mountain. In late August, Murie found 150 reindeer wandering near his camp on the Savage Fork. He herded them north and away from his caribou trap and sent word to the herders to come get them. A year later stragglers were still showing up. In July 1923, Murie saw several more at the head of Maurice Creek, many blind in one eye.[14]

The summer of 1922 was a busy one for Superintendent Karstens. Not only did road work, maintenance, and administrative duties fill his time, but he also met with the park's first adventurous visitors. A party of seven arrived on the train as an advanced scouting party for a 70-person contingent that would

HENRY P. KARSTENS COLLECTION, #1460, KARSTENS LIBRARY

*On the south bank of Riley Creek, just before leaving on a poaching patrol, Harry Karstens howls with his excited team.*

visit the park the next summer and dedicate it to the American people. These wealthy New Yorkers, representing the *Brooklyn Daily Eagle*, were the first to sign the park's guest book.

Karstens also prepared for the July visit of W.F. Chandler of Fresno, California, a wealthy rancher, vintner, and Republican politician. Well in advance of Chandler's visit, Karstens had tried to hire J.E. Van Kirk to take Chandler into the park but Van Kirk was contracted to support Abbey's survey crew. Karstens then attempted to buy a few horses from him but the animals he offered were in very bad shape. Van Kirk then demanded that Karstens buy his whole string of horses, or none, to which Karstens replied "... out of the question." When Chandler arrived at the park he found himself without horses or a guide. He telegraphed Director Mather and asked that Karstens be assigned to take him into the park. After several telegrams, Karstens took an approved leave of absence to guide Chandler. Karstens hired his old acquaintance Dan T. Kennedy to provide horses and services.[15]

In mid-July, Chandler, Karstens, and Kennedy left on a trip to the base of Mt. McKinley. Chandler was a regular visitor to national parks but was especially thrilled by the mountain and the park's varied wildlife. In all he saw "596 sheep, three grizzly bears, one moose, and caribou too numerous to count." After his trip Chandler donated, through the National Geographic Society, $1,000 to the park for trail construction. " ... when you feel a new route should be opened I ... trust your judgment," he said. Karstens eventually used the money from "McKinley Park's first visitor," to build a good wagon road to the head of Savage River.[16]

Visitors like Chandler helped the park cause, others hurt it. Major W.C. Gotshall, whose donation had funded Karstens' preliminary efforts, visited in late summer. His parting comments infuriated many Alaskans and sorely strained Karstens' relationship with the ARC. Gotshall, a good friend of Charles Sheldon's, was a wealthy New York railroad engineer, investor, and avid hunter, who appears to have visited the park, in part, as Sheldon's proxy. For a week Karstens accompanied Gotshall as far as west as Igloo Creek, then returned to headquarters with him after a stop at Murie's camp. Gotshall spent the month of September crisscrossing the park, much of it through deep snow, on "an independent expedition to study [park] boundaries." Just before leaving Alaska he told a reporter that "Game conditions in McKinley are such that if steps are not taken to change the boundary no animals will be left in a few years. A peculiar condition exists there. The park is essentially a sanctuary but the eastern line is such that unscrupulous hunters are able to come in and shoot all the goats and sheep and caribou they care about with no danger of interference."[17]

Gotshall also said that he, along with other "influential sportsmen," would soon pressure Congress to shift the park boundary all the way east to the Nenana River, and northward five miles to include an area "teaming with wild life." The extensions he outlined precisely mirrored Charles Sheldon's original proposal for the 1922 expansion, but which had been rejected for the sake of compromise. He also seemed to advocate shooting poachers when he said "fill [them] full of birdshot." This comment, and a report in the press that he was doing this for "the benefit of trophy hunters," enraged many Alaskans, who believed that preserves were the work of elitists looking out for their own special interests. Gotshall's "buckshot" comment incensed European immigrants who well knew the violent methods employed by Old World nobility to protect their lands and wildlife.[18]

"Were it not for the fact that Major Gotshall has an influential following in the east," began one news editorial, "the news would be inclined to ignore his recent utterances . . . but under the circumstances it might be dangerous to let the Major go unchallenged else . . . [his views] be regarded as reflecting the general sentiment of Northerners.

"Alaskans believe the park is already larger than need be for the protection of game and the amusement of special privileged trophy hunters. The reservation of any additional area will not benefit anyone and the Major should be set right before he succeeds in adding to the burdens of real residents of the Territory."[19]

Nearly identical arguments and language would be heard again during both the 1932 and 1980 park boundary expansions, with similar rhetoric used in Alaska to this day in nearly any federal lands reclassification squabble.

Unfortunately, ARC's Major John Gotwals mistakenly bore the brunt of criticism from irate Alaskans. The similarity of names and rank resulted in identity confusion. Gotwals, a civil engineer who had commanded the 56th Engineers in France, quickly announced that in his capacity with the ARC, the park's boundaries did not concern him and he had never discussed the issue with the press. Superintendent Karstens stayed out of the public debate but no doubt got an earful from Gotwals.

Another trophy hunter who visited the park that summer also caused a stir. Charles Sheldon's adventures on the Toklat River had made the drainage famous with sport hunters around the world. Prior to the establishment of the park, Belmore Browne and other wealthy sportsmen had queried Karstens about guided trips to hunt Dall sheep there. Sometime in 1919, New York tycoon William N. Beach had asked Karstens to guide him into Sheldon's old hunting grounds, completely ignoring the fact the area was now inside the new park. Karstens declined, explaining "[I'm] making [enough] money operating an auto stage line between [Fairbanks] and Chitina."[20]

"Billy" Beach, a Yale graduate, amassed a fortune as President of Pennsylvania Cement Company which supplied concrete for New York subway construction. His wealth allowed him to indulge his twin passions of hunting and collecting sporting art. His stories of hunts in exotic locales were widely published. He lived at Great Neck, on Long Island, and his trophy room displayed the original artworks of Carl Rungius, James L. Clark, and Frederick Remington. Beach was a member of both the Boone and Crockett Club and the Campfire Club, the influential sportsmen's organizations that had led the fight for the park's establishment. He described Sheldon and Belmore Browne as close friends. Browne, in fact, had encouraged him to hunt in Alaska but his connection to Sheldon seemed one of competition more than friendship.

When Karstens returned to Alaska in the spring of 1921 to assume his position as park superintendent, he told a Fairbanks reporter that several hunters from Outside had applied for permits to hunt "the animals within the park destructive to other animals and bird life." At that time the Interior Secretary had the authority to issue permits for hunting wolves, coyotes, and bears in the parks. Karstens emphasized that no special trophy hunting permits would be granted for McKinley Park, an attempt to reassure park opponents that the area wasn't set aside as a playground for Outsiders.

Prior to his trip, Beach had attempted to gain a special permit. He petitioned Edward W. Nelson, head of the Biological Survey, to intercede with the park service on his behalf for a permit to hunt inside the park, not just for predators but for other animals, too. Nelson refused. Karstens whole-heartedly agreed, adding in a letter to Beach that "there will be more satisfaction to you [in visiting the park] than all the heads and capes you have got heretofore." The response infuriated Beach. He desperately wanted a special hunting permit. In a follow up, Beach ripped into both Gotshall and Sheldon, allegedly calling Sheldon a "Game Hog."[21]

To ensure the success of his trip, Beach also requested assistance from outgoing Governor Thomas Riggs, Mears, Steese, and Gotwals. His connections paid off. The railroad changed its schedule for him and provided a special car for his use. Major Gotwals assembled a party of former ARC employees to accompany Beach. Arno Cammerer, NPS Assistant Director, drafted a letter of introduction, advising Karstens to do "everything you can to assist Mr. Beach in his undertaking." Both men thought Beach's primary goal was the photography of park wildlife and scenery.[22]

Beach, with his friend George Godley, arrived at McKinley Station in late summer, now ostensibly to tour through the park to the western boundary, where they would then hunt sheep outside the perimeter. Due to scarcity and high prices, the party had failed to procure horses in Fairbanks, and arrived at McKinley Station in need. J.E. Van Kirk offered to sell his pack horses to them for an almost extortionate sum. Without options, Beach bought the horses but fumed that "it went against the grain to be held up by this northern Pirate." Karstens seemed amused noting that Beach "got the 'bump' proper . . ."[23]

Additional insult compounded the injury. The horses needed shoeing and the tack was in total disrepair. Karstens lent them hay and grain, which Gotwals promised to replace. After a delay necessitated by a search for a farrier, the expedition finally left their camp at Lynch's Roadhouse and headed west for the park, toting with them a complete developing and printing outfit that allowed them "to see their photographs within hours of exposure."[24]

Beach and Godley's party consisted of guide Guy Burch, Bill Simpert, teamster Jim Gibson, cook Walter Eng, and Ed Woods, a former Valdez mayor and a childhood friend of Teddy Roosevelt's. En route west they passed Harry Lucke's old market hunting camp on the Savage where "many old sheep heads and quantities of skins lay scattered about, all evidences of the early-day slaughter." They also visited Murie where he was building his capture corral at the head of the river.[25]

Westward progress was slow because the packers had to make several relays to move the expedition's mountain of supplies and horse feed. On one stop they met "Pix" Wood and learned of Van Kirk's duplicity regarding the survey crew. Other passersby included Jim Burrows, U.S. Marshall James Buckley, and Fairbanks attorney Collins, returning from an investigation of a miner's peculiar death in the Kantishna district. During their travels they encountered prospectors, surveyors, and long-time area residents.

Beach and Godley stopped often to take photographs and motion pictures. They filmed sheep, bear, and caribou. As they approached the mountain they marveled at its stupendous size. They made a pilgrimage to Sheldon's old cabin on the Toklat but were downcast to see it nearly "obliterated by the river overflow."[26]

At the far point of their trip they hunted Dall sheep and caribou and hunted unsuccessfully for what Beach described as a "glacier bear, the meanest animal in all of Alaska." Besides returning to McKinley Station with exposed film, the party also packed out caribou meat and three sheep heads that they said were killed west of the park. On their return to McKinley Station, something apparently aroused Karstens' suspicions and he quizzed the packers and guides but found nothing amiss. The trophies appeared to be legally taken.

Based on Beach's initial comments, his month-long expedition through the park to the Tonzona River was a great success. "In reading your letter of Oct 18th," Karstens wrote, "it afforded me great pleasure to know that your moving pictures of game in the park turned out so well . . . you are bound to reach the right people and in that way promote the advancement of this park." That winter, as a token of appreciation, Beach sent Jim Burrows and Karstens each a new Mauser rifle.[27]

That winter in New York City, at the annual Camp Fire Club dinner, Beach made a terrible gaffe. He revealed to his dinner partner that he'd shot a Dall sheep in the park. "This is one case where a man, by talking too much, has gotten himself into a pretty deep hole," Arno Cammerer later remarked. Beach's dinner partner was Horace M. Albright, Yellowstone National Park Superintendent and assistant field director of the National Park Service.[28]

"Received a notice from my Service," Karstens soon wrote, "that Beach has admitted poaching a sheep." Based in part on Sheldon's advice, and his own reluctance to accept a "tainted" gift, Karstens returned the Mauser.[29]

Beach asked Karstens to "reconsider and accept it as it embarrassed him very much, also that certain ones in Washington and New York were trying to discredit him and he was very desirous of knowing who they were." Karstens did not relent nor did he reply to Beach's effort to shift blame to others.[30]

After attempting to circumvent the ban on hunting by invoking the rights of prospectors to kill game in the park for meat—Beach lamely claimed to be a business man investigating mining opportunities—Beach signed a written statement owning up to the sheep kill but admitted no wrong doing. With his admission, however, pertinent, disturbing facts surrounding the case began to surface.

Game Warden Burrows had actually seen the poached sheep and took no action. In fact the two men had engaged in friendly banter over the firearm used to kill the sheep. "After [Beach] had killed the sheep he had an argument with Game Warden Burrows about shooting the sheep through the heart with a .22 caliber bullet. Burrows wouldn't believe it. He walked over to the carcass, picked up the heart and said, 'you did shoot him through the heart, didn't you!'" Karstens told current Governor Scott C. Bone.[31]

Burrows' lack of an appropriate response to the shooting was no surprise to Karstens and others familiar with territorial game wardens. Burrows main interest was his various quartz claims, especially the discovery he made with Mike Lodi near the headwaters of the Toklat River. Most of his energies were not bent toward law enforcement. "A reading of the governor's correspondence with their wardens leaves the unmistakable impression that wardens were selected and retained for political reasons, that they performed partisan political jobs while in office, that they were often unqualified—sometimes barely literate—and reluctant to arrest violators," writes historian Morgan Sherwood. "Game law violations were widespread. The system was, as charged, 'negligent and incompetent' between 1908 and 1925, and Alaskans who paid attention knew it."[32]

Even Beach did not appear to think much of the warden. "Burrows came into the country as a prospector," Beach wrote, "had developed into the proprietor of a music and gambling hall, drifted from place to place as the various strikes were made, and, I imagine, as a last resort got the appointment as Game Warden of the Kantishna."[33]

In January 1923, while in Fairbanks on other business, Karstens met with the district attorney and laid out the Beach affair. He offered Burrows' complicity as an example of the lack of local cooperation he was receiving. The prosecutor responded that in his opinion the case would be a long, drawn out affair, with a jury conviction doubtful. He thought it best to seek a guilty plea in return for a nominal fine.

Authorities in Washington also waded in. According to Cammerer, Beach had laid out "all the facts relating [to the] killing frankly and openly [and] admitted the killing of one mountain sheep for food at Igloo Creek on the west side of the park. The Service believes that the most satisfactory handling of this situation would be the demand by the Department on this man to pay an amount equal to the maximum $500 fine for violations of the law into the Mt. McKinley Park fund as a donation toward trail work in the Park; in other words, settle the case out of court."[34]

In September 1923, after much negotiation, Beach pled guilty in Fairbanks to killing a sheep in the park. In sentencing, U.S. Commissioner M.R. Boyd said that Beach "had suffered considerable mental punishment," and because the shooting was for "meat and not a flagrant violation" fined him $10.00 and $5.80 in costs. "The fine is pretty low but it is quite a feat to get a conviction for illegal hunting in this country," Karstens reported.[35]

The news of Beach's poaching did not dampen local beliefs that sportsmen were rich, two-faced, game hogs who promoted their ethics and scientific collecting at the expense of people who really needed the meat for basic survival. It also made it abundantly clear that Harry Karstens was alone in enforcing the park's hunting regulations.

Officially, just seven people visited the park in 1922, but the actual total was nearly double. The superintendent met with almost every visitor and had the chance to explain his plans for park expansion. Besides the handful of visitors, Karstens also had to deal with local residents, many of whom lived, at least in part, off of game meat. Probably less than 40 people lived at, or near, McKinley Station that summer. With the exception of Maurice Morino, most of them had moved there within the preceding year. That summer saw an influx of new faces. Just as railroad boosters and the Government had hoped, the railroad spawned new resource development. In the autumn, mining engineers identified a commercially developable, bituminous coal seam just six miles south of McKinley Station.

Local investors quickly capitalized the Mt. McKinley Coal Corporation, with Joe O'Connor President, W.B. Reaburn Vice-President, and Alex Fowler, a Nenana druggist and storekeeper, as corporate agent. By the spring of 1923, the 2,560-acre coal claim was a beehive of activity. Skilled miners drove tunnels into the seams, while other laborers erected a tram, feeder tramways, coal bunkers, mess house, office, blacksmith shop, and outbuildings. Healy businessman J.M. "2x4" Smith started work on a hotel and laundry. In addition, the railroad, anticipating a revenue stream, began work on a siding needed to load its coal cars. A wagon road was cut high into the slope above, and parallel

HENRY P. KARSTENS COLLECTION, #874, KARSTENS LIBRARY

*In front of their Igloo Creek camp, (l-r) Harry Karstens, Joe Clark, Joe Quigley, and Major W.C. Gotshall, wait out a sudden and fierce storm that struck in September 1922. Gotshall, on a fact-finding trip for his friend Charles Sheldon, stirred up local park opponents with his intemperate remarks.*

to, the railroad tracks and ran from the mine north to Smith's cabins, located on a flat bluff just south of Triple Lakes. The road doubled as a logging road to the dense stands of timber needed for construction.* Game meat was soon a staple in everyone's diet.[36]

The coal mine was just one of several small endeavors that lured people to McKinley Station. When Rufus Nichols accepted the job as railroad agent, he sent for his wife Martha and five children. They arrived from Washington State in September. Just as some of the pioneer tourists were making their way out into the park via horseback, application was made and approved for a McKinley Station school district. Martha Nichols was elected clerk with Louise Karstens as treasurer.[37]

At least four people approached the superintendent that year to discuss the park concession. In early spring, Frank D. Quigley, no relation to the Kantishna miner, announced plans to build a $250,000 hotel somewhere in the park. Quigley, a tour promoter, and his investors, suggested a site some 25 miles into the park depending on the ultimate location of the planned road. Apparently Quigley failed to provide Karstens with satisfactory details of his project and consequently his permit application died a quiet death.[38]

Next, Casey McDaniel, a railroad contractor, applied for a permit to build multiple accommodations within the park, including a hotel near the base of Mt. McKinley. Access to these hotels would be by horseback and eventually by automobile. Perhaps anticipating a long wait for an adequate road, or for financial reasons, McDaniel abandoned his project.

Van Kirk, the "pirate" on horseback, also approached Karstens about a concession. He wanted permission to develop a pack string and a freight wagon operation to support the Copper Mountain mining ventures but said he would "haul tourists" into the park, utilizing pre-established tent camps. Karstens, quite familiar with Van Kirk, gave little credence to the proposal. The man simply could not be relied upon. Within days of selling his horses and tack to Beach "in order to quit the freight business," Van Kirk was using a new pack string to haul freight on the Kobe to Kantishna trail.

Woodbury Abbey's proposal met strong opposition from Alaska's GLO chief, George A. Parks. Parks cited as main reasons for his opposition, Abbey's lack of experience in the hotel and tourism industry, and vague financing details. He also mentioned that Abbey's open disdain for Karstens made success unlikely. (What caused the rift between Abbey and Karstens remains murky, but their friendship had foundered.) Perhaps Parks' was miffed by Abbey's

* Parts of this old road, last brushed out by rangers in the 1950's, now serves as the Triple Lakes Trail.

resignation, or some other private disagreement, but in the end Parks convinced Karstens to let the permit application die.

As Autumn 1922 rolled into winter, an early and deep snow covered the land. The Riley Creek bottomlands were colder than the surrounding elevations and Karstens spent much of his time preparing for the long, dark, frigid months ahead. His days were spent hauling and cutting firewood and coal and upgrading his family's living standards. His home cabin was by his own admission crude and frontier–style with handmade and scavenged furniture. Just getting ready for winter, caring for horses and dogs, as well as unconquerable administrative paperwork, demanded his full-time attention. After Ranger Powless quit, shifting the entire work load to Karstens, he had little if any time left for his family, let alone to train the dogs for patrol work. A week after Powless quit, Karstens hired Robert S. Bragaw, Jr., of Anchorage, to take his place as "ranger-clerk." Karstens described the young recruit as "honest, active, conservative, and fond of the hills and wildlife . . . just such a young man as the Park Service wishes to enroll." Later he explained that "Bragaw has been employed by the Alaska Railroad Accounting Department for some time, he is getting at least $80.00 or $90.00 a month less here than he was with the railroad but he likes this life and believes in this park's future and wishes to grow with it. The railroad people are trying to get him back offering him an executive position at an increase of salary."[39]

Extreme weather, low pay, and endless, back-breaking labor, drove Bragaw and other pioneer rangers, to resign. Years later Fritz Nyberg explained the situation: "The office work was something that just drove [Karstens] crazy. He didn't trust his clerks at all. Clerks all quit because they didn't like working conditions, living conditions down on Riley Creek. They didn't quit on account of him." The rangers, he said, slept in tents or small, crude cabins with spruce boughs or caribou hides for bedding. I "don't blame them guys for not wanting to stay around," he added. "Nobody wanted to put up with life around McKinley Park then, in those days."[40]

At some point during his first year and a half on the job, Karstens must have felt like he'd been sentenced to a term of hard labor. Not only was he an administrator, but also a lobbyist, law enforcement officer, laborer, tour guide, maintenance man, wrangler, and dog handler. As the little community of McKinley Station began to grow, he must have felt overwhelmed. Poaching patrols, one of his main priorities, got repeatedly shoved to the back burner. He barely had time to keep an eye on his neighbors, most of whom were openly hostile to the park and his position. Escalating tensions with Riley Creek pioneer Maurice Morino would occupy much of Karstens time and energy.

# 5

# Maurice Morino, Pioneer

Maurice Morino was a man of varied temperament. One moment he could be charming, articulate, and gracious; the next moment, gruff, foul, and recalcitrant. The gender, or social position, of the person he dealt with often determined Morino's demeanor.

One woman described this 5'10", 190-pound, blue-eyed, gray-haired pioneer as "very handsome." Another said that, "even in his rough clothes, he had a courtly manner and bearing." When working outside, this "marvelous fellow," as she described him, always wore a red bandanna and Italian cap, and inside his establishment, a blue eye-shade. He loved to philosophize and often quoted passages from the bible and had a "charming way with words." One young woman, who was considering a solo winter stay at McKinley Station, asked Morino for advice. "It's better to eat salt pork than eat with errant kings," he told her. On another occasion she knocked on the hotel door for mail and when Morino finally answered, she said, "Oh, did we come to the wrong door?" He replied, "No, all our doors are open to you, as are our hearts."[1]

Morino's musicality also attracted women's attention. In "a beautiful, cultured voice Morino sang Italian arias all day long," recalled Denise Abbey. He "had been something of an opera singer," added Jean Simmons Wear, a park visitor. "He had a *Victrola* on which he played lots of opera arias all the time, not something the workers on the railroad especially relished."[2]

Men were not usually as impressed. "A rough customer," one man said. "A rather illiterate Italian," huffed Harry Karstens. At times, Morino was rather haughty. He claimed he had been a Colonel in the Italian army before coming to Alaska. "He always walked straight as an arrow and gave orders like an officer, even to patrons," Walter Teeland said.[3]

"Morino wasn't especially well-liked," added Teeland, who worked on the railroad bridge. "In heavily-accented English, he kidded young chaps: '*You're not working hard enough. If you were in the old country you'd know how to work!*'" The truck driver he was ridiculing worked 7 days a week, 12 hours a day. In the 1930's, Maurice's nephew, Joe Morino, spent a year managing the hotel while his uncle went outside for medical treatment. Joe ended up loathing the man and had little good to say about him.[4]

As a representative of the hated federal government, Superintendent Karstens, no matter what he did, would never have gained Morino's acceptance. "In most other matters—particularly financial ones—Alaskans have the free and easy ways of all frontiers," Grant Pearson explained. "Maurice had come to Alaska in 1898, and had no use for anything resembling red tape." A clear personal animosity between Karstens and Morino exacerbated the situation. "Morino had no use for Karstens," said Fritz Nyberg, who had rented a cabin from Morino, "and he didn't want anything to do with me after I went to work [for Karstens.]"[5]

No person dominated McKinley Station more than Morino. Maurice, pronounced "Morris," was born in Bosaio, Italy, on October 27, 1870. When he came of age, he joined the French Foreign Legion, and in the Belgian Congo rose to the rank of Captain. Of these early exploits Morino said, "I could have learned a lot more, but . . . I was young . . . and fifty-horse-power."[6]

Morino immigrated to the United States from Liverpool, England, via Quebec, Canada, on the vessel *S.S. Bavarian*. He soon caught "gold fever" and in 1900 stampeded north to Nome, storming onto the "golden beaches" as part of a wave of 18,000 gold seekers.

Morino's countryman, Felice Pedroni (aka Felix Pedro), struck gold in the Tanana Hills in 1902. Trader E.T. Barnette exaggerated and fanned news of the strike. Hundreds of people stampeded to the hills north of Barnette's Chena River trading post. The diggings at first produced little gold but within three years the area's gold production topped $6,000,000.

Maurice Morino rushed to the Fairbanks strike but arrived a little late. Most of the richest ground had already been staked. In May 1906, Morino filed claims on Vault Creek, twenty miles from Fairbanks. Two years later, Joe Conta, on a neighboring claim, worked gold-bearing gravel that yielded $200,000 in a single clean-up. Morino's property, on the other hand, produced poorly and he was quickly going broke.[7]

Over time, Morino used his limited resources to buy or lease eight claims, including the "*Sierra Association*," on Vault Creek. In its heyday, the boomtown of Vault City, with a population of 200, consisted of nine mining outfits, three saloons, four mercantiles, and three roadhouses, one of which Morino partly owned.

ALASKA ENGINEERING COMMISSION COLLECTION, #G1444, ANCHORAGE MUSEUM AT RASMUSON CENTER

*Returning from a Dall sheep hunt, Maurice Morino pauses in front of his original roadhouse. For anyone traversing the Nenana River canyon, the cabin, built in 1914, offered a welcome respite from the treacherous journey. After railroad construction began, Morino called his home the "Park Gate Roadhouse."*

Exaggerated tales of the richness of Vault Creek, and nearby Dome Creek, led to claim-jumping, ownership squabbles, and fraud. Legal battles hampered development and drained area miners of their precious working capital. Two years of legal disputes cost Morino dearly.[8]

Vault Creek was difficult, expensive ground to work. Most of the actual excavation took place in winter, in temperatures to -50°F, and colder. Here the gold layer was 125'-to-200' deep in soil often frozen year-round. Steam points thawed the ground for excavation by pick and shovel. It cost miners $10 a foot, or more, to sink shafts to bedrock. At bedrock, tunnels, or "drifts," branched out from the main shaft. Laborers hoisted the gold-bearing gravel to the surface where they piled it in cone-shaped dumps for sluicing in the spring.

Morino did not have the money to fully develop his claims. He could not afford to dig a $1,500 hole in the ground. Most of his partners were equally poor, some illiterate. One of his partners, Anthony Tonucci, who had been a fisherman and Klondike stampeder, labored on at Vault Creek long after Morino departed, and, at age 66, died in Fairbanks, penniless and "insane."[9]

"The miners of Vault and Treasure Creeks have gone to a great expense in opening up their ground, and a shortage of water works a great hardship on them," read a 1908 mining report. "The depth to bedrock is so great that it requires a great deal of money to even prospect the ground." Although Morino's 1909 spring cleanup netted between 300 and 400 ounces of gold, he failed to turn a profit, floundering deeper into debt.[10]

Early in 1910, Morino announced the discovery of "good pay" from a new shaft on Vault Creek, perhaps a ploy to stave off creditors. His survival depended on a big spring clean-up but the gold was not there. Immediately after emptying the sluice boxes, Morino declared bankruptcy. He owed $34,222.96 to almost 80 creditors, mostly laborers and suppliers, and another $6700 to the Northern Commercial Co. Some of his laborers, working for $5-to-10 per day, had not been paid in over two years.

Vault Creek's total annual output had declined sharply. As "a sign of the times," many of the buildings in the town of Vault were hauled away and moved to Chatanika. Over the ensuing seven years the banks paid Morino's creditors a total of about $800.

After his Vault Creek debacle, Morino roamed west and then south into the central Alaska Range. In 1910, he followed a trail cut by packer Dan T. Kennedy up the Nenana River to Riley Creek from where he prospected the surrounding drainages.

In 1914, at the peak of a small gold rush to Broad Pass, Morino built a "miner's cabin" on Riley Creek where he spent the winter. In May 1915, Morino left his cabin to go prospecting, not knowing that one month later, President Woodrow Wilson selected the Seward to Fairbanks route, via Broad Pass, for the government railroad. Quite by chance Morino had selected a perfect spot to profit from railroad construction. The AEC began surveying and locating the route later that year.

"During this period 1914 to 1919, I was prospecting in this region and lived on [Riley Creek] during the winters only," Morino later explained. "From 1919 to 1927, I lived on the land continuously conducting a small store and roadhouse for the accommodation of miners, trappers, etc."[11]

Curiously, Morino, who owned other prospecting cabins in the area, never filed a mining claim on Riley Creek itself. In fact, Lee Stillwell, Leo Nebil, and Kay James staked the only claim on Riley Creek, the Ouida Quartz Claim, a 20-acre bench claim on a bluff about 900 feet downstream and south of Morino's roadhouse.

Located just south of the treacherous Nenana canyon, and astride the rigorous route to Broad Pass, Morino's cabin on the north bank of Riley

Creek offered respite to prospectors, trappers, and travelers. A sign nailed to a tree at the confluence of Riley Creek and the Nenana River directed travelers upstream to his cabin.

Sometime in 1916, Morino built a barn and roadhouse, a three-room log cabin topped with a pole and sod roof. In case of chimney fire, he kept a ladder leaning against the eaves and cut his firewood on a sawbuck near the front door. A galvanized wash tub, gold pan, and the skins of fox, ermine, caribou, and other animals, hung on the outside walls. Morino's roadhouse rose from a stump-littered clearing just downstream from the future site of the railroad viaduct.

Like many era roadhouses, Morino's was crude, but at the same time a God-sent reprieve from the elements. "All Morino had was caribou hides for bunks," Fritz Nyberg said. He also described the bill-of-fare as always "beans and caribou meat."[12]

The roadhouse could accommodate twelve people, but was seldom full. In the last five months of 1918, 75 people passed through the roadhouse, including the first railroad trail-blazers and workers. The roadhouse likely was doing record business. As an indicator of his new prosperity, Morino made a donation to Nenana's Red Cross chapter of $7.50—ten cents per customer—and a grizzly bear skin for their fundraising efforts.[13]

Morino's business dwindled to nothing in the warm months and he relocated for summer employment. In 1920, Morino, then 50, ran a roadhouse and prospected at a small camp somewhere on the Tanana River. On April 30, just before his summer sojourn, he officially staked his Riley Creek homestead.

When Morino returned to Riley Creek that autumn, he found the area buzzing with activity, as well as competition. Patrick J. Lynch was building a roadhouse upstream of the trestle site and adjacent to the budding AEC camp.

When Karstens arrived at Riley Creek in 1921, he found Morino and his helpers hard at work on a new 40'x70' "*Mt. McKinley Park Hotel*" on the bluff at the north end of the soon-to-be-built trestle. Visitors described the unusual, flat-roofed two-story log building as "Italian-Alaskan." When complete it featured exposed balconies, glass windows, and electric lights. Inside were 20-to-25 sleeping rooms, a post office, a mercantile, lunch counter, kitchen, and store room. Under the building was a tunnel which opened onto the bluff overlooking the creek. The tunnel accessed cold storage rooms and a room for a Kohler generator. Morino served the first meal in his new hotel, which locals referred to as a roadhouse, on Thanksgiving Day, 1921.[14]

During bridge construction when "both roadhouses at Riley Creek were crowded to capacity. [Morino] . . . made as much as one thousand dollars a

ALASKA RAILROAD COLLECTION, #B88-52-44, ANCHORAGE MUSEUM AT RASMUSON CENTER

*Maurice Morino's Mt. McKinley Park Hotel opened on Thanksgiving Day, 1921, serving its first meal to workers building the Riley Creek trestle. The following summer, Morino proudly poses in a dark suit and hat in front of his hotel.*

day," said one visitor. "It wasn't much of a place…but [with little] competition everybody was satisfied." Observers described Morino's relocation as a shrewd business move. Not only would his new location best serve the army of bridge workers but it would "take care of the volume of [park] travel that is bound to pass that way in the future." Railroad construction would soon end but Morino expected an influx of tourists, road workers, and miners.[15]

In 1922, Morino ran half-page ads in various newspapers trumpeting his running water and electricity. A generator provided the power and Morino piped water from McKinley Pup Creek (later, Hotel Creek) to his hotel. "During construction days, when fellows boarded and roomed there . . . Morino had to carry the water from below the hill for his drinking water. In the summer time . . . he had running water . . . somebody asked him how long he would have the [water] . . . or who shut it off—'Jesus shuts it off,' Morino answered."[16]

Morino essentially abandoned his old roadhouse when he moved to the bluff top but someone served meals in it until 1923. The abandoned roadhouse had napkins and ketchup on the table, and "dead flies all over the inside." A variety of new businesses operated near the old roadhouse or on adjacent property.[17]

An inveterate builder, Morino eventually constructed 10 rental cabins, a school house, two machine sheds, renovated a box car into a cabin, and added a new kitchen. The "annex" enlarged the dining room capacity to 100. In 1925 Morino had his horse barn and old roadhouse torn down for materials to build a log post office on the back of the hotel and to build his *"Chicken-coop Apartments,"* a crude conjoining of three cabins and a shed. The apartments had washrooms and baths, with space for 60 people. In winter, Morino hauled water from the creek and filled the interior water barrels by throwing bucket loads through an open window.

Some of Morino's cabins were built by locals in exchange for five years of rent. In this manner, road commission foreman Elmer Hosler, and his wife, Maude, who would one day be postmaster, built a cabin on the river terrace below the hotel.

Both the road commission and the railroad contracted with Morino to feed their workers but he'd often skimp on meals. Morino would buy a case of pork chops, or whatever else was on sale in Fairbanks, and serve chops every meal until they were gone. Morino then would order another case of chops. Sometimes he served eggs in the same way. "By the end of the crate, if you were lucky, the eggs didn't have any taste at all," said the road commission's Pete Bagoy.[18]

Due to the high cost of beef and chicken, and without adequate refrigeration to preserve fresh meat, Morino regularly served game meat. "Hunter Steak," a euphemism for sheep and caribou meat, was always on the menu. Harry Lucke, who ran a tab at the hotel, paid his debts to Morino by hunting. A typical meal—steak, potatoes, tomato soup, bread, and mince pie—cost $1. While Wood Abbey lived at the park, his mule, named *Jack*, routinely showed up at the back of the hotel to eat stale bread and table scraps. Later, a red fox, named *Marconi*, made nightly foraging visits.

Meals also included fresh vegetables from Morino's gardens. Near his original roadhouse he tended a half-acre garden and on the bluff he annually tilled an acre, which eventually expanded to five acres. "I had no market other than my own road house for vegetables and I supplied that from the start," he said. "I kept clearing land ahead for future use."[19]

In the mid-1920s Morino bought a Caterpillar 30, harrow, disk, and plow. To fulfill the requirements of the Homestead Act, Morino hired a man to clear and till 100 acres and plant 30 of them with hay and barley. Over the course of one exceptional summer a crop of wheat matured. The tilled fields surprised arriving tourists.

Dressed in "hip boots and parka," Morino worked in his kitchen night and day. "By today's standards, he was pretty crude," remarked Walter Teeland. Morino's rustic offerings prodded some itinerant laborers to work extra hard in order to finish the job early. "We'd probably have stayed a little longer," Teeland said, "if the accommodations were a little better, but we got our work done . . . as quickly as possible."[20]

Morino cooked on a five-foot army range with a wire drying rack stretched over it. People wandered in and hung their socks over the stove to dry. Pete Bagoy once saw Morino, who was cooking pancakes on the griddle, grab a sock and wipe the stove down with it before pouring another batch of batter!

Late one winter Morino, suffering from ptomaine poisoning, caught the train to Nenana. No doubt the locals guffawed over that one, but the malady was actually acute appendicitis.

"His coffee pot—a five-gallon can—was continually on the stove," Denise Abbey recalled, "and each day he merely poured in more grounds and then egg shells to settle the grounds. When the pot filled up, he threw out the contents, then started all over again." [21]

The cooks that Morino hired seldom lasted very long but almost all of them were an improvement over the boss. Some of them surprised local customers with excellent meals. In 1922, Mrs. Edgar Brooker, formerly of the Healy Roadhouse, cooked briefly at Morino's before going out to Kantishna. Workers often jammed the hotel for one of her meals. Verna Close was another superb cook and baker who worked for Morino. In autumn her blueberry pies and muffins elicited raves.[22]

One visitor left this vignette of a typical evening at Morino's hotel: "It was suppertime on a hot mid-July day," he wrote. "The doors of the roadhouse . . . were open and a refreshing breeze swept through the sultry kitchen. At the kitchen counter sat several men tardily devouring the last of an excellent meal. The lady of the house was busy with the dishes. Outside, a man was putting up his dogs. As he entered, removed his coat, and found a stool next to mine, the proprietress and several of the oldtimers greeted him with enthusiasm and affection." The man was miner Billy Taylor, who had climbed to the north peak of Mt. McKinley in 1910.[23]

Despite the lice, dirty linen, muddy rooms, flies, marginal food, and un-holy coffee, Morino's "hotel" was not unusual by Alaska roadhouse standards. Perhaps somewhere out in the vast wilderness, with it -30°F and heading for -50°F, Morino's hotel would have been considered luxurious, a welcome respite from the deadly wind and the threat of frozen limbs. Located at the gateway to Mt. McKinley National Park, however, tourists, fresh off the train and satiated with cookies and lemonade, found the hotel wholly substandard and often disgraceful.

Morino sold hardware, traps, gloves, groceries, and, at times, perishables from one of his two gardens. He bought trappers' furs and outfitted itinerant prospectors. For tourists he stocked what he called "gee-gaws."

"Morino had a funny way of selling things," Norma Hoyt remembered. "If you wanted one candy bar, it was five cents, but if you could afford a quarter's worth, you got four for a quarter. A can of soup was 15 cents a can, but three for 50 cents because 'if you could buy three you could afford to pay more.'"[24]

Apparently Morino did not believe in unpacking boxes and shelving his goods. "His stock of groceries was curious to behold," said a visitor. "If a customer asked for a box of crackers he would be sent to Room Four, for a pound of coffee to Room Eight, and so on." [25]

Morino had a supply of straw hats that a salesman had unloaded on him during railroad construction. One year, a U.S. Senator from Connecticut, while in the park on vacation, jokingly bought a hat. Later, someone asked Morino if he'd ever sold any of his hats, and he said: "Yes, I sold one last year to a drunk man and one this year to a United States Senator."[26]

Desperate men could scrounge machine parts from Morino's old car, held together with rope and wire, which was parked on the hotel's porch. People who needed spare parts just came and got them. Morino said that "even the engineer of the train had used parts for emergency repairs!" Years later, minus many parts, and "after a lot of concentrated tinkering on his 'ritzy' automobile," Morino got it running. "This *sick*-cylinder wagon" once belonged to the road commission but they "threw it away or gave it away . . . It has no license plate . . . no starter . . . Sounds like a freight train . . . [but is] all paid for and appears to use soft coal for fuel."[27]

When Martha Nichols declined re-appointment as postmaster in 1925, Morino accepted the position which he held until his death, 12 years later. The post office, which originally operated out of a hotel room, relocated to a log cabin behind it. Morino ran the post office as informally as his other enterprises. Once a postal inspector paid a surprise visit and demanded to see the books and money. When the two did not balance, he approached Morino with the discrepancy. Morino brought out a roll of currency about four inches in diameter, handed it to the inspector, and remarked, "Maybe she's here." The inspector took the necessary amount to balance the books and handed back the rest. According to Grant Pearson, "Maurice's attitude was, 'if the post office needs more money, let it help itself; it's an honest business, and won't take more than it deserves.'"[28]

Like other era roadhouses and hotels, Morino's provided not only food and shelter, but a place to read year-old magazines, month-old newspapers, and socialize. All night community parties, some fired by moonshine, were "well attended and enjoyed by all." A traveling minstrel show, featuring "two scantily-clad ladies," attracted an enthusiastic audience of bachelors.

Morino's dances often made the Fairbanks papers. "The Morino Roadhouse . . . is anticipating the tourist season by providing the setting for an increasingly popular series of good old-fashioned dances . . . The large comfortable ballroom, commodious lounging rooms, and the convenient lunch counter, with the good music . . . brings out practically 100 per cent of the local population besides many from points both ways on the Alaska Railroad . . . A cordial community spirit is being worked up here . . . with no decrease in pep until 3:00 a.m."[29]

COURTESY OF ALICE MORINO

*A former captain in the French Foreign Legion, Maurice Morino, stampeded to Nome in 1900. Nine years later, his search for gold ended in bankruptcy on Vault Creek, north of Fairbanks. Pictured here in later life, Morino made his living at McKinley Station as a roadhouse proprietor.*

The "McKinley Station Bachelors Club" sponsored some of the dances. "The Morino hostelry was the scene of another jolly time last Saturday night . . . this dance featured live music, dancing on the new polished floor, and two cases of Matanuska strawberries."[30]

Maurice Morino gladly supplied the venue for holiday celebrations. "Exceedingly fine time at dance last evening [the Fourth of July], thirty-five people present, among them a number of tourists who had a good time and were very much interested in our little rustic hall which we decorated with flags and spruce boughs. An excellent lunch was served at midnight," Karstens said. "[The] good time was somewhat marred by some of the men being full of moonshine."[31]

During the long dark winters the hotel was an important gathering place. "The majority of the people of McKinley Park have decided to get together and hold a dance to create a better feeling and make the isolation more livable," Karstens explained. "The dance and luncheon at Morino's roadhouse tonight was enjoyed by everybody but was marred somewhat by a free-for-all fight between ex-agent Nichols and some railroad men."[32]

Morino's relationship with Karstens veered from cordial to rancorous, sometimes with reason, other times on trifles. Maurice Morino not only shared, but also inflamed, his neighbor's attitudes toward Karstens and the park. "You, I am sure, can realize the attitude of the people here regarding a man who is practically a watch dog on their hunting expeditions and deportment in the park," Karstens wrote Sheldon.[33]

When rangers, as federal law required, began investigating liquor law violations, Morino exploded in anger. Morino never forgave Karstens for his role in the boot-legging bust. Instead of citing Morino for every liquor violation, however, Karstens more than once looked the other way. In early 1922, shortly after Marshall Hagan had arrested Morino for violating provisions of the Bone Dry Law, Karstens saw one of Morino's employees in the hotel dining room bottling home brew "which Morino [had] been selling to his patrons." Karstens informed Morino that this practice must be stopped in order to establish a working relationship. "Throwing up his hands in an Italian gesture, [Morino] said 'no–no–no—there would be no more of it.'" Convinced by Morino's apparent sincerity, Karstens took no action.[34]

Morino's promises did nothing to curb drinking and fighting at the roadhouse. "No ladies stop there," Karstens said, "preferring to go to Lynch's roadhouse one quarter of a mile from the station, where there is some semblance of decency."[35]

While Morino seemed to turn a blind eye to illegal drinking and drunken antics, he absolutely forbade local prostitutes to come anywhere near the roadhouse. "He was very strict about that," said Pete Bagoy.[36]

HENRY P. KARSTENS COLLECTION, #1486, KARSTENS LIBRARY

*Despite its frontier ambience, Morino's hotel hosted numerous functions, including a 1923 visit by a 65-person Congressional delegation. Local residents welcomed and mixed with the visiting dignitaries. Ranger Gus Buhmann (l) shakes hands with a military officer. Congressman E.W. Sproul, of Illinois, and a colleague, stands at center facing the camera. At right, Harry Karstens, in campaign hat, speaks with a visitor and a local family. At far right, Maurice Morino, in white shirt, emerges from his hotel.*

Tension between Morino and Karstens developed early on. AEC chairman Frederick Mears and Morino were friends and Karstens sensed that the contretemps over the poaching letter somehow kindled Morino's hostility. He felt that Mears would always side with Morino, right or wrong. As Karstens already knew, Mears could be either a powerful ally, or a formidable opponent

In 1921, Mears approached Karstens in support of Morino's concession bid to set up a string of tourist camps in the park. "Morino at all times has ignored my position here," Karstens wrote, "but seeing that the putting up of temporary stopping places would help things considerable in the park I consented [to Mears request] to arrange matters." A few weeks later, Karstens reversed himself, citing the liquor violations.[37]

Karstens soon gave up entirely. "In the case of Maurice Morino whose [concession application] is to put in six tents through the park…I recommend the Service cancel, [Morino] has proved he is not a fit person to be permitted to conduct any business within the park," Karstens reported. "His road house … has been a center for the rough and drunken element in this section, having frequent fights in his place of business it became so bad…that on February 12, 1922, the Marshal made a raid and arrested Morino on the charge of breaking the dry law."[38]

The main bone of contention between the proprietor of the Mt. McKinley Park Hotel and Superintendent Karstens was the physical location of Morino's land, which dominated the railroad depot and thus, the gateway to the park. "The matter of the Morino homestead is blocking the development of a permanent entrance to the park," Karstens wrote, "Morino has been a pet of Colonel Mears and Mears has been out to help him . . . to the detriment of this park."[39]

Woodbury Abbey surveyed Morino's property in 1921, adjusting the boundaries from the original staking, an action upsetting to Karstens. "Abbey the surveyor moved Morino's original lines west in the direction of the park one thousand feet or more up to the foothill taking in all the level ground I wanted and barred me out completely, forcing me to build my headquarters down in the valley . . ." Karstens complained. (Abbey's survey was eventually rejected and a section of Morino's claim vacated.) The conflict over the survey may have been the issue that estranged Abbey and Karstens.[40]

The park service clearly needed to secure land adjacent to the railroad for future use and preserve a route westward to the park boundary. Consequently, the Interior Department drafted Executive Order #3617 which withdrew portions of eight sections, nearly 2,440 acres, "for use in connection with the administration of the Mount McKinley National Park and to protect a right of way for a proposed road into the park." Morino only learned of the federal land withdrawal after President Harding signed the order in January 1922. With the additional land withdrawal, Morino's property was then bounded on three sides by federal reserve. When Morino learned that Karstens had helped George Parks, of the General Land Office (GLO) draft part of the order neither Woodbury Abbey nor Frederick Mears could quell Morino's fury. "Moreno [sic] is still hostile and does not care to have anything to do with this office . . ." Karstens lamented.[41]

Washington's instructions for the strip were clear: "Regarding the stretch of land between the park and the railway withdrawn for administrative purposes . . . the best thing to do is for you to assert jurisdiction for the National Park Service over this strip and manage it the same way as the Park area," Assistant Director Cammerer told him.[42]

Despite the withdrawals, Morino's bluff-top homestead still commanded the best ground. Karstens questioned the legality of Morino's homestead. According to Karstens, the GLO said that "Morino has no right to the ground here . . . [so] I notified my service that I had acquired all this ground. More than a month later the Land Office then notified me, verbally, that Morino did have a right here." Because Morino was not yet a U.S. citizen, Karstens requested an additional ruling. The U.S. District Attorney in Fairbanks agreed that Morino could be evicted. After much wrangling, and despite the fact Morino was not naturalized until January 12, 1925, his homestead was ruled valid.[43]

"I have told Morino a number of times that if he had a right there I could not

COURTESY OF ALICE MORINO

*John Romanov, with a puppy, and Joe Morino, wear two of the Panama hats that Maurice Morino stocked in his store. Morino once said that he sold only two hats, "one to a drunk . . . and one to a U.S. Senator."*

or would not want to cheat him out of his rights, but, if he did not have a right I was going to get such ground as the park needed," Karstens said. "Morino has an insane dislike for me which is fanned by the majority of hangers-on here. He claims he will relinquish such ground as the park needs but not through me."[44]

In the failure of the negotiations with Morino, Karstens saw the work of an old foe. "Mears is the man behind this Moreno [sic] homestead trouble I am having," he informed Sheldon.[45]

**Trading Post**
**McKinley Park Station**

*Tourists, Hunters, Trappers and Prospectors*
**Outfitted. - - Guides Furnished**

*Prices Reasonable* *Mary Thompson, Prop.*

**Mt. McKinley Park Hotel**

Situated on the Government Railroad at the Entrance to
MOUNT M'KINLEY NATIONAL PARK
COMFORTABLE ACCOMMODATIONS—RATES REASONABLE
MAGNIFICANT SCENERY—BIG GAME HUNTING
ELECTRICALLY LIGHTED—PHONE CONNECTIONS
TOURISTS' HEADQUARTERS—GUIDES FURNISHED
Parties can be furnished with pack horses to a limited extent, arrangements for which must be made in advance
Moose, Caribou, Mountain Sheep and Bear in Season, can be found Within easy distance of the Hotel
MEALS SERVED MAURICE MORINO, Proprietor

THE NENANA NEWS NOVEMBER 26, 1921

*Maurice Morino and Mary Thompson competed for goods and services.*

Karstens tried several times to smooth over his differences with Morino. One evening at the roadhouse, Karstens "talked on the park, its present and future developments . . . cited the necessity of eliminating personal animosities, using that energy on the greater problems of the park's development which will benefit everyone."[46]

The superintendent also met with station residents to explain why he wanted parts of Morino's homestead. He explained how valuable the park would become to all concerned and again appealed for understanding and cooperation. He might as well have been baying at the moon.[47]

With resentment running high, Karstens faced enormous opposition and challenges to his authority. Local hunters and trappers impacted by park rules despised him, and personal antagonisms grew into vendettas.

Karstens had more to worry about than just the local festering situation. He heard rumors of illegal hunting and trapping out west near Kantishna, but the two communities at either end of the park were just too far apart for one man to cover. The Kantishna Mining District was booming with activity and completely unmonitored. In the spring of 1920, Karstens had staked a gold claim there and had witnessed first hand the nascent boom. He knew the stories filtering out from the mining district were likely true, and intensely troubling.[48]

## WHO WERE HINES AND RILEY?

AN ENDURING MYSTERY is the identity of the people for whom Hines Creek and Riley Creek are named. The confluence of these two creeks is located almost directly below the railroad trestle, a historic landmark. Originally, Hines Creek was known as Maurice, or Morris, Creek, after Maurice Morino. The first written use of the name "Hines" appears in April 1922, in Harry Karstens' diary, and is used in the monthly Superintendent's Reports for the first time in December. He last used "Morris Creek" in his diary entry of July 26, 1922. Throughout the rest of the year he used both names in public, but not the following year. Hines Creek is labeled as such on a 1923 hand-drawn survey, but another map from that same year uses the original name. By 1925, only a few people used the name Maurice Creek.

SO WHO WAS HINES? No such local name turns up in either period newspapers or existing, known documents. Since the first government use of Hines Creek appears in park service communiqués, we can assume that Karstens changed the name. Barring other candidates, Harry Karstens may have named the creek for his colleague and friend, Frank J. Hines. Hines, who had mined near Deadwood and Dawson City, stampeded north in the great Klondike rush of 1898. Hines first came into Interior Alaska over the Copper River trail, making the trip with Frank Morell, Frank Wiseman, and "Too Much" Johnson. For many years, Hines hauled the mail with Johnny Palm from Chatanika to Circle City, where he likely relayed his freight to mail carrier Karstens. The two also might have met earlier in Dawson.[1]

Hines and his partner Oscar Morell, a French-Canadian, disappeared in the latter part of May 1922 on Birch Creek near the mining camp of "Jump Off." In mid-June, searchers found Hines' body on Birch Creek. It appeared that he and Morell had drowned when their canoe capsized. Morell's body was never found.[2]

Hines was a member of Pioneers of Alaska, Igloo No. 4, and the Arctic Brotherhood, Camp Cleary. McKinley area residents Mason Farrar, Ed Jern, and Harry Karstens, also were members of the Arctic Brotherhood, Camp Cleary.

The connection between Hines and Karstens is clear, but it is not conclusive evidence. Perhaps Karstens, no admirer of Morino, did in fact rename the creek for his friend Frank Hines but such is only speculation. On this point history has drawn a veil.

WHO WAS RILEY? The source of the name Riley Creek, a significant park landmark, also remains unknown. Perhaps an itinerant miner or traveler? Or maybe the well-known riverboat captain and miner, Harry Riley, or the man who grub-staked the first miners to enter the Broad Pass region, Patrick "One-eyed" Riley? Or was it the real estate man from Nenana? The latter Riley is easily eliminated as he came to Interior after the creek acquired its name. Two people who lived at McKinley Station in the 1920's, Walter Teeland and Denise Abbey, said Riley's first name was "George." In an era when almost everyone had a nickname, that is not sufficient to establish identity.

The first government maps of the Nenana River drainage do not identify all of its tributaries by name. In circa 1910 maps, Riley Creek is shown but is not named. The name first appears on an AEC map from late 1914, the year that Morino built his first cabin on the creek. It suggests that Maurice Morino named the creek in honor of a friend or important associate.[3]

A long connection is documented between Morino and miner J.E. Riley, of Fairbanks. Unlike many prospectors Riley possessed both the knack for finding gold and the business sense to succeed. In 1905, Riley owned a claim, Caribou Creek #2, in the Kantishna, but he also prospered from his many profitable claims north of Fairbanks. Riley was both smart and lucky. In 1907, he picked up a 12-ounce nugget on the Discovery Claim of Dome Creek.

J.E. Riley had extensive holdings. His partner on his Pedro Creek and Goldstream claims was Pasquale Manconi, who was also a partner of Morino's on Vault Creek. At one point, Riley and "unidentified partners" worked the *Sierra Association* on Vault Creek, the claim that later pushed Morino into bankruptcy. Morino and Riley also shared adjoining ground on nearby Modock Creek. [4]

In autumn 1908, J.E. Riley followed Dan Kennedy's pioneer trail up the Nenana River to Valdez Creek. The journey, especially in the Nenana canyon, proved arduous. Riley spent the winter at Valdez Creek studying the new diggings. Bedrock here was 100' to 200' below the surface and he knew that it would require a large infusion of capital to recover the gold. In late June, with his evaluations completed, Riley joined a group returning to Fairbanks.[5]

Some of the miners tried to float the Nenana River, but soon gave up when one of their boats disintegrated in the rapids. Prospector J. K. Solomon teamed up with Riley who was hiking the route. Somewhere upriver of the Nenana gorge, Solomon disappeared while attempting to cross a flooding creek. According to the newspaper, "Riley did all he could to try and find the man, but was so short of grub he had to hurry to get through and save himself." Riley believed that Solomon had succumbed to starvation or exposure.[6]

Ten days after Riley arrived in Fairbanks and reported his partner missing, Solomon walked into town. "After getting separated from Riley I built a raft and started to float down the Nenana but the river is nothing but a series of rapids, so I had to give up the idea of reaching the Tanana in this way," Solomon said. "I made through to the second canyon the day after the separation from Riley. There I blazed a tree stating, 'I am two days out of grub and have gone up this stream to try and find a pass over the mountains, and a short cut to the Tanana.' I had not been gone five minutes when I heard a gun shot, from the direction I had left, so I started back in double quick time. On arriving I found three men who had seen my notice, and having noticed the camp fire I had left was still burning, fired the shot to try and attract my attention. Food at Last."[7]

The men built a raft below the second canyon, but swamped two miles downstream, all four men nearly drowning and losing everything except the clothes they wore. After four days without food they found a well-stocked cache which saved their lives. (While the term "second canyon" is open to interpretation, for downstream travelers, it roughly describes the river's course above Healy.)

J.E. Riley next joined the rush to the Iditarod district. By 1911 he, and various partners, owned claims on rich Otter Creek. In 1913, he installed a dredge there which transformed him into on one of the most prominent and wealthiest mining men of the new district.

On Sunday, May 5, 1918, J.E. Riley was at work in his boiler house when a Montenegran wood cutter, named Mailo Steguro, confronted him over a $300 debt. Riley refused to pay or sign a promissory note. An argument ensued. Gun shots rang out.

Miners rushed to the scene and found Riley dead, with three bullets in the back. Steguro ran a short distance but was quickly captured. Only the prompt action of Marshal Geraghty prevented the incensed miners from lynching Steguro. Geraghty seized a .38 caliber pistol, and took Steguro into custody.[8]

The Marshal's investigation revealed that, at the time of the shooting, Steguro had $1,800 of his own money and had killed in anger over $300. A Coroner's Inquest ruled J.E. Riley died by gun shot wounds "from a gun held in the hands of Mailo Steguro."[9]

The murder trial, convened in Iditarod on July 14, 1818, with Judge Charles Bunnell presiding. Steguro, ably defended by Leroy Tozier, pled self-defense.

Witnesses testified that all three shots struck Riley in the back after an argument over a simple debt. Witness Thibault testified that he saw the defendant fire the last shot into the prostrate body of the deceased. Witness Keen testified that the defendant had said, "I will kill the s--- of a b----[sic]."

The trial lasted five days. After deliberating just four hours, the jury rendered a verdict of guilty, ruling the killing "wholly without excuse, justification or any mitigating circumstances." Judge Bunnell sentenced Steguro to death by hanging, the sentence to be carried out in Fairbanks, on October 4, 1918.[10]

Five times Steguro's attorneys and relatives secured reprieves. Finally, on April 15, 1921, he walked on to the improvised gallows in downtown Fairbanks. Steguro fainted when his feet struck the sounding boards but after being revived he was strapped to the hanging board. His last words were a mumbled request for "more of that whiskey." Steguro was pronounced dead at 1:39 p.m.[11]

Was J.E. Riley the man Riley Creek was named for? Perhaps, but again we have nothing definitive, only intriguing speculation. Clearly, J.E. "George" Riley" (also sometimes referred to as Edward) had long known and associated with Maurice Morino. In fact, it has been inferred several times that Riley re-financed Morino after his catastrophic bankruptcy. In 1913, Morino, with a grub-stake from J.E. Riley, visited Valdez Creek. The next year, during the 1914 Broad Pass stampede, Morino built his first cabin on the stream that was soon named Riley Creek.

# 6

# All that Glitters

As placer gold output on Glacier and Eureka Creeks, the two richest streams in the Kantishna Mining District, plummeted sharply in 1906, prospectors began exploring the slopes and benches for lode deposits. The discovery of pebble-to boulder-sized galena (lead ore) and stibnite (antimony ore) in their sluice boxes fueled the search for other metals. Joe Quigley prospected the Kantishna Hills and soon found mineral veins extending 35 miles, from Moose Creek to Stampede Creek. In response to the high price of antimony prompted by the Russia-Japan War of 1904-1905, Quigley shipped twelve tons of stibnite from his Last Chance Mine on Caribou Creek to an Outside smelter. High freight costs and a plunging demand for antimony doomed this pioneer lode project.[1]

Of all the Kantishna pioneers, Joe Quigley and Fannie McKenzie became best known, their story inseparable from Alaska's gold rush history. Both had stampeded to the Klondike and from there to other strikes in Yukon and Alaska. Fannie had missed the 1905 Kantishna stampede, but in the following two years, she staked multiple claims there. She and Joe, acquaintances from earlier strikes, quickly teamed up, and on February 2, 1918, U.S. Commissioner J.C. Van Orsdel married them at Glacier City.

Together, the Quigleys staked a number of the best antimony, silver, gold, and copper-bearing veins on what was then called Mineral Ridge, now Quigley Ridge, which forms the divide between Friday and Eureka Creeks. Soon after their wedding Joe and Fannie built a cabin on their Silver Pick claim located on a high bench over-looking Eureka Creek. Here Joe discovered a new vein of galena that showed promise of surpassing anything yet found in the district. Some of their other claims—the Little Annie, Banjo, and Red Top—also

DENALI NATIONAL PARK & PRESERVE, MUSEUM COLLECTION, #11236

*Owen "Red" Grant's cabin at Copper Mountain. A mineral strike there sparked a small stampede and attracted the attention of large mining companies. A proposed rail spur through the park to Copper Mountain was never built.*

looked promising. By 1921, the Quigleys had built another, more substantial, home cabin on their Red Top claim above Friday Creek. Unfortunately, neither Quigley was an experienced hard-rock miner, nor did they possess the capital to properly assess and develop their discoveries.[2]

For both Quigleys, hard–rock mining was "learn as you go." Joe enjoyed reading and was always eager to learn something new, studying and collecting books on hard-rock mining, geology, and mineralogy. He purchased an assaying outfit and soon became a more scientific prospector. By hand, and usually working alone, Quigley ran his drifts, or shafts, far into the rocky hillsides. Following one ore lead that measured almost 30 feet wide, Quigley eventually dug "600 feet into the hillside . . . with 200 feet of cross-cut tunnels." The mine was a monument to hard labor and persistence fueled by optimism.[3]

Underground work was both difficult and dangerous. The country itself conspired against the lode miners. Permafrost lay just below the surface and had to be melted by fires. In summer, the frozen ground inside the tunnels sometimes melted and slumped. Extensive timber shoring was needed to prevent mine collapse. Some tunnels filled with water. Working alone underground was a form of Russian Roulette, and in 1930, the odds would finally catch up with him. Joe was badly injured in a tunnel collapse on his Banjo Claim, effectively ending his mining career. The mere fact that Quigley

COURTESY OF CANDY WAUGAMAN

*In the wake of the Copper Mountain stampede, the Mt. McKinley Tourist and Transportation Company set up a tent camp to serve its guests.*

worked as long as he did without major accident, attests to the skill of this resourceful pioneer.*

Mining engineers suspected that Quigley's lack of capital, rather than low–quality ore, prevented large-scale mineral recovery. Consulting geologist Harry Townsend, working for the Anaconda Copper Co., inspected Quigley's lode properties and declined investment because of the lack of reliable transportation.

Other veterans of the 1905 stampede stayed loyal to the Kantishna. Billy Taylor worked ceaselessly to secure financing for large scale mining ventures. Joe Dalton, who struck it big on Eureka Creek, remained bullish on the district, for years predicting that large quartz and placer mining operations would ultimately reveal the hidden Mother Lode.[4]

By summer 1918, only 36 people lived in the district, with over half of them original stampeders. The American war effort had literally drained the Alaska Territory of manpower. Mining throughout the territory faltered for lack of laborers and prospectors. At the end of the war claim owners and mining interests were trolling

*Eventually the large Banjo quartz–sulfide vein became the largest tonnage hard-rock producer in the district's history, yielding for its new owners $15 to $18 dollars a ton of free gold from panned crushed ore. At peak operation the Banjo Mine, re-named Red Top Mining Co., included a 24 ton–a–day ball mill and employed almost two dozen miners

for new blood. "There is room in the Kantishna hills for many more prospectors than are there at the present time, and more room for large–scale operations," a reporter said. "The McKinley Park country is a good mining district and the regrettable truth of its slow development is lack of prospectors. When the hills are filled with prospectors the country will begin to open up," said mining engineer E.J. Costello, a representative of Anaconda Copper.[5]

The general demobilization following the Armistice, coupled with national economic woes, spurred a population influx that ended Alaska's chronic labor shortages. The construction of the Alaska Railroad, seen as the answer to the Kantishna district's debilitating transportation problem, spurred new interest in mining there.

After the war a steady trickle of gold-seekers filtered into the Kantishna Hills to join the old-timers working there. Floyd "Kid" Marsh turned up in Eureka Camp and was pointed in the direction of an old claim on Yellow Pup. Here, after consultation with Rainy Creek old-timers Perry Blue and Jack Ritter, he said he discovered an 18-inch-wide quartz vein which "assayed at over $500 a ton in free gold," an almost preposterous value. He later boasted of taking $2,000 in nuggets back to Fairbanks that fall. If true, it was fabulous luck for

## WILDERNESS CHRISTMAS

Glacier City had never seen a Christmas party like the one Billy Taylor hosted in 1922. On that frigid Christmas Day guests from as far away as Nenana assembled at his cabin, the headquarters of Mt. McKinley Gold Placers, Inc. Although his cache bulged with moose and caribou meat, Taylor wanted something special and was determined to create a memorable Christmas for all. In late autumn, Taylor had ordered a turkey from a farm in Washington. Just getting the bird to Glacier had been an incredible adventure. Taylor's efforts were rewarded when everyone gathered round the decorated table and chef Frank Kawasaki served up turkey with all the trimmings, and a dessert of fresh-baked pies.

After dinner, the 20 guests retired to the bunkhouse to light the Christmas tree candles. The pungent spruce was ostensibly decorated for the two children present, but it was the greybeards, men from the stampede of '05, that had tears sparkling in their eyes. Dancers careened around the cabin into the early morning hours. Later, guests like old-timers Peter Lish and Billy Folger, called the festivities "the best Christmas celebration they'd ever had in the north."

The Kantishna's mining revival fueled a sense of optimism and hope, especially in those associated with Taylor's well-financed venture. At dawn they toasted their renaissance, the long years of hardship nearing an end, and the birth of a viable and vibrant community.

a *Cheechako* working picked over ground. The next winter, he claimed to have single-handedly removed 25 tons of high-grade gold ore from his Oklahoma Claim and sold it for $8,000.[6]

In 1919, geologist Stephen R. Capps, an early booster of the park, made a trip through the Kantishna and according to one report, "seemed highly impressed…and thinks that if anything like adequate transportation facilities are provided the district can be developed and made to support a large community." Prospectors' impact on the region's wildlife disturbed him greatly and he reported "wholesale slaughter" of caribou.[7]

Intense prospecting led to new discoveries and excitement. Newspapers trumpeted the finds in the Kantishna, Broad Pass, and in McKinley Park itself, attracting ever more prospectors eager to strike it rich. "Experts" were quoted at length, mirroring similar reports published at the peak of the 1905 gold rush. "There have been found lately a number of very fine looking prospects…which we will soon develop into mines," said J.A. Haney, a pioneer miner working a lay on Charles McGonagall's claims. He estimated that over 100 men were at work in Kantishna in the summer of 1920, and by autumn would top 200.[8]

Just as it had in 1905, every positive account of the district attracted attention. "The next big mining camp of Alaska will be in the Kantishna district," predicted William Layman, another well-known old-timer. The Fairbanks and Nenana newspapers, as promoters of their respective towns, had a vested interest in booming any new strike. An increased population and a strong, mining-based economy translated into advertising revenue for the papers. Consequently, even scant commentary was given a positive spin. When famed Nome musher Leonard Seppala passed through the Kantishna in 1921, en route to the Kuskowim drainage, he mentioned that he thought the Kantishna looked "promising." This comment inspired an entire newspaper story that said little else.[9]

The rebirth of the Kantishna Mining District as a hot mining locale relied only in part on the surge of new prospectors. It was the old-timers like Taylor, Quigley, Dalton, and Hamilton, who made the exciting strikes and found the investors to fund the big projects. Spurred by their reports, many of the original 1905 stampeders sent word that they were on their way back "home." After years in the lower 48, many former Kantishnans returned to take part in what they saw as the redemption of the district. One of the returnees, Charles Griess, had volunteered for military service in defense of his adopted country, and despite being over the age limit, joined the Army for the duration of the war. Pioneer miners throughout Interior lauded their Kantishna peers for their determination. "Men like Jack Hamilton, Joe Quigley, and Billy Taylor . . . have held on to their claims for 17 or more years stretching out their mere tinseled existence on a diet of sowbelly and beans . . ."[10]

The growing excitement spared no one, not even those with potentially lucrative positions. U.S. Commissioner J.C. Van Orsdel resigned his post to partner with Billy Taylor in a hydraulic mining venture. An increasing population and nascent mining boom in the district necessitated his immediate replacement. Federally-appointed Commissioners acted as coroner, judge, and mining recorder, often the only authority in a vast region. Instead of receiving a fixed salary, they charged a fee for each transaction—the larger the volume of activity, the greater the income. In 1919, Judge Charles Bunnell appointed Charles Herbert Wilson to replace Van Orsdel and ordered the Commissioner's office moved from Glacier City to Glen Creek, then the largest producer of gold in the district. Wilson, born October 7, 1892 in Seattle, was "one of the prominent young civil engineers" hired and sent to Fairbanks in 1916 by the Alaska Engineering Commission (AEC). He and his wife Anna were well-known and liked in the Fairbanks area.

Despite the rumblings of war in Europe, the Wilsons' classic love affair made news in Alaska. Both were from Washington State where Wilson played high school football. C. Herbert, as he was called, met his future bride, Anna L. Elsemore, in Aberdeen during school vacation. In 1916, Anna boarded the *S.S. Mariposa* for the long trip to Fairbanks and her waiting fiancée, keeping a promise to wed made two years before.

After a steamship voyage, two railroad trips, and a long river journey, Anna arrived in Fairbanks in late June. The story of their romance was no secret. Papers described Miss Elsemore as "one of the prettiest and most accomplished young women to ever go into the Interior . . . Her eyes are of deep blue, and her head crowned with a mass of beautiful Titian hair . . . the possessor of a highly cultivated soprano voice of great sweetness and purity."[11]

Their quiet Episcopal marriage at the home of Bess Milum on Fifth Avenue in Fairbanks was followed by an elaborate dinner at the *Arcade*. The couple spent a romantic, but brief, honeymoon in a wall tent somewhere along the railroad right-of-way near where Wilson supervised a crew grading the right-of-way.[12]

After working three years as a railroad construction supervisor, Wilson quit to develop his own silver and business prospects in the Kantishna. On May 20, 1919, Fannie Quigley sold Wilson a house lot in Eureka Camp for $1. The old boom camp then boasted about a dozen log cabins, a few tents, a small

JOHN M. BROOKS COLLECTION, #68-31-87, ARCHIVES, UNIVERSITY OF ALASKA, FAIRBANKS

*The Kantishna Hydraulic Company dammed the outlet to Wonder Lake and diverted the flow into a hand-dug, 12,000-foot-long ditch that carried water to their operations at the confluence of Moose and Eureka Creeks. Nozzles, called "giants" washed away overburden and provided water to the sluice boxes.*

store and 29 year-around residents. Wilson, acting as agent for the Quigleys, who owned the old mining town, renamed it "Kantishna City," with lots for sale at reasonable prices. (This was the second name change in two years. In 1918, Eureka was called "Shamrock City." Neither name stuck.)

Wilson soon ordered tons of supplies for a new store there and another he had in Glacier City. The Wilsons sold out their entire stock as soon as it was unpacked, despite flour and sugar going for a hefty 50 cents per pound. Not to miss out on the boom, Evelyn Grant bought a washing machine from Tom Aitken and opened a laundry near the Wilsons' new store. That winter, in preparation for the 1920 mining season, Wilson built a two-story log cabin in Eureka for use as a home and unofficial office. (Wilson's log home still stands and although called the "Kantishna Roadhouse" it never was a formal roadhouse.)[13]

Wilson and three others teamed up to develop silver claims on Alpha Ridge northwest of Eldorado Creek, not too far from the Neversweat Mine. They hauled nearly 10 tons of high-grade ore down to Moose Creek and on to Roosevelt on the Kantishna River for shipment Outside. Their silver ore, which included some gold, assayed at $200 per ton (the value of silver at that time was one dollar an ounce.) Prospectors Mace Farrar and Edgar Brooker

Sr. developed another mine near theirs that produced a slightly richer silver ore. However, the remoteness of the mines and high cost of shipping made the ventures unprofitable.[14]

On December 23, 1921, Judge Cecil Clegg appointed Edgar Brooker, Sr. to replace Wilson. Mr. and Mrs. Brooker had extensive mining and roadhouse experience. Brooker estimated that about 100 whites lived year-around in his jurisdiction, covering "an area as large as the State of Washington." After receiving a petition signed by 40 area miners, Clegg ordered the commissioner's headquarters moved from Glen to Friday Gulch where Mary Brooker had just opened a "first class roadhouse."[15]

Without telegraph service, and far from Fairbanks, the Kantishna seemed dangerously isolated. Within weeks of his appointment he wrote the U.S. Marshal in Fairbanks requesting the assignment of a deputy to the Kantishna District, or at least enlargement of the duties of his Nenana deputy. " . . . the majority of the people in the Kantishna Precinct in the past were men who had located here about 1905 . . . These people were typical Alaskans, law abiding and honest . . . I regret to inform you that conditions have changed and an element has crept into our district entirely foreign to the old-timers' conception of what constitutes a good citizen." Either Brooker was unaware of the sometimes violent and often brutal nature of the Kantishna, or conditions had perilously deteriorated.[16]

ALBERT JOHNSON COLLECTION, #67-32-32SN, ARCHIVES, UNIVERSITY OF ALASKA, FAIRBANKS

*Sacks of lead-silver ore stack up at the entrance to Red Top Quartz Mine and next to the Quigley cabin further down the hill. The high cost of transporting the ore doomed several efforts to make the Mineral Ridge claims profitable. Below is the Friday and Moose Creeks confluence.*

Brooker blamed an influx of ex-railroad construction workers, and renewed interest in quartz development for an upsurge in crime, mostly thefts of prospector's caches. "Investigations show conclusively that these are all traceable to the new element," he said. As an example of everyday problems, Brooker mentioned that former Commissioner Wilson had caught two men "sniping"—a miner's word for sluicing or panning on another's claim—on Yellow Creek. Brooker could do little other than file a report with the U.S. Marshal's office.[17]

With World War I finally over and the AEC ramping up efforts to complete the Alaska Railroad, a new breed of mining entrepreneurs moved into the district. Production of high-grade lead-silver ores did not begin until early 1919, when the Quigleys optioned out their claims on Mineral Ridge to Tom Aitken, who had mined similar deposits at Keno Hill in the Yukon. Aitken leased the Quigley claims on a part cash/part royalty basis, for a total price of $230,000, paying $10,000 up front, which Joe and Fannie divided evenly. Newspapers erroneously claimed the deal was for an initial cash payment of $300,000, with the potential royalty totaling $1 million. After signing the papers the Quigleys went on "vacation" to the foothills of Mt. McKinley and announced plans to go Outside in December. "They plan to go Outside and stay as long as they can stand it and then beat it back North," said one friend. It would be Joe's first trip out of Alaska since 1891, and Fannie's first since 1895. They planned to visit Joe's hometown in Pennsylvania, Fannie's in Nebraska, her sisters in Oregon and Washington, and tour silver and lead mines in Missouri.[18]

After signing the papers, Aitken wasted no time in getting to work, sending in a power launch and scow loaded with eight men, horses, and supplies. He instructed foreman Billy Grant to excavate Quigley's galena ledge above Friday Creek and extract sample ore. Initial tests showed the silver content to be 250 ounces per ton, with 40 percent lead and some gold. Expectations for huge profits ran high. "With the opening of the Quigley mine on an extensive scale," opined one editorial, "the old town of Roosevelt will again have a population and the mining game in this region will be stimulated."[19]

To the delight of old-timers, the boom restored a semblance of regular freight service to the district. Despite the high rates charged, miners embraced the flotilla of launches and steamers plying the rivers as harbingers of a new, prosperous era. Whenever conditions allowed, usually in spring high water, big sternwheelers like the *Shushana* hauled huge loads up river to Roosevelt. Shallow draft sternwheelers, and a gaggle of smaller gasoline launches, including the *George Black, Moody, Moore, and McGonagall,* hauled modest loads up the main river and its smaller tributaries. At the height of the new boom, *The Mutt*, a small, gas–powered sternwheeler and the most reliable of them all, made two round trips a month, carrying both passengers and freight.

Renewed activity also restored monthly mail service. Summer shipments were initially dumped in an abandoned cabin at Roosevelt for delivery by whoever happened by. In response to local protest, the postal service contracted with George Black to deliver the mail to a *locked*, abandoned cabin. George Duncan won the bid for winter service, the contract stipulating one round trip per month, the carrier "not to exceed 400 pounds of mail a single trip each way, leaving Nenana (with a turn around time for outgoing mail) at Kantishna of not less than 24 hours." To pioneers like Taylor and Quigley, it seemed like old times. The mail arrived by dogteam in winter, riverboat in summer, same as it had in 1905.[20]

Kantishnans saw a boom in the offing and took steps to exploit it. Wilson, and pioneer Alois Friedrich, staked an 80-acre claim over the old town of Roosevelt, and renamed it Town of Quigley. Which, according to Wilson "was chosen as a tribute to the man whose perseverance has made the camp of Kantishna a success." If indeed the district boomed as expected, this town on the Kantishna River at the head of navigation would become prime real estate.[21]

Throughout the summer the ore from the "Aitken tunnel" continued to improve with depth. Before freeze-up, Aitken shipped in 200 tons of cargo, with more on order. He also sent in six more laborers to sack ore, which they stored either in an ore house at the tunnel mouth, or on the open hillside. Two shifts of workers drove the tunnel deeper and by December they had extended Quigley's old tunnel 150 feet into the mountain and had removed 700 to 800 tons of ore.

Transporting the ore was Aitken's biggest challenge. Just getting the ore off the ridge and down to the creek bed was difficult. Ore bags weighed 100 pounds, or more, and there were hundreds of them. Aitken hired teamster Ed Bartlett to do the hauling. Bartlett immediately assigned one of his men to begin transferring the sacks by pack horse downhill to a storage site on Moose Creek. After freeze-up the silver ore would be hauled by horse-drawn sleds to Roosevelt.

Before cross-country freighting to Roosevelt could begin, however, Bartlett needed to clean up and improve the old road that was built in 1905. As soon as the road was cleared, and two relay camps established, Bartlett's teamsters began hauling ore. In short order, his three four-horse teams were delivering ten tons of ore per day to Roosevelt. On the return trip the wagons and sledges

JOHN M. BROOKS COLLECTION, #68-32-314, ARCHIVES, UNIVERSITY OF ALASKA, FAIRBANKS

*Ed Bartlett contracted to haul Tom Aitken's silver ore across country to Roosevelt on the Kantishna River. Before Aitken's mining operation shut down, Bartlett's teamsters transported over 300 tons of ore to the river's edge for summer shipment.*

carried fuel and supplies as well as timber for tunnel shoring. The ore pile grew throughout the winter, awaiting river shipment after spring break-up.[22]

With Fairbanks 341 river miles from Eureka, the lack of dependable, year-round transportation had long been the Kantishna's Achilles Heel. Despite the fact that the district's rivers might only be navigable for less than 12 weeks a year, the water route was the only practicable way to transport large loads. Even the smallest boats found the route difficult. After one typical trip, J.C. Van Orsdel, a river pilot, gave this report: "Owing to the very low stage of the water and the abundance of dangerous snags in the river, navigation was rendered difficult and tedious and it took two days to make the distance of fifty miles down the Bearpaw River to its outlet on the Kantishna River."[23]

Van Orsdel went on to describe the usual procedure. "All supplies are freighted up the river to Diamond, or Roosevelt if water levels allow, and cached there until the coming of the snows and then they are freighted to the neighborhood of the mining country. As the Bearpaw River can only be navigated at a fairly high stage of water, the necessary supplies have to be rushed into the country early in the season."[24]

The 35-mile trail from Roosevelt to Eureka, first brushed out in 1905, led across muskeg swamps and through otherwise impenetrable black spruce and alder thickets. In 1917, financed by a $4,000 ARC contract, miner Thomas Lloyd, who had organized the 1910 Mt. McKinley climb, began to cut and build an "all-seasons" corduroy road over the original route. The funds were inadequate to do much more than repair some of the worst trail sections. Despite additional work by the road commission crews, Ed Bartlett found the trail in dire need of repair.

Winter's fearsome cold and the district's isolation had long exacted a gruesome toll in lives and lost limbs. The mining resurgence at least brought new people into the country, slightly improving everyone's margin of safety. While hauling ore on a frigid mid-winter day, Bartlett came upon a crumpled body in the snow. Fearing the worst, he charged forward, finding the man alive but unconscious. Unable to revive him, Bartlett loaded Bill Hunter, a pioneer prospector, in his sleigh and raced to the nearest occupied cabin. He carried him inside and sent for Nurse Pande Bagley who was a guest of the Quigleys. Bagley revived Hunter, finding him partially paralyzed. Although Bagley was scheduled to leave for Nenana the next day, she canceled her departure in order to treat the stricken miner. When Bagley finally returned to town, she reported her patient restored to health. Without the mining boom no one would have found him.[25]

Tom Aitken planned to use the shallow draft sternwheeler *Reliance* to move his ore to the Tanana River, where a succession of bigger vessels would barge the ore to the mouth of the Yukon River for shipment south. Normal shipping costs from the Kantishna to the Selby, Montana, smelter hovered around $57 a ton, but despite a special rate offered by the Alaska-Yukon Navigation Company, Aitken's ore had to be worth at least $165 a ton just to break even. His miners were under orders to dump anything of less value into the tailing piles.[26]

Late in the summer of 1920, the *Kestrel*, another shallow draft steamer, was pressed into service but by freeze-up over 100 tons of sacked ore remained scattered on the banks of the Kantishna River, mute sentinels to unseasonably low water levels. At the mine, ore began to accumulate in an ever–growing backlog.[27]

This first production of lead-silver ore in the Kantishna generated much interest. Adding to the excitement of the mining district's rebirth was the arrival of geologist Livingstone Wernecke, a representative of the powerful Alaska Treadwell Mining Company which for 30 years had operated the most successful hard rock mine in Alaska. With Billy Taylor as his guide, Wernecke left Nenana intending to examine every major ore ledge in the Kantishna. The tight-lipped geologist would not say which claims he was most interested in, but the locals believed that he was there to investigate Aitken's project.

A few months later, in January 1920, Aitken made the unusual public announcement that reports of the value of his ore "do not run as high as the public has been encouraged to believe." Although known as a conservative mining man, his remarks raised a few eyebrows. What the public did not know was that due to mining and transportation costs, his venture was a losing proposition.[28]

Aitken, and others, developed their hard rock propositions in Kantishna years ahead of any dependable and economical form of transportation "at an expense which is enormous compared with the immediate returns." These hard–rock miners faced a stark conundrum: they had to ship substantial tonnage before the transportation companies would establish regular service at reasonable rates, but without substantial profit from large ore shipments, they would go bankrupt from the exorbitant shipping costs.[29]

Although the Mineral Ridge claims produced quality ore, the project continued to operate in the red. With the easy–to–find, high–grade, lead–silver ores exhausted, Aitken substantially reduced operations. In February 1921, he stunned Kantishna boosters with the announcement he was quitting the district and heading back to his gold dredge on Candle Creek. In the aftermath, Quigley argued with Aitken over their lease agreement, claiming the decline in ore output resulted from "careless mining." With the dispute unresolved, Aitken invoked a closure clause in his lease and returned the 22 claims on Mineral Ridge to Quigley with no further payment due. When he quit the Kantishna, Aitken left behind 400 tons of sacked ore.

The Quigley claims did not remain dormant. Hawley Sterling leased Red Top, and several others, employing a small work force to remove the lead–silver ore. He hailed the claims as "the most promising silver discovery" in Alaska. For two years Sterling shipped 184 tons of ore overland via tractor–pulled sledges to the railroad stop at Kobe. (The use of motorized transport was Sterling's attempt to secure profitability.) The ore yielded 43,664 ounces of silver, 187 ounces of gold, and 93,200 ounces of lead, but the total value still less than $60,000. Over the course of five years, Sterling and Aitken had wrested 1,435 tons of ore from eight deposits on Quigley and Alpha Ridges. In total, the 253,000 ounces of silver, and at least 450 ounces of gold, and other metals, were worth about $300,000, but actual profits were negligible.[30]

Aitken's hard-rock operation, the catalyst for the district's mining rebirth, was not the only big project underway in the Kantishna during the early 1920s. With the easily recoverable placer gold removed, and the promise of an end to the district's labor and transportation woes in the offing, interest turned toward an industrialized approach to gold recovery. With the days of pan and rocker gone forever, Kantishna pioneers and their backers developed two hydraulic operations.

Hydraulic mining, or hydraulicking, is a form of placer mining that employs water under very high pressure to wash away overburden or excavate a bank of gold-bearing gravel. A system of ditches and riveted pipe carried water from higher elevations to a spot above the area to be mined. From that point the water was directed downhill through tapering pipe and passed through iron nozzles called monitors, or "giants." Miners systematically waved the monitors back and forth, the pressurized water sufficient to blast away entire hillsides. The loosened soil then ran downhill into a series of sluices, the gold removed through traditional mining techniques.

Dr. John Sutherland's Kantishna Hydraulic Company controlled 890 acres of placer ground, embracing 45 claims, on Moose Creek and extending from just above the mouth of Eureka Creek to one and a half miles below Friday Creek. Work on the project was originally slated to start in 1918 but low water the year before prevented equipment delivery. In June 1918, tons of supplies still sat on the bank of the Tanana River at the mouth of the Kantishna awaiting shipment upstream. The first 20 tons of pipe and heavy equipment finally made it to Roosevelt in the summer of 1920, but the poor condition of the haul road to Eureka delayed hauling until after freeze-up. With somewhat limited capital to work with, the delay was a serious financial setback for Sutherland.

Preliminary work commenced in 1921. Teamsters hauled in 40 more tons of pipe and laborers built a five-foot dam at the outlet of Wonder Lake to divert water into a freshly-dug, two-foot-deep, and six-foot-wide, 12,000-foot-long ditch. On the mining site opposite the mouth of Eureka Creek, laborers assembled 4,000 feet of riveted steel pipe tapering down from 26 to 18 inches in diameter, as well as hundreds of feet of sideline and feeder pipe. They also built sluices, sheds, and at least one cabin. In all, the company employed a total labor force of 20 men, each paid $5 per day plus board.

If the venture proved lucrative, the company planned to pipe water all the way from the McKinley River. In preparation for the work, the company built a cabin at Big Timber. Such a pipeline would obviate the low water that historically hampered area mining.[31]

Hydraulic mining began on Moose Creek in 1922, slightly downstream and across from the mouth of Eureka Creek. The first few claims on Eureka had been the richest in the entire district and it made sense that gold might have been deposited in the buried gravel opposite it. That summer, a seven men crew, working eight-hour shifts, washed away a layer of over-burden ten feet thick, exposing 50,000 square feet of bedrock. Five "giants" washed the gravel and sand into a long line of sluice boxes. The nearly 600-foot-wide pay streak had a preliminary value of fifty cents per square foot, but "recovery . . . fell considerably below the estimated value of the ground." These poor returns, and delays when the dam and ditch washed out, doomed this operation. Sutherland's multi-year gamble ultimately failed to produce the wealth he had sought.[32]

Such industrialized mining obviously required substantial capital. In 1920, Billy Taylor and J.C. Van Orsdel attracted Outside investors in their hydraulic venture, Mount McKinley Gold Placers Inc. Taylor, Van Orsdel, and Bill Julian controlled all the claims on Caribou Creek from its mouth to one mile above its confluence with Crevice Creek but they needed big money to exploit their advantage. Finally the partners secured an investor, Charles Johnson, an Ohio capitalist, who was also a friend of the new President, Warren Harding. With Johnson's money Van Orsdel bought and shepherded the initial shipment of hydraulic equipment from Seattle to Kantishna. After freeze-up, horse-drawn sledges and a motor tractor hauled the 77 tons of pipe and other tonnage from Diamond to Caribou Creek. Mining engineer, K.E. Casparis, who was Johnson's on-site representative, examined the ground and directed mining operations. His preliminary survey found that bedrock varied from two to fourteen feet below the surface with a spotty, ill-defined pay streak with wide variations in value. After Casparis identified bench claims on the upper creek as the best ground, preliminary work by a 40-man crew began. Laborers dug 450 feet of ditch, laid 4,000 feet of steel riveted pipe, and built an eight-foot–high, 200'–long dam near Crevice Creek that diverted water into the ditch and flume. They also built three sluice boxes for each of the three "giants." In 1922, the crew cleaned over 70,000 square feet of ground down to bedrock, washing away a six-to-eight foot thick layer of overburden. Test pannings in mid-July promised returns far larger than expected but low water volume abruptly ended the season. The partners anticipated big returns in 1923. *[33]

---

*Neither of these two large–scale hydraulic operations produced enough gold to be profitable and quickly shut down. Late into the decade Taylor and Julian continued to operate a small hydraulic operation on Caribou Creek but it proved more of a "grubstake" operation than a big money maker. Taylor's belief in his claims was not misplaced. In the late 1930s, William Dunkle's Caribou Mines, a dragline operation, finally tapped the drainage's full potential becoming the most successful mining venture in Kantishna history.

JOHN E. ANDERSON COLLECTION, COURTESY OF JAY HATHAWAY

*As the Kantishna's placer gold played out, miners developed ingenious contraptions to maintain water levels and move ever larger quantities of overburden. This self-dumping dam on one of Paula Anderson's claims was typical of such innovations.*

In the fight to establish a Mt. McKinley National Park, James A. Wickersham, Alaska's Delegate to Congress, demanded that the borders of the proposed park exclude the Kantishna mining district. Wickersham, who owned claims on Glen Creek, initially opposed the park's creation unless language was inserted that guaranteed the rights of miners to locate claims within the park. Although he recognized the park's tourism potential, Wickersham strongly resisted any attempt to inhibit mining activity. He also demanded hunting rights in the park for all miners and prospectors. Many parks in the Lower 48 provided for mining activity, but McKinley would be the first to give miners hunting privileges. Reluctantly, park advocates gave in to Wickersham's boundary demands, but were spilt over the miners' hunting exemption. The key to securing Congressional passage was a specific statement acknowledging the mineral laws. "My objection to including this area in a park has been very largely overcome by the provision in the bill which extends the mineral-land laws there," Wickersham testified during Congressional hearings.[34]

The act signed into law read: "For necessary development it is permitted that prospectors and miners engaged in prospecting or mining in said park may take and kill therein so much game or birds as may be needed for their actual necessities when short of food; but in no case shall animals or birds be killed in said park for sale or removal there from, or wantonly. No animals shall be killed within the park limits primarily for the purpose of dog food, except with prior permission . . . but when animals are killed for food by prospectors, or miners, the excess portions may be fed dogs without such prior permission."[35]

Thus empowered, prospectors examined every drainage in the new park. Two claims were staked not far from Charles Sheldon's old cabin on the Toklat. A gold strike there at the beginning of the war had gained some attention, but the mini-stampede fizzled as miners went off to fight. On the periphery of the park, prospector Ed Kerns staked his Echo Lode Claim and Savage Lode near the confluence of Savage and Teklanika Rivers. Lou Powless, with partners J.C. Felix, J.K. Moore, and Rufus Nichols, filed multiple claims on Jenny Creek, Savage River, and Dry Creek. One small copper find at the head of the Teklanika proved too small to justify development.

The biggest find within the park came in 1920, when Joe and Fannie Quigley staked lead, copper, and zinc claims at Copper Mountain, south of the confluence of the Thorofare and McKinley Rivers. That winter Frank Giles and partner O.M. Grant also discovered rich mineral deposits there and staked another 23 claims. Their ore samples assayed at $400 a ton. Expecting another Kennecott-like copper bonanza, a stampede ensued that staked the entire lode line.

How many stampeders reached Copper Mountain is unknown. In April 1921, Major John Gotwals issued public notices advising against a greater stampede. "From what I can learn the [find] is spotty and covers a wide area, and those going in seeking placer deposits would do well to [wait] as there will be little work for them."[36]

Many men did not heed Gotwals' advice. One traveler who stopped at Copper Mountain at the height of the stampede said he was greeted by the barking of "600 sled dogs." Although likely an exaggeration, his report suggests the extent of the rush. Obviously wildlife suffered greatly during the stampede as mushers and prospectors lived off the land and fed their dogs game meat.

Copper Mountain, south of today's Eielson Visitor Center, was then an isolated, physically challenging site, accessible only by foot, horse, or dogteam. It was a place where winter came early and the treeless high tundra offered no shelter. An early and heavy snowfall in late September 1922, the same storm that blocked Karstens and Gotshall's expedition, pushed miners down out of the mountains. During a break in the storm Billy Grant and Ed Jern, an old

JAMES GORDON STEESE COLLECTION, #3028351484, DICKINSON COLLEGE ARCHIVES

*In 1922, the post office at Eureka Camp was located in Herbert and Anna Wilson's two-story log home. The Wilson's cabin is still standing today and is called the "Kantishna Roadhouse." Wilson ran a store and developed promising silver claims.*

friend of Karstens and Alaska's champion wrestler, left their Copper Mountain claim bound for Eureka. While breaking trail on the McKinley River ahead of Jern's dogteam, Grant suddenly called out for a rest stop, "complaining that everything was turning black." Jern stopped the team to give his partner a rest and the two sat down side-by-side on the sled. While lighting his pipe, Jern heard a groan and turned to see Grant pass out. Within seconds, Billy Grant died in his arms.[37]

A few miles southwest of Copper Mountain, Willard J. "Wild Bill" Shannon struck high–grade ore on Slippery Creek, sparking yet another small stampede. In June 1920, he and his wife, Anna, staked their first lode claims near Slippery Creek. When Shannon and a group of Kantishna old–timers reported the discovery of "large deposits of copper, cinnabar, and antimony on ledges traceable for over 12 miles," it sparked a mini-stampede that resulted in the staking of 40 new Slippery Creek claims.[38]

The early 1920s were a heady time in the Kantishna Mining District. The new strikes, plus the industrial mining of existing claims, hinted at great riches and lured newcomers from far and wide. The potential seemed enormous but the lack of reliable transportation was an obvious obstacle to full development.

The railroad offered the first real hope for cheap shipment of ore and freight but it was nearly 90 miles away over a rugged stretch of mountains and tundra. Many miners hoped that the involvement of one of the huge mining concerns would have the clout to get a road built quickly, perhaps even a rail spur.

From the outset of railroad construction, district miners, and their supporters in Nenana and Fairbanks, lobbied federal authorities for construction of an all-weather road to the Kantishna. Most of them felt that a road was the key to unlocking the district's genuine, but hidden wealth. Geologist Stephen J. Capps agreed. "With better transportation that will be made available by the completion of the railroad…mining costs may be so reduced that placer gravels heretofore unavailable may be mined at a profit," he said.[39]

Four proposed routes competed for dominance. Boosters in Nenana wanted a road built directly from their town to Eureka. Lengthy editorials in the *Nenana News* explained the apparent advantages of such a year-around road but also minimized the obvious and astronomical cost. In 1921, ARC crews cut a winter trail to the Kantishna from Kobe (now Rex) railroad station, following in part the old winter trail from Knight's Roadhouse to Diamond, Glacier, and Eureka. An upgrade the following year developed 70 miles of trail with 20 new bridges suitable for four-horse teams. ARC teamsters hauled twenty tons of freight over the road that winter and reported "it is now possible to drive with a load of freight [in winter] from the railroad to Quigley mine." Once again, the cost of turning this winter haul road into a year-around road would be prohibitively expensive and was a stop-gap measure at best.[40]

Of the two routes proposed for park use, the majority of Kantishna miners favored the Lignite to Kantishna route over the mountain route from McKinley Station to Eureka. "That route does not pass through the central portion of the district," miner John Zimmerman explained, "and is too much exposed during the winter months."[41]

The miners wanted a year-round, all-weather road, and they wanted it immediately. What they saw instead was the decision to build a park road through the high mountain passes which would *eventually* connect to Eureka.

The Territory of Alaska was truly America's last frontier, and it continued to be as wild and remote as it had ever been. Kantishnans led what was even then an anachronistic lifestyle. America had moved on from its frontier origins. Life in cities like New York and Chicago then was not all that different than today. People rode the subway to work. They had electricity. They went to movies and Broadway shows. They worried about diet and paying bills. The disparity between rich and poor was vast and parts of the country were incredibly racist. While the rest of the country was reveling in the excesses of the Roaring 20s, life in the Kantishna scarcely had changed since the days of the first stampede. Men, without women, lived in isolation, subsisting off a harsh land, seeking the elusive pay streak that would make them rich. Each day they faced daunting challenges. If they didn't hunt, they didn't eat. Even by Alaska's modest standards, Kantishnans led a tenuous, grueling existence, life held hostage by the implacable winter.

# 7

# The Deadly Kantishna

Many of the original stampeders who settled into the Kantishna clung to their claims, partly hoping for the ultimate strike, but also because they had connected with this challenging place they now called home. While city dwellers celebrated winter holidays, Kantishnans living in the hills and along the rivers sat alone and silent, in dimly-lit cabins, likely unaware of the date or day of the week. Even during the best of times, life in the Kantishna could be daunting.

Johnnie Busia was one of those who married the Kantishna. When Busia came to America from Croatia in 1911, he was just 20 years old, migrating to the Kantishna around 1918, to join his uncle, Tom, and father, Marko, a 1905 stampeder. "Old Marko," as he was known, was a celebrated teller of tales. The Abbeys knew him as "Old Michael" and often repeated this story: After a short absence Old Michael returned to one of his claims and found his stakes replaced with someone else's. He pulled up the claim-jumper's stakes, re-set his own, and went back to work. Later, after another absence, he again found his stakes uprooted. This time he hid in the bushes and waited for the miscreant to return. He didn't wait very long before a man walked up the creek and rudely yanked up the first stake. Busia sprang from hiding and approached with leveled rifle. "You like my ground?" he asked the startled claim-jumper. "If you come back again I'll give you six feet of it."[1]

No doubt Johnnie heard many such stories from his father. In summer the two men prospected together and in winter ran a trapline out of Marko's McLeod Creek cabin. That first year, Johnnie Busia could not have known that he would spend the rest of his life in this isolated spot.[2]

In the mining days most everyone had a nickname, and at 5'4", and 120 pounds, Busia picked up the moniker, "Little Johnnie." Some old-timers, like

Karstens, initially called him "Johnnie Marko." After his father died in 1923, Busia moved into Eureka, trapping, and living a subsistence lifestyle. He lived in the once-abandoned cabin built near the mouth of Eldorado Creek by Dr. Sutherland as a mess hall and bunk-house for his defunct hydraulic mining venture. A man of maximum practical application, Busia could fix almost anything, even without a manual. He'd spend hours, days even, tinkering until he got a piece of machinery up and running. To cross Moose Creek, Johnnie built a homemade, hand-propelled cable tram which he called an *"Armstrong."* Going west, the tram went uphill and required strength to keep it in motion.

Busia lived off the land, eating what he grew, caught, and shot. "He lived 95% off the country," according to one ranger, "mostly moose and potatoes, and we wondered how he made it. Other than a few marten skins to sell, he seldom had money." He killed only what he needed for food. Since he didn't eat bear meat, he left bears alone, saying "bears don't harm me." In his old age, he usually waited until a moose wandered passed his cabin, but sometimes he hunted caribou in the nearby hills. His garden produced bumper crops of potatoes, his winter staple, which he kept along with his homebrew in a root cellar beneath his cabin. What little money he had came from trapping and pay for manual labor. When he had cash, he ordered his winter staples—200 pounds of sugar, 100 pounds of flour, two cases of malt, a large bag of oatmeal, and incidentals like salt and yeast. As Busia aged, he dismantled and burned some of Eureka's old cabins, bits of history rising into the cold winter air.[3]

A self-trained naturalist, Busia could intimately describe the habits of the local wildlife, many of which "he didn't even know by common name." Although he had a few run-ins with the local deputy marshal and park rangers over hunting violations, he seldom got into any real trouble. He trapped Moose Creek and ran a line that crossed Big Timber to the McKinley River and on to the Muddy River. Although some of his trapline crossed into the park, rangers never seemed to notice, perhaps because he was a good trapper who would quit the season early. "I leave plenty, and there's always plenty for stock," he explained to one ranger.[4]

For all his years in the Kantishna, Busia staked very few claims. He bought marginal mining properties but sold better prospects. He sometimes ran a one-man sluicing operation on Moose Creek but apparently preferred to work for wages. His only notable claim was the "Neversweat Mine" at the confluence of Eldorado and Rhinehart Creek, a drainage named for a murdered miner, but a real pay streak there eluded him.[5]

Late in his life, when Busia was Eureka's sole resident, rangers supplied him with a surplus, two-watt, U.S. Forest Service radio and established a weekly schedule

STEPHEN FOSTER COLLECTION, #69-92-714, ARCHIVES, UNIVERSITY OF ALASKA, FAIRBANKS

*From 1919 to 1921, C. Herbert Wilson served as U.S. Commissioner for the Kantishna Mining District.*

with park headquarters, his only connection with the outside world. Busia seldom talked much about local affairs but rather recited radio newscasts and asked visitors endless questions about the world beyond. He railed constantly about the conditions in his homeland, which he called "Titoslavia," a slam at its iron-fisted dictator. Patrol rangers always stopped in to check on him, but often dreaded it. "He'd start talking the minute he saw you," former ranger Bill Nancarrow remembered, "and you'd fall asleep and wake up to him still talking."[6]

Famous hunters, climbers, scientists, and passersby visited Johnnie and were treated with typical warmth. Busia, the wryly-dubbed "Mayor of Kantishna," always offered guests a drink of his homebrew made of molasses, rice, hops, and sugar, which ranger Grant Pearson dubbed "Kantishna Champagne." The brew had a legendary kick. "After one drink you started talking to yourself," Pearson wrote, "after two you answered yourself."[7]

Johnnie Busia and his friend Fannie Quigley lived on Moose Creek longer than anyone else. Joe and Fannie Quigley had grown apart over the years with Joe often wintering Outside. Whenever he was asked about Fannie, who often promised to go with him but never did, Joe diplomatically replied that Fannie stayed home because "she was afraid someone might steal Mount McKinley, or the park, or some of her mountain sheep if she left them there alone." On one trip Outside, Joe, who Busia described as " . . . my oldest and dearest friend," was quoted in the press as saying, "We have a good camp in the makings and I am feeling quite optimistic . . . for the future." What a revealing comment! Even after almost 32 years of hardscrabble life in the Kantishna this old time prospector was still "optimistic."[8]

## KANTISHNA HERO: "WILD BILL" SHANNON

In the winter of 1925, a Nome doctor diagnosed an outbreak of diphtheria, an often-fatal contagious disease, and immediately telegraphed Nome's plight to the outside world. Alaska Governor Scott Bone decided the quickest way for the stockpile of diphtheria vaccine in Anchorage to reach the isolated town was by train to Nenana, then by dogteam to Nome. Between the two towns stretched 674 miles of frozen rivers, tundra, forest and a few scattered villages. The only people to travel those frigid miles were dog mushers, mostly hardy trappers and mail carriers.

On January 27, the U.S. Marshal in Nenana hammered on the cabin door of Willard "Wild Bill" Shannon and begged his help to prevent a deadly epidemic. Shannon immediately readied his dog team. After midnight on the 28th, a railroad conductor handed Shannon the insulated, 20-pound cylindrical serum package for the first leg of the relay. Shannon and his nine dogs immediately left Nenana, the temperature sixty below, on the 52-mile trip to Tolovana. Less than 24 hours later the frost-bitten musher handed the serum off to Edgar Kalland. Over those cruel miles three of Shannon's dogs perished from frost-bitten lungs. Thanks to the efforts of 20 stalwart mushers and their dogs the serum package reached Nome in five days, seven and a half hours. After the vaccine thawed, Dr. Welch inoculated the populace averting catastrophe. The Nome quarantine was lifted on February 21st, one month after the first diphtheria symptoms appeared.

The emergency mush to Nome captivated the country. All of the mushers became world-renown, some personally famous. Bill Shannon and his wife Anna, and their seven dogs, were booked on a year's lecture tour of the lower 48 where they were feted like genuine heroes. Touched by celebrity, Shannon announced at the end of the tour that he was leaving Alaska and taking his surviving dogs to Hollywood "to enter the movies." Stardom eluded the man who was "blackened and scarred with the frost and showing the intense strain of the biting cold." In less than a year he was back in Alaska again grubbing for gold.

"Wild Bill's" life was typical of era prospectors and mushers, a mix of high adventure and hardship. Shannon came to Alaska as a sergeant with the Fourteenth Infantry and after mustering out became manager of the N.C. Co. store in Nenana. Gold fever drew him into the Kantishna. In June 1920, Bill, Anna, and his brother Edward, staked their first claims on Slippery Creek. Additional finds sparked a small stampede.

Although shy, the brown-haired, blue-eyed Anna could be coaxed to tell her own stories of wilderness exploits. One story Anna recounted was of an incredible journey around Mt. McKinley. Early one spring the Shannons left their cabin in the Kantishna on a three-week prospecting trip through Rainy Pass. An early

A few years after his mine accident, Joe sold his portion of the Red Top Mining Company and in a divorce settlement, split the take with Fannie. Joe moved to Seattle and remarried, Fannie stayed in the Kantishna Hills for a total of 38 years.[9]

What better friends could Little Johnnie have had there? The Quigleys were

break-up caught them deep in the mountains and forced them to abandon their sled and non-essentials. One by one their dogs died. They struggled on foot through deep, melting snow. With the rise in spring temperatures the mosquitoes hatched and attacked in dense clouds. The wind offered only the briefest respite with sleep impossible on calm nights. Under the constant assault Anna feared for her sanity. Emerging on the southeast side of the Alaska Range, the Shannons lost the trail but battled on through vast, nearly impenetrable alder thickets. They built crude log rafts and risked their lives to cross surging rivers.

In mid-June, with their food exhausted, their exposed flesh bleeding from countless mosquito bites, the Shannons stumbled into a cabin on the Yentna River. The meager food they found inside saved them. Three weeks later they reached a mining camp on Dollar Creek in the Cache Creek district. After a few days rest and treatment they walked into the railroad town of Talkeetna. Anna estimated that in three arduous months they had traveled 600 miles. "All I know now is my mind was full of just one idea—to get out!" she said later.

A year after his leg of the serum run, Shannon reported "staking extensive deposits of high grade silver bearing copper ores, carried in a vein two hundred feet wide . . . and quicksilver ore immediately north Mount McKinley . . . the field is practically unexplored." In the end, the riches he imagined again eluded him.

In 1937, Shannon discovered gold on the left limit of Muldrow Glacier, about six miles south of Mile 75 on today's park road. Territorial Assayer William T. Burns examined it and found values ranging from $7.10 to $115.30 per ton, the higher figure another tantalizing hint of wealth. A few months later Bill Shannon disappeared.

Shannon's wife and friends feared that he'd been killed by a grizzly bear. He'd had close shaves before. On a previous hike to his mine Shannon saw his pack dog suddenly stop and whirl around with raised hackles. Shannon swung around just in time to shoot a grizzly bearing down on him. He credited the dog with saving his life.

While locating claims on Slippery Creek in 1941, three prospectors found hewn stakes lying on the riverbank. Suspecting foul play they summoned Deputy U.S. Marshal John J. Buckley and an ensuing search turned up scattered human bones. Later, Shannon's widow identified a rifle, shovel, pick, part of a pack sack and articles of clothing as belonging to her late husband. His brother, Edward Shannon, then employed by the Alaska Railroad, somehow identified the remains as his brother. Because the bones were in an exposed stretch of tundra, Buckley listed the cause of death as "exhaustion and exposure."

One reporter asked the appropriate question: "Who really knows what happened to Shannon? Just another man lost to the great alone, in the great lonely region that claimed many unknown men, their dogs the only witnesses to tragedy."

FANNIE QUIGLEY COLLECTION, #80-46-220, ARCHIVES, UNIVERSITY OF ALASKA, FAIRBANKS.

*On the slopes of Mineral Ridge, later re-named Quigley Ridge, Fannie Quigley stands in front of her home cabin. She carried soil for her gardens from Moose Creek far below. In this modest cabin she entertained visitors from far and wide, all of them either amazed, or alarmed, by her cooking which varied according to her mood.*

loyal, honest, and generous. Surely he learned much from these two pioneers, especially how to survive and thrive in such a demanding environment. "Joe had no enemies," Busia said. "Do you know, I've never heard Joe speak a bad word about anyone. I wish he'd come back here." Their friendship was mutually beneficial and endured despite the usual strains common to small, isolated communities. Busia lived in the Kantishna nearly four decades, longer than any other person, besting Fannie Quigley's mark by two years.[10]

Life in the Alaskan bush was never easy. Trappers and miners faced all the same challenges of early-American pioneers—a rugged, demanding landscape, extreme cold, protracted darkness, wild animals, and the threat of starvation, accidents, and disease. To survive and live in the Kantishna Mining District, which included most of the western half of McKinley Park, took daring, experience and skill. The wilderness was unforgiving of weakness and exacted a terrible toll on the inexperienced, or unlucky. Winter travel could be perilous even for veteran mushers and freighters.

The few existing diaries kept by era trappers and miners all contain terse comments on weather, wildlife sightings, fur catches, or other daily events. A life-threatening encounter with overflow ice at 40 below, for example, might earn a brief comment: "Broke through. Had to build a fire and dry out." The un-written law of the bush, but scrupulously observed, required anyone using a cabin to leave behind a supply of dry wood, kindling, and a little food.

Inside one well-stocked cabin, a traveler found this creatively-spelled sign: "TO THE TRAVELING PUBLIK. Make your silw at home You vil find some grub ind the cabin, and some more ind the chas [cache], take what you wondt, and hvat silver you tink es right. Plase bi carefuld ved fire. Live kendeling under the stove, the es alvays sombody behind you. Sign you name and amount of monny you living. Plase be carefuld ved fire. Ed Knudson."[11]

An unlocked cabin and firewood could make the difference between life and death. On the trail, far from shelter, the ability to build a fire was crucial. One winter while mushing across a frozen lake, trapper Ed Kammersgard, who owned a roadhouse near Lake Minchumina on the McGrath-Nenana trail, broke through thin ice, dumping him into paralyzing water 40 feet from shore. His frantic commands to his lead dog kept the team going long enough to pull him to safety. Just then an Athabascan trapper happened by, built a hot fire, and helped Kammersgard into dry clothes. He escaped without injury.[12]

Daniel B. Libby suffered a similar, but more tragic mishap. Libby was no Cheechako but an experienced pioneer. While setting a trap on a small stream about two miles from his cabin, Libby fell into an overflow and was immersed to the armpits. Before he could reach camp, and his wife and son Robert, he froze both feet. Parts of his feet were crudely amputated, necessitating later corrective surgery and treatment.[13]

Severe frost injuries were fearsome but common hazards of the trail. One misstep could maim a person for life. Eli Borach, a prospector and freighter, left Nenana in mid-winter with supplies for the Kantishna. Somewhere west of Knight's Roadhouse, his team broke through overflow. Before Borach could reach the apparent safety of 12-Mile House, an un-tended shelter cabin, he froze his hands, face, and feet. Even worse, someone had broken the code of the trail and had failed to replenish the cabin's firewood supply. Unable to collect wood for a fire, or care for his dogs, Borach rolled up in a sleeping bag where he lay for three days before trapper Chris Nelson discovered him. A relay of teams rushed Borach to Nenana, then to Fairbanks where doctors at St. Joseph's Hospital amputated both thumbs and his right leg midway between the knee and ankle.[14]

Cut off and far from help, many pioneers learned to doctor themselves, even performing minor surgery and setting bones. Sometimes the problem was beyond self-cure. Game warden Sam O. White, the first warden to use an airplane, once stopped in to see Johnnie Busia. White took one look and blanched. One side of Busia's face was blackened and swollen twice its normal size from a broken tooth. At 30 below zero, White loaded Busia into his open-cockpit biplane for the flight to Fairbanks. Busia's first flight ever culminated in a painful tooth extraction.[15]

Accidents were common. Every prospector and trapper on the trail carried a sharp axe for building shelters and gathering firewood. Seasoned pioneers were never without an axe, but sometimes those very tools were the cause of accidents. One winter while camped on the McKinley River, Mace Farrar slashed open his lower leg when his axe glanced off a frozen tree limb. To stop the bleeding, Farrar smeared sugar on his wound and his partner Jim O'Brien mushed him the 180 miles to Fairbanks.

During spring break-up one year, trapper Slim Carlson chopped off his left thumb while splitting kindling. He rushed into his cabin and stanched the bleeding with rags. With no way to get to town, Carlson gathered needle and thread, and while holding the severed thumb in his mouth, tried sewing it back on. His crude attempt failed.

For two long weeks he endured horrendous pain that prevented sleep and limited activity. When he finally reached Fairbanks, the doctor cleaned the stump and applied antiseptic. For years Carlson proudly displayed his preserved thumb to "sometimes-horrified victims."[16]

Even old-timers like the Quigleys suffered accidents. Fannie once broke her leg and after a long, cold, ignominious, sled ride, had it set in Nenana. Her husband Joe was injured in a summer plane crash. In Fairbanks on business, he chartered Joe Crosson to fly him and his supplies back home. Quigley told Crosson that there was a flat-topped hill near the mine suitable as a landing strip. (Miners notoriously underestimated what constituted an adequate landing field.) Crosson made one pass over the alleged "airstrip" and bypassed it for a gravel bar along Moose Creek. He overshot the landing and went into the river. The biplane nosed up, bending the prop and breaking the crankcase. Joe was thrown out of the open cockpit and smashed face first into a wing strut, splitting his nose wide open. From her cabin Fannie saw the whole thing. Fearing the men might be trapped she grabbed an axe and ran down the trail. Joe, bleeding and holding his nose together, met her on the way. "What are you doing with that axe?" he asked. "I was just coming down to finish the job," she retorted.[17]

Back at the cabin she gave Joe a big drink of whiskey, got out a needle and thread and, with Joe yelping in pain, sewed up the wound using a baseball stitch. "Stop bellering like a damned baby," she ordered while painting his wound with iodine.[18]

FRITZ NYBERG COLLECTION, #1500, DENALI NATIONAL PARK & PRESERVE, MUSEUM COLLECTION

*At the peak of the Copper Mountain stampede, trapper and miner Ed Jern posed for pictures in front of his cache, which also served as an emergency shelter. In 1922, his partner, Billy Grant, died in his arms as they tried to escape from here in a fierce September snowstorm.*

"That was the first time I ever sewed up anyone, and I sewed it the same as I do my moccasins," Fannie recalled. Quigley's nose "swelled up like a balloon afterwards but healed with only small scars." Without a radio to call for help, Crosson and his mechanic, Ed Young, were forced to walk out to the railroad to procure parts.[19]

Illness claimed many lives that with proper treatment might have been saved. Perry Bigelow died of pneumonia despite the care of a miner "who had considerable [Army] experience nursing during two or three flu epidemics." Bigelow and his partner, Alois Freidrich, had just built a cabin on their Moose Creek claim opposite the Aitken mine and were in the process of moving in when Bigelow fell ill. Seven days later he was dead. At the time of his death, he believed the ore on his claim to be worth an extraordinary $1000 per ton. His estimate was wildly in error but he did not live to see yet another dream shattered.[20]

Carl Hult, who had trapped in British Columbia, migrated to Alaska in 1923 to trap and prospect. With most of the prime trapping grounds in the Kantishna claimed, Hult teamed up with John Folger, 75, a veteran of 41 years in the North. The second year of their partnership, Hult left Folger, who was complaining of a stomach ailment, in camp alone, while he ran a 50-mile segment of their line. When Hult returned to camp he found Folger dead.[21]

Lack of witnesses complicated Hult's loss. More than one partner had been killed over a bundle of furs. After considerable dithering, and mushing from one person to another seeking advice, Hult strapped his partner's body into his sled and headed for Nenana, arriving three weeks after Folger's death. Judge Clara C. Heid, known as "Ninety Day May," for her sentences to drunken trouble makers, gave Hult a severe tongue-lashing for wasting her time and effort, then issued a death certificate ending what Hult later recalled was a 450-mile odyssey with a frozen corpse.[22]

In 1908 or '09, Richard Knight, a handsome, dapper man, and his wife, built a roadhouse at the confluence of the Toklat River and Sushana River. Because their roadhouse was located at the junction of several trails, the site quickly became a beehive of activity. On his homestead, the industrious Knight tilled the ground, planted crops, raised livestock, chickens, and tended a fur farm, somehow preserving enough time to work his claims in the nearby hills.

Knight's wife, long praised by travelers for her kindly disposition and the extra care she bestowed on all who came by, died on July 25, 1919, and was buried near the roadhouse. Some thought she'd worked herself to death. Less

COURTESY OF CANDY WAUGAMAN

*The Kantishna Mining District was largely male. The isolation, weather extremes, and lack of companionship, led to high rates of violence, alcoholism, insanity, and, in some cases, suicide. Friends tried to intervene when old-timers began talking to themselves and "shaking hands with the willows."*

than three years later, Richard succumbed to pneumonia and was buried by his wife's side. News of the actual circumstances of his death reached Nenana six months later and by then a rumor claimed that he had taken ill and froze to death on the trail. His nephew, Henry Knight, who had an adjacent 320-acre homestead, took over the roadhouse, serving travelers through the early 1940's. Natives remember the Knights for their kindness and hospitality.

Cabin fires claimed the lives of many miners and trappers and are even today greatly feared. A sudden inferno consumed not only food, equipment and clothing, but also critical shelter from the elements. A cabin fire cast hapless survivors into the sub-zero twilight, with death and frostbite lurking at the edges of the cooling ashes. One frigid night, Slim Carlson let his young pups into his cabin. Just as he settled in for the night, a pup knocked a candle onto a pile of kindling, igniting the cabin.

"I yumped [sic] out in yust [sic] my underwear," he said, and scrambled outside. He watched helplessly as the cabin, with the pups inside, burned to the ground. Carlson, dressed only in long-johns, and his feet clad in the bottoms cut from shoepacs, considered his options. He thought of killing some of his remaining dogs to make clothing but he'd "rather freeze to death than do that." Instead, as the coals burned down, Carlson frantically hooked up his team and raced for his Birch Creek cabin. "One good thing, it wasn't too cold—only about 12 below zero," he said, "but I had a hard time to keep from freezing." Despite a vicious headwind, he reached the cabin and quickly built a fire. Even though the temperature inside rose to almost 100°F, "I still was freezing, laying in my sleeping bag with canvas and blankets on top." Carlson writhed in agony as his frostbitten fingers, face, and frozen heel began to thaw. He later said that if it had been 30°F or 40°F below, he would have shot himself.[23]

Carlson's thawed toes turned black and he feared gangrene. With his sterilized knife, he peeled off the rotting tissue. Throughout the rest of his life Carlson meticulously donned protective footgear.[24]

Winter's intense cold victimized seasoned pioneers like Joe Dalton, who while mushing the old Minchumina trail broke through thin ice and froze his right foot. He spent nearly two months in the Nenana hospital, recuperating in Fairbanks.[25]

Summer brought different hazards. Mosquitoes made life miserable for all living creatures. Travel across muskeg or through thick timber could be a "living hell," as Judge Wickersham once said. Smudge fires, head nets, gloves, and tight-woven clothing offered the only relief. "In those days, we had no dope for mosquitoes. You had to wear something over your nose, a hat, big gloves and heaviest underwear you could think of," Carlson recalled. He thought a suit of armor might have offered the best protection, but instead he made a concoction of creolin, a disinfectant deodorizing fluid, and lard or tallow, and smeared it on. It partially worked, but "a man was smelly as the dickens."[26]

One prospector nearly perished from his bout with mosquitoes. Prior to crossing the McKinley River he took off all his clothes and stuffed them into his backpack. He got part way across before the surging river rolled him, sweeping away his pack. Naked and defenseless he faced the peak of mosquito season. After a torturous scramble through dense clouds of stinging insects he stumbled into one of Johnnie Busia's trapping cabins. Before continuing on, he clothed himself in what little he could find, two small towels. A day later he made it to Eureka, staggering into camp covered so thickly in bugs that he looked like he was "wearing a fur coat." It took two full days for the swelling to subside and his strength to return.

In summer, prospectors shared the hills with grizzly bears. Most times the encounters ended peacefully, but others sometimes resulted in serious injuries or even death. While hunting caribou, miner Charles Trundy was attacked from behind by two grizzlies. One slashed a six-inch gash in Trundy's leg. As he rolled away, Trundy fumbled for his rifle and killed the bear, the other ran off. Trundy ripped up his clothes and bandaged his wounds. It took eight hours to walk two miles to his cabin and days more to recover from what he described as "an unprovoked charge."

Late one afternoon, Henry Knight, who was hunting moose on Chitsia Mountain, ran smack into a female grizzly squatting outside her den. He at first mistook the animal for a moose but when the bear rose up, he opened fire. After his third shot, the wounded bear retreated into its den. In the gloaming, Knight decided to leave and come back the next day. In the dark he mushed to Sam Feddersen's cabin on nearby Hot Creek. The next morning the two men discovered a well-defined blood trail leading from the den and followed it on snowshoes, Feddersen in the lead. The bear suddenly burst from a thicket and attacked, knocking Feddersen to the ground, sending his gun flying. Knight, just a few feet behind, rushed forward and fired two quick shots, killing the bear atop Feddersen. Knight then helped Feddersen to the roadhouse for first aid before the two mushed into Nenana for further medical treatment. Two weeks later Knight hauled his friend home by dogsled.[27]

Everyone carried a gun on the trail, usually a rifle, but not everyone was proficient. As one old-timer said, the firearms motto of the Kantishna seemed to be, "Better to have and not need, than need and not have." Mace Farrar and Jim

O'Brien spent several summers prospecting Copper Mountain. One autumn, just after the first snow fall, they hitched their dogs and struck out across the lower Muldrow moraine. Prior to leaving camp, Farrar had carefully cleaned and loaded his .256 Newton. Early on the first day, they surprised a "glacier bear," a local name for a grizzly, at close quarters. O'Brien, who was breaking trail, looked up to see the bear charging down on him. He turned and ran. The grizzly plunged into the dogs. Farrar grabbed his rifle from the sled, and began shooting into the melee. Before it died, the bear shredded and killed two dogs.

Besides the usual risks posed by fire, frost, famine, illness, accident, or wildlife, people also posed substantial danger to themselves and others. Crime was not unknown but theft rarely included violence. Travelers, including miners and fur buyers, often carried large sums of money or gold. Ed Kammersgard's roadhouse on the McGrath to Nenana trail was a regular stop over for miners coming from the headwaters of the Kuskokwim River. "I can still remember the time when one official of a large gold mine stopped over night," he wrote years later, "and left a half million dollars in gold brick on the dog sled outside!" On another occasion, however, two mushers discovered a $50,000 mine payroll missing from their mail load. A woman who'd stopped off at Kammersgard's that same night was the only suspect but she was never convicted.[28]

Isolation, deprivation, and hardship exacted a terrible toll on people's sanity. Imagine life in a tiny, dingy, nearly window-less, dirt-floored cabin. Picture, too, a constant diet of moose meat and beans, and sourdough biscuits, broken only by periodic famine. Then imagine cold so severe that the occupant, or occupants, might be confined inside for days, or even weeks at a time, completely cut-off from human contact other than their trapping or mining partner. No wonder that insanity seemed almost of epidemic proportions in the territory. A few pioneers completely lost their senses and posed a threat to themselves and those few around them.

The declaration of insanity was so commonplace that it raises many questions. Were these people genuinely ill? Or was the diagnosis a convenient way to explain horrific crimes or inexplicable behaviors? Or, in some instances, was the declaration a way to get rid of unwanted neighbors? Ranger Bill Myers said that Alaska had more insane people, per capita, than any other state. Even the steamers had special rooms equipped for the mentally ill. "There are supposed to be three sides to Alaska," he said, "the Inside, Outside, and Morningside—the insane asylum."[29]

Alaskans generally coped with the implacable winters in two ways: they either went south on the last steamer of the year or toughed it out. For those that stayed behind, the isolation of trap lines and mining claims, and the rigors of the trail, where a misstep could mean death or lost limbs, exerted a terrible mental strain. Men who led lives of isolation and poverty, it was believed then, either became quiet and humane or ended up going mad, "shaking hands with the willow," as they described it in the gold fields. Today a person suspected of mental illness, prior to treatment or commitment, would be subjected to a battery of tests, receive a psychiatrist's evaluation, and have the benefit of adequate legal representation. Back then the process was simple and direct. One year a Glen Creek old-timer, a German, went "off his rocker" and started shooting at his neighbors with his Mannlicher rifle. Commissioner Edgar Brooker summoned a "posse" from Fairbanks and captured the man without incident. In Fairbanks, the miner was jailed, fed, cleaned up, and sent to the lower 48 with an unofficial warning never to return to the Kantishna. It was never explained if the man's problem was insanity or "the demon rum" but nevertheless he got the miners' infamous "Blue Ticket," a one-way ticket Outside and never came back.

In 1922, Fred Hauselmann, of Little Moose Creek, began behaving erratically, turning sullen and moody. A miners' posse arrested him and turned him over to the deputy marshal. In Fairbanks, Assistant District Attorney Collins, who headed the investigation, believed that Hauselmann had been driven insane by the deaths of his two friends, Rudolph Lambert, who had disappeared in late-May, 1922, and Alois Keim. Three weeks after he disappeared, Lambert's decomposing remains were found on Chop Creek. A coroner's jury ruled Lambert's death was due to unknown causes with "no evidence of foul play." Hauselmann, however, claimed that Lambert had been murdered. In response, Lambert's body was exhumed. An inquest jury, which included miners Sam Feddersen and Charles Christensen, ruled that Lambert had died of natural causes.

The second death struck Hauselmann especially hard. Keim, his trapping and mining partner, suffered from stomach cancer and his final five days were spent in excruciating agony. Alone in their remote cabin, Hauselmann could only watch his friend's final throes, powerless to help.[30]

In the spring of 1923, after a hearing in Nenana that heard Charles Christiansen testify to Hauselmann's insanity, Hauselmann was declared mentally ill. But was Hauselmann really insane as everyone thought, or simply overwhelmed and despondent over the loss of his two friends?[31]

Authorities remanded Hauselmann to the care of physicians at Portland's Morningside Hospital. Little more than a year later, doctors declared him cured and he returned to the Kantishna, retrieving his property from his court-appointed guardian, James Burrows.[32]

Suicide, given the population of the area, seemed inordinately common. On the morning of August 18, 1924, Joe Quigley noted a lack of smoke from the chimney of his neighbor Peter Lish. Quigley investigated and found Lish, 61, dead on his bunk. The Swiss miner had been ill for several months, and had futilely spent some time in the "restorative" waters of Chena Hot Springs. Two days earlier, Quigley had visited Lish and found him despondent and paranoid. He thought people were talking about him and complained of his declining health and poor gold cleanup. The afternoon before he died Lish seemed in a better humor and accepted Fannie's gift of fresh meat and vegetables.

On the table near Lish's corpse, Quigley found a note and poison-filled cup. An open straight razor lay next to the body. Quigley sent Johnnie Busia to Glen Creek to notify the commissioner. A coroner's jury took evidence, examined translations of the note, and ruled Lish had committed suicide by poison. Lish was buried at the mouth of Friday Creek. Otto Bossart, appointed administrator of Lish's estate, ended up owning Lish's Friday Creek claims and possessions when no one offered to buy them.[33]

A few years later Otto Bossart also ended up "shaking hands with the willows." Bossart's life had been a grubstake affair, never really striking it big. In the winter of 1929, he showed up at Copper Mountain and told quite a tale. People in the Kantishna were "bothering" him and he was getting out. He claimed a trapper was stealing his fur and yet another was "stealing his butter."[34]

"Yeah, does people run me out of Kanteeshna [sic]," Otto said. He told rangers Fritz Nyberg and Bill Myers that a neighbor had a "witch in his pipe" and the smoke caused strange things.[35]

"Well, Otto was crazy. He had lived alone too long . . . he had gone daffy sitting in that dinky little cabin of his with nothing to do except imagining neighbors had been pilfering his food and robbing his trapline," Myers said.[36]

Even on the less-isolated eastern periphery of the park near the railroad, similar tragedies occurred. Mining engineer Ernest Patty once spent New Year's Eve with trappers John Fern and Joe Gagnon in their Healy River cabin. "Joe, a good cook, had a fine dinner ready for us," he said, and brought out several bottles of homemade beer for a New Year's toast. Suddenly, Patty's companion, Andrew Anderson, leaned forward with a peculiar look and asked if his friends thought he was losing his mind. Stunned silence greeted the remark and Fern glanced at the loaded rifles on the wall. Patty surreptitiously gripped his prospecting pick. After a bit, the three men were able to quiet the powerful Anderson, but the rest of the night passed fitfully. The next day Anderson, again rational, accompanied Patty to Healy where Patty boarded the train.[37]

On June 2, one of Anderson's friends in Healy called Fairbanks to tell Patty that Anderson had gone crazy and was threatening to shoot himself. Anderson had asked him to call Patty and say goodbye. Patty phoned Healy Roadhouse owner Jack Singleton and relayed the news. "Sorry, you're too late, Singleton said. "He shot himself [in room four] ten minutes ago."[38]

Well into the 1930s the solitude of the Kantishna continued to exact its terrible toll. The "bard of the Kantishna" Alex Mitchell, came to the Kantishna in 1908. He mined and trapped out of his cabins at Big Timber, Spruce and Moose Creeks. By all accounts Mitchell was an able woodsman, musher, and trapper. "Mitchell...is now the champion fox trapper," Karstens wrote Charles Sheldon (who had met Mitchell in 1906), "whenever he sees a track he gets the fox."[39]

After visiting in 1922, Mary Lee Davis waxed eloquent about Mitchell's ability to deal with "Silence, Loneliness, and Space." She said, "Mitchell loved the intimate winters, too, when trap-line was his business even when, [as Robert Burns said,] 'bleak December's winds insuin.' Alec's [sic] valley at the foot of the Most High is like a withdrawn place of sanctuary, consecrate set apart, silent, untouched, unshaken—a place to take breath after hurried living." In such a place, Davis wrote, "severe, prolonged and fundamental thinking" had to be maintained throughout a long winter alone, "if spring is to find our [Alec] healthy, sane, and living!"[40]

"So the old trapper in his cabin by the Wonder Lake sits winter-long," Davis concluded, "holding his own life close in his two hands."[41]

In February 1938, Pilot Leon Brennan of Pollack Flying Service flew over Mitchell's cabin at the mouth of Willow and Spruce Creeks and saw no sign of life. On a flight three weeks later, Brennan again saw no one. A week before, Mitchell's sled dogs had showed up at Johnnie Busia's cabin, 15 miles away. Brennan contacted ranger Lou Corbley.

"I found outside the cabin no evidence of recent activities . . . Doors were fastened from inside. Looking through the windows I could see his body lying partly on the bed," Corbley later reported. Forcing open the door, the ranger found Mitchell, 71, "shot dead," in an obvious suicide.[42]

Davis' words penned 16 years before—"holding his own life close in his two hands"—proved prophetic. With his own two hands, Mitchell loaded his rifle, placed it in between his knees, and used a string to pull the trigger. Carl Hult, who retrieved the body, testified that Mitchell "might have had a spell of craziness." Or, maybe the "Bard" had finally gone blind, or sickened, and despaired.[43]

Insanity even drove some men to murder. One cold December day, Charles Christiansen mushed into Knight's Roadhouse and told a chilling tale of shooting his trapping and mining partner Sophus "Sam" Feddersen, 56, a 16-year-long Kantishna resident, at their cabin on Little Moose Creek, a tributary of the Clearwater Fork of the Toklat River. Prior to the murder, area residents had grown ever more alarmed by Christiansen's odd, often violent behavior, and Feddersen began to fear for his life. A few weeks before the murder, Christiansen had fired 120 shots into the air, explaining to a neighbor that he was "sinking the English battle fleet." [44]

Christiansen claimed that he killed Feddersen on the orders of park ranger John Rumohr, who was in no way involved. He said that he believed Feddersen was "gassing" him. Christiansen marched Feddersen at gunpoint out of their cabin, where after a brief struggle he killed him.

Afterward, Christiansen returned to the cabin and broke out all the windows to "dissipate the gas." Kantishna's Dewey Burnett found the body and cabin just as Christiansen had described. The U.S. Marshal flew to Moose Creek and recovered Feddersen's body. In subsequent confessions, Christiansen described the murder this way: "I went out and shot down the moon and the stars and the next night I shot Sam Feddersen."[45]

COURTESY OF BAYLES MAULDIN

*Despite their idyllic settings, scattered mining camps, like this one on the Clearwater Fork of the Toklat River, were the scene of madness and murder.*

HENRY P. KARSTENS COLLECTION, #E060, KARSTENS LIBRARY

*Knight's Roadhouse on the Toklat River was located at the junction of several trails to the Kantishna. Alaska Natives remembered the Knights as honest and generous in their dealings. When temperatures dropped to 60 below, and colder, travelers hurried to the safety of this well-run roadhouse.*

Ernest Patty offered some insight into the murder. "They were partners but had separate cabins about one hundred yards apart. Both of them were well past middle age. One was tall and rawboned with a rather truculent manner and the other was a small, colorless fellow.

"I have seldom seen messier cabins. When they skinned the animals from their trapline they threw the carcasses out only a few hundred feet from their cabins. A nauseating stench hung over the area. They were living almost like animals themselves, it seemed to me.

"Clearly, they were getting on each others' nerves, too. The tall man [Christiansen] would snap at his partner and the little man would cringe. Later, when we were alone, he would tell me what a 'mean bastard' his partner was," Patty recalled.[46]

A Nenana probate jury declared Christiansen insane and on January 21, 1932, committed him to Morningside Hospital, where he died twenty-five years later.[47]

For all those that stayed on in the gold fields, dozens more came and left. An eager, vibrant Floyd "Kid" Marsh arrived in 1919 and met several old-timers.

Jack Ritter asked Marsh if he wished to see his dead partner, Perry Bigelow. "Jack said that it would be several months before they buried Perry. He told me that the body was in a tent down at the diggin's and would stay frozen all winter." After viewing the body, Marsh pondered his future. "I asked myself if I wanted to stay in the north and live the life of . . . Perry who came up here a young man in the prime of life and now lay frozen in a tent at the diggin's [sic]." His answer was no, and he moved on.[48]

Considering the difficult, dangerous, and base existences that many Kantishnans lived it is easy to see why few of them had any sympathy for, or understanding of the national park concept. To them, the land provided meat and furs, gold and silver. The notion that wildlife was to be left alone, unmolested by hunters and trappers, and forests left uncut when timber was needed for logs and firewood, was ludicrous, the snobbish conceits of Eastern millionaires. Even after Harry Karstens arrived on scene, park boundaries were regularly violated by hunters and trappers alike, often under the guise of "prospecting." Many prospectors and miners spent their winters trapping, filling their caches with the furs that provided cash for summer grubstakes. Spurred throughout the 1920s by high fur prices, increasing numbers of trappers went afield, often trespassing onto park land, to trap as many as animals as they could catch.

ALBERT JOHNSON COLLECTION, #1989-166-76, ARCHIVES, UNIVERSITY OF ALASKA, FAIRBANKS

*Prior to the Great Depression, fur trapping employed miners and Alaska Natives who had no other source of winter income. Silver and black foxes rose in value until the 1929 Wall Street crash. In front of a Fairbanks mercantile a fur buyer displayed his furs, many of them caught in the Kantishna district.*

FABIAN CAREY COLLECTION, #1975-0209-84, ARCHIVES, UNIVERSITY OF ALASKA, FAIRBANKS

*The reality of weather and wilderness necessitated that trappers and miners partner up for safety. Here, Slim Avery (l), who trapped in the Kantishna from 1918 to 1950, sits in front of a tent with George Hilary (r), a prospector.*

# 8

# Of Traps and Snares

Frank Giles knelt between the sled tracks on the hard-packed trail and with a rusty trowel dug a small depression in the frozen snow. He then took a Newhouse #2 double-spring trap out of his rucksack and wired the end of the trap chain to a small sapling near the trail. He pried open the jaws of the trap, carefully setting the trigger to match the light tread of a fox. He centered the trap in the hole he'd dug and cautiously covered it with a waxed cloth. Next Giles used his knife to cut a thin, six-inch circle of snow from the wind-packed crust next to the trail and shaped it into a thin lid that he laid gently over the trap cloth. He then cut a tiny trench in the snow and buried the chain and wire right up to the base of the sapling. Finally, he scooped up loose snow and sprinkled it over the chain and trap until even he could not tell where it lay hidden.

From a pocket inside his trail parka Giles fished out a small bottle filled with an amber fluid. Briefly he bared one hand to the -30°F wind chill and removed the stopper. He swore aloud when he accidentally smeared some of the foul-smelling substance on his palm. Then, like a cook adding ingredients to a batter, he dribbled a few drops of this scent lure, concocted from fox urine, rotten meat and fish, in front of the hidden trap. After replacing the corked bottle in his pocket so that it would not freeze, he stood up and backed away from the trap using a spruce limb to brush away his tracks. A few yards away he paused to examine his handiwork. Maybe, just maybe, a silver fox—worth $350, or more—would trot down the trail, investigate the scent, and step on the trap, caught in the deadly grasp of what trappers of the era called the "kiss of steel."

In seasonal mining areas like the Kantishna, the fur trade became an economic mainstay. With little else to do in winter, almost everyone set at least a few traps or snares. After World War I, fur prices dropped but surged in value from 1922 until the 1929 Wall Street crash that ushered in the Great Depression. Foxes brought the highest prices: silvers were worth $350–$800, cross foxes $150, and reds $80. (Black, silver, and cross, are color phases of the red fox.) The boom saw the number of Alaska trappers triple. From 1923 to 1929, the most successful Kantishna trappers made upwards of $6000 a season, a small fortune. Most trappers made much less but earned enough to buy badly needed goods to see them through the winter and to the start of the mining season.[1]

Frank B. Giles (or Jiles) was one of the district's most successful trappers. By mid-winter one year, his catch totaled 43 red fox, 22 cross fox, 24 mink, 24 muskrats, 17 lynx, 35 ermine, 1 wolverine, and 1 wolf. Giles, was born in Virginia in 1886, and orphaned at eight when his parents died of typhoid fever. He worked his way north from Virginia to Alaska via Colorado and Wyoming, arriving about 1920. An energetic, hard-working woodsman, over the years he built an impressive and well-developed trapping territory northwest of the park. Harry Karstens described Giles and his partner Ed Knudson as "good prospectors and trappers," a high accolade from him.[2]

Trapping was illegal in Mt. McKinley National Park, but, until 1921, few Alaskans knew the regulations or even the borders of the new park. The few that did know the park rules or boundaries didn't care and kept on hunting and trapping as before. Even after Karstens' appointment and the dissemination of park regulations in 1921, some trappers, spurred by booming fur prices, continued to trap in the park anyway. The illegal trapping was not curtailed until the mid-1920s when Karstens was finally able to employ several experienced and dedicated rangers. The enforcement effort took years to have an effect on the trade. Even then the park's northern boundary was ringed with trap lines, some encroaching on the park boundary.

Most trappers were hard-working men trying to eke out a living, but pelts were currency in the Far North and their increasing value lured the unscrupulous into the wilderness. "There is though, a problem presenting itself, which will require very careful attention and that is, the use of poison to procure furbearing animals in this Park. It is a well known fact that trappers in the central and western portion of this park, are resorting to this means of obtaining their catch . . . not only being detrimental to the animals which are caught but to those who will [be poisoned] . . . in the future," Karstens reported. "Also it is very dangerous for rangers' dogs who might scent a piece of poisoned meat, eat it and die in the harness, leaving the ranger at the mercy of the wilds and the elements and thusly endangering their lives. A solution to the problem must be found in the near future."[3]

Karstens knew who was using poison. "There are a few men from Fairbanks and Nenana whom I am going to keep mighty close tabs on . . . two of them have virtually exterminated the fur bearing animals in the park some years ago by poisoning," he said.[4]

Although a revision of the Alaska Game Law in 1925 outlawed the use of poison, and forbade its sale and possession by trappers and hunters, its clandestine and devastating use continued into the 1930s.* In March 1930, legendary game wardens Jack O'Connor and Sam O. White, acting on an anonymous tip, entered and searched Alex Mitchell's Moose Creek cabin and seized two vials of strychnine. The seizure landed Mitchell in the Nenana jail and a "heavy fine" of $100.[5]

In the McKinley region, the poison ban was seen as "too little, too late." According to one report, "In the Kantishna fur bearing animals [last winter] had become practically extinct by poisoning and excessive trapping."[6]

*The 1925 law stipulated one exception: "Game wardens or predatory animal hunters under the supervision of the commission may use poison to kill wolves, coyotes, and wolverines . . ." (Government hunters used poison to control wolves until outlawed at Statehood in 1959.)

FABIAN CAREY COLLECTION, #1975-209-88, ARCHIVES, UNIVERSITY OF ALASKA, FAIRBANKS

*Carl Hult and dog team in front of a small trapline shelter. While Hult was out setting traps one winter, his trapline partner, John Folger, 75, died alone in their main cabin.*

The use of poison to procure furs was nothing new in the district. The year following the 1905 stampede saw "wholesale destruction of game, and trapping of fur" and the use of poison in the "most reckless and unscrupulous way." In the wake of every northern gold stampede were destitute men who needed a way to survive the winter or to buy a ticket home. Some of them saw furs as a source of quick cash. Poison was the preferred tool of the desperate, incompetent, or unscrupulous. These so-called "trappers" spread poison baits along animal trails or laced carcasses with poison, returning later to collect their victims. Since poison kills indiscriminately, loss and waste was enormous, with more animals than just the targeted being killed.[7]

Real trappers shunned poison. (Those that used poison were generally loathed and consequently worked in secret.) Most used steel leghold traps and snares. Foxes, because of their value, were highly sought after but trappers also targeted lynx, ermine, beaver, and, in the lowlands, the easily-trapped and abundant marten. Trapping was grueling work, conducted in hostile weather extremes. Before fur prices spiked, some trappers lost money, or barely broke even. The surge in prices changed all that. "Trappers are doing exceptionally well in the Kantishna this winter," Joe Quigley reported. "John Busia has already caught 18 fox. About half of them were red and the rest cross skins. Others who are obtaining good catches include Alex Mitchell, Charles Greiss, the Hanson Brothers at Roosevelt, and John Dyke and Gus Hurgess."[8]

High fur prices also stimulated fur farming. The business of pen-raising fur-bearing animals had begun in the Kantishna as early as 1914. A number of old-timers raised and bred high value silver foxes. Paula and John Anderson raised them at their homestead at Wonder Lake. They thought the region's prolonged cold ideal for raising animals with dense pelts. Like other fur farmers, they fed their foxes almost anything edible, including fish netted out of the lake, ptarmigan, caribou, moose, hares, and porcupines. Throughout Alaska, the localized over-hunting of small birds and animals was the inevitable by-product of fur farming.

Each spring trappers sold their furs in Fairbanks or traded them for supplies at remote outposts. Some sent their catch to Seattle, London, or New York. One year Ed Kammersgard took his prime fur to Los Angeles but thieves broke into his hotel room in Long Beach and stole $7,000 worth of fox and marten.[9]

Itinerant fur buyers also wandered the country. In the Bush, ready cash bought furs for a price well below that paid in town. Most fur buyers traveled by dog teams driven by professional freighters.

One miner who embraced the trapping life was Hjalmar "Slim" Carlson. During his first summer in the district, Carlson labored in the diggings for less than one dollar an hour. In following years, he hunted and sold game meat, and freighted with dogs, but trapping became his lifelong occupation.

Trapping, as with prospecting, usually was the work of two partners. The rigors and challenges of the country demanded it. It was a basic understanding that each man would look out for the other in time of danger, share the work and expenses equally, and split the rewards, usually down the middle. Tales of abandonment and treachery were well-circulated. Consequently some men drafted and signed detailed contracts that spelled out the duties and responsibilities of each partner.

Slim Carlson once partnered with Slim Avery, a former Wyoming cowpuncher who drifted into Alaska about 1910. Avery was a dog musher, prospector, freighter, mail carrier, and trapper. At a time when only a handful of whites had preceded him, he prospected up to within a short distance of the West Fork of the Foraker River. Avery boasted that from 1918 to 1950, he was self-employed, except for two days when he worked as head packer on a section of the railroad project. William N. Beach vividly remembered him. "At about six feet three . . . we called him Skyline Slim as he always traveled the skyline."[10]

Life in Alaskan winters was challenging at best and Kantishna lore is rife with stories of partnerships gone bad. An oft-repeated tale concerned two trappers who, after a falling out, drew a dividing line down the middle of their small cabin which neither man could cross. Each ignored the other and lived as if alone, never speaking.

The two Slims' experience was similar. One day, while camped in a wall tent, one of them failed to cut his share of firewood, so the next day, the other retaliated by also refusing to cut firewood. A test of wills ensued with neither of these stubborn men cutting wood. Their firewood supply quickly dwindled in the sub-zero weather. One frigid morning, with no wood left to start a fire, both men stayed in their sleeping rolls until finally Carlson exploded in frustration. He got up, dressed, and stomped outside to gather and chop wood. Back inside he fired and stoked the stove until it was blazing hot, forcing Avery out of his sleeping bag "and I kept it up until he had to crawl out of the tent." Afterwards the partners pitched two tents side-by-side. Later Carlson expressed no interest in having another male partner but said he "wouldn't have minded a woman partner, of course."[11]

Except for his early partnership with Avery, Carlson lived alone in the foothills and forests north of Minchumina Lake for *57 years*!

Having a partner offered a margin of safety that often meant the difference between life and death. Nonetheless, prospecting and trapping, because of human foibles, often turned into a solitary pursuit. Many of the lone men, who ventured into the wilderness in search of fur, or gold, vanished without a trace. In 1919, in what papers called, "Another Mystery of Silent Places and Another Man Gone," trapper Edward Lahato disappeared without a trace somewhere near the Kantishna River and not far from the long-abandoned McKinley City. Five years later, Nels Stole vanished, leaving behind a cabin, his fur catch, and supplies. Searchers Jim Burrows and Ed Jern found the cabin ransacked by a bear and his chained dogs dead of starvation. (Not many years later Burrows himself vanished without a trace.)[12]

Gold fever and trapping led many men, some woefully ill-prepared or inept, into the wilderness and an unknown fate. Alaskans were well-aware of the daily hazards and built a unique northern ethos. One writer left a classic written example of the era's mystique: "But, Alas! what about those old weather-beaten prospectors who have left their bones to bleach on those lofty peaks, after years of dancing to the weird music of the timber wolf and the uncanny hissing of

ALASKA RAILROAD COLLECTION, #BL79-3-1843, ANCHORAGE MUSEUM AT RASMUSON CENTER

*Harry Karstens, Ed Jern, Bob Degen, and Ray Dame, pose in front of Jern's tent–cabin at Copper Mountain. Though un-insulated and spare, Jern's camp was an important haven for winter travelers.*

FREDERICK B. DRANE COLLECTION, #1991-46-700, ARCHIVES, UNIVERSITY OF ALASKA, FAIRBANKS

*In late November, miner and game warden James Burrows carries "Poker" Green across open water on the Toklat River while their two female companions wait by the dogteam. In 1929, while hauling freight in the Kantishna, Burrows disappeared and was never seen again.*

the Aurora . . . . Though their names are being forgotten . . . their deeds are as lasting as the old mountains themselves. . . ."[13]

Despite endless hardships and dangers, Kantishnans enjoyed their own quirky sense of humor. One popular tale began: "Joe Canuck was on the trail out. His grub was low, his cartridges gone . . . fear lending wings to his feet. The [wolf] pack followed him, at first afar, but ever coming nearer . . . Stopping, he hastily built a fire . . . Darkness fell, and with it the realization to the poor traveler that many eyes were upon him . . . In desperation he piled wood on his fire . . .

"Ghostly forms were crowding in closer. In a frenzy of despair Joe dashed to a tree twenty yards away and hurled himself into its branches, determined to be found frozen among the knotted limbs rather than be a feast to the hungry circle below.

"At the first light of dawn, however, he took heart: only one wolf, keeping a sleepy guard, remained. But the hope was false and short lived. The rest of the pack returned with a captured beaver and put him to work cutting down the tree."[14]

Illegal trapping was, and is, a much more difficult practice to curtail than illegal hunting. In timbered areas, trap line trails are obvious and easily followed, but in open, wind-blown terrain, the whereabouts of concealed traps and snares are only known to the poacher. As fur prices soared, the rewards from poaching, or the use of poison, far out-weighed the risk of getting caught and the resulting fine. For that matter sympathetic juries might even refuse to convict the accused.

In Alaska, where year-around employment was scarce and many people lived a hand-to-mouth existence, money was a huge incentive to break the law. Law-breaking for profit wasn't always just a matter of greed for some, but of subsistence. The "Roaring Twenties" appeared to be a time of increasing prosperity in America. It fact, it was this increasing affluence, coupled with era fashion trends, that helped to inflate fur prices. Excluding Alaska, from 1923 to 1929 the per capita income of Americans rose 9%. (The top 0.1% saw their income rise an astounding 75%.) In the contiguous 48 States, the average yearly income rose to $7,505 in 1929, a new record. (By comparison, today's average yearly income is $18,506.) Trouble was brewing. The top 0.1% of Americans had a combined income equal to the bottom 42%! This incredible imbalance of wealth, with a visible and vast chasm between the rich and poor, not only led to the Great Depression but fueled latent hostility between the haves and have-nots.[15]

Marxist rhetoric and publications were popular and widely circulated in Alaska's mining camps of the 1920s. In several such publications the conservation movement, sometimes labeled "Pinchotism," named for pioneer conservationist Gifford T. Pinchot, was held up as just another example of the rich oppressing the proletariat.

From the very beginning the notion of a national park, with its guiding principle of preservation, did not sit well with Alaskans. Even mainstream Alaskan politicians, like Judge James A. Wickersham, railed against the "conservation fad" that was "locking up Alaska." The vast majority of Alaskans did not need a formal political philosophy to oppose the park: it was enough to believe that it hindered development and prevented the pursuit of traditional Alaskan endeavors, such as mining, market hunting, and trapping. Money might be a powerful lure to break the law, but a general contempt and disdain for the park and the Federal Government paved the way for widespread violations and a public willingness to look the other way.

Illegal trappers rarely got caught red-handed. Most arrests occurred after the fact, not during commission of the actual crime. Sam Fedderson, who ran a line well into the park, was cited by the territorial warden for trapping without a license. Alex Fowler was fined for possessing illegal furs. J.P. Sherman was cited for illegal trapping but the case was dropped due to improper search and seizure. Deputy Marshall Hagan cited Carlson for dealing furs without a license. Carlson was fined $250. In 1927, Game Warden Frank Dufresne also arrested Carlson for the out-of-season shooting of a white bull moose on Birch Creek. Carlson had no hunting license and also possessed illegally-taken beaver. The commissioner's court levied a fine of $200.[16]

Late in the 1920s, Ranger Grant Pearson hounded one poacher he called "Grubstake Bill" but was never able to catch him. According to Pearson, "Grubstake Bill," likely a pseudonym for Willard Shannon, once used a shooting demonstration to intimidate him. Pearson was unimpressed but there is also no evidence he ever apprehended Shannon.[17]

The growing trapping pressure, both in the Kantishna district and adjacent to the park's northern and eastern boundaries, coupled with illegal trapping within the park itself, presented a difficult challenge for Karstens. Because he needed to make a strong showing on the eastern line and halt widespread hunting in that sector, he had almost no time to deal with the trapping issue. One man could only do so much. The one trip he made to the Kantishna in 1921 to make contact and "show the colors" was not enough to stem the surge in illegal trapping. Before he could halt the trapping carnage, he had to first establish a strong presence at McKinley Station and deal with the vexing hunting situation.

By law, prospectors were free to stake new claims, develop existing ones, build cabins, and cut firewood within park boundaries. They were allowed to hunt for meat, both for themselves and their dogs, as long as the meat was not sold or transported out of the park. The miners' hunting exemption was exploited by many people who had nothing to do with mining, including a few small-scale market hunters, to continue hunting in the new park.

One major problem was that the legislation did not define, or limit, the terms prospector and miner. Almost anyone could buy a pick and gold pan, claim to be a prospector, and go hunting in the park. The Copper Mountain strike brought large numbers of stampeders into the heart of the park. Hunting, there, as everywhere in the northern mining districts, was not recreation, but a necessity of life.

For people living on the margins of the park in established camps like Glen Creek, Eureka, and Glacier City, the local availability of game dictated the extent of their hunting within the park. Frank Ten Eyck and Pat Kinnaley,

Friday Creek miners, built a moose-hunting cabin on Bear Creek north of the park. When caribou were present in large numbers there was no need to hunt in the park, but when moose and caribou were scarce, hunters went after the park's sheep herds. For many old-timers, certain spots in the park were their traditional hunting grounds. Joe and Fannie Quigley hunted Sable Mountain for sheep well into the mid-1920s. One winter, John Bowman, who lived in Eureka, accompanied by a young friend, mushed to Mace Farrar's claim on Copper Mountain in order to hunt Dall sheep. At -40°F the well-stocked tent there seemed a god-send. Neither man prospected or mined within the park but both apparently claimed the miner's exemption.

Through simple expediency some miners and prospectors routinely hunted in the park despite the availability of game elsewhere. One traveler, who stopped at a miner's cabin wrote: "I smiled as I saw sheep meat hanging in the cache . . . A meat saw and cleaver hung from a purlin . . . The owner came in and soon had some juicy sheep steaks frying in the pan."[18]

Prospectors and miners kept large numbers of sled dogs inside the park boundaries. In 1924, for example, Karstens counted seventy-five sled dogs, not counting pups, living within the perimeter, all of them fed wild meat. William N. Beach described what he saw in 1922. "We rented an outfit from the Alaska Road Commission . . . The territory was overrun with prospectors all of whom had good-sized dog teams that were being fed off the country . . . ."[19]

Trappers hunted for food, dog food, and trapping bait. One trapper left a brief but vivid record of his take. "No caribou for dog feed this fall," Carl Hult recalled, "I've shot as many as thirty a day on these slopes [Chitsia Mountain] when they were going through." From April through June 1924, he and a partner shot 18 caribou and three sheep.[20]

Clandestine market hunting continued within the park even after Karstens' appointment as park superintendent. One of these illegal hunters was Frank Glaser, who relocated to the park to work for Olaus Murie. During the winter of 1922-23, Glaser teamed up with Harry Lucke. "Once Lucke and I took two dog teams into the head of Riley Creek, which flows into the Nenana River, and killed a couple of sled loads of Dall sheep for the Fairbanks market," Glaser told an interviewer. Lucke also killed sheep on Riley Creek to pay off a debt to local roadhouse owner Maurice Morino.[21]

On his first patrol into the park, Karstens noted the impact of over-hunting. Dall sheep seemed to be in decline. In 1924, he estimated the population at around 3,000, citing diminished numbers due to hunting. Almost from the outset of his park tenure, Karstens felt the only way to stop excessive hunting

STEPHEN FOSTER COLLECTION, #1969-92-267, ARCHIVES, UNIVERSITY OF ALASKA, FAIRBANKS

*Joe Gagnon's cabin on Home Creek, a tributary of the Healy Fork, served as both a trapping and prospecting camp. A dozen or more trappers, headquartered near the town of Healy, set up camps along the north boundary of the park, with foxes their primary target.*

was to close the loophole that allowed miners special hunting privileges. "Sheep are being hunted extensively in distant portions of the park," he wrote, "piles of sheep hides and horns are to be found at different points." He also reported that "many loads of sheep were hauled to the railroad from Riley Creek which runs parallel with the eastern boundary." The closure he advocated would not take place until 1927.[22]

The enforcement of park regulations, and curbing exploitation of the hunting loophole, would sorely test Harry Karstens. Even though old-timers resented park rules, they knew not to trifle with him. "There has been quite a lot of hunting along the northern boundary of the park last winter [1921] . . . ," Karstens wrote, "but my comming [sic] has put a stop to that. The market hunters don't like it a bit but are taking it pretty well at that, some of them think they can slip something over on me but I told them they would be the loser." A closer examination of the situation indicates that Karstens was deluding himself. The old-timers he knew altered their practices in response to his arrival but by 1923 they were in the minority. The imminent completion of the railroad attracted large numbers of prospectors. Some of these newcomers exploited the loopholes to hunt and build cabins in the park: their only "prospecting" was for more bullets. These men did not share an allegiance to an old, respected friend. Many of the newcomers were war veterans, steeled on the bloody fields of Flanders. A few were hard cases, their past lives concealed from the law by fake names. It took tough, hardy people to live in the northern wilderness year-around. Despite their toughness, they more than met their match in Harry Karstens.[23]

# 9

# Murie on the Savage Fork

McKinley Station residents were abuzz. Olaus Murie, supposedly a biologist, was building a camp at the head of the Savage Fork* with plans to catch caribou. Rumor had it that Murie, actually a fur warden, was working undercover for the U.S. Marshal to snare liquor law violators. Harry Karstens, who heard the rumors, snorted "Nonsense!" But what was Murie doing there? No one had ever heard of such a thing. Catching caribou?

While mineral development spurred most early Alaskan scientific efforts, pioneer wildlife studies centered on specimen collection, predator control, and rudimentary counting. For example, Charles Sheldon's collections on the Toklat were sent to C. Hart Merriam, of the National Academy of Sciences, for taxonomic classification. Dr Edward W. Nelson, Chief of the U.S. Biological Survey (forerunner to the U.S. Fish and Wildlife Service) was eager to learn more about Alaska's wildlife, especially the habits and migrations of caribou. In 1920, he hired biologist Olaus J. Murie to investigate and record everything he could about the territory's caribou. At Nelson's bidding, Murie left Fairbanks on March 22, 1921 bound for the upper Tanana River.

Murie, 32, a second-generation Norwegian, hailed from Moorhead, Minnesota. From his father, a former Army Officer, he'd learned dedication and perseverance, traits invaluable in the wilderness. Influenced by the writings of naturalist Ernest Thompson Seton, the young Murie studied biology at Fargo College near Moorhead. When his biology professor took a position at Pacific University in Forest Grove, Oregon, Murie followed, graduating in 1912. After

* In that era, the word "Fork" was used instead of "River" to denote minor tributaries of larger water courses.

graduation he worked two years for the Oregon State Game Commission. From 1914 to 1917, he served as Field Naturalist and Curator of Mammals for the Carnegie Museum of Pittsburgh, making two expeditions into Hudson Bay and across the Labrador Peninsula. When World War I broke out, he enlisted as a balloon observer. Soon after the Armistice, he accepted Nelson's invitation to work in Alaska as an "assistant biologist and fur warden." Some suspicious Interior residents believed Murie's "caribou study" concealed his "real" work of enforcing liquor laws.

Murie's boss, the legendary and notoriously grouchy E.W. Nelson, was a demanding taskmaster with vast Alaska experience. In 1877, he had established a meteorological station at St. Michael, explored the Bering Sea littoral, the Yukon delta, and voyaged to Barrow on the revenue cutter *Corwin*. In the dead of winter, he and Charles Peterson mushed across the Yukon Delta to the Kuskokwim River, the first white men to use the route. He expected similar effort and dedication from Murie and other field biologists in his employ.

Nelson possessed extensive knowledge of reindeer, then being introduced into western Alaska to benefit Alaska Natives, and believed them to be inferior to indigenous caribou. He surmised that their strength, size, and disease immunity could be improved by cross-breeding prime caribou bulls to reindeer cows. In 1921, he directed Olaus Murie to capture sixteen bulls and ship them down the Yukon River to Nome. If all went as planned, the animals would then be moved to Nunivak Island in the Bering Sea.

"There are probably about 200,000 reindeer in Alaska. Eventually the reindeer industry will be an important resource," Murie explained. "The Biological Survey has undertaken to encourage this industry in every way possible-by studying the diseases of the reindeer, food and range problems, methods of handling, etc. Introduction of native caribou in the herds, with careful control of breeding, will tend to effect these results."[1]

"[My] investigations among the caribou have had as one object to find out where the largest species are to be found," Murie explained, "in order that bulls might be captured for breeding with the reindeer." Murie's initial investigations led him from the Alaska Range to the Brooks Range and back again, much of the research conducted in the heart of winter.[2]

During his initial wanderings Murie had found "a number of [caribou] snare fences . . . the most perfect examples in the Ketchumstuk country, where caribou migrate regularly. Near the Indian Creek village was a more elaborate structure," he said. "A line fence extended westward about 6 miles. The whole structure, fastened entirely by willow withes, was well built, and the parts still standing were firm. The inner corral or pocket [a 510'-long pole corral] was more than 6 feet high and reinforced by vertical poles close together. A band of caribou, following the lead fence, would be led into the corral. Then the entrance was guarded by a number of Indians, while one on each side shot caribou with a bow and arrow. Caribou are [also] snared by the Indians at the mouth of Old Crow River, in Yukon Territory. A missionary at that place showed [me] samples of snares made of twisted rawhide." Native hunters also built and used similar fences in the drainages north of the new park.[3]

Murie believed a fence patterned somewhat like the one at Indian Creek could be used to effectively capture live caribou. "I visited several localities in an endeavor to locate the caribou herds and to find good crossings, where caribou might be captured for domestication," he wrote.[4]

Trapping and shipping wild caribou presented numerous challenges, paramount of which was the need for reliable transportation. At Nelson's suggestion, Murie first scouted for a capture site near Black Rapids on the Richardson Highway, a place where Nelson had seen large herds of caribou. Murie quickly learned that the caribou migration there was unreliable, so he turned his attentions to McKinley Park, which he had first visited in November 1920. He quickly decided that the railroad offered the best method of transporting live animals.

During a late winter, 1921, foray into the park, Murie walked from the government railroad to the Toklat drainage. There, he rendezvoused with Jim Burrows, the district game warden, at his claim on Little Moose Creek, and together they mushed to the head of the Toklat River where they looked for caribou. Murie rejected that location because of its isolation, but in the process Murie assuaged his curiosity about "Sheldon's country."[5]

On July 14, 1922, Harry Karstens accompanied Murie to the head of the Savage Fork, a locale Karstens considered perfect for the task at hand. "Murie & I left Savage Fork and traveled to the upper forks. Before arriving we saw numerous bands of caribou between two and three hundred but don't think there were 25 calves in all. Blowing hard & showers of rain in the afternoon but we went up the right fork about two miles & then through a low pass in the high mountains into Sanctuary River. We continued to see caribou on our way down Sanctuary to our camp about four miles above timber line and expect to get a bull caribou specimen tomorrow. The caribou range quite high in the summer with few of them in the lower range," Karstens said.[6]

After their jaunt, Murie agreed with Karstens' assessment, noting several well-worn caribou trails and two topographic features at the head of the Savage that naturally funneled moving animals into an area suitable for a trap. In early

HENRY P. KARSTENS COLLECTION, #2122, KARSTENS LIBRARY

*In 1922, Olaus Murie built a pioneer road to the head of the Savage River, where he established a camp and built a corral to capture caribou. Later, workers with the Alaska Road Commission, pictured here, upgraded the road to "Caribou Camp" for use by tourists.*

July, Murie and Karstens began work on a pioneer wagon road to the Savage Fork. By late August, construction of the capture corral and camp was well underway, its completion hindered by a delayed shipment of wire fencing.

Murie's construction crew consisted of Sam Ivey, Bob Perkins, Joe Cunningham, brothers Ted and Jule Loftus, and Frank Glaser, the latter three of whom were to stay on as "caribou wranglers." Each man was paid $5 per day, and the cook got $5.50. In addition, Murie hired local teamsters to haul freight to the head of the river. Jule Loftus had come to Alaska in 1921 to join his brother Art. The brothers, described as "experienced cattle men and woodsmen," found immediate work with the AEC. In the autumn of 1921, they bought dog teams and hunted sheep for the Allred Roadhouse and AEC camps in the Nenana canyon. They spent the rest of the winter trapping on the Yanert Fork, where they were joined in March by their younger brother Ted. Jule and Ted hired on to work with Murie until the start of the autumn semester at the college in Fairbanks.[7]

Glaser was hired on the recommendation of Dr. Nelson, thus beginning a long, and sometimes contentious, association with the park. Glaser, a veteran market hunter and former operator of the Black Rapids Roadhouse, brought to the project his considerable wilderness skills and wildlife knowledge. In previous years, he had supplied meat to the large road commission force turning the Richardson Trail into a highway, recalling that they "would take all the meat I could kill." Earlier, he'd hunted for both the U.S. Army Signal Corps crews building the military telegraph line and the Copper River Mining Company. Glaser said that from 1915 to 1923, he killed around 280 sheep, a lesser number of caribou, and every moose he saw. From 1924 to 1937, Glaser lived and trapped on the Savage River just outside the park's northern boundary.[8]

The crew spent the last half of the summer of 1922 building the capture corral at the head of the river, about six miles above the last timber. Their base camp was located 1.5 miles below the corral. Murie modified the Athabascan model by shortening the wings of the trap, which he extended upstream so that animals could be driven downstream into it. "Using some wire, and some poles that we had to cut and haul in," Glaser recalled, "we built a big circular trap with lead wings six-feet high that ran about a mile up the mountainside." Bushes and trees were cut to camouflage the wings and catch pen.[9]

"The corral itself, which is circular, [has] a diameter of about sixty yards," explained Jule Loftus. "At the end opposite the main entrance there is a small pen one rod square into which individuals are driven for treatment such as dehorning and hobbling. A small chute serves as an exit."[10]

"The endeavor of the Bureau of Biological Survey to build up the market quality of the Alaskan reindeer is taking active form. O. J. Murie [took] with him a party of experienced cattle men and woodsmen who will attempt this fall to corral a number of bull caribou for breeding purposes," reported the news. "Mr. Murie hopes to secure about fifteen bull calves. He will winter them at McKinley Park station, where the main corral will be placed. Captured bulls will be shipped to Nunivak Island the next spring."[11]

Early expectations proved overly optimistic. "We caught no caribou with the trap that [first] year," Glaser said. The shortage of wire fencing prevented use of the capture corral.[12]

Murie, accompanied by his half-brother Adolph, returned to the park in October to collect caribou specimens for the Biological Survey. The brothers hunted and explored the upper Savage drainage and succeeded in killing several mature bulls, giving the meat to the ranger staff. "From on top of the hill we saw several herds of caribou . . . In the last herd we saw a reindeer . . . he was easily distinguished from the caribou by his short legs and small size," Adolph wrote. "Olaus followed this herd [to Maurice Creek] in an effort to get the reindeer but could not."[13]

COURTESY OF LOUISE MURIE-MCLEOD

*Olaus Murie brought his younger half-brother, Adolph, to the park to work on the 1922 caribou project. "Ade," pictured here in the mid-1950s at the East Fork cabin, returned later to complete landmark studies of the park's wolves and bears.*

The outing provided an unexpected bonding experience for the half-brothers. Martin Murie, Olaus' brother, originally had been scheduled to assist in the caribou project but he succumbed to a virulent form of tuberculosis. Adolph, or "Ade" as he was called, then an under-graduate, was a logical choice to replace Martin.

The younger Murie eventually obtained his M.S. and Ph.D. degrees in natural science from the University of Michigan and later worked for both the Fish and Wildlife Service and the National Park Service. His later research into the relationships between Yellowstone coyotes and elk, and McKinley's Dall sheep and wolves, led to both condemnation and praise, but also recognition as landmark studies. Over the course of his 40-year-long association with McKinley Park, Ade became one of the most influential voices in its development and preservation.

As part of the capture crew, young Ade Murie enjoyed no special favors from the boss, working as hard as anyone else. Catching caribou proved to be more arduous than anyone assumed. "One day while doing some work on the fence some one exclaimed, '*Caribou!*' and pointed to a ridge," Olaus Murie recounted. "A cow and calf were sauntering along, feeding. We hurried to our stations and waited. This was just after dinner. The afternoon slowly passed, and still the cow and calf fed leisurely on the same slope. Then they lay down and we waited patiently. The sun went low, evening came on, but the cow was in no hurry. A cold breeze had been coming down the valley and we shivered as we lay in hiding. Late in the evening the cow arose and began feeding again; then actually started down the valley.

"Suddenly a bull appeared, from nowhere it seemed, and all three fed quietly for a time, while we could hardly control our chattering teeth. When our patience was about gone they started definitely downstream, fairly between the lead fences. We let them go as far as they would before disturbing them, and they marched nearly up to the corral gate. Then we all leaped into action running toward the gate, five abreast. The caribou tried to turn back, but seemed to meet a man wherever they went. They turned again, and after prancing around a bit, undecided, entered the corral. Now we raced in earnest, each one eager to close the gate. I lost out in the scramble, but heard the slam of the gate, a welcome sound!

"It was late, but we decided to rope the animals at once, for fear the calf might be trampled by the others. After driving them into a smaller compartment, some one pounced on the calf and had it hog-tied; another had the cow down and some one else had a rope on the bull, a fine three-year-old. Halter and hobbles were placed on the cow and calf and they were tethered for the time being in the large enclosure. The bull was not so easily handled, and we were thoroughly warmed before we had him in control. His menacing antlers were sawed off, hobbles fastened to his front feet, and he was given the freedom of the small pen. We returned to camp well satisfied with the day's work."[14]

Because the cornered caribou fought wildly to escape, the second field season sometimes resembled a summer-long rodeo. "Often the animals would pitch headlong into the wing fences and be thrown back," Loftus said, "various nooses [were] hurled at them from every post in the pen fence where a puncher could safely perch. The caribou can dodge very efficiently, and for this reason it sometimes required several minutes to get them stretched on the ground and securely hog-tied. When finally unwound, and standing, they were each equipped with a pair of leather hobbles and a leather halter to which their tie rope was fastened. The hobbles were fastened to the front legs, between the knees and the ankles, purposely causing the animal to jump instead of trot as is its habit."[15]

Failed attempts out-numbered successes. "Olaus drove a large bull caribou almost into the corral. He tried several times to jump the fence. . . . The fence post broke off, the caribou and fence going down together. The bull got up and jumped over the busted fence running up the mountain," Ade Murie recounted.[16]

A reading of Olaus' journal reveals his mounting frustration. "We found several caribou above the corral and missed driving them in by a hair's breadth. Failure was due to hasty judgment on my part . . . [On another occasion] three came up the river . . . they passed the end of the lead fence—we tried driving them, but they were too much in a hurry and sped up the opposite mountain before we could surround them. Then came another. He came on the run, stopped on the bar near the corral and lay down for a long time. Then he got up and seemed to be rubbing his horns on the fence . . . suddenly he dashed off around the corral as if greatly frightened . . . The Caribou were traveling the wrong direction today for a capture."[17]

On one occasion, frustration turned to tragedy for one of the animals. "While Frank [Glaser] went up a mountain to get a caribou specimen," Olaus wrote, "I went up to the corral and had not been there long when I saw two large bulls coming down the creek. I let them go all the way up to the corral gate, then slipped in behind them. When they saw me they tried to run through the wire netting and both were knocked down. One tried it again, fell down and lay there. The other ran into the corral. I shut the gate, then ran down to the one who fell and tied his feet together with my handkerchief. But it was no use—in a few minutes he was dead."[18]

On another day, a band of several cows with calves and one young bull wandered into sight, moving slowly, grazing here and there. The crew hid and waited. When the animals were near the trap, the men stood up, arms outstretched. The animals stopped and stared. A large, mature cow bolted. Olaus sprinted from hiding, trying to turn them back toward the trap. The frightened animals easily outran him.

"After several such experiences, we learned to be more subtle," Glaser said. "Instead of standing and showing themselves when caribou were between wings of the trap, Olaus and Adolf remained crouched and waved a hand at the animals to get their attention. This made them nervous, and they'd edge away from the Muries and toward the trap entrance. When the animals were at the entrance, Olaus and Adolf would leap up and run towards the animals—and as often as not the deer would flee into the trap. When they were well inside I yanked the gate shut.

"We caught a few big bulls, but mostly we caught cows and calves. The animals were terribly wild in the trap. Most could climb the fence; they simply hooked their feet into the wire in the fence and climbed over.

COURTESY OF JIM REARDEN

*Frank Glaser, a one-time market hunter and former owner of the Black Rapids Roadhouse, worked on Olaus Murie's caribou project. Afterward, he built a cabin on the lower Savage River where he trapped from 1924 to 1936. Here he paused by one of the road commission's notoriously incorrect mileage signs.*

CLARA RUST COLLECTION, #67-110-395, ARCHIVES, UNIVERSITY OF ALASKA, FAIRBANKS

*The caribou corral construction crew in front of their camp on the Savage River. (l-r) Unidentified, Adolph Murie, unidentified, Ted Loftus, Jule Loftus, Frank Glaser, Bob Perkins. The unidentified are likely Sam Ivey, and, Joe Cunningham, the other members of the crew.*

"When the animals were inside the trap we had to rope the young bulls we wanted. I did most of the roping, using a regular lariat. Often, with the loop hanging right over the head of a bull, just about to drop on him, he'd leap to one side, and the loop would land on the ground. Then the animal would attack the rope with his sharp hoofs. If I did get the rope around a bull's antlers, he'd usually lower his head and charge, and I'd have to dodge. I had some very close calls. In the end I had to snare most of the bulls by a front leg.

"We sawed the antlers off of the dozen young bulls we did catch, put halters on them, and staked them out around our camp with ropes. They tamed quickly. We used about 40 feet of rope tied to a heavy, movable, dry spruce toggle and frequently moved the toggle to put the animals on better grazing.

"Not one of those caribou ever became tangled with their picket rope. They were afraid of the rope, and wouldn't step across it, and always kept out at the end of it. They learned to move their toggle a short distance with a sideways pull so they could get fresh grazing. Then they'd feed in a wide circle as far as the rope would allow before yanking the toggle again. We kept some of them that way for more than a month.

"The cows weren't difficult to handle. When we roped them they usually stood while we walked down the rope and put our hands on them ... We didn't keep any of the cows."[19]

The men treated the picketed caribou like domestic livestock. "A pail of water and a sack of moss were always left with the animals when tied out," Jule Loftus said. "After being fed Eagle Brand milk for a short while the calves became quite tame and would follow the feeder . . . the milk-fed and tamed animals are preferable in this experiment to the bulls captured when they are several years of age."[20]

One bull broke its halter and got away but was recaptured. "Had '*Harding*' [a bull named after the President] down today. We changed his halter and placed a rope around his neck for emergency. After we let him up, we fed him some moss which he evidently enjoys very much," Ade explained.[21]

In August, Karstens escorted W.C. Henderson, assistant chief of the Biological Survey to the head of the Savage River to inspect the operation. Karstens remarked that the corral, "located 10 to 12 miles south of Savage Camp, would make an excellent side trip for visitors ..." In contrast to the two-day horseback trek needed to reach the site originally, Karstens drove his Model T in three hours and 15 minutes to within a mile and a half of the corral. Henderson and Olaus Murie discussed the project and his plans to ship the captured caribou to Fairbanks, the first stage of the trip to the coast.[22]

HENRY P. KARSTENS COLLECTION, #1422, KARSTENS LIBRARY

*A snowstorm on August 31, 1922, buried the camp on Savage River and temporarily halted work on the corral. Visitors, including Helen Franklin, by tent door, and a child, were stranded for a short time. Harry Karstens loads the wagon at right.*

The onset of the caribou rut in late September 1923 ended the capture work. The hobbled animals were led out of the mountains and down to the station where they were loaded into a box car for transfer to a corral on the College campus. That winter, Murie hired George Flood and another local man to gather and sack lichens at the head of Maurice Creek for caribou feed. In all, they collected 100 burlap bags of lichen.

Late that following winter, Robert Degen and Harry Lucke rescued a bull caribou from a hole in the ice on the upper Riley Creek. The weakened and injured bull was kept in the horse corral at headquarters and quickly recovered from its near–fatal entrapment. "Caribou doing nicely, feeding him on moss. Does not care for oil meal and bran mixed, hay or grain," Karstens explained. "Is not haltered but runs loose in a small corral. We work around him but he does not appear to mind."[23]

Karstens called Dr. Charles E. Bunnell, President of the Alaska Agricultural College and School of Mines, where the caribou were being kept, to gain assistance and funding in shipping the bull to Fairbanks. "That was a fortunate incident, for now breeding experiments . . . may be carried on by the college on a small scale. The animal seems to be doing well and is tame, considering the time he has been kept in captivity," Murie soon wrote Karstens, "We shall not be using the corral on Savage River this summer . . . But Dr. Nelson said he had not given up that project." In 1925, the captive caribou were finally shipped to Nunivak Island. The Savage Fork corral was abandoned due to high costs and limited success.[24]

INCIDENTAL TO HIS PROJECT, Olaus Murie also compiled and classified "the flora, fauna and natural phenomena of the park," the area's first such systematic listing. He also recorded an ornithological first. On July 1, 1923, Gus Buhmann, while driving a buckboard on Savage Fork about five miles above the confluence with Jenny Creek, flushed a wandering tattler. When he saw the bird flutter away he stopped the team and quickly located the nest, a small, relatively elaborate affair of sticks and twigs, just "six inches from the wheel track!" The nest of this shorebird, at about 4000′ elevation, was the first wandering tattler nest known to science.[25]

Olaus Murie's three year capture effort included an event that transformed his life and helped shape the future of American conservation. In June 1921, Fairbanks friends, Jess and Clara Rust, introduced Olaus to a young woman, Margaret "Mardy" Elizabeth Thomas, returning from two years at Reed College to join her beloved step-father, an assistant U.S. Attorney. When the Rusts

HARPER'S FERRY COLLECTION, #8-27-40, NATIONAL PARK SERVICE

*In 1950, Adolph Murie (l), and biologist L.J. Palmer (r), re-visited the Savage River caribou capture corral. To this day, remnants of twisted wire and poles remain on site.*

introduced Murie as an employee of the U.S. Biological Survey, young Mardy innocently asked, "What's that?"

The following winter, while conducting his wildlife studies along the Koyukuk Trail, the smitten Olaus expressed his feelings in several letters to Mardy. "How I wish you were with me right now," he wrote. "We are up on a summit; the night is silver clear, with twinkling stars and a pure crescent moon. I was out a moment ago to look at it and think of you at the same time . . . Oh, the sweetness of a moonlight night!"[26]

In late July 1923, Mardy, now 21, and her family visited the caribou capture camp at the head of Savage River. "At the end of five days of tramping about in a rosy haze in those enchanted mountains," Mardy wrote, "we both knew there was no life for us except together." On August 18, 1924, Olaus and Margaret were married in a log mission at Anvik on the bank of the Yukon River. In 1963, when Olaus, then 74, died of cancer, Mardy called their luminous life together "a fairy tale." Throughout the rest of her long life she persevered in the struggle to protect wilderness and wildlife, her efforts, she said, dedicated to "her beloved Olaus."

HENRY P. KARSTENS COLLECTION, #6001, KARSTENS LIBRARY

*In 1923, the cast and crew of* The Chechahcos *[sic] gathered for a portrait at the McKinley Station depot. On the right, Harry Karstens, stands at the handlebars of the dogsled, while Fritz Nyberg holds the park team still for this publicity photograph. Behind the center dogsled is the famed "Malemute Kid," Frank Tondro.*

# 10

# The Nation Comes Calling

"Camera! Action! Start the dogs!" When the director shouted the command, Harry Karstens, dressed in a fur parka, pulled the snow hook and mushed his eleven dogs down a steep hill above a frozen creek. That he managed to reach the bottom without a spill was testament to both skill and luck. When the dogs lined out on the hard-packed trail, they quickly built up speed and pulled away from the camera crew. As the lead dog took the team around a sharp bend in the trail, the director began yelling and flapping his arms. *"Cut! Cut! That's a take!"* Hollywood had come to McKinley Station.

While Karstens halted his team and laboriously turn them around, the cast and crew of *The Chechahcos* [sic] moved their camera and positions to begin filming yet another scene in front of Maurice Morino's log hotel.

In early March 1923, Harry Karstens had received a letter from Austin E. "Cap" Lathrop of the Alaska Moving Picture Company and owner of Anchorage's *Empress* Theater, requesting his assistance in shooting sequences for the first feature film ever to be shot entirely in Alaska. Lathrop, also Chairman of the Healy River Coal Corporation and future owner of the Mt. McKinley Bituminous Coal Corporation, was one of the territory's most powerful entrepreneurs. His letter explained in detail what he was doing and what he needed. His film, he said, boasted an Alaskan crew working in spectacular locations, all filmed with the latest Hollywood techniques. Lathrop wanted Karstens' help with location suggestions along the railroad and the staging of dog mushing sequences.

A few days later, Lathrop's representative phoned Karstens, then in Nenana, to explain that the film was more than a drama, it was also to be a promotional effort for Alaska. He said that the film company would distribute publicity pictures of scenic Alaska, including the park entrance. He went on to say that, although the U.S. Army Signal Corps and the Alaska Railroad were donating their services, the company also needed Karstens' expertise. Karstens, aware of the film's publicity value and the importance of helping "Cap" Lathrop, agreed to assist as best he could. He warned also that, "I will take care of the dogs [but] will not allow cheap melodrama pictures to be taken in the park." He was assured that the script was of the highest quality.[1]

Although this silent picture's incomparable Alaskan landscape set it apart from other era films, the story in fact was hokey melodrama. In it, Horseshoe Riley and Bob Dexter save Baby Ruth Stanislaw from a calamitous boiler explosion aboard a steamer. Another survivor, Richard Steele, a gambler, encourages Ruth's mother to believe her little girl has drowned. He then offers the bereaved mother protection. Steele buys a gambling house and forces the young mother to "entertain." Meanwhile, Ruth grows to young womanhood and marries Dexter. Riley and Dexter discover her mother in the gambling house and decide to attempt a reunion. Learning of the plot Steele binds Dexter to a chair and sets fire to the cabin. Dexter escapes and goes after Steele, who is killed by a collapsing glacier during an exciting dogsled chase. Mother and child are tearfully re-united.

In late March, a special train delivered Lathrop and his crew to McKinley Station. For this segment of the film, two legendary mushers, Frank Tondro, the famed "Malamute Kid," and Harry Karstens, the equally famous "Seventymile Kid," doubled for the actors mushing their teams across the frozen terrain. Tondro, famous for his fur attire, mushed his dogs both at McKinley Station and through Broad Pass for pay. Karstens loaned eleven dogs, two sleds, and four days of his time, as public relations for the park. In the finished film, several exterior scenes of Morino's hotel cut away to lavish, stylized interiors built on a stage in Anchorage. Even though Morino profited from the shoot, and appeared briefly as an extra in front of his hotel, he seemed to resent Karstens' involvement and limited screen time.

After shooting at McKinley Station, Lathrop gave Karstens two thumbs up for his able assistance and promised to provide photos of the park team and his future cooperation. As elsewhere, the film company made a good impression on locals. "The company, which is composed of some of the finest actors and actresses to be found anywhere, has been at work for several months at Anchorage, McKinley National Park, Nenana, Fairbanks, Seward and Valdez," the news reported. "The members of the cast have made friends everywhere among Alaskans . . . whatever Hollywood may be, they are fine, clean ladies and gentlemen."[2]

In contrast to his first two years as park superintendent, Karstens faced entirely new challenges in 1923. Although the park was not yet ready to host visitors, the year would introduce it to the nation. If successful, *The Chechahcos* would promote Alaska, and McKinley Park, to tens of thousands of Americans, some of whom would be enticed north. In spring, three important delegations would descend on McKinley Station—a Congressional delegation that controlled railroad funding, an entourage from America's largest and most widely-read newspaper, and in July, the U.S. President and much of his cabinet. Until spring break-up, for Karstens the only respite from his never-ending work load was involvement in the film.

Working with the film crew was a big change of pace for Karstens, who had spent much of the winter of 1922-23 on construction projects. Beginning in early October, Karstens began salvaging lumber from two log cabins at the abandoned AEC camp to build a school near the railroad depot. Working alone, or with the help of one other volunteer, Karstens finished the new school by mid-November. Then he cut and hauled a winter's worth of firewood for the school's modest woodstove. The school project may not have been part of Karstens' job, but he needed to build the infrastructure necessary to support a family in this isolated spot.

The territorial government required a minimum enrollment of six children before it would provide a teacher and supplies. Eugene Karstens and the children of station manager and telegrapher Rufus "Red" Nichols, Frances, Bro, Orrin, Ralph, and Marion, met the minimum, with the Abbey children due to join them after the first of the year. With the woodstove installed, school started on November 13, 1922. Basic illumination was provided by Aladdin-type kerosene lamps.[3]

In early January 1923, Woodbury Abbey and his family returned to McKinley Station from Nenana with the intention of building a permanent home. Abbey had applied for a permit to operate a hotel and transportation concession within the park and was anxious to begin the groundwork. The first order of business was to find a temporary place to live. Lined up at right angles to the railroad tracks were five old boxcars, one of which served as a crude depot. Another was the home of the Nichols family. Two others housed and fed transient railroad workers. The Abbeys moved into the fifth one, an insulated refrigerator car heated by a small coal and wood stove. Here they lived for two months before moving into one of Morino's cabins.

In spring, Abbey, assisted by family friend Al Wigand, a stalwart veteran of various surveys, began work on a log cabin northwest of the depot. In mid-summer, accompanied by clouds of mosquitoes, the Abbeys moved into their new home.

While Karstens worked on the school, Ranger Robert Bragaw finished building several dog houses at the park headquarters. Together they salvaged lumber from the abandoned camp in order to renovate Lynch's Roadhouse for their own use. In early January, Karstens began serious training of the park's two dog teams. Twice the rangers took the teams to Igloo Canyon on patrol and to prepare a camp for Major Gotshall's up-coming winter trip. Karstens used his own money to buy dogs to build a seven-dog team for Gotshall. When he learned in March that Gotshall had taken ill and would not be returning, he sold off the new dogs.

Reports of illegal hunting and trapping out west greatly alarmed Karstens. "From reports [game] is getting thinned out around Copper Mountain where quite a number of prospectors and miners have been located," he informed National Park Service Director Stephen Mather. "There has been trapping of fur animals going on in the western portion of the park. The men in that section of the park are doing pretty much as they please." Even though Karstens reported that a "northern boundary patrol is urgently needed," budget and appropriations deadlines, endless winter chores, and various construction projects kept him chained to headquarters.[4]

News of excessive hunting and trapping did not surprise Karstens. "The general run of people seems to think this Reservation was created for the benefit of Big Game Hunters from the states," he said, and they expressed considerable antipathy to the park. Alaskans would not easily give up their hunting and trapping privileges, even in a national park.[5]

Karstens detailed the park's urgent infrastructure and personnel needs. "My plans are for six cabins with barns and caches along the Northern Boundary," Karstens wrote. He said he needed at least four rangers, one for the east boundary, one for the area south of Riley Creek, and two on the north boundary. By April, he was begging for help. "We will do our best," he pledged, "and are eager to cope with any situation that may develop; but is it fair to the Park [to operate so short-handed]?"[6]

A business deal at Copper Mountain set off alarm bells that reached all the way to Washington and highlighted the park's desperate situation. In March 1922, miners Giles and Grant optioned their copper claims to Jack Price and Tom Aitken for $500,000. Less than a year later, Aitken, that shrewd and experienced miner, bonded these claims to the Guggenheim Brothers for $1,000,000. The "Guggs," as miners called them derisively, also showed interest in other Copper Mountain claims. The Guggenheims consolidated Aitken and Price's 23 claims, totaling 440 acres, and hired W.E. Dunkle to supervise the initial development.[7]

Daniel Guggenheim, a partner in the firm of Guggenheim Brothers, was one of the leading figures in the U.S. copper industry, extending the firm's activities to include Alaska gold. In 1906, tycoon J. Pierpoint Morgan joined with the Guggenheims to form a partnership soon known as the *Alaska Syndicate*. The *Syndicate* built a railroad from Cordova to their Kennecott Mine properties and bought up the Alaska Steamship Company to control coastal shipping. It also purchased twelve of Alaska's largest salmon canneries; opposed home-rule for Alaska; and appeared on the verge of monopolizing the territory's vast coal reserves. Ordinary Alaskans viewed the "Guggs" with distrust, fear, and hostility. Morgan was equally loathed. A decade earlier, Morgan had been one of a group of New York tycoons that unsuccessfully attempted to corner the copper market. Throughout his career, Congressional Delegate James Wickersham steadfastly opposed their monopolistic ploys.

The Guggenheims clearly had the necessary capital to develop Copper Mountain and the Kantishna District claims, *if* any proved rich enough to justify full development. Not only were the "Guggs" wealthy enough to build a private rail link to the mines, but they had the power to force it through the park. At that time, the Secretary of Interior, Albert B. Fall, who was described as so "crooked he had to be screwed into the ground when he died," surely would have acceded to, if not championed, any such proposition. Only time would reveal the true value of the claims, but the news certainly fired deep concern among park advocates.

Karstens was bogged down with paperwork that winter and spent critical time studying various applications for the park concession, including Woodbury Abbey's plan to build two hotels. In January, Dan T. Kennedy met with Karstens to discuss his application for transportation privileges in the park. Kennedy wanted a 10-year permit, and promised to provide first class equipment and horses. Abbey, Kennedy's junior partner, would provide financial support. Karstens suggested that Kennedy apply directly to Assistant Director Arno Cammerer. Karstens knew and respected Kennedy but for multiple reasons wanted to exclude Abbey.

Kennedy seemed to be an ideal choice for the transportation concession. Few people possessed his knowledge of animals, outfitting, and cross-country travel. After a stint in the Klondike gold fields, Kennedy moved to Valdez in 1901, where he contracted to freight supplies for the military telegraph project.

ALBERT JOHNSON COLLECTION, #89-166-658, ARCHIVES, UNIVERSITY OF ALASKA, FAIRBANKS

*Dan T. Kennedy, "the Gold Dust packer," was awarded the park's first tourist concession. Prior to that, Kennedy had made his name transporting gold dust and bullion throughout the Alaska wilderness. In this 1906 photograph, Kennedy, third from the right, stands guard over1,200 pounds of gold. Completion of the railroad put teamsters and packers like Kennedy out of business.*

He used his horses to move supplies, summer and winter, over a rugged trail through Thompson Pass to the Copper River valley.[8]

Kennedy arrived in Fairbanks in September 1904, and inaugurated an independent freighting business on the Richardson Trail that flourished despite stiff competition. Townspeople eagerly anticipated the arrivals of the various stage lines. In Fairbanks one spring Kennedy was hailed as a hero for bringing in three tons of sugar to "relieve the sugar famine." The headline story did not mention that sugar was a vital ingredient in homebrew.[9]

Due to Kennedy's skill and implacable courage, word quickly spread that Kennedy Stage Lines, was the outfit to move gold from Fairbanks to the coast for shipment south. The most successful miners soon sought out the "Gold Dust Packer" to transport their "pay." In an era photograph, 14 men and two women posed in front of the St. Elias Hotel in Valdez with 2,800 *pounds* of Fairbanks gold brought to Valdez by Kennedy and his heavily-armed men.

In 1906, Kennedy, Frank Manley,* and "Silent Sam" Bonnifield, and two gun-toting wranglers transported 1,200 pounds of gold—worth $16,320,000 in 2008—to Valdez. Kennedy led the way on his favorite riding mule, his rifle resting across the pommel for quick use. Later that year, Kennedy and Bonnifield transported an additional 1,350 pounds of gold bullion over the road. Highwaymen left Kennedy and his heavily-guarded pack strings alone.

Kennedy also possessed first-hand knowledge of the upper Nenana River region. Kennedy, his crew, and 24 horses, were on board the steamer *Florence S* in 1908 when it pulled away from the Pioneer Dock in Fairbanks bound for the Kantishna to pick up Karstens' and Sheldon's crates of hunting specimens. En route to the Kantishna, the steamer dropped off Kennedy's outfit at the mouth of the Wood River for their cross-country trek south to Valdez Creek in the Upper Susitna drainage.

Prospectors first discovered gold on a remote creek near Broad Pass in 1897. After a hurried trip back to the coast for supplies, they returned but could not re-locate their find. The site remained "lost" for the next five years until re-discovered by Peter "Laughing Ole" Monahan, a veteran prospector. The 1904 stampede to the newly-named Valdez Creek yielded disappointing results, but Monahan and James S. Smith persisted. Two years later they arrived in Valdez with 118 ounces of gold that they had panned from a bench claim in just 52 hours.

Like the Kantishna, inaccessibility hampered development of the find. The nearest jumping off point was Paxson Roadhouse on the Richardson Trail about 70 miles to the east. Kennedy's mission in 1908 was to build a new access trail to the diggings. He expected the task to take twelve days. Three weeks later he was still hacking out a trail through the slab-sided Nenana canyon, almost 80 miles from his destination. After almost two months of back-breaking work, Kennedy finally returned to Fairbanks, the return journey from Valdez Creek taking less than ten days. In the end Kennedy's independently-financed trail "proved too long and difficult a route to be profitable." In 1914, Kennedy's over-grown trail was used during another strike, but at no profit to him. "The Broad Pass Mining District [in 1914] is the subject of much excitement . . . gold-bearing ore is now reported in enormous quantities, but unfortunately, nothing definitely is known." Prospectors and mining engineers flocked to the area in 1914 and 1915, but the stampede was short-lived. It was during

*Frank G. Manley's real name was Hilliard Bascom Knowles, a fugitive from California. He made a fortune in Alaska and died wealthy.

the waning days of the stampede that Morino opened his first roadhouse on Riley Creek.[10]

Kennedy later said that part of his interest in building a trail up the Nenana River was to find prime hunting grounds in order to guide hunters. Proposals to build a bridge over the Nenana near Riley Creek "which will give hunting parties access to a paradise of big game," captivated Kennedy.[11]

In 1910, Kennedy sold his freight business to the powerhouse Northern Commercial Co. He subsequently mined on Cleary Creek and freighted from Fairbanks to various new strikes. Like many other era teamsters, Kennedy contracted to haul supplies for the AEC, and in early 1921 freighted between Healy and Broad Pass.

Competition from the railroad, and a general decline in mining, put Kennedy out of the freight business. McKinley Park's roadless wilderness seemed an ideal business opportunity. Kennedy found himself vying with Morino, Abbey, and others, for a park concession. After meeting with Superintendent Karstens, Kennedy headed Outside to confer with Assistant Director Cammerer. Kennedy's acknowledged expertise with horses and wilderness travel, coupled with his pioneer experiences that tourists would have loved, made him an apparent ideal candidate for the transportation concession.

As spring wore on, McKinley Station residents eagerly anticipated two important upcoming events. In the first week of July, a group sponsored by the *Brooklyn Daily Eagle* newspaper would arrive to formally dedicate the park. A week later, President Warren G. Harding would stop en route to Nenana where he would drive the Alaska Railroad's "Golden Spike" signaling its completion.

Early planning for the two visits vexed Karstens. When an AEC official called Karstens in January 1923, and asked what visitor facilities the park offered, Karstens tersely replied "None!" After a lengthy conversation, the AEC promised to erect mess and sleeping tents to accommodate the numerous travelers expected to stop at the park that coming summer. In April, Karstens learned that the road commission would expend a small amount of money to improve the trail to Savage River "to get the road in as good shape as possible before the arrival of the Brooklyn Eagle party in July." Neither funding nor tents materialized, leaving Karstens scrambling.[12]

Severe spring flooding washed out the Riley Creek wagon bridge and thoroughly trashed park headquarters. The pioneer road up Hines Creek was impassable and once the flood waters subsided, it was in dire need of reconstruction. Repairing the road damage would take days, if not weeks. Intense effort would be needed to get everything cleaned-up and ready for the dedication. Karstens likely could clean up his own facilities in time but he could do nothing about Morino's homestead and development which dominated the depot area. The year-old hotel was already cluttered and dirty, and the surroundings dotted with ramshackle outbuildings and construction detritus, hardly comparable to the grand hotels that welcomed visitors to other national parks. The hotel itself, unfinished and crude, was a dump.

Karstens also needed help with the ceremonies themselves. He wanted to hold the dedication ceremony inside the park at the headwaters of the Savage River which would "afford an excellent view of sheep and caribou, as well as rugged scenery," he explained. The "success of transporting these parties far enough into the park to observe the game and scenic beauties [will depend on Dan Kennedy]," he added.[13]

Back in May 1923, Kennedy had been awarded a five-year transportation permit and the right to establish three camps as far as 50 miles into the park. The permit also stipulated that he supply a minimum of 30 horses and be open for business by July 4. After satisfactorily negotiating the terms of his permit, Kennedy roamed around Washington State buying saddle and pack horses, which he then brought north by steamship.[14]

En route to the park, Kennedy met George Flood in Anchorage, a farm boy and expert horseman new to Alaska, and hired him as a packer and guide. While he stayed in town to conduct business, Kennedy sent Flood and the horses north on a freight train. "All of the inhabitants, which numbered perhaps around 10 or 15 at that time, were at McKinley depot to meet the train," Flood recalled, "so I had much assistance in unloading the horses." Instead of the 30 horses stipulated by contract, however, Kennedy shipped just 16 to McKinley Station. Already he was off to a rocky start.

In early June, Colonel James Steese invited Karstens to join the Presidential party on the trip to Fairbanks. Both men saw it as an opportunity to educate the many influential participants about the park. With less than a month to go, Karstens hired two laborers to help clean up around headquarters and begin repairs on the pioneer road. Even with this temporary hire, the park's staff were wholly inadequate for the immediate task at hand. Ranger Bragaw*

*After he resigned, the college-educated Bragaw returned to Anchorage where he, and others, founded Alaska Guides, a company that brought hunters to Alaska. He opened a photographic studio in 1926, and became a prominent photographer who subsequently made many trips to the park to photograph scenery and wildlife. Karstens always greeted him warmly.

HENRY P. KARSTENS COLLECTION, #1414, KARSTENS LIBRARY

*In 1923, Harry Karstens, facing the group, welcomes the* Brooklyn Daily Eagle *newspaper entourage to Mt. McKinley National Park. At the behest of the Secretary of the Interior, the group formally dedicated the park to the American people.*

had quit in April, citing his poor annual salary, $2,000, with "no prospect for better salary in the next year." (By comparison, Karstens only made $3,600 per annum.) As his replacement Karstens hired August B. "Gus" Buhmann.[15]

To Karstens' surprise and relief, Morino hired extra help to prepare his grounds for the up-coming events. Morino planted saplings in front of the hotel and did a through cleanup of the hotel and its surroundings.

On June 7, Karstens had the opportunity to practice his speaking skills when a 65-person Congressional delegation, on a railroad inspection tour, stopped at the station for a brief respite. The Superintendent regaled them with the story of his ascent of Mount McKinley and described the park's needs.[16]

The Congressional visit was a good tune-up for the big events to come. Each year, the *Brooklyn Eagle* supported jaunts to various western parks, dedicating new ones "for the rightful owners, the people of the United States." This newspaper, first published in 1841, was the most popular afternoon paper in the United States. The 70-person entourage included wealthy New Yorkers, socialites, and celebrities like famed author Rex Beach, each person paying a share of the expenses. Before accepting the Interior Secretary's invitation to dedicate Mt. McKinley National Park, the newspaper's publisher required assurances that the trip could be "made in complete comfort and within a reasonable period of time." Both Karstens and NPS Director Mather worked overtime to fulfill the bargain, anticipating a windfall of favorable publicity.[17]

On June 14, Director Mather wired Karstens that it was Kennedy's responsibility, as a demonstration of his abilities as concessionaire, to provide food, transportation, and lodging for the *Brooklyn Eagle* party. Karstens immediately caught the train to Anchorage to inform Kennedy. The news did not sit well with the new concessionaire, who was severely cash-strapped. Karstens then conferred with Colonel Steese and Major Gotwals who were handling travel logistics for both the dedication and the presidential visit.

During a second meeting, Kennedy informed Karstens that he would not feed the *Brooklyn Eagle* party because he had no cooking facilities or money to do so. He would only supply the transportation and sleeping tents, nothing more. A heated exchange followed but Karstens had little recourse. Short of options and time, Karstens shouldered the burden and spent well over a week in Anchorage borrowing dishes, utensils, and buying food and cooking equipment from the AEC. He hired Anton J. and Florence Wendler, and their supper club staff, to prepare the gala barbecue.[18]

Once Kennedy finally arrived at the station, he started work on a tourist camp on the east bank of the Savage River. For the season he employed six men, including Flood, Abbey, and Harry Lucke. All worked overtime to get the camp ready for the dedication.[19]

Olaus and Adolph Murie had been encamped at the headwaters of the Savage River since early spring, attempting to capture caribou. With time running out, Karstens asked Murie to supply wild meat for the upcoming barbecue. In response, Olaus and his brother Adolph, assisted by Frank Glaser, shot five sheep on Jenny Creek and Savage River, and transported the butchered carcasses to the Savage camp.

On July 7, the day before the dedication, and despite intense effort by all concerned, the camp was still not ready for the two-day event. At 7:30 that night, ranger Gus Buhmann hiked in from headquarters to relay the group's latest demands. In total frustration, Karstens threw up his hands and made the decision to relocate the ceremony back to the station. Karstens and Buhmann feverishly set to work tearing down the camp for the big move. After a hectic all-nighter everything was finally in place for the train's arrival. When the train pulled in at 9 p.m., a blazing bonfire welcomed the *Eaglets*, as they called themselves, to the hastily-erected tent camp where they'd spend the night. The next morning, after the superintendent's welcoming address, William V. Hester, Jr., son of the newspaper's president, gave a speech dedicating the park to the American people. A cheer went up and the party was on. Hikes, horseback riding, and fishing trips followed the obligatory speeches. The Murie brothers hiked in from their Savage River camp just in time to enjoy the festivities and sheep barbecue.[20]

Anticipating high demand for wagon rides, Kennedy and Flood had prepared two wagons and teams. The youthful *Eaglets,* however, preferred horseback riding so Kennedy hurriedly saddled several horses, some of which hadn't been broken to ride. Flood quickly "green broke" some of them and handed them off to the more experienced riders in the group. "The Brooklyn Eagle party was only at the station for about a day but we took them up as far as the divide between Maurice Creek and Savage River, a distance of six miles, and returned them to the station," he said.[21] As they waved good bye to the train carrying the *Eaglets,* everyone involved in the ceremony breathed a sigh of relief. Superintendent Karstens, however, had little time to relax and savor the moment. The President of the United States was already on his way to Alaska and he would arrive in one week.[22]

En route to Alaska, President Harding, at Director Mather's instigation, first visited Yellowstone and Zion National Parks where he reveled in their wonders. Nothing, however, prepared him for the majesty of Mt McKinley. The President caught his first glimpse of the mountain from the train. When the train paused in Broad Pass for him to view the new reindeer herd, the gleaming summit prompted Harding's oratory. "Above its towering head there is never-ending sunshine in summer," he intoned, "and in the long winter its unchanging garb of white reflects a sheen of glory no darkness can wholly dim."[23]

On July 15, the presidential train pulled into McKinley Station at 10:30 a.m., and was greeted by the entire community augmented by miners and trappers who had hiked in from outlying camps. The crowd assembled in front of Morino's bunting-bespangled hotel cheered when the President emerged waving from the train. After a formal introduction, Superintendent Karstens welcomed the President and Mrs. Harding to the community. The presidential entourage included the new Secretary of the Interior, Hubert Work; Agriculture Secretary Henry Wallace; Commerce Secretary Herbert Hoover; Secretary of War John W. Weeks; Speaker of the House Frederick Gillette; Governor Scott C. Bone; prominent military officers; and a horde of reporters. Never before or since has such a high-ranking contingent of the U.S. Government visited Alaska in one group. Notably absent was Colonel

COURTESY OF DENISE ABBEY

*Denise Abbey, then 13, took this photograph of President Warren G. Harding when his train stopped at McKinley Station, en route to Nenana in 1923 to drive the Golden Spike signaling official completion of the Alaska Railroad.*

COURTESY OF DENISE ABBEY

*First Lady Florence Harding posed for photographs with a sled dog in front of the Mt. McKinley Park Hotel. The Presidential party mingled with locals and enjoyed a Dall sheep barbecue hosted by Harry Karstens.*

Frederick Mears, who had been unceremoniously relieved of duty as AEC Chairman, and replaced by Colonel Steese.

The entire community, dressed in their finest, lined up beside the tracks to shake the President's hand. Just before the train arrived, Harry Lucke rushed to his cabin and donned an old, faded shirt, pants, beat-up sweater, and slouch hat cut full of notches. Lucke always carried a belt knife, but for this occasion he chose a wider belt and hung a big butcher knife in a sheath in the middle of his back. By all appearances he looked to have just arrived from some hazardous trek or a tussle with a grizzly.[24]

At 6'2", Lucke towered over the President. When his turn came to shake the President's hand, Lucke pulled him close, loudly proclaiming his delight in their meeting. A nearby Secret Service agent reached over and yanked Lucke's big butcher knife out of the scabbard, then stood there looking at it dumbfounded, which provoked general laughter. When Lucke turned, the agent returned the knife, supposedly saying, "That's a nice knife you have, Mr. Lucke!"[25]

At least one person refused to shake the President's hand. Young Bud Abbey came running up from the tracks and on the rock steps cut into the bank by Morino's hotel, crashed into a stranger in a gray suit. The stranger smiled and offered his hand but the boy refused to shake, much to his father's chagrin. Harding thought the pint-sized snub hilarious. "Why should I shake hands," Bud Abbey recalled thinking, "he didn't buy me anything."[26]

For twenty minutes, the President and Mrs. Harding wandered about visiting with locals and sampling the local produce and Dall sheep steaks again grilled by the Wendlers. About 40 locals partook of the barbecue and mingled with the presidential party. Florence Harding greeted everyone and was remembered as a "nice friendly lady." She asked Flood if she could pet the sled dogs that were tied near the hotel. She seemed genuinely intrigued by them and asked numerous questions: "How fast can they run? How much weight can they pull? What do you feed them?" Mrs. Harding wanted her picture taken with one of the dogs and while a gaggle of newsmen fired away, Denise Abbey took a frame-filler.[27]

Denise Abbey, 13, desperately wanted the President's picture. Clutching her Kodak Brownie she struggled through the adults and finally settled for a picture of the President partially obscured by the crowd around him. Harding noticed her and waved everyone away and smiled while Denise took the coveted picture. A few minutes later Denise's mother introduced her to Herbert Hoover who held out his hand and said, "I don't believe I have had the pleasure to meet this young lady." Hoover was elected President six years later.[28]

At promptly 10:50 a.m. the President's train pulled out for Nenana, with Karstens on board. Just after it left, the Murie brothers, who again had provided the Dall sheep for the day's barbecue, hiked into the station from their caribou camp, only to find the schedule changed and the President—and the entire barbecue—long gone. Later they wryly nicknamed one of their captive caribou *Harding*.[29]

On the train to Nenana, Karstens had the opportunity to speak with the Secretary of the Interior about the "Morino problem." (Morino's homestead prevented development of a more appropriate park headquarters and entrance station.) Secretary Work promised to have George Parks, of the General Land Office, take care of it. Work's predecessor, Albert B. Fall had resigned over the Teapot Dome Scandal. Before his resignation, Fall had been conniving to gain control of Alaska's Tongass Forest Reserve and the National Petroleum Reserve. On this trip, Alaskans had many questions for the new Interior chief. In that light, Secretary Work must have viewed Karstens' provincial request with a degree of disinterest because apparently he took no action.[30]

Just north of the new Tanana River Bridge, Harding delivered a resounding speech and drove the Golden Spike. Afterwards Karstens continued on to Fairbanks and returned to McKinley Station two days later.

In the wake of Harding's visit, Karstens had time to take stock and catch up with neglected office work and chores. On the very day he returned to headquarters, Ranger Buhmann handed in his resignation, effective immediately, in order to go to work for Kennedy. In August, with advice from Washington, Karstens hired Major Edward R. McFarland as his new ranger. McFarland possessed impressive credentials. He came to Alaska in 1910 by way of Skagway and Dawson. From 1912 to 1915, he worked on various communications projects before accepting the position of chief of the AEC telephone and telegraph department. At the outbreak of World War I, McFarland, a veteran of the Spanish-American War, shipped out with the Signal Corps to France where as a brevet Lieutenant Colonel, he oversaw railroad communications for the American Expeditionary Force.

"After his distinguished service overseas, his host of Alaskan friends welcomed him home with great cordiality . . . While in France there was no place too hot for him to venture and while in Alaska there has been no trail too cold for him to travel."[31]

Prior to his ranger appointment, McFarland, and his wife, the widow of John Vachon of Tolovana, and her two daughters, Rita and Mary Vachon, were living in Santa Cruz, California. Apparently two years of cultivating a garden and pulling weeds convinced McFarland "to stick with Alaska, where it is worth while living."[32]

The Park Service approved McFarland's hiring, precisely because of his military and managerial skills, thought an invaluable asset to Karstens. The pairing would prove volatile.

In early August, Superintendent Karstens reviewed Kennedy's operation and found it lacking. In the spring the two men had tussled over the 4% concession fee, which was eventually waived for the first year. Karstens also could not get Kennedy to provide a satisfactory fee and camp schedule. When Kennedy did set his prices, Karstens felt they were too high. Kennedy also provided fewer horses than stipulated and was always borrowing equipment."I had known Kennedy for 20 years," Karstens said,"and knew he was an excellent man with stock, but that handling an undertaking of this kind was different." [33]

Immediately after the departure of the *Eaglets*, Kennedy confronted Karstens. He declared that Karstens obviously did not want him in the park and that he was trying to run him out. Karstens denied his claim and retorted that,"[You] are simply short of funds and a poor manager."[34]

Kennedy also had failed to establish all the camps as stipulated in his permit. He claimed the use of Jack Donnelly's prospecting camp on the Toklat River as one of his own. Karstens described Donnelly's' camp as"a 12'x14' tent in awful shape, a poor excuse of a place [even] for a prospector to stay." Karstens felt the main guest camp at Savage River was little better."I have observed that you have only one big tent established at Savage River," Karstens wrote Kennedy in mid-July,"[neither] do you have any facilities for serving meals to tourists, or beds of any kind." Karstens also noted that Kennedy only had 16 horses, instead of the required 30, and had not established a camp of any kind at Igloo Creek as required by his contract.[35]

Kennedy characterized Karstens comments as"unreliable and misleading." He felt he had sufficient equipment and personnel to handle a large group of tourists in the unlikely event that any showed up. He submitted a written and detailed description of his Savage River camp which "consisted of two 10'x12' tents, one 8'x10' tent and one 20'x60' tent all to be used for sleeping tents, and one 16'x20' tent which was being used as a cook tent . . . There has been a grocery supply at this camp for the last two weeks valued at about $300 . . . [but] only one tourist has visited this camp." He also claimed to have established camps at Igloo and"Toclap" and, in addition, had purchased Jack Donnelly's shuttered restaurant on Riley Creek, the source of the tents and his kitchen equipment.Gus Buhmann waded into the fray and claimed that Savage Camp had "all the comforts of an up-to-date hotel!" At least two of the tents Kennedy claimed actually belonged to Abbey, who used them for his family while employed there.[36]

By early September, with tourist season long over, Kennedy began removing his gear from the park. Only 34 people made the trip to the Savage River camp and, according to Flood, the only overnight tourists that first summer had been a Dr. and Mrs. Sudler from Lawrence, Kansas. Flood guided them to Savage River and remembered his guests fondly. "They were very gracious people," he said, "and wrote me a very kind letter after their return to Kansas."[37]

At season's end, to make ends meet, Kennedy contracted to transport mining supplies to Copper Mountain and the Kantishna. Joe Quigley hired him to freight twenty ton of supplies into Copper Mountain and back-haul 30 tons of ore per trip, the work to be done in winter using three- and four-horse teams. Each round trip from McKinley Station to the mine took six days. Kennedy's men also packed in powder for the Kennecott Copper Company (the "Guggs") then running a tunnel on Copper Mountain. On one trip, Flood and Kennedy were joined by prospector John Depp. At one point young Depp, who Flood described as "rather awkward," carelessly led a horse between the stacks of powder and knocked over the bags. "It happened to be the 90% powder," Flood recalled, "the powder didn't explode but Mr. Kennedy did!"[38]

After leaving the park Kennedy guided hunters in Broad Pass. He may not have known it at the time, but two individuals, Ruth Reit, who was involved in the Cantwell reindeer project, and Gus Buhmann, were independently vying for his concession permit.

From the very beginning Kennedy's operation was hampered by poor funding and planning but Buhmann self-servingly declared Kennedy's transportation company's first season "a success." At season's end, he told reporters that Kennedy had spent a considerable amount of money, including almost all of his profits in "outfitting of the three main camps and the [purchase of a] large amount of equipment, including thirty head of horses . . . Mr. Kennedy feels the result has perfectly justified the expenditure of a considerable sum for further improvements." Although Kennedy had done no advertising that first year, Buhmann said, plans were made for "an extensive national campaign."[39]

By early autumn, with the summer tourist season over, Karstens turned his attention to the immediate problems at hand. A lawless, rambunctious faction embroiled the community in endless jousts with federal marshals. As a federal officer, Karstens was expected to do his part in enforcing liquor laws, no matter how minor the transgressions. More importantly to Karstens however, was developing a respectable community and controlling the illegal hunting that was taking place almost under his very nose.

JAMES GORDON STEESE COLLECTION, #3043377685, DICKINSON COLLEGE ARCHIVES

*Near Nenana, on July 15, 1923, a hatless President Warren G. Harding prepares to take another swing at driving the Golden Spike signaling completion of the railroad. Harry Karstens, in campaign hat and open jacket, is in the middle of the photo. Next to him in gray suit and sport cap is Herbert Hoover.*

# 11

# People of the Station

Pandemonium in the dog yard at three a.m. roused Harry Karstens from a deep sleep. Dressed only in a nightshirt he grabbed his rifle and rushed outside, thinking a grizzly was in among the dogs. In the cool June twilight he saw nothing amiss, just the dogs barking and circling wildly on their chains. He shouted them into silence and lingered to watch as they slowly settled down. Sudden shouts and drunken laughter echoed from downstream near the Riley Creek trestle. Karstens, muttering under his breath and batting away squadrons of whirring mosquitoes, trudged back into his cabin.

Less than half an hour later, the dog yard erupted a second time. Karstens again jumped out of bed and rushed outside but found nothing amiss. With heavy steps he went inside once again, fully awake. Karstens put the coffeepot on, reassured Louise that all was well and, with further sleep impossible, dressed quietly for the day ahead. It was just after four a.m., only five hours since he'd gone to bed the night before. "Oh well," he shrugged, "an early start to the day." What he didn't know was that someone had disturbed the dogs, and his sleep as a practical joke.

The dogs were normally very quiet. "Except at feeding time," Eugene "Skippy" Karstens said, "the only other time we heard from the dog area was during those nights with a full moon. Then about three in the morning one lonely howl would start—then another dog would come in and another and another until all 60 would be in full howl for about an hour and then it would stop." The Karstens never knew the whole story.[1]

The station began to expand in 1923, a trend that continued for about ten years. Seasonal roadwork, mining, trapping, and tourism brought new people to the area. By mid-decade, as many as 60 people over-wintered with dozens more in summer residence. Some worked only one season before moving on; others lingered. Despite the transient nature of the populace, Superintendent Karstens tried to foster a sense of community. Each year, on the summer solstice, Harry and Louise hosted a party for all local residents and anyone else who happened by. "It was a big event [attended by] friends of the family, dignitaries from along the railroad, Nenana, and Fairbanks," Eugene Karstens recalled. "Everybody ate, drank and danced until the wee hours of the morning in complete light. Then there would be a big breakfast and people would then head home."[2]

Karstens tried to be a good neighbor. He lent out his crosscut wood saw that he built and powered with an old Ford engine acquired in 1921. "Because there are no privately owned horses in the community I am occasionally granting the use of the park teams for various little services such as hauling logs, fuel, etc." he said.[3]

The "McKinley Colony" saw many holiday celebrations and parties. The McKinley Station Bachelors Club hosted dances at Morino's hotel. The school put on a Christmas social, occasional musicals, and plays. Each year Maurice Morino decked his hotel in piles of spruce boughs and decorated a huge tree. A local man dressed up as Santa. "The spirit of Christmas is in the air and all have been remembered," Karstens reported, "the stock also receiving special attention."[4]

In this growing, rough-hewn community, Harry and Louise worked to make a real home for their five-year-old son, Eugene. They gave him his first dog, Kenai, a wolf-malamute hybrid. The boy and his dog explored their small world and got into the usual scrapes common to such friends. When he was older, Eugene strapped on skis, harnessed his dog, and skijored "like the wind."[5]

Boy and dog grew up together wrestling on the floor. One winter night Eugene snuck up on the sleeping dog and grabbed it around the neck. "He awoke with a start and snapped at me, his eye tooth went in just below [my] left eye, just missing the eye and the tear bag," he recalled. "I guess he realized what had happened and laid perfectly still. Father speaking quietly told me to not move, came and slowly lifted the dog's head away and tooth out of the wound and separated us." Karstens sliced a sliver off his shaving stick and inserted it into the puncture of his son's cheek. "The pain was terrible but Father said it was the only way to cauterize the flesh to prevent infection." After the accident Kenai appeared "crushed."[6]

Eugene Karstens helped his father, acting as an unofficial junior ranger. He helped exercise the dogs and clean up after them. Over a wood fire in the cookhouse, he cooked a mixture of cornmeal and smoked salmon, using a canoe paddle to stir the brew, and then helped feed about 30 dogs, usually the puppies.

HENRY P. KARSTENS COLLECTION, #1426, KARSTENS LIBRARY

*A 1923 summer gathering in front of the Superintendent's Office on Riley Creek. Adults (l-r) "Ray," Beatrice Abbey, Ann Fairburn, Louise Karstens, Helen MacDonald, Mary Vachon (Edward McFarland's step-daughter,) Harry Karstens, Denise Abbey, Major Edward McFarland, Mrs. McFarland, and Mrs. McDonald. In the front row, (l-r) Eugene Karstens and Bud Abbey.*

Harry rewarded his son's work with the gift of a half-size birch sled and a three-dog team, all young dogs undergoing their initial harness training. Young Eugene would mush his team out of the dog yard and be gone from headquarters for several hours. Not surprisingly the puppy team would bolt after wildlife, especially snowshoe hares. "It was a good thing I had a brake on the sled or else there would have been no controlling them," he said.[7]

Karstens sometimes bundled his young son in blankets and furs and took him on patrol, often for several days at a time. "I could look out and see the fifteen dogs over the top of the canvas cover and then look back and see my Father standing on the runners and hear him talking to the dogs. [He] never let the dogs go too long without a word or two and he had a commanding voice. I saw cases where the discipline in the team was maintained by the leader without even a word from my Father. The leader would come around and administer a good nip in the hindquarters of the offending dog."[8]

After a fresh snowfall, or on melting trails in early spring, Karstens used a loose leader. "Normally the leader would be tied to the team, but when a bad part of the trail was upon us," Eugene explained, "Father would unhitch the lead dog, take his

ALASKA RAILROAD COLLECTION, ANCHORAGE MUSEUM AT RASMUSON CENTER

*Telegrapher and depot man Rufus Nichols sits with his family on the steps in front of one of the boxcars that served as McKinley Station's first railroad depot.*

harness off, and then before turning him loose they would have a short conversation and Father would actually tell him what he wanted done."[9]

Running up to 300 yards ahead of the team the loose leader searched for the best routes around open water or thin ice, and even locate a trail hidden under two feet of fresh snow. "But the uncanny thing was how he would ignore all wild animals except those that could cause us harm, like grizzly bears in the early spring or late fall, and also wolves," Eugene said.[10]

Multi-day trips, in -40°F weather, required planning and exercise to stay warm. Eugene, at his father's instruction, sometimes ran alongside the sled "to keep the circulation going," before crawling back into the blankets for a nap.

On patrol, Karstens cooked for his son, who remembered that, "Father was the best cook on the trail . . . he would make his slumgullion stew with either beef or caribou . . . and the biggest and fattest sourdough pancakes for breakfast, along with heaps of bacon and coffee for him and diluted Eagle Brand [milk] for me. Then he would make our [trail] lunch of sourdough bread and cheese and jelly and meat."[11]

Thanks to his father, even part of the most ordinary chores could be exhilarating for Eugene. "The most fun was going with Father in the cutter [a small light sleigh] and one horse, through the deep snow to get the mail and telegrams and supplies at the roadhouse, because this meant I could have some candy out of the big glass bowl," he said. "Father and I, and sometimes Mother, would sit down at the counter of the small restaurant and have something to eat. In later years Father would lament how we barely survived Morino's greasy cooking."[12]

Karstens regularly warned Eugene to stay away from Riley Creek. Thin ice was always a danger, and in summer, sudden floods washed out the wagon bridge. A two-day downpour during spring runoff one year caused considerable flooding. "The creek began to rise and rise until big boulders, some the size of a car, were tumbling down the creek in front of the cabin," Eugene remembered. "The awful roar of the rushing river combined with the noise of the boulders slamming together was very frightening." A huge boulder hit one of the concrete bridge piers and cracked it. Karstens warned the railroad immediately. The next day engineers warily allowed a train to slowly cross the bridge while they kept an eye on the crack. The next day they dispatched a work crew to repair the pier with reinforced concrete.[13]

Despite the somewhat strained relations between Harry Karstens and Woodbury Abbey, their wives and children shared many adventures in this pioneer community. Beatrice Abbey thrived despite the lack of modern amenities. She heated and cooked on a woodstove, and hauled water from McKinley

HENRY P. KARSTENS COLLECTION, #0297, KARSTENS LIBRARY

*Harry Karstens and his family, and friend Helen Livingston, wait at the depot for arrival of the train.*

Pup Creek, the feeder stream of Horseshoe Lake. To discourage mosquitoes she burned Buhach, a pungent aromatic. She ordered her children's clothes from Sears and Roebuck's and Montgomery Ward's catalogs, and hers from more fashionable New York stores. All of their groceries, supplies and mail came by train. Some Fairbanks friends once surprised the Abbeys with a five-gallon can of fresh milk, which they and friends drank all in one day. Denise "Dolly" Abbey savored the treat. "The powdered milk of that era was awful," she recalled, "and like drinking powdered chalk." When the leaves began to turn colors, Beatrice and Louise Karstens joined forces to pick and can berries for winter use. Because Wood Abbey did not hunt, Beatrice ordered beef and chicken from Fairbanks, augmented by wild meat procured from local hunters. During the winter there was no problem keeping food cool or frozen, but perishables often suffered. Summer provisions were stored in a log ice house insulated with sawdust, the blocks of ice cut from Horseshoe Lake.[14]

The Karstens' supplies and groceries also came by train, but Karstens was a subsistence hunter. "[Hunting] was done in the fall to supplement the domestic meat that Father [purchased.] Father would hitch up the team, get an early start and be home late the next day with a caribou, all dressed and ready to be butchered," Eugene said.[15]

The most mundane tasks sometimes required considerable effort. To get a haircut, Wood Abbey had to hike the tracks to Healy. Beatrice preferred her husband not to be alone. He suffered from poor vision and severe headaches, which he believed were caused by Vitamin A deficiency. Beatrice, an avid and fast walker, usually accompanied her husband on his "strolls."

Neither Abbey drank liquor. This well-known trait became the basis for a huge practical joke played on Deputy James Hagan. The Abbeys owned a white mule, Jack, a faithful servant during the park boundary survey. Locals soundly disliked Hagan because of his enforcement of the liquor laws. When Abbey loaded Jack onto a boxcar for stabling in Fairbanks, someone telegraphed Hagan and told him that "Wood Abbey is shipping 1600-pounds of white mule to Fairbanks." The informant told the absolute truth, but knew that bootleg whiskey was also called "white mule." The miscreants howled long and hard when they heard that Hagan and an armed posse had met the train in Fairbanks, "faithful Jack surrendering without a fight."[16]

Each day, Eugene trudged up the steep hill leading out of Riley Creek and walked by the hotel on his way to school. Usually one parent or Kenai accompanied him to school. Occasionally he went alone. "Sometimes Father would hitch up the horses and take me in the cutter," he recalled. "If I walked alone I always had to check in with Mister Morino at the roadhouse before going on . . . and also on the way back. When it got too cold, there was no school."[17]

Mrs. Louise Ann Fairburn, a retired teacher from Fairbanks, with twenty years of teaching experience in Alaska, was hired as McKinley's first teacher. She was a disciplinarian who emphasized the "three r's" — reading, writing, and arithmetic but did not neglect the fine arts. Fairburn initially taught grades one, five, and six, and added curriculum for other grades as needed. Adult classes met three times a week. She read the children works by Robert Louis Stevenson and other luminaries. Each month, she focused on a specific poet and poetry, which the children loved. The school, as often happens in rural communities, quickly became a social center.

The entire community filled the school for poetry readings, songs, and skits. Hard-bitten oldtimers, tears freely running down their cheeks, would watch enactments of such classics as *The Courtship of Miles Standish*, and *The Lion and the Mouse*, with Bud Abbey as the Lion. One such evening drew 42 people, who afterward feasted on coffee, sandwiches, and ice-cream served by the students and the McKinley chapter of the Camp Fire Girls. The show was described as a "brave, almost pathetic, tho [sic] successful, efforts to do the things those other schools in palatial buildings do . . ."[18]

COURTESY OF DENISE ABBEY

*The McKinley Park school was built of lumber and logs salvaged from the abandoned AEC camp. Teacher Louise Ann Fairburn taught elementary students in the day and held adult classes at night. School programs, musicals, and plays, attracted nearly the entire community.*

COURTESY OF EARL PLUMB

*Les Plumb built this cabin on the slope above McKinley Pup Creek, a home typical of McKinley Station.*

Denise Abbey, at her teacher's suggestion, studied Sir Walter Scott's *Lady in the Lake*, a long narrative poem about a lovely girl courted by the Scottish king, but who chooses another. She read all six of James Oliver Curwood's books that her father gave her for Christmas. Curwood, then more popular in North America than Jack London, spent the summer of 1923 in Fairbanks writing the gold rush-epic *The Alaskan*. His visit to McKinley Station that summer drew a sizable crowd. Al Wigand, who occupied the lean-to attached to the Abbeys old boxcar, and Doc Kirby, who wanted to write like Curwood, borrowed and read all of Denise's books. Passionate book discussions enlivened many winter nights in the Abbey cabin.[19]

During her tenure Mrs. Fairburn enchanted the community. "Her exceptional ability as a teacher and her delightful personality has endeared her to this rapidly growing community [which] has found her equal to the task of turning out a brand of Alaskan youth of which we may be very proud," Karstens wrote Charles Sheldon. Late in her life, Denise recalled that she was given a "remarkably good education for being out in the wilderness."[20]

After school the children played outside, usually along the railroad tracks, but were forbidden to go downstream of the trestle to the area called "the Hole."

One of their friends, "Little Jimmy," who lived there but rarely attended school, told lurid tales of moonshiners, gamblers and painted ladies. Francis Nichols and Denise Abbey were the same age and became best friends. In winter, they sledded down the tote road that zigzagged up out of Riley Creek. Bud Abbey and Skippy Karstens often joined them. In summer, the children played on the gravel slope above Horseshoe Lake. They explored all the local rock formations and gave them names. The yellow rock outcropping just upstream from, and between, the confluence of Riley and Maurice Creeks, was called the "Castle of the Owl." Mount Healy was known as "K-2." Everyone called the little rise at the northeast end of the trestle "Cat Mountain," because of the lynx that seemed always to wander there.

Another favorite pastime was berry picking, a hot spot being the railroad maintenance station at Lagoon, Mile 344. On such outings Beatrice and Dolly visited the camp cook, "Happy Jack" Winzenreid. When Happy Jack left to work on the park road, he was replaced by Ragna Haugen, a Norwegian who had followed the gold rushes along the Yukon and Tanana Rivers, working her way from strike to strike as a cook. She lived in the back of the cook shack and never complained, no matter how bleak the conditions. Once a year, around Independence Day, she spent a few days in Fairbanks, otherwise she stayed in the Bush. One of her typical meals for the section gang consisted of beans, bread, and coffee, with canned peaches, or raspberries fresh from the nearby patch, for dessert.[21]

Throughout the 1920s very few families settled in at McKinley Station, which was mostly a bachelor community. Some miners over-wintered there and others came looking for work. One of them, Karstens' old friend "Mace" Farrar, shod the park horses and did odd jobs until start of the summer mining season. One year, he guided two women on a sightseeing trip to Cantwell. "The ladies are looking for thrills," read a news account, "and it is believed at Cantwell they will find them." At the station, and at Cantwell, they met miners, railroad men, and rascals—a fairly typical Alaska community.[22]

During railroad construction, mushers from all over the territory gathered to work on this gargantuan project, hauling tons of freight and passengers up and down the line. One of them, Frank Tondro, the "Malamute Kid," operated a roadhouse south of Broad Pass near the confluence of Coal Creek and the middle fork of the Chulitna. This 5'3", 100-pound, Klondike veteran sometimes drove teams of up to 30 dogs. Jack London met Tondro in the Yukon and later fictionalized his story. Tondro could often be found late at night playing cards with Maurice Morino. Afterwards, with little or no sleep, Tondro would mush off down the trail on a heavily-loaded sled. After completion of the Broad Pass segment of the railroad Tondro closed his roadhouse and hauled freight from the new Kobe station to the Kantishna.

"Geepole" Larson was another of those who freighted for the railroad. He drove a team of quarter-breed wolves, described as one of the "craziest dog teams . . . ever seen." All the local dog mushers avoided Larson's team. "The moment they were . . . turned loose, that team lit out in whatever direction they happen to be headed and nothing would stop them," Frank Glaser recalled. "Invariably when leaving Morino's, Geepole's dogs ran under that [garden] fence and pulled it down with the sled. Morino would patiently rebuild it, but the next time Geepole was there, his dogs would tear the fence down again. Morino was angry at Geepole all the time."[23]

One spring, Larson somehow talked Morino, who apparently hated sled dogs, into caring for his team while he worked at a Kantishna mine. Morino tied the dogs in front of the hotel but they were noisy and disturbed Morino and his guests.

Harry Lucke and Glaser loved to pester Morino. The men shared a cabin below the hotel, an ideal spot for their antics. Late one summer night, Glaser stepped outside the cabin and howled like a wolf. Larson's nine dogs answered. Morino in his underwear rushed angrily out of the hotel and silenced the dogs. Just as things quieted down, Lucke cut loose with another howl, provoking similar results. The men, "relaxed and happy from the effects of [Lucke's] fig wine," fell asleep quite pleased with themselves. During spring breakup the two would sleep all day and stay up all night which allowed plenty of time to harass Morino and Karstens, their favorite targets. "Lucke was full of the devil," Glaser said, "and I never knew what he was likely to pull."[24]

Morino eventually outwitted them but at the expense of the dogs. He built a four-foot-high board fence and threaded the dogs' chains through holes he drilled in it. He then tied a rope to each chain and ran the ropes to his door. If a dog so much as barked once, Morino pulled a rope, yanking the dog against the fence. As often as not, Morino punished the wrong dog. If the barking persisted, Morino started pulling ropes until "he succeeded in curing those dogs of making noise," Glaser explained. "In the end I could howl all I wanted, but those nine dogs would simply sit there quietly eyeing the roadhouse door and Morino's ropes."[25]

Lucke, a seasoned market hunter, lived at McKinley Station for nearly a decade, providing meat first to the railroad, then to Morino's hotel. Lucke had lived in Interior for over 20 years but there was still an air of mystery about his past. One rumor claimed that he was nobility, a "Count Von Lukkee." Another claimed that he had been an American hero in the Spanish-American War. Neither tale was true.

Johann Heinrich Lucke was born in Vechta, Germany, on August, 18, 1875, to George and Josephine Lucke, neither of whom were aristocrats. Lucke did serve in the U.S. Army. After emigrating from Germany, Lucke, 23, enlisted on June 6, 1898, in M Battery, the First Artillery, located at Sullivan's Island, South Carolina. He served the duration of his tour, 8 months, 13 days, in South Carolina and never fought in the Spanish-American War. On March 8, 1899, Lucke reenlisted joining Company F, 7th Infantry and arrived in Alaska in 1900, with assignment to Fort Gibbon. He spent the next two and one half years in Alaska working on the military telegraph line. "I was on the first boat that landed [in Valdez]," he said. "I jumped out and grabbed an axe and chopped down a tree and said, 'this is the first log for Fort Liscum.'"[26]

Lucke was honorably discharged Outside with the rank of private on March 1, 1902, and returned to Alaska. Like most Alaskans Lucke took any available seasonal work. In summers he cut firewood for steamboats, which burned one to two cords of wood per hour. Getting the wood was difficult, hazardous

DENA #3484, DENALI NATIONAL PARK & PRESERVE, MUSEUM COLLECTION

*In 1926, the local community assembled for a summer party at the Lagoon railroad camp, Mile 344. In the back row, on the far left, is Edward McFarland. Mrs. McFarland is third from left with Harry Lucke, smoking a cigarette, seventh from left. On the right, Fritz Nyberg poses with his arm around a young boy. Louise Karstens, in a white, checked, dress, is in the middle row. In the front row, Frank Alba cradles his guitar, ready for the party to begin.*

work. In March, 1905, while working as a woodcutter for John J. Healy's trading company at a woodlot 180 miles from Fort Gibbon on the Tanana, Lucke split open his left thumb with an axe, rendering it permanently useless.

A year later, Lucke contracted to haul mail between Fairbanks and Manley Hot Springs. On one trip, because of frightful trail conditions, he abandoned an 800-pound load several miles from Chena. The exhausted carrier arrived in town on foot seeking fresh horses to retrieve the load.[27]

Lucke prospected on the Cody Fork of Wood River and also on Gold King Creek. In 1914, he and George Comstock used a poling boat to transport four tons of supplies up the Wood and Tatlanika Rivers for a group of government surveyors. For most of the first two decades of the 20th Century, Lucke supported himself as a commercial hunter, killing hundreds of animals for the market.[28]

In 1922, Dan T. Kennedy hired Lucke to guide tourists into the park. Lucke, a polished storyteller, possessed a dry sense of humor. While escorting three young tourists through the park in 1925, Lucke encountered the second William Beach expedition and shared a meal. "The evening passed rapidly as we took particular pains to relate all of our wildest bear stories," Beach wrote. "Harry Luckey [sic] was at his best, and that is going some." Lucke, while living in one of Morino's cabins, earned his living through hunting and guiding. He hunted grizzlies with imported bear dogs and no doubt exaggerated those already outrageous tales.[29]

In a strong German accent, Lucke regaled tourists with hunting and boxing stories. In Germany he'd learned to box, and as an adult he liked to fight both in and outside the ring. He didn't like to lose. "How do you suppose it looked to invite a girl friend to the fight," he would say, "and be sprawled out there on the canvas?" A tattoo etched in German on his left shoulder, reflected his life's philosophy: *"Learn and Suffer Without Complaint."* [30]

Harry Lucke was one of Interior's worst wildlife scofflaws laws and delighted in both eluding rangers and bragging about his exploits. One winter Karstens dispatched rangers Fritz Nyberg and Robert Degen up Riley Creek to investigate a report of poaching.

"A man and a woman have located in a cabin about seven miles up Riley Creek," Karstens wrote. "The man is Harry Luckie [sic] who worked for the park transportation company as a guide last summer. The woman is Kate Smith of doubtful reputation. Mr. Morino told Ranger Nyberg that Mr. Luckie [sic] was out to get meat for him to pay a debt he owed him." The rangers found part of a caribou next to the cabin. "Following up one of Luckie's [sic] trails they found where he had been close to the park line."[31]

Lucke's cabin was located in a popular local hunting spot. During railroad construction the supply road, called the "tote road," from Cantwell to Riley Creek, followed the west bank of the Nenana River to a low pass locally known as "Riley's Pass"—roughly west of Milepost 226, Parks Highway—and crossed over into Riley Creek. In winter the tote road then followed the frozen waterway downstream to Camp Riley. In summer, pack strings transported heavy loads over the same route. This detour was necessitated by the blasting and rock work conducted on the slab-sided hillsides along the Nenana between the pass and Riley Creek. Locals used the old tote road to access the upper creek and bring out their game.

Later in the decade, Lucke and an unnamed partner got caught with several sheep that they'd shot in the park. Without a jail they couldn't be locked up but the sheep were confiscated. "The sheep were put up in a big cache high off the ground," recalled one of Lucke's old friends. "In the middle of a big, howling storm, Lucke and his partner sawed the legs off the cache and when it tumbled to the ground they got all the sheep and loaded them in big freight sleds and took off. The snow of course covered up their tracks and they got away with the evidence."[32]

Harry Lucke was not well liked but at McKinley Station he had an important friend, Woodbury Abbey. The two had become acquainted in Nenana in 1918 when war fever was running high. After the U.S. declaration of war on Germany in 1917, German-Americans were persecuted and harassed. Many Alaskans held virulent anti-German sentiments. Deputy Marshal Hagan posted a circular from the U.S. Attorney General which read: "No German alien enemy . . . who has not been hitherto been implicated in a plot against . . . the United States need have no fear . . . as long as he observes the following warning: *OBEY THE LAW; KEEP YOUR MOUTH SHUT.*"[33]

In 1918, Kantishna trapper Carl Nigl was arrested for treason, declared an enemy alien and sent Outside for the duration of the war. Although a long-time resident, Nigl fully supported the Kaiser and had painted *Villa Hindenburg* and an Iron Cross on his cabin. Trial testimony indicated he was openly pro-German, anti-American and had failed to register as an alien as required by law.[34]

Harry Lucke was arrested and jailed in Nenana that same year for "seditious utterances" made at his camp on the Middle River. He was simultaneously charged with "malicious injury to animals" for spreading poison baits to kill fur-bearing animals. Trial witnesses quoted Lucke as saying, "I don't give a damn which side wins or loses, but I would like to see the States licked for going into [the war.] I am a German and a damn good one, too, and if any one wants to lick a German he's got to lick me first."[35]

Lucke was found guilty on the sedition charge and sentenced to one year in jail and fined $1,000. He pled guilty on the poisoning charge and was sentenced to six months in jail, the sentences to run concurrently.[36]

Before and during the trial, Abbey, then living in Nenana, befriended Lucke and at the risk of public censure spoke publicly on his behalf, calling him a "real, American patriot," perhaps, in part, influenced by the Spanish-American "war hero" tale.

Station children found the tall, lanky hunter to be a friendly man and imaginative storyteller. Lucke once told them how he had snuck up on a moose and with one shot "severed its neck from his body." The kids thought this hilarious with Denise Abbey wanting to know, "What happened to its head?"[37]

Karstens had known Lucke for years and knew him for what he was, a rascal who would violate the park laws at any opportunity. The two eyed each other warily but remained on relatively friendly terms. On a few occasions, Lucke borrowed the park dog team and exercised the dogs when Karstens was otherwise occupied.

When the road commission began fielding large crews to build the park road, a number of its seasonal employees settled in the area. Peter Bagoy moved to McKinley Station in 1927 to work as a seasonal laborer for the commission. Bagoy, just 19, was a strong and willing worker who turned his summer job into a year-round position, driving trucks, road-graders, tractors, shovels, and a rock crusher. He helped build the East Fork cabin and worked on the original bridge over the Toklat. As a cook, he once worked for 30 straight days, arising each morning at 4:30 a.m. His wage varied between $4.00 and $4.50 a day, paid monthly, including room and board. He lived and worked at the station for 10 years.

Bagoy was the son of a northern pioneer, John Benedict Fabian Bajoye, a Croatian, who, like Karstens, earned his Klondike grubstake by backpacking loads over the Chilkoot Pass for one dollar per pound. His trail led from the Klondike to Nome; from the Tanana Hills to the Kantishna Hills; from Eureka to the Iditarod. The Bagoy family, including five children, settled in Flat where they toiled in the gold fields, unloaded barges, ran a series of roadhouses, and developed a six-acre farm which provided the area's only fresh produce. In August 1921, the Bagoys moved from Iditarod to Anchorage where they operated a successful greenhouse, selling flowers and vegetables on the local market.

Bagoy, friendly and out-going, socialized with most of the locals. According to Bagoy, William Allman, an Englishman, was a "remittance man" who was paid by his family to stay away from home. Allman overhauled heavy equipment in summer, and in winter, ran a trapline along the Nenana. One autumn, rushed by the onset of winter, Allman hurriedly built a cabin near Horseshoe Lake. Haste necessitated shortcuts and he left a large tree stump rooted in the middle of the cabin. Sometime the following spring Allman asked Bagoy for a stick of dynamite to uproot the stump. Fearing that he'd blow the entire cabin up, if not himself, Bagoy refused but Allman insisted, claiming that since he'd been in the army he knew how to use explosives. Bagoy relented and gave Allman a stick of dynamite. A short while later a tremendous blast reduced the cabin to splinters, the roof blown sky high. The chastised Allman moved into a cabin on McKinley Pup Creek.

In 1920, 28,500 whites lived in the territory, 43% of whom were foreign-born. With so many unfamiliar and difficult names to pronounce, nicknames became common. For example, the road commission at McKinley Station employed two Smiths—"Silent" Smith and "Whispering" Smith. "Silent" Smith, from Talkeetna, never stopped talking. Oliver M. "Whispering" Smith seldom spoke unless spoken to, then only briefly. Another Smith, "2x4" Smith, worked at the Mt. McKinley Bituminous Coal Mine and got his nickname because he was "two feet tall and four feet wide."[38]

The man who spent winters in Kennedy's cabin, "Snotty-Nose Frank," a Finn, never took a bath and consequently reeked. Frank, who chewed tobacco relentlessly, got his nickname from the brown stain that ran down his beard and shirt. Old and feeble, he could not work. "There was no welfare in those days," Pete Bagoy explained, "and since we didn't want him up at the mess hall because of his runny nose and [because] he never took a bath, we carried food, all the leftovers, on down to his cabin by the tracks." When the old bachelor fell gravely ill in 1933, he was sent to Fairbanks for treatment, but died a week later.[39]

William "Hobo Bill" Dickinson labored for the road commission in summer and trapped in winter. Dickinson first showed up in the area in 1919 to work on the railroad. His ultimate goal, he said, was to earn a grubstake and quit Alaska for good, but he never quite made it. For a short while, he worked his own gold mine near the old Allred Roadhouse. He and his friend Jack Donnelly spent part of the winter of 1924 prospecting on the Toklat River.

In November 1920, Olaus Murie met Dickinson, then 36, and hired him to freight supplies with his two-dog team to the pass above Maurice Creek. Murie described Dickinson as the area's "number one character," and that was saying a lot given the people gravitating to Riley Creek.[40]

COURTESY OF DENISE ABBEY

*Denise and Bud Abbey play on the railroad tracks in front of the McKinley Station depot, 1923.*

When the road commission hired him in 1923, Dickinson was extremely skinny but by summer's end, after feasting on camp cooking, he'd gained probably 100 pounds.

Dickinson's clothing and habitation earned him his nickname. He wore patched overalls and all the old discarded clothes he could scrounge. He lived in a tar-paper-wrapped wall tent on the Nenana River below the Healy railroad bridge. At the end of each construction season, he bought two rolls of tarpaper and layered his tent with them. The walls eventually measured two inches thick. Inside the tent he had a stove, table, and bunk arranged in such a manner that he could reach everything from his bunk, with little room to move among the clutter. "I never saw anything like it. It was filthy," Pete Bagoy said. "On one visit he said, 'I'll make you a cup of coffee', and I politely said, 'No I don't think so.'"[41]

One cold winter night in Healy, a traveler met Dickinson in Singleton's Hotel, a place where old-timers gathered daily around the pot-bellied stove, and left a vivid description. Singleton's had long ceased to be an inn but housed a spotless post office and general store run by Anna Shannon. "And yet there is comfort at the store, even when the mercury stands at thirty—forty—even forty-five degrees below zero . . . at such times those who would be warm must wear heavy clothing, even indoors. No one, however, needs be quite so well protected against the cold as Hobo Bill, who nightly comes to sit near the stove at the store. There he sits, wearing a woolen shirt (none can say what is underneath), covered with a heavy red sweater and, over that, a wind-proof miner's coat. On his head is a wool cap with the flaps pulled down. There he sits, close to the roaring stove, now and then getting up to expectorate outside—for this is the land of chewing tobacco."[42]

In 1932, Dickinson and Jack Wizenreid helped engineer Donald MacDonald locate the 22-mile long section of the park road that finally connected Kantishna with the outside world. Dickinson lived in Healy into the 1940s.

In winter, McKinley Station became a major supply point for area trappers and hunters, with Moody Creek being a favorite destination for hunters. In 1925, the road commission built a suspension bridge over the Nenana River, much like the one at Curry, but without "the disagreeable swaying while being crossed," which allowed transit via Montana Creek, "to the prime game fields east of the park." The 320' bridge spanned the Nenana from a point just south of Riley Creek to a point just south of Montana Creek [43]

Two Russian émigrés lived near the bridge. Jack Hoheff, 5'10", slim, graying, and handsome, spoke very poor English but was an energetic and hard worker. He would flex his arms and say "me strong." Hoheff built a very good cabin just north of the mouth of Riley Creek, on the west side of the Nenana. Born in Russia in 1892, Hoheff immigrated to Alaska in 1914, his country already in turmoil. Before working for ARC, Hoheff had worked on the railroad and in a Healy coal mine. In winter, he trapped along the Nenana and up the Yanert River. Some local parents disciplined their children by threatening to turn them over to Hoheff, whom they called "the Bogeyman."[44]

A former market hunter, John Romanov, lived in a cabin on the east bank of the Nenana River downstream from its confluence with Montana Creek. Because of his short build, extra long arms, heavy accent, and flaming pipe, local children avoided him. Romanov immigrated in 1910 and lived in Nenana prior to joining the "Kestly Camp" hard rock crew clearing the railroad right-of-way through the Nenana canyon. In winter, he trapped upstream on the Nenana and along its feeder drainages.[45]

After the suspension bridge failed, Romanov, an extremely hard worker, helped build and maintain a cable crossing over the Nenana River. The west end, just south of Riley Creek, was anchored in a 8' x 8' log crib filled with crushed rocks, with the east end anchored on the bluff south of Montana Creek. Locals used a handcart to cross the river to reach the game fields of the Wood River and Yanert drainages.[46]

Residents of McKinley Station were a varied, colorful lot, most of them harmless characters, but a few guarding sordid pasts. The area below the trestle called "the Hole," the site of Maurice Morino's original roadhouse, developed during railroad construction as the locus of "sinful excesses." At the height of

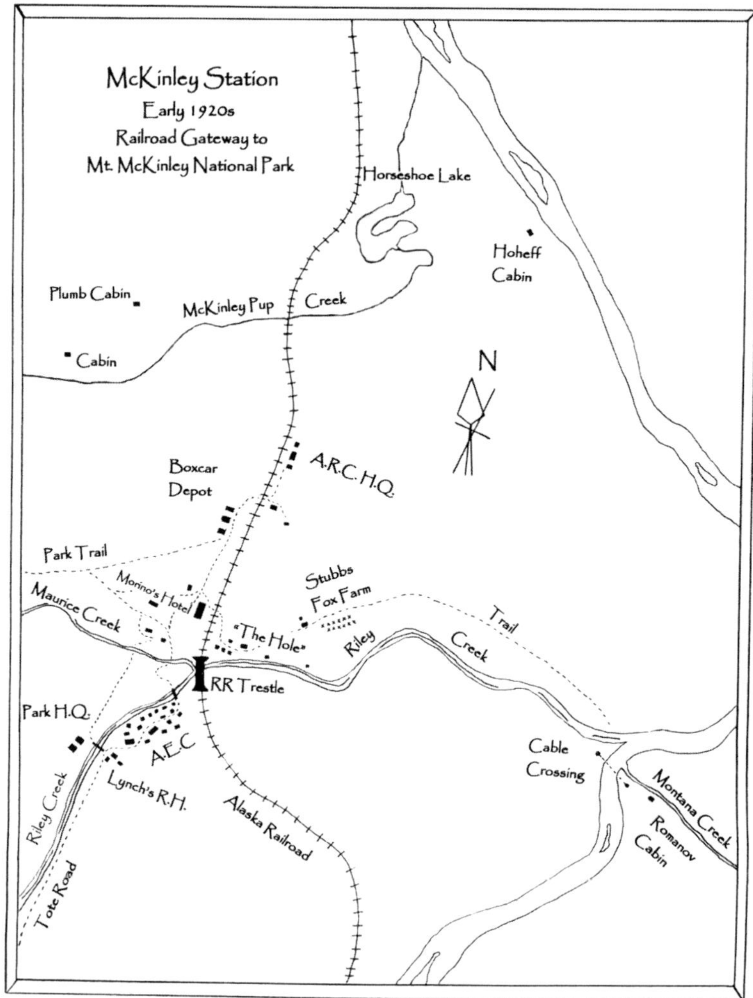


railroad and trestle construction, a host of "undesirables" gathered there. The influx of workers needed to build the park road revived the old haunts.

Since the time of the construction of the great western railroads, a carnivorous horde of rounders, sharpies, and painted ladies had followed the builders west. The same characters descended on the northern gold camps and construction projects, bent on relieving miners and workers of their gold and pay. Roadwork, like mining, was nothing but hard, monotonous, and sometimes dangerous work. To relieve the fear, pain, and anxiety, of the daily drudge, the road workers availed themselves of the frontier temptations. Unless you were looking for trouble, or wanted to step beyond respectable behavior, "the Hole" was a place to avoid.

# 12

# Life and Death in "the Hole"

On a glorious mid-September day in 1923, with the autumn foliage decked in brilliant red and yellow beneath snow-tipped mountains, two grim-faced lawmen trudged silently along the railroad tracks two miles south of Riley Creek. Frosty leaves crunched under foot while sandhill cranes circled overhead. Deputy U.S. Marshal James A. Hagan and Liquor Enforcement Officer Henry E. Seneff had no time to enjoy the autumnal spectacle. Earlier that morning they had searched the cabins of Michael Joseph Sullivan, a notorious moonshiner, but they failed to find the still they believed hidden there or in the surrounding woods.

Just when they were about to give up for the day and return to McKinley Station they saw a gray puff of smoke in the hills to the west of the cabins. They headed toward it, checking their sidearms. They separated slightly then crept forward through the open woodland, homing in on the smell of wood smoke. Through a gap in the trees, they spotted a still and three men, only one of whom, Sullivan, they immediately recognized.

As the officers closed in, they kept a wary eye on the men. One man stood tending the still, the other two sat or reclined a short distance away. Sullivan was the first to spot the officers and shouted to the man at the still, "Here comes Hagan!" In unison the lawmen yelled, "Raise your hands and don't move!" Sullivan, now standing almost between Hagan and Seneff, immediately raised his hands. His prostrate companion never moved. The man at the still pulled a black cap down over his face and started to run. "Don't run, John," Sullivan hollered. "What in hell's the matter with you?"[1]

The man ran toward a rifle leaning against a nearby tree. Hagan fired a high warning shot and commanded him to stop. When the man stooped for his rifle, Seneff yelled out a warning. Two quick shots rang out and the man crumpled to the ground. The lawmen rushed over. Kicking the rifle out of reach, Hagan bent to examine the man and found him critically wounded. He ordered Sullivan to run to the station for a doctor. Less than an hour later the wounded man died.

Late that day Seneff telephoned the news of the shooting to the Fairbanks District Attorney. The D.A. hastily assembled a party of investigators and caught the night train south, arriving at Sullivan's cabins at Mile 345 at about three the next morning. At dawn the investigators proceeded to the scene of the shooting which the officers had guarded throughout the night. After a careful examination of the site, the men carried the dead man back to Sullivan's cabin, where they convened to hear testimony and collect statements.

The deceased was officially identified as John Bernard, 45, a Norwegian, who had emigrated to the U.S. in 1882. Before settling at McKinley Station, and working for the road commission, he had been employed by the Healy River Coal Corporation. Deputy Hagan had previously arrested him for a minor liquor violation. Since that arrest, Sullivan testified, Bernard had long threatened "that if any deputy came into that country they would not get out alive."[2]

Further testimony revealed that all three suspects were known to Hagan. Earlier that summer at Riley Creek, Hagan had caught Sullivan distilling "white mule," whiskey. In fact, reports that Sullivan, out on bond and awaiting trial, was again making alcohol were what had prompted the search of his cabins. Sullivan, 53, from Ontario, Canada, was another veteran of the Klondike stampede. Well-known in Interior Alaska, Sullivan had mined at Eagle, Nome, and Manley Hot Springs. He was out-going and affable, and a non-stop talker when drinking. Years before, at Rampart, prospectors had tied him up for a week to prevent him from spreading the word of a strike and sparking a stampede.[3]

Sullivan first came to Riley Creek to work on the railroad, and later, for the road commission building the park road. Despite chronic alcoholism Sullivan was "held in high repute as a worker . . . notwithstanding the fact that he was far past the age at which many less vigorous men are compelled to give up heavy toil." In the spring and fall he operated a large still near his cabin in The Hole until repeated raids from law enforcement officers forced him into hiding his operation further down the tracks.[4]

Sullivan testified that on the previous morning John Bernard had invited him to Bernard's still to sample a run of whiskey. Sullivan said he initially declined but changed his mind. He said that when he arrived at the still he found the third man, "Hootch" Albert Fortier, already intoxicated. Sullivan further testified that prior to the shooting he had imbibed two or three drinks and was not under the influence of liquor to the extent that he did not understand what had happened. Bernard had been drinking, Sullivan said, but was not insensate. He stated that on previous occasions Bernard had threatened to fight the deputies. Sullivan also said he did not know which deputy fired the first shot, or how many shots were fired. He said Bernard was stooping over when he fell, but he did not know Bernard had been hit until he saw blood.[5]

Fortier, an infamous moonshiner from the Circle City area, was also a seasonal road worker. Fortier, a long-time friend of Bill McPhee, migrated to Alaska in 1884. In the towns of Circle and Central, he was well-known for making high quality whiskey from dried fruit and fresh berries which sold for an unheard of $75 a gallon. Fortier said he was so drunk that he knew little or nothing of the shooting. He testified that about all he could remember was Sullivan yelling, "*There comes Hagan!*" but did not know that Bernard had been shot until the following morning. He said that he had gone to Sullivan's cabin the previous day to borrow a hand-saw and some nails, but found no one there. Bernard, carrying his rifle, soon arrived and produced a bottle of whiskey which they drank. Bernard then invited Fortier up to his place but Fortier could not remember the location. Both Sullivan and Fortier denied any involvement in the still or its operation.[6]

Dr. J.A. Sutherland next testified that the apparent cause of death was a wound from a .45-caliber bullet that entered six and a half inches to the left of Bernard's backbone. He speculated that the line of the wound indicated the man was in a stooping position with his left arm extended when shot. Both deputies testified that they had fired a total of three shots, Hagan twice with his .45 automatic, and Seneff once with his .32 revolver. Both said they aimed high, in front of Bernard, neither intending to hit him, and at first thought Bernard had escaped injury.[7]

The investigators knew the two law officers to be tough, determined men who pursued law-breakers with relentless tenacity. Seneff, a man of unquestioned honesty and integrity, served as prohibition agent for northern regions. James Hagan, a Klondike veteran widely-known throughout Interior mining camps for his strike on Engineer Creek, was a controversial figure. In 1907, he'd been fired from his position as Fairbanks police chief after a prostitute allegedly used his gun to commit suicide. He was first deputized in 1910, and since 1917 had served as Deputy U.S. Marshal for the Nenana region. He was well-known at Riley Creek for frequent raids. In spring 1923, Hagan, assisted by Special Agent William Bader, arrested Leo Nebil at his cabin in The Hole for shooting at a neighbor with the intent to kill. They also took into custody

John Bain for a liquor violation. Due to their zealous enforcement of the hated liquor laws, neither man was popular. The pugnacious Hagan, in particular, made a number of enemies. One newspaper trumpeted Hagan's narrow escape in a "20-round" bloody battle with a "murderous land otter," a parody of an alleged incident of Hagan's public intoxication.[8]

On September 25, 1923, a Fairbanks coroner's jury ruled that Bernard had died from a bullet fired by Deputy U.S. Marshal James Hagan in the official discharge of his duty and "That the blame for the aforesaid death is to be attached to no one." This almost unprecedented shooting of a moonshiner shocked Alaskans. One headline summed up the public reaction: *BOOZE-MAKING IS NOW PUNISHED BY DEATH.*[9]

With the passage in 1920 of the Volstead Act, the national Temperance Movement won a victory in their decades-long struggle for sobriety. By then, however, prohibition had a long, but checkered, history in Alaska. In 1908, the U.S. Congress passed legislation outlawing the sale of liquor to Alaska Natives. The so-called "Bone Dry Law" of February 14, 1917, extended the prohibition to all territorial residents. Many, perhaps most, McKinley Station residents ignored the law and made homebrew and wine, while others made the local moonshine, or "hootch." It was relatively common for old, debilitated, or unemployed men to engage in whiskey-making. "Moonshine was an old age retirement system for old-timers," Walter Teeland said, "and they were pretty much left alone, and caused no problems."[10]

The area near McKinley Station, near the Riley viaduct, was a volatile place populated in part by moonshiners, ne'er-do-wells, and prostitutes, and was known as "The Hole." Drunken brawls, thefts, and vicious cursing marred spring nights. The crack of big guns firing in the winter darkness woke residents on the bluff and engendered fear. The volatile mix of sloth, greed, and illegal alcohol led to fights and injuries that quickly drew the attention of the marshals. No wonder parents forbade their children that unsavory place. Frequently, inebriates were the first people that park tourists met when descending from the train at McKinley Station.

"There is an element living close to the depot who have just squatters rights and living in any old cabin that has a roof on it. They realize about 30 gallons to the acre and have no scruples as to whom they sell it to. Fights and drunken brawls are a common occurrence in this district . . ." explained Harry Liek, the park's second superintendent.[11]

Although hootch and homebrew was widely imbibed, it could be lethal. "Jerry McCarthy was a fairly indolent person, a moonshiner, who stayed drunk

HENRY P. KARSTENS COLLECTION, #2297, KARSTENS LIBRARY

*The large log structure in the middle is Maurice Morino's original roadhouse. The flat roofed building is a barn. Other structures sprouting around the clearing are small businesses and homes. The cabin perched downstream on the riverbank, and partially hidden in the trees, belonged to the gambler Sam Coddy.*

all winter," said Pete Bagoy. "They had a still and the residue at the bottom was like syrup and they couldn't wait to distill that, they would dip it out and drink it." He was found dead in his cabin in The Hole; his death attributed to that potent residue. In a rather macabre twist, one of McCarthy's friends appropriated the dead man's false teeth and whittled them with a knife to fit his own mouth.[12]

Most of The Hole's residents lived in shacks or tents near the site of Maurice Morino's original roadhouse. John "Jack" Cronin, 56, operated a small store and "amusement place" in a cabin built by railroad workers in 1922. "Amusements" included gambling, drinking, and meals. This veteran of the 1898 stampede was a renowned chef, often called the "King of Cooks." In early February 1923, just before he died at Riley Creek of liver failure, the hard-living proprietor sold out to his partner, Mary E. Murphy Thompson. When laid to rest in Nenana, it was said that "he was known as a man with a good heart who was never known to turn anyone away from his kitchen hungry, generosity being one of his many virtues."[13]

Thompson took over full-control of the business, which she called a trading post. In 1925, she added on to her building which "justified a considerable

DENA #11-119, DENALI NATIONAL PARK & PRESERVE, MUSEUM COLLECTION

*Near Riley Creek, Duke and Elizabeth Stubbs raised foxes for their furs, or to sell as breeding stock. Their Mt. McKinley Silver Fox Ranch attracted buyers from around the territory. In this photo, the Stubbs' home is on the right, the work and pelting shed is on the left, with the fox pens in the background.*

HENRY P. KARSTENS COLLECTION, #294, KARSTENS LIBRARY

*Several businesses opened on the banks of Riley Creek downstream from the trestle. (l-r) McKinley Park Cigar Store, Donnelly's Restaurant, and Mary Thompson's Trading Post. Prostitution and illegal liquor sales and consumption persisted in "the Hole" until the early 1930s.*

addition to the stock carried." She also took in laundry and offered guided trips into the park and surrounding areas.[14]

Thompson came north in 1913 with her husband and son Ted in a thirty-five-foot salmon troller, one of the first in Alaska. The four Thompsons (daughter Helen was born in Ketchikan) moved to Anchorage in 1916. After her husband's death in 1918, Thompson ran a roadhouse on the railroad where it crossed the east fork of the Chulitna, at Mile 292. Four years later she moved to McKinley Station.[15]

Thompson sold out to Mrs. Elizabeth Stubbs in 1927, and moved to Suntrana near the Healy coal seams where she opened another roadhouse, store, and cabins to service miners and timber cutters working for the nearby mines. On her 15-acre "goat ranch" Thompson raised goats and gained her nickname, "Goat Mary." A two-story brothel and beer parlor near the "goat ranch" featured five to seven working girls, and according to old-timers, Thompson was their business manager. "Just before payday each month, the gals would come down from Fairbanks on the train and encamp at Mary's and stay until the miner's money ran out before going back to town," one old-timer explained.[16]

The first prostitutes arrived at Riley Creek in 1921, and did a brisk business until completion of the trestle. Road construction drew a small number of prostitutes back to the station. In an era when men vastly outnumbered women, prostitution was matter of fact. Prostitutes trailed the northern mining stampedes and every large construction project. These women's lives were never easy, and sometimes ugly, but some gained a degree of respectability often unheard of elsewhere. A few married influential and successful men and retired to leisure. They were the lucky ones.

Apparently a handful of prostitutes lived at Riley Creek until the 1932 park boundary extension forced them out. A few road workers considered one unnamed, "300-pound woman" especially enticing, describing her as "warm in winter, shady in summer." Two others, "Texas Rose" and "Goat Annie," shared a cabin in The Hole throughout the 1920s. Annie became less attractive as she aged, Pete Bagoy said, and to make money, "she made booze in her bathtub, using her own bath water." One detail of Texas Rose's life is documented. In 1909, in Fairbanks, a liaison between P.J. Lynch and Texas Rose, who lived in the red light district at that time, prompted Christina Lynch to divorce her husband.[17]

"Mary was one of the 'gals' who located in the McKinley Park Station area in 1922. She also sold some supplies, including moonshine," wrote Grant Pearson. "She vacated from the area in 1926. Catherine, who ran competition to Mary, also left in 1926 when business dropped off." Although it has been widely repeated that this "Mary" was Mary Thompson, there is insufficient evidence to support that conclusion.[18]

P.R. #18031, ALASKA STATE ARCHIVES

*Deputy U.S. Marshal James A. Hagan, based in Nenana, vigorously enforced the liquor laws. His surprise raids on Healy, McKinley Station, and Cantwell, resulted in numerous arrests and citations. In a search for a hidden still, Hagan shot and killed John Bernard, a moonshiner who had previously threatened the lawmen.*

At Riley Creek, as in all boom towns, gamblers mined the workers with a variety of card games, like solo, fan-tan, and the local favorite, panquinque, or "pan." (Pan is a variation of *Corquian*, a game of Mexican origin that was a predecessor to the game of rummy.)

Heated arguments and fights accompanied liquor-driven card games that always favored the professional gambler. More than one gambler frequented the area during bridge construction. Sam Coddy, then 70, moved to the station in 1922 or '23 and lived in a squatter cabin near Thompson's store. He slept days, tended a garden in evenings, and gambled at night. He said he was a laborer but it was widely known that, due to his age, he made a "precarious living as a gambler."

Mixed in with the illegal business flourishing in The Hole were a few respectable ones. Jack Donnelly ran a restaurant near Thompson's trading post. "Donnelly's Roadhouse" consisted of a shack, three tents, and $250 worth of groceries. Later, Tom O'Hara ran "Donnelly's Restaurant," his "masterpiece" was a dish called *Kasha Veriniskkaes* served with side dishes of chulent, momaliga, pirogen and salmon bellie [sic]. These traditional Jewish, eastern European foods were vastly superior to typical roadhouse fare. Sam Coddy often helped himself to two or three platefuls of this choice fare. Road builders placed orders days ahead for a favorite ethnic dish. Eventually D.E. "Duke" Stubbs assumed ownership from O'Hara for payment of a debt.[19]

Throughout Harry Karstens' career as park superintendent, Stubbs was one of the most vexing residents of The Hole. The politically active Stubbs, a one-time newspaper man and former U.S. Commissioner at Aniak in the Kuskokwim District, arrived in the spring of 1923 to open a fur farm. Over the previous 16 years, he had dabbled in fur farming part-time and after rejecting sites at Wasilla and Seward, selected Riley Creek as an ideal spot for a fox ranch. The long, cold winters, coupled with the availability of year-round water and timber for construction and firewood, seemed a perfect combination for such an enterprise. In addition, the railroad offered a convenient way to ship furs and breeding stock, as well as a supply of tourists eager to buy furs. In the belief that a railroad branch line to the Kantishna and Kuskokwim regions would begin nearby, offering further business opportunities, Stubbs wasted no time in making his land entry, staking 83.3 acres east of and adjacent to Morino's homestead. He surveyed the property on July 28, 1923, and filed on it three weeks later. Under the terms of the Homestead Act, only four people, Stubbs, Morino, Thompson, and Dan Kennedy legally acquired land at McKinley Station, everyone else was either a squatter or renter.[20]

In the summer of 1924, Stubbs officially opened the "Mount McKinley

Silver Fox Ranch", his pens stocked with the finest breeding pairs of silver foxes in Interior. He built a cabin, fox pens, pelting shed, barn, warehouse, light plant, and cook house, and connected them with a Stromberg-Carlson telephone system. In 1925, he purchased a herd of pure-bred Swiss Toggenburg milk goats to supply milk for his foxes and seeded a portion of his land for pasture. The foxes were fed dried salmon and the raw carcasses of porcupines, snowshoe hares, squirrels, as well as chopped moose and caribou.

Duke and Elizabeth Stubbs lived in a two-room log cabin located near the pens. Each fox "nesting box" was equipped with a microphone—an innovation in the territory—that transmitted every sound the foxes made to a loudspeaker in the house. "Any unusual noise registered at whelping time is given prompt attention," Stubbs said, "because breeding foxes are easily disturbed by people or wandering dogs." Agitated foxes sometimes kill their own pups, a substantial loss in an era when a pair of foxes could bring $1,000, or more. Stubbs fenced his fox pens and during spring breeding season posted a 24-hour guard. It didn't take long before the locals ran afoul of the ex-commissioner who was "very severe" to anyone disturbing his foxes. In May, at whelping time, "great care [must be] . . . exercised to exclude any undue excitement . . . as possible destruction may ensue if the foxes are subjected to any noise or . . . strangers," Stubbs said.[21]

Until the Stock Market Crash of 1929, the fox farm was a financial success. Each summer, Elizabeth Stubbs exhibited silver foxes at the Tanana Valley Fair, garnering multiple awards. In 1928, a black fox owned by Stubbs whelped a record litter of ten pups. Buyers came from around the territory to buy breeding stock or share trade secrets. Albert A. Burglin, owner of a fox farm at the head of Kachemak Bay, was one of many who bought his breeding stock from Stubbs.[22]

Perhaps seeking a quieter, more secluded area, Stubbs built a second set of pens and structures at the north end of his property on the bluff not far from Kennedy's cabin, a somewhat surprising selection given the distance from running water. For use as a hunting camp, Stubbs bought the old Allred Roadhouse and renamed it the "Canyon Roadhouse Cabins." In 1927 the Stubbs up-graded and re-stocked Thompson's old store, hiring a "Mrs. Palmer" to run it.

Stubbs often became embroiled in situations that clearly did not involve him. Once three prospectors complained to Stubbs that Karstens wanted to force them out of their cabin on Maurice Creek about one mile upstream from the trestle. They said they had proof that they had built there prior to the administrative act that reserved the land for park use and pleaded for Stubbs

COURTESY OF THE EARL BEISTLINE COLLECTION

*"Hootch Albert" Fortier, a notorious moonshiner from the Circle area, moved to McKinley Station and was present during the shooting of John Bernard.*

assistance. "[Karstens] has been molesting and annoying them by coming to their cabin," Stubbs wrote Director Stephen Mather, "and demanding [they] 'get out' and other intimidating, overbearing, insulting remarks." Stubbs also alleged that Karstens was interfering with locals' normal way of life and subjecting prospectors to "ridicule and embarrassment."[23]

Stubbs' comments only faintly concealed his personal disdain for Karstens' authority. Karstens, in fact, had the power to ask the cabin builders to cease work and vacate, and was only following orders to police the reserve in the same manner as the park itself. When Karstens began enforcing park laws adjacent to McKinley Station the resentment that had been simmering boiled over.

Stubbs seemed to rile people up wherever he went. No one seemed surprised when it was reported in 1911 that he had been murdered in Iditarod by "Bismark Joe" after a bitter quarrel. A month after that story made news, Harry Bismark sent out this correction: "My attention has just been called to an article in your paper . . . I presume this report is the result of a josh, as there was absolutely no truth in it. Stubbs and I did have a few words over a lot . . . but he is alive and well."[24]

In 1921, Stubbs, a political gadfly, provoked anger and outrage when he caused to have introduced in the U.S. Congress a bill that would have prohibited resident aliens and naturalized citizens from holding any government position in Alaska. Most people saw this move as self-serving, speculating that "Sometime, somehow, somebody who might not have taken out his last papers obtained an office that [Stubbs] wanted . . ."[25]

Events in 1922 reveal a potential source of Stubbs' antipathy toward the federal government and its representatives. On March 17, 1922, Commissioner Stubbs was indicted for receiving funds from the Federal government under false pretenses. He was arrested at Bear Creek, near Aniak, and released on $2,000 bail. A jury later acquitted him of all charges. This may explain why Stubbs sided with anyone in conflict with Karstens, the local government man. He clearly loathed the park and its rangers.[26]

During the fur farm's ten years of operation Stubbs heatedly complained about rangers disturbing his foxes by mushing dogs on the trail that led past his pens. In one fracas with Karstens, over an incident involving Ranger Edward McFarland, Judge Charles Bunnell weighed in with his opinion of Stubbs: "I tolerated him as Commissioner [of the] Kuskokwim Precinct for several years. Finally fired him. He is absolutely cultus, wholly dishonest, utterly worthless, contemptible, despicable, and despised by everyone ever having anything to do with him. I cannot be mistaken I know him thoroughly," wrote Bunnell, who also warned that Stubbs was a "prolific letter-writer," a skill that eventually brought his land conflict with the National Park Service to Congressional attention.[27]

Stubbs always seemed eager to do battle with the park service. Harry Liek, Karstens' replacement, especially infuriated Stubbs. When Liek accused Stubbs of hunting and trapping on park lands to feed his foxes, Stubbs exploded. "Both you and all the rangers have known . . . that I kill porcupines for fox feed, and that I use a .22 rifle. Mr. Karstens . . . heartily approved our methods. You have the rangers in the Park kill thousands of porcupines and allowed them to lay to rot," Stubbs wrote Liek. "I have lived in Alaska for 25 years and have never owned or set a game trap in Alaska nor anywhere else. I am a lover of all wildlife . . . I am probably the first United States Commissioner in Alaska who used every possible means to stop trappers using poison bait . . ."[28]

It seems clear that Stubbs was not telling the truth. According to Karstens' journal entry of December 29, 1924, "Mr. Stubbs has been up Riley Creek rabbit strangling [snaring]. He has made a round trip for last few days and he must have Hines Creek trapped out."[29]

Stubbs' feuds extended beyond the park service to include his neighbors. Morino and Stubbs despised each other. Morino strongly disapproved of prostitution, and if through nothing more than mere proximity, he held Stubbs responsible for the presence of the working women. On a more mundane level the two competed for retail sales, food, and some services. Both turned a blind eye to the liquor law, but the cabins in The Hole near and on Stubbs' property were "often the site of drunken brawls," something Morino tried to quell when increasing numbers of tourists began to visit the park.[30]

Since so many of the people living in The Hole were involved in illegal endeavors, it is not surprising to learn that many of them also illegally hunted and trapped in the park. Many Alaskans held the "Sin Laws" in open disdain, to them poaching was more a "sport" than a crime. Even the most law-abiding citizens did not see hunting, especially violation of the bag limits, as criminal. If you got two moose instead of one, you weren't illegal, you were "lucky."

Jack Donnelly, who hunted and prospected in the park, was another resident of The Hole that rangers kept close watch on. In 1922, Karstens intercepted Donnelly as he mushed up Maurice Creek bound for the Savage River and gave him the park regulations. Although Donnelly at that time was still operating his roadhouse, he claimed to be going on a "prospecting trip," which Karstens saw as merely an excuse to go hunting in the park. During their conversation, Donnelley told Karstens that he intended to build a cabin on the Savage River and prospect downstream to, and including, Ewe Creek.[31]

For more than two years, Donnelly, and other local "prospectors" thumbed their noses at Karstens and continued to hunt in the park undeterred. On one occasion while Harry Karstens was Outside on official business, Ranger McFarland blundered into a case that illustrates the difficult situation that he and Karstens faced.

At the railroad depot McFarland saw Donnelly mushing in from the direction of the park with a heavily-laden sled. He refused to allow McFarland to inspect his load. The next morning, McFarland backtracked in fresh snow to a point three miles inside the park boundary and found a trail that appeared to be where "a soft, unfrozen animal had been dragged to [the sled] from the heights above."[32]

The blood trail eventually led McFarland to the entrails of a caribou, a small herd grazing nearby. After Karstens returned to the park and conferred with McFarland, he went to Fairbanks to confer with the District Attorney "and

HENRY P. KARSTENS COLLECTION, #2275, KARSTENS LIBRARY

*According to Harry Karstens, Charles Armour, a road commission laborer, was a bootlegger, and related to the founders of Armour Meat Packing, Co.*

get his opinion as to whether prosecution would be justified with this kind of evidence." The D.A. advised that McFarland should go to Healy and swear out a warrant before U.S. Commissioner John J. Donovan. Another attorney advised Karstens that "in his opinion we had a clear case and did not see how Donnelly could escape punishment."[33]

Karstens wasn't so sanguine. Other investigations had led nowhere. In an earlier case, railroad station agent and telegraph operator Rufus Nichols, who Karstens once described as "our prize trouble maker," reported a case of illegal hunting. Karstens, who suspected Nichols was forging a cover-up, deemed it "not worth the paper it was written on." At Stubbs' instigation, Nichols fired off letters to the Interior and Justice Departments complaining of Karstens' alleged misdeeds and mishandling of poaching cases.[34]

While the Donnelly case was pending, McFarland developed evidence of another poaching incident. This time he spotted a sheep hindquarter in the dunnage of "Hobo Bill" Dickinson who was waiting for the train to Healy. Dickinson claimed to be coming in from his prospecting camp at the confluence of the Kantishna and Toklat Rivers, a totally unlikely route for someone bound for Healy.

McFarland recited the law prohibiting removal of game meat from inside the park. At first Dickinson denied having any, but under further questioning, he said that someone had given him the meat but he couldn't remember who. Once again, without any iron-clad evidence, Karstens had no legal recourse.

"After I left him, he raised the deuce, calling all the boys residing around McKinley Park informers and stool pigeons, and worse," Karstens said, "accusing them of being instrumental in giving him away. Dickinson is more or less a traveling partner of Jack Donnelly."[35]

On February 11, 1923, Donnelly pled not guilty before Commissioner Donovan and demanded a jury trial. The next day, with the temperature at -50°F, McFarland and Karstens boarded the weather-delayed train for the short trip to Healy. The commissioner called Donnelly's case at 6:30 and seated six jurors. Donnelly, representing himself, testified that he had been on a prospecting trip, and headed out of the park for supplies, when his sled broke down. While stalled, a dog broke loose and could not be caught. He said that he found the dog at the carcass of the caribou which had been killed by someone else or by a wild animal. He dragged it down to the sled and took it out of the park. When reminded by Karstens that the law did not permit hauling game out of the park and asked him why he didn't report the matter, he replied, "What in hell would I do that for? That is your business to find out."[36]

Karstens read the park regulations and testified that the year before he'd warned Donnelly to cease all hunting in the park. The jury deliberated for only a few moments and returned the predictable verdict of not guilty. During the brief deliberation, Donnelly told Karstens that he "was not leaving the country and wasn't through with him." Karstens bristled: "I asked him if that was a threat, but he did not answer, though the question was repeated several times."[37]

Before the trial, Commissioner Donovan, well aware of the attitude of the local populace, had warned Karstens that he would probably lose the case. "The prosecution failed because of the reluctance of the people to convict anyone for illegal hunting," Karstens wrote. "This general disinclination to punish illegal hunting is recognized by everybody and the park seems destined to suffer along with the rest of the territory as a consequence. It is very discouraging for those appointed to protect game and who feel responsible for the results.

"Once we get enthusiastic sympathy for our aims—and no thinking, unselfish person denies that they are right—cooperation will follow. The process of swinging the attitude of these people to recognizing the importance and value of conservation of wildlife . . . promises to be a slow and tedious one requiring much missionary work."[38]

Karstens sorely lacked diplomatic skills and his straightforward attempts to enforce the law undermined his "missionary work." A powerful sense of duty, and the influence of Charles Sheldon, kept Karstens from dealing with the rough element in a manner that, in early territorial days, would have been considered honorable. "If I were a private citizen I know I would take care of a few of these rounders and political hangers-on. The only thing that restrains me is the thought of the work you put in getting me here," Karstens wrote Sheldon.[39]

Donnelly's brush with the law did not deter him. In April 1924, Dr. and Mrs. Gregory and Dr. Edith Hook, guided by Paul Borak, embarked on the first winter "pleasure trip" into the park. Since Mrs. Gregory, a lecturer and author, could do much for park tourism, Karstens loaned them a dog team for their 10-day trip as "I am anxious to see how winter visitors may enjoy themselves." On the Savage River they ran into Donnelly and saw fresh meat hanging from a rack near his camp.[40]

In late April, Ranger McFarland found fresh caribou meat near Savage Camp and guessed the animals were killed for dog food. "The only other person in the eastern portion of the park," Karstens noted, "was Jack Donnelly." A month later, McFarland found the carcasses of three caribou along Jenny Creek. The unknown poacher had taken just the hindquarters of one caribou; the others "simply killed and left to rot." No charges were ever filed in either incident. [41]

The poaching incidents exacerbated growing tensions within the local community. In early 1924, Interior Secretary Hubert Work reported to the President that "the caribou and mountain sheep are being destroyed in [the Park] at a rate which promises to defeat the principal purpose for which the park was established." The blame, he said, rested with "prospectors who are hunting for the hidden treasures of the region, [who] do not observe the rules."[42]

The territorial press, while admitting that "there is possibly too much destruction of the game," leaped to the defense of Interior prospectors. "It will be hard for Alaskans to believe that the prospector . . . practices any wanton destruction of game anywhere . . . If any prospector is following that practice in McKinley Park he is not the genuine Alaskan kind . . . It is always hard to believe while game is still plentiful, that there is possibility of its becoming exterminated." Although press accounts failed to name Work's informant, numerous fingers pointed at Karstens, increasingly viewed locally as a ham-handed bureaucrat representing an uncaring government.[43]

Over the course of his first few months on the job, Ranger McFarland made a good impression on his demanding boss, Karstens. Not only did McFarland and his wife seem to enjoy living on Riley Creek in the renovated Lynch's Roadhouse cabin, but he also pursued poachers with zeal, such help long overdue. While he did not possess the knowledge and experience to conduct long-distance winter patrols by dogteam, he seemed willing and able to learn. Unfortunately, these two strong-willed men would butt heads in 1924, igniting a row that enflamed the simmering passions of Interior residents and threatened to undo everything Karstens had worked so hard to achieve.

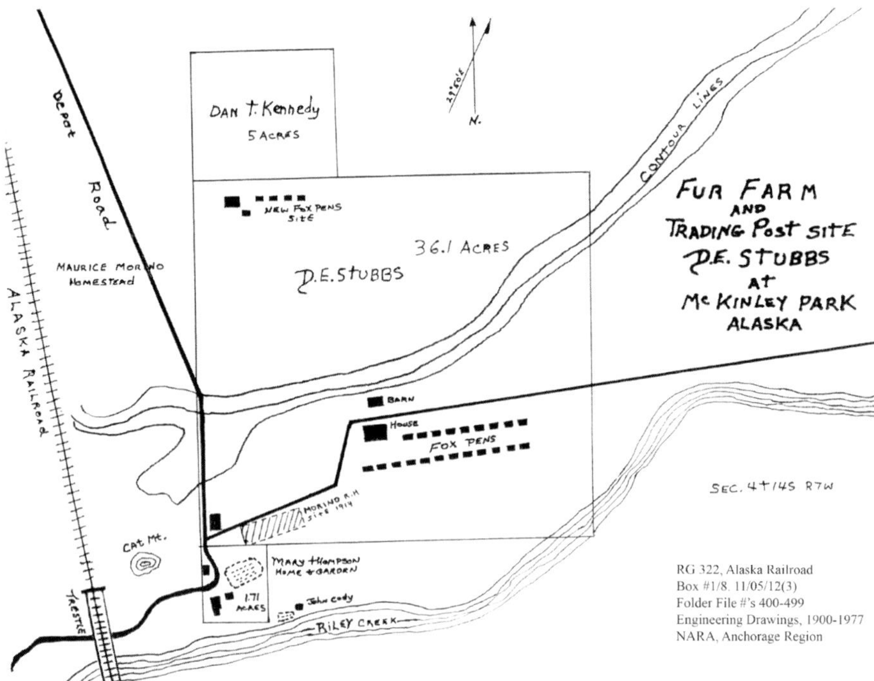


*An Alaska Railroad engineering sketch shows the boundaries of private property in The Hole downstream of the Riley Creek Bridge.*

# 13

## Up in Smoke

In Interior Alaska, summer temperatures near 80°F send powerful cumulus clouds soaring and seething above the Alaska Range. Afternoons often turn dark and ominous, the landscape blasted by thunder and arrows of lightning. Fierce winds fan small lightning-induced flames into infernos that engulf huge swaths of tinder-dry spruce. In 1924, over a million acres of the Interior's forests went up in smoke.

On a hot afternoon in late June, drifting smoke and the acrid scent of fire interrupted the park headquarters routine. Superintendent Harry Karstens and Ranger Edward McFarland dropped their tools and rushed off down the tracks to locate the source. Just three miles to the south they found a wildfire raging before the wind. Recognizing the danger, they raced back to sound the alarm. This was a powerful inferno, and unlike the smaller blazes that had sprouted and died earlier in the month; this blaze could devastate the entire village.

With the fire bearing down on Riley Creek, the able-bodied rushed out to cut a fire line. Women with small children packed their belongings for evacuation by train to Healy. A sudden, almost miraculous, afternoon shift in the wind turned the fire back on itself. Later, Karstens described the accompanying sense of helplessness. "Large forest fire immediately south of headquarters but outside of park," he said. "We were all out fighting fire most of the day but could do no good as we had no equipment . . . a portable force pump and sufficient hose would have solved the problem . . . Rangers McFarland, Jon Way and myself went back in the evening and fought the fire long into the night. Before leaving we had it pretty well corralled."[1]

Low humidity, high temperatures, and wind renewed the fire again the next morning. Flare-ups sent everyone back to the fire lines, with the fight lasting all day and into the early morning hours. A weather change helped beat back the immediate threat.

HENRY P. KARSTENS COLLECTION, #2722, KARSTENS LIBRARY

*The wild fires of 1924 consumed most of the spruce in the Nenana Canyon. One inferno threatened to destroy the community of McKinley Station as well as the wooden portion of the railroad trestle. Strong winds pushed the fire to the very edge of park headquarters.*

In the early afternoon of July 14, rangers McFarland and Way, stringing temporary phone line near Savage Camp, saw dense smoke rolling up canyon. Fearing the worst, they raced home only to confront a massive fire topping the Riley Creek bluff. It seemed then that only a miracle could prevent the destruction of McKinley Station.[2]

For two long, wearying days, the community beat back the flames that threatened homes, Maurice Morino's hotel, park headquarters, and the wooden trestle itself. "This past week, July 15–20, has been a continual grind day and night fighting fires. The morning of the 15th a strong wind came up from the south again, bringing a raging furnace of flame and smoke to within a hundred feet or so of Ranger McFarland's quarters, the barn, warehouse, and blacksmith shop," Karstens reported, "Most everyone . . . assisted in digging a trench and carrying water including 10 railroad section men, the women and children carried water and put out sparks carried over among the buildings.

"The next day the fire came around from the west and jumped Riley and Hines Creeks and was raging on all sides of us. We had to move horses, household goods, and office out on the bars of Riley Creek where they were left for two days. No one at McKinley Park could assist one another. Everyone had to care for his own, [and] until the 20th we did not leave headquarters as we had to fight the fire back day and night."[3]

When it appeared that the McFarlands' cabin could not be saved, his family hastily moved their possessions to the open area along the tracks north of the hotel.[4]

"To see that wall of fire come over the top of the hill behind the cabin was the end of everything," remembered Eugene Karstens, then 6. "Father moved Mother and me out to the center of Riley Creek, which was now a knee-deep rushing stream. Then he and five other men set about saving the two cabins by backfiring and throwing water on the sides of the cabin."[5]

Fearing disaster, Dan Kennedy used his wagons to haul away the road commission's vast store of dynamite and powder. He and his crew then hauled wagon loads of water and supplies to combat the fire near Morino's. "Had it not been for Dan Kennedy and the force of the McKinley Transportation Service," trumpeted the Fairbanks newspaper, "the fires which recently threatened the town of McKinley Station would in all probability fully have destroyed the place."[6]

On the 19th, with the danger easing, McFarland and Karstens moved their families back indoors, grateful to have saved their homes. The next day they drove an automobile two miles out the new park road to assess the damage. Karstens described the first half mile as "a black scar, completely burned over . . . the next half mile is burned in patches and is still burning, working in the direction of the park line and over a large scope of country." Heavy rains in late July finally extinguished the threats but not before the fires had consumed an estimated 30 square miles, and to as high as 2000' on the hillsides.[7]

"Old-timers here say that although they have witnessed many forest fires in the North they have never seen any so vicious and spectacular as the ones which have been raging here lately," intoned the news.[8]

The cause of the fire became a topic of fierce debate. Lightning was the obvious culprit but many locals blamed the park service, specifically Ranger McFarland. Back in early June, some children playing near Michael Joseph Sullivan's home, had "reported Mr. Sullivan as asleep on the ground outside one of his cabins," Karstens explained. "They looked into the other cabin and saw a big copper kettle and several tubs with a sour, white stuff in them. Evidently . . . moonshine." Despite witnessing the fatal shooting of John Bernard, Sullivan had not mended his ways.[9]

Two days later, Ranger McFarland paid an unexpected visit to Sullivan's cabins. "Ranger McFarland informs me that he had been up to M.J. Sullivan's

HENRY P. KARSTENS COLLECTION, #293, KARSTENS LIBRARY

*This photo, looking downstream from the Riley Creek wagon bridge, shows the fire raging out of control and destroying the timber on the east side of the Nenana River.*

and that he had destroyed the big copper boiler and set fire to the cabins," Karstens said. "I do not like this taking the law into one's own hands." Sullivan eventually filed a grievance demanding $2000 compensation.[10]

McFarland's vigilantism, coming at a time when fires were breaking out all along the northern segment of the railroad, displayed a monumental lack of common sense. Locals quickly blamed McFarland's arson as the cause of the disastrous fire. A close review of the record does not reveal a direct cause and effect. The burning cabin did not immediately trigger a wild fire. Instead, the disaster was likely generated by one of two sources, lightning or sparks from a passing train. Indeed, bush pilot Noel Wien blamed steam engines for the fires burning along the tracks.[11]

That spring, huge fires burning well north of Healy had produced layers of heavy dense smoke that had blotted out the sun, and seared eyes and lungs. In fact, McFarland had seen several small fires along the new park road, one of which he single-handedly extinguished. Regardless of the actual cause, the fire only added to the growing community resentment of the park service.

HENRY P. KARSTENS COLLECTION, #E001, KARSTENS LIBRARY

*Even before the 1924 fires, the spruce forest surrounding McKinley Station was more open than it is today. After the fires, the landscape underwent a radical transformation, with aspens replacing the spruce and dominating many of the south-facing slopes.*

The fire further estranged Karstens and McFarland, a relationship already strained by a series of incidents. In early October 1923, the Karstens family went Outside to attend the first ever park superintendents' conference held at Yellowstone, followed by a 28-day leave, which included working visits to Yosemite, Sequoia, Crater Lake and Mt Rainier. On a train trip between the parks, a thief stole $400 from Karstens' berth.[12]

Even while on vacation, Karstens was nagged by park concerns. "It was evident that [Acting Superintendent] McFarland, being alone at headquarters, would not be able to leave camp for any length of time," he wrote, "there is no safe to protect our papers or other valuables, and [it being winter] a number of fires had to be kept going which added to the fire hazard. There were also four horses and thirteen dogs to be cared for which meant a close monotonous grind for one man."[13] When Karstens returned to the park on December 28, he found Ranger McFarland and his family living in Karstens' cabin rather than the Lynch cabin that McFarland had spent some of his own money to fix up. Karstens also found one of his dogs dead in the yard. McFarland admitted shooting the dog but offered no adequate explanation.

Karstens had initially placed considerable trust in McFarland, especially following the Donnelly and Dickinson poaching incidents. Their children played together and their wives shared similar interests. Mrs. McFarland served as president of the Mount McKinley Club with Louise Karstens as vice president, the two exchanging positions on the school board.[14]

McFarland was a hard worker, but the ceaseless demands of the job tested his resolve and patience. In spring he helped cut and haul one and one-half tons of ice from Riley Creek to the storehouse. He and Karstens built a bridge over the creek and demolished old cabins and shacks and salvaged the lumber. Dogs, horses, and tack needed daily care and feeding. Preparing and preserving dog food took considerable time. In his "spare time" McFarland assisted with voluminous paperwork.

The relationship between Harry Karstens and Lt. Colonel McFarland—his reserve promotion, which he flaunted, arrived in the wake of the destructive fire—soured as the summer wore on. On August 4, McFarland told Karstens that the previous November while he was Outside, ex-ranger Buhmann had killed five caribou on Riley Creek, just outside the park boundary. Buhmann and Kennedy had used the park's horses to retrieve two of them, but had left three to rot. The two Russians living near the mouth of Riley Creek had found the wasted caribou and signed an affidavit to that effect. "Why did he not inform me of this sooner?" lamented a puzzled Karstens.

On July 1, the start of the fiscal year, Karstens hired a new ranger, Jon E. Way, with the livestock his principal responsibility. The park's 1924 budget totaled $8,000 and authorized a staff of three rangers. The previous February, Louise Karstens had been officially hired as a "ranger," with an annual salary of $1.

Ranger Way actually had reported for duty a month earlier, working just for room and board. "I decided to board him personally, until the position is open, letting him get familiar with the duties of a ranger in this park," Karstens said.[15]

Way had only been in Alaska a year. In that time, he had cruised timber near Seward for the U.S. Forest Service, herded reindeer at Cantwell, and worked in a Healy coal mine before hiring on with the park.[16]

Even after Way hired on, Karstens and McFarland continued to work side-by-side, seven days a week, 12-hours a day. Rangering in the fledgling park resembled a stint on the chain gang rather than an idyllic outdoor life. One Sunday, for example, Karstens almost apologetically took a short break from work. "Part of the day in office," he said. "Taking afternoon off for a run up Hines Creek with dogs." On his "afternoon off" Karstens went prowling for poachers.[17]

In early July, Way helped Karstens salvage lumber from abandoned buildings which he then helped McFarland haul to a proposed new headquarters site near Rock Creek. Way and McFarland paired up on a variety of projects. The inexperienced Way followed the lead of his older partner.

That spring the Alaska Road Commission finally began full construction of the park road. Karstens regularly checked on progress and commented on locations for gravel pits and brush disposal sites. The foreman of the road crew did not take kindly to his "butting in" but Karstens demanded extra care as this was a *park* road with specifications uncommon to other Alaskan roads and trails. Helter-skelter brush piles and numerous gravel pits visible from the road simply weren't acceptable to him. The pioneer road builders saw his demands as ludicrous. McFarland and Way were directed to keep an eye on the road builders and help rectify problems. Consequently, the two often found themselves in conflict with hostile road workers.

On July 30, Karstens assigned Way a menial task. Later, finding the work undone, he went in search of Way and found him asleep in the feed house. The next day, Way again abandoned his duties in favor of a stealthy, mid-day snooze. When Karstens woke him up, Way complained of being ill.

Two weeks later, Louise Karstens returned from Fairbanks accompanied by Ms. Shirley Turner, NPS Director Mather's cousin, and Turner's traveling companion, Mrs. Ethel S. Newton. On August 12, Karstens drove the three women to Savage Camp, navigating the rugged road right-of-way in his indomitable Model T. In case of a breakdown or impassable road conditions, Karstens instructed Way to follow with the park horses and wagon. After a short break at the tourist camp, Karstens drove on to Murie's old camp at the head of the river. Later that evening they returned to Savage Camp and Karstens found the park team standing in the cold, soaking-wet. "They were still hitched to the wagon and not tied," he explained, "and ranger Way nowhere in sight." While Karstens' guests went on to the dining tent he remained at the corral to unharness and wipe down the horses. Just as he was feeding them, Way arrived, explaining that he'd gone to dinner. Karstens verbally lit into him, demanding that the livestock always be taken care of first.

The next day the party returned to headquarters, with Way invited to dinner at the Karstens home. Colonel Steese, and another road commission official, fresh in from an inspection trip, joined the gathering. During dinner Turner and Newton attempted to relax the young ranger and include him in the conversation.

"In the evening Ranger Way [at first] was rather quiet and morose. The ladies [tried] to put [him] at his ease by including him in the conversation," Karstens later explained. "Ranger Way took advantage of this kindness in what I consider a nasty, insulting way by criticizing things pertaining to my guests unmercifully." In the early 1920s the nation had experienced a shift in public standards. Women bobbed their hair, smoked cigarettes, drank, and wore short skirts. The traditional values—centered on work, discipline and self-denial—had been replaced by what some people felt was a culture of self-indulgence. During dinner Way criticized "modern women" in general, and the attire and attitudes of his dinner companions. His chauvinistic remarks insulted the women, and infuriated Karstens who, by sheer force of will, remained silent during Way's rude commentary.[18]

When Way left the cabin, Karstens followed him outside and accosted him at the barn. "What followed I can hardly be responsible for," Karstens later allowed. When Way smarted back, Karstens knocked him down, fired him, and ordered him off park property. "I know I should not have struck him and will have to take the consequence," Karstens admitted, "but no man can come into my home and insult my guests and get away with it."[19]

When Karstens returned to the cabin the outraged ladies berated him for remaining silent during Way's tirade and asked why he had not thrown Way out of the house!

The next day, U.S. Commissioner John J. Donovan called to tell Karstens that Way had filed a criminal complaint, and in response he'd issued a warrant for Karstens' arrest. At a party at Morino's that night, Way approached Newton and Turner and threatened to call them back from the States as witnesses. His comments further insulted and angered the two women but Karstens assured them that he would plead guilty to prevent any such inconvenience. Karstens liked and respected these two, describing them as "Mighty fine women, Jolly and full of fun."[20]

On August 16, Commissioner Donovan, attended by Deputy Hagan, convened court in the park schoolhouse. Before any testimony was heard, Karstens pled guilty and Donovan, who respected Karstens, fined him $20 plus $11.36 in court costs. "The court stated to Way that he knew me to be a good citizen," Karstens said, "therefore he would give me a light fine." Afterward Way confronted Karstens and demanded payment for the work he'd done prior to his appointment.[21]

The next day, Kennedy hired Way to work at Savage Camp. "Manager

Kennedy is surrounding himself with men who are absolutely against this park administration. He has three of them now in his employ," Karstens complained. Although his comments appear somewhat paranoid, the sentiment against him was very real. His relentless dedication to the park made many enemies, some now out for blood. Some of the discontent he brought on himself. At times he seemed unable to grasp that diplomacy worked better than confrontation. In the aftermath of his firing, Way sided with anyone opposed to Karstens.[22]

"Ex-ranger Way visiting Ranger McFarland, also others who are antagonistic to me. I do not understand his actions," Karstens said. "McFarland seems to take sides with Way, though he knows nothing of the circumstances."[23]

In the following days, Karstens chided McFarland for turning in his reports late, being sluggish in his duties, and lax in his patrols, the latter especially important due to the seasonal influx of hunters along the park boundary. He described McFarland's behavior as "morose."

In the last week of August, Karstens dispatched McFarland to investigate a hunting party camped near Cantwell. Two days later McFarland returned on the 2:45 a.m. train but did not report to work until noon. Karstens upbraided his ranger for failing to follow his instructions to track the hunters. McFarland responded with indignation, raving at Karstens for making unfounded assertions and accusations. "I'm sure the man tried to goad me on to strike him," Karstens said, "as later on he told me he would have filled me full of holes if I had . . ."[24]

Two days after the confrontation with McFarland, Karstens hired Fritz Nyberg, then working for the road commission, to replace Way. Karstens immediately sent Nyberg to Cantwell to find the hunters, and make sure they were hunting outside the park boundary. En route, Nyberg passed McFarland on the Windy Creek trail but kept on going. An outraged McFarland filed a report stating that Nyberg had been dispatched to spy on him.

Ranger Nyberg soon returned to headquarters with the news that the hunters had gone east and away from the park. In Cantwell, he learned that "they were warned of his coming over the phone. No one knew of Nyberg being sent to Cantwell but McFarland and I," Karstens said.[25]

The conflict soon came to a head. Prior to taking the train to Anchorage, Karstens exchanged words with McFarland over unfinished duties. On the train south Karstens met an old friend, Kantishna miner Eli Borach, recovering from amputation of his leg and both thumbs due to freezing. "He informed me that [last winter] he saw Ranger McFarland shoot a [loose park dog] several times, that the dog broke loose and McFarland could not catch him . . . McFarland got crazy angry, got his gun and shot the dog," Karstens reported. "Mr Barich

[sic] states that he himself ran [away] as McFarland was so angry that he was afraid . . . Also he stated that any man who would shoot a dog like McFarland did is bad and no good."[26]

Karstens mulled his options before making a decision. "I have been thinking [McFarland's] case over for some time and have finally decided to discontinue his position . . . Looking through [his] file I found that it had been rifled as his appointment and several papers were missing," Karstens said. "He denied taking the appointment but later sent it over to me with some other papers . . . His methods are not in accordance with my ideas of honest administration of this park."[27] McFarland at first refused his dismissal, and only belatedly turned in his field binoculars and compass. He then moved his family from headquarters into a furnished cabin near Morino's, one recently vacated by the Abbey family who just had moved to Fairbanks. (McFarland lived at the park through the early 1930s, working as railroad station agent, apparently waiting for an opportunity that never came. "One day I will have Harry's job," he once told Louise Karstens.[28])

Happy as he was to resolve the McFarland issue, Karstens was also pleased to see Woodbury Abbey move on. The last vestiges of Abbey's dream of becoming park concessionaire had been dashed earlier in the year when Dan Kennedy introduced his new partner, Fairbanks attorney Thomas Marquam.

Karstens and Abbey had gotten along well at first, but their friendship had slowly eroded. "We were the best of friends and he was my disbursing agent and was to drill me so I could do my own disbursing in the fall," Karstens explained. "He is a very likable fellow, most of the men he has had in his parties swear by him and he is a most capable surveyor and accountant." In 1921, Abbey was asked to tutor Karstens in the government's Byzantine funding practices. Within a short time Karstens seethed over what he saw as Abbey's corrupt advice on the use of government funds, but which in reality were standard practices. He saw Abbey's technique as "spend, spend, spend," an affront to the frugal Karstens.[29]

In addition, Karstens attributed an imagined change in Abbey's behavior to his failure to obtain appointment as Territorial Surveyor General. When "he heard Carl Thiel was appointed Abbey was a changed man," Karstens said. Lingering resentment over Abbey's survey of Morino's homestead, which complicated Karstens' development plans, also played a part in the rift, as did Abbey's employment with Kennedy. When Kennedy and Abbey fell out over management of Savage Camp, the fair-minded Karstens supported Abbey's position.[30]

Karstens had also learned that in the wake of William N. Beach's stormy

1922 park visit, Beach had returned to New York and had lobbied for Karstens' dismissal as superintendent, nominating Abbey to take his place. Karstens saw it as an act of revenge by Beach, with Abbey as a co-conspirator. Consequently, Karstens was not sorry to see Abbey go.[31]

The hiring of Fritz Nyberg was a breath of fresh air for Karstens. In Nyberg, he found a physical equal, a man at ease on the trail or with a drawknife in his hand. "The Swede," as he was called, first came to the area in 1921, to go bear hunting on Riley Creek, but he never got one. "They overslept that year," Nyberg explained. That summer, he mined in Kantishna and prospected near Copper Mountain. He then freighted with horses between Hurricane and Lignite for the AEC, and the following winter hunted big game for the construction camps.[32]

The affable Nyberg was an expert outdoorsman, the type who carried out directives with skill, courage, and tenacity. Nyberg knew he had a lot to live up to. "Harry was a good outdoorsman," he said. "There wasn't a finer man to be on the trail with." [33]

Nyberg quickly proved himself to his boss. One dark December day, after posting paraffin-coated boundary signs on the northern perimeter, Nyberg headed back to headquarters. "Left lower Savage cabin at 8 a.m. [Went] up through canyon, very difficult getting through. Ice had broken, got wet, stopped at upper cabin, dried out, hauled two loads of wood," he reported. The report was typical of him. No complaining, no exaggeration, just do it and move on.[34]

"Fritz was a pleasant, easy-going fellow, hard to ruffle, doing his job quietly and efficiently—including making sure he got enough food to keep up his strength," said Grant Pearson. John Rumohr added that Nyberg "was a truthful, good man. If he said something, it was so."[35]

With park road construction underway, Karstens was desperate to establish a new headquarters adjacent to it. "I have always had in mind the erection of permanent buildings on the high bench, on a level with the railroad and immediately west of the railroad station, from this point the road into the park will begin," Karstens wrote in 1922. "The idea is to . . . erect a large rustic gateway for entrance . . . Within the gate there will be a main thoroughfare, on either side of which will be park buildings located with an eye to efficiency and beauty. In the near future this office expects to induce Mr. Moreno [sic] to relinquish such portions of his claim as this park needs." [36]

In late April 1924, Karstens received permission to move headquarters out of the Riley Creek bottom to a more suitable and accessible site. Initial discussions with Morino seemed promising. At one point, according to Karstens, Morino "agreed to turn over to us about 600' frontage on the railroad, extending back through his homestead to the park reserve." When Morino changed his mind, Karstens then approached the railroad, which owned the adjacent property.

Colonel Lee H. Landis, a decorated war hero, was now the railroad's general manager. His initial contacts with Karstens were cordial and encouraging. He clearly saw the potential for the park to benefit the railroad's bottom line and viewed development of visitor amenities as crucial. Landis believed that McKinley Park needed a first class hotel, not dissimilar to the grand railroad hotels built in western parks. One of his first moves was to request government funds to build a 72-room hotel near the depot and for construction of 50 miles of park road. He ordered the park depot upgraded in 1924 and hired workers to build a story-and-a-half house for the station agent, who, until then, had lived in a decrepit boxcar. Landis was amenable to providing railroad land for development of a new headquarters.[37]

Landis' good intentions quickly bogged down in controversy. In an attempt to make the railroad solvent Landis eliminated four influential administrators, who immediately cried foul, touching off a Secret Service investigation. Landis was forced from his post in mid-1924, replaced by Noel W. Smith, the very man assigned to investigate the charges.[38]

With Landis out, negotiations for use of railroad land at the depot ground to a halt. Karstens then began clearing land at a location west of the railroad. "I have had in mind . . . for our new headquarters . . . a site with a commanding view, drainage, water, and sufficient room for expansion, this I found on the west side of First Creek [Rock Creek] about two miles from the railroad . . ." he told his boss. In September, after Governor George A. Parks officially scotched the use of railroad land, work on the Rock Creek site accelerated. "This I am now getting to think is the best solution of the problem of a permanent headquarters," Karstens said.[39]

"The Park Service will spare no efforts in making the grounds and buildings a creditable exhibit and fitting the project they are designed to serve," a reporter said. Karstens, already cash-strapped, would need all of his ingenuity and resolve to relocate park headquarters. Throughout the summer and fall he and Nyberg dismantled derelict buildings and salvaged materials for the new headquarters.[40]

When Robert H. Degen reported for duty in early October, Karstens now had two exceptional employees. Degen enthusiastically pitched into the endless list of tasks. On October 16, in the middle of a severe blizzard, Nyberg and Degen began clearing the new site but routine chores interrupted their work.

While Nyberg cut and hauled logs with the park team, Degen repaired horse tack and dog harnesses and salvaged lumber for a coal bunker to be built at the depot. In one day Nyberg single-handedly unloaded five tons of hay from the train. After the bunker was built, the two men shoveled a railroad car full of coal into the new 12'x50', 60-ton coal bunker.

Despite limitless chores, poaching remained Karstens' biggest concern, and he made time for the two new rangers to conduct patrols. On one patrol Nyberg saw 3,000 caribou above the Savage canyon and another 500 downstream near the park boundary. In addition, 2,000 caribou wandered near Cantwell, and another large herd lingered along the railroad between Healy and McKinley Station, where local hunters were able to kill all they wanted. Even so, road commission laborers and Kennedy's employees hunted up Riley Creek and close to the eastern boundary. "It does not seem proper that parties working for park activities should hunt along the park boundary as it encourages others to do so," Karstens fretted.[41]

"This fall has seen the greatest run of caribou that has occurred in this section in many years," he said. "The reports of prospectors in past years, of seeing a herd of 10-to-20,000 animals in the western portion of the park, sounds more reasonable now, though I had my doubts at the time." (Estimates were notoriously unreliable. For example, Frank Glaser estimated a herd of caribou that came through Healy in 1927, as numbering "a half million." Based on other reports, a newspaper article estimated the same herd at 5,000.)[42]

Degen and Nyberg set out in a late October snow storm to look for tracks of hunters leading into the park. "Rather severe weather to send them out but they were willing to go which shows the right spirit," Karstens said, "I want the people along the boundary to know that we are on the job, which is having a good effect. It is to be regretted that we have not two or three more rangers to extend patrol to the Kantishna district . . ."[43]

Two days later, Karstens received a cryptic phone call from Degen at Cantwell designed to foil eavesdroppers. "Ranger Degen . . . stated he did not know when he would return to headquarters as he had information he would like to look into," Karstens said. Exhibiting confidence in his new ranger, he added, "I advised him to take as much time as he needed." The next day, Degen returned, having followed a tip that two men were hunting Dall sheep in the park. The allegation proved false—one of the men had already left for the Valdez Creek mines. "Saw about 500 caribou," Degen reported, "total distance patrolled [on foot] 61 miles."[44]

The next day, Degen and Nyberg left on an extended patrol from Cantwell to Healy. On their return from that trip, with no time off, they again cut and hauled logs near the new headquarters site. "They are picking them over a large area well back from the road," Karstens said. "We are in hopes of having sufficient logs and material on the ground to begin construction very early in the spring."[45]

While Degen continued logging, Nyberg and Karstens caught the train to Fairbanks to pick up the park's dogs. They found the dogs "soft" but in good condition. On November 5, in anticipation of the winter patrol schedule, Degen and Nyberg hauled supplies to a tent camp on the Savage River. Upon arrival they found that someone had stolen their stockpiled provisions. "We can leave nothing in the park and depend on it," Karstens sighed.[46]

Next, the two rangers broke trail to Windy and Cantwell, a one way distance of over 30 trail miles, and returned in just four days. "That is very good traveling considering the softness of the dogs, which arrived home feeling playful and in good shape," Karstens said.[47]

The frequency and duration of patrols increased as the dogs toughened. Degen and Nyberg bought a good lead dog for the team and donated it to the kennel. Trail breaking introduced the two men to the park's boundaries and trails.

Just before Thanksgiving, someone reported poachers at work above Maurice Creek. "Sent Ranger Degen . . . to see if the three men living there had moved yet, also to see if there was any hunting going on as a man named Stubbs living on Morino homestead is making frequent trips . . . dressed in white and carrying a gun," Karstens said.[48]

Karstens clearly felt that something more than patrols were needed to protect the caribou's winter range. "It is my hope that in time, the eastern boundary will be extended to the railroad and follow the course of the Cantwell [now Nenana] River on the southeast corner of the park," he wrote, "also that four or five miles be taken in along the northern boundary from the railroad to the Toklat River. These extensions . . . would eliminate considerable poaching . . ."[49]

On November 15, Karstens received a phone call from Enock John in Healy. John, an Athabascan from Nenana said he had been caught hunting in the park by rangers he did not know and wanted Karstens' help as he had meant to do nothing wrong. Karstens promised to meet him in Healy early the next morning.

Alaska Natives had not been consulted prior to the establishment of the park nor had their traditional land uses been recognized. Local Athabascans, whose history on the land stretched back nearly 11,000 years, found the basic park concept unfathomable. Survival, not recreation, dictated their hunting and land use. Karstens knew many of the Natives who frequented the park and they apparently shared a mutual respect. Throughout Interior Alaska, Karstens carried a reputation for fair dealings with Alaskan Natives, one of the few whites "always invited and welcome at potlatch."

Early the next day, Karstens hitched up four dogs and headed for Healy, leaving Louise to care for the horses, kennel, and camp. Karstens contacted John at noon and heard his side of the story. Without artifice, John explained that he and his partner, Titus Bettis, had been caught shooting Dall sheep. After an initial contact, he said, the two rangers had heard shots and had gone off in pursuit of another hunter.

After dark, Nyberg and Degen mushed into Healy, their sleds loaded with dead sheep. That evening in a tiny, unkempt cabin, the three rangers met with the two Natives. John, ill and partially blind, explained that he needed help to procure meat for his wife and three children and had summoned Titus Bettis, 28, from Nenana to assist him. John said that he did not think he was doing wrong in hunting where he did. "White men had told him that he could hunt along the hills close to Healy," Karstens explained, but they had killed four sheep just inside the northeastern boundary.[50]

"All indications were they had no wish to do wrong and were repentant," Karstens said. "They gave us information as to where we could find the other hunter and other information that is useful to us. They promised to observe the park rules and be more careful. I told them I would decide their case in the morning."[51]

The next day, Karstens wrote out a statement for John and Bettis to sign but declined to cite them "seeing it was their first offense and that it would be impossible to get the conviction of a hungry Indian with a family who pleaded ignorance." Karstens was willing to overlook these men's earlier brushes with the law and judge the situation on its own merits.[52]

Acting on information supplied by John, Nyberg and Degen set out in search of the third hunter. The rangers soon located a cabin two miles inside the park near Dry Creek and saw a dead sheep on the roof and a man dragging another down off the mountain. After dark the rangers returned to Healy with the two sheep and James Paul Sherman in custody.

Unlike other local residents, Sherman did not claim the prospectors' hunting exemption. "Mr. Sherman admitted having killed the two sheep in the park," Karstens said. Sherman produced an old map, professed ignorance of the 1922 park expansion, and said that he was hunting for his "more or less demented wife and three children," who were wintering in Nenana. Karstens, though not

DENA #17-5, DENALI NATIONAL PARK & PRESERVE, MUSEUM COLLECTION

*In 1923, Harry Karstens guided Ray Dame and C. Blanchard, of the Bureau of Reclamation, into the park to photograph wildlife and scenery. In front of the Sanctuary River cabin, (l-r) are packer Bob Degen, C. Blanchard, and Harry Karstens. Photo by Ray Dame.*

an admirer of Sherman's, congratulated him for not claiming to be a prospector but rather hunting in the park accidentally. In lieu of charges, Karstens required Sherman to sign a notarized and witnessed statement admitting his act.[53]

When Judge Wickersham insisted on the park's special hunting exemption, he no doubt had people like Sherman in mind. The Wisconsin-born Sherman arrived during the Fairbanks strike, and as early as 1903, had prospected the north side of the Alaska Range from the Little Delta River to the Nenana. He staked claims throughout the Nenana district and as far south as the upper Susitna country. In 1908, he pushed for the construction of a winter trail from the Wood River, across to the Nenana River and upstream to Broad Pass. In 1910, Sherman, 31, and his wife, Agnes Eckert, 20, mined on the Totatlanika River where they found gold. His discovery of diamonds there in 1906 had sparked a mini-rush.

Sherman lived off the land but possessed a greater conservation ethic than most prospectors. For years he had lambasted the "shameful" work of market hunters who worked so ruthlessly that the "legitimate prospector suffered for the lack of meat." In 1908, Sherman helped form a miner's committee to end the slaughter by market hunters. At the time of his arrest, Sherman maintained an interest in a fish wheel on the Nenana River and had a homestead near some of his claims at the confluence of the Healy and Nenana Rivers, the site of the modern day power plant. When caught in the park, he was truthfully hunting for his family, including a newborn son.[54]

Karstens' returned to headquarters quite pleased with his rangers' work. "The two young huskie [sic] rangers are doing excellent work," he reported, "they are both very much interested in the park and their work and deserve much credit for their willingness under all conditions." To Karstens it appeared that he finally had the help he needed to end poaching in the park.[55]

Karstens decisions in these two incidents drew praise from his superiors. "You are to be congratulated on the excellent manner in which you handled these cases," acting director Arno B. Cammerer told Karstens. "In such cases where you are convinced that it was a first offense and there was nothing malicious in their attitudes and they were truly ignorant of the park boundaries ... you will make more friends for yourself and the Park Service by getting their cooperation ..."[56]

The rangers spent the early part of Thanksgiving Day cleaning up around headquarters before sitting down to a "big turkey dinner enjoyed by the park personnel, the school teacher, and Mrs. [Polly] Anderson of Wonder Lake." Thanksgiving marked a high point in staff relations, but Degen, however, soon disappointed Karstens.[57]

"He is very much attached to a young lady who is going from Fairbanks to the states on today's train," Karstens wrote, "he wishes to accompany her as far as Anchorage and will return on the next train. Permission was granted without pay."[58]

Degen spent the first week of December hauling coal and firewood for the park stoves, and on the afternoon on December 10, handed in his resignation, effective the next evening. On December 12, the temperature hovering at -52°F, Degen boarded the southbound train. "It was quite a surprise to us," Karstens lamented, "as Degen was getting on fine and liked the work, it is a case of either the girl or the job and the girl won ... The resignation of Ranger Robert H. Degen is to be regretted as [he] was a loyal and energetic ranger who was very interested in the park and the work."[59]

Degen's departure was a minor blow for Karstens, compared to what was to happen next. Complaints to Congress from former rangers Way and McFarland, and others, had finally resulted in the opening of a government investigation.

In the spring of 1925, Director Mather ordered Karstens to immediately stop work on the new headquarters project and travel to Seattle to meet with his assistant, Arno Cammerer. Mather also informed Karstens that the Interior Secretary had requested that the Post Office Department's Office of Inspections undertake an unbiased review to determine Karstens qualifications and ability as park superintendent.

# 14

# Get Karstens!

Karstens is out!" "He's finally getting what he deserves." "He'll be lucky to get run out of the country!" "Hawley Sterling will be the new Superintendent. He'll treat us right." A wild variety of rumors about the investigation of Harry Karstens' actions as park superintendent raced through the region, getting wilder and more distorted as they traveled. In early 1925, in response to numerous complaints, and precipitated by the fight with Jon E. Way, the Interior Secretary ordered an official inquiry.

Early in 1925, the Post Office Department's Office of Inspections, began a probe to determine Karstens "qualifications and adaptability for the position" of superintendent. Karstens' accusers alleged that he was temperamentally unfit for his position due to his arrogance, violent nature, and pettiness. Dan T. Kennedy's multiple complaints that Karstens wanted to get rid of him in order to secure the concession for himself also figured into the probe.[1]

Over a span of three months, the two Inspectors in Charge, C. Riddiford and P.L. Neil, conducted extensive interviews, traveling to Seattle, Ketchikan, Juneau, Anchorage, Fairbanks, and McKinley Park. Rather than being solely based on recent events, the investigation was the climax of a long hap-hazard effort to oust Karstens. Two years earlier, park supporter John Burnham had returned to New York from a seven-week trip to Alaska and informed Charles Sheldon that "There seems to be a concerted effort to put [Karstens] out of his position . . ."[2]

Rumors of Karstens' imminent firing or resignation circulated long before the official inquiry began. Stories that Karstens had lost his support in Washington prompted the submission of numerous applications for his job.

Former ranger Lou Powless submitted his application on January 2, and included letters of recommendation from Delegate Dan Sutherland and

#79-G-11F-21, NATIONAL ARCHIVES AND RECORD ADMINISTRATION

*Incensed by rude remarks made to his female dinner guests, Harry Karstens followed his ranger, John E. Way, outside and physically assaulted him. The fight led to charges of assault and battery, to which Karstens pled guilty. The incident led to an official government enquiry.*

John Baker of the U.S. House of Representatives. Baker said he believed that Karstens would be leaving the park because he had been "designated as one to represent the United States in an endeavor to climb Mt. Everest."* [3]

Hawley Sterling's application, dated mid-January, carried the endorsement of Governor Scott C. Bone, and was submitted "based on persistent rumors" of change. Sterling concluded his cover letter with these words: "This application is not made with the idea of attempting to oust another man from his posi-

* In early 1924 Harry Karstens learned that he'd been nominated as one of two Americans to accompany the British expedition to climb Mount Everest. With the North and South Poles conquered, Everest, the highest peak in the world, ranked as the Earth's last great challenge. Adventurers of all stripes clamored for the chance to join the third British summit attempt. William Colby, former President of the Sierra Mountaineering Club, recommended Karstens.

Ascending to Everest's north col then required a minimum of two full days of step cutting. The "staircase" Karstens had cut into the high ridge above the Muldrow Glacier during the 1913 McKinley climb was widely admired by climbers around the world.

Karstens, 45, was not sure that he still possessed the stamina for high altitude work. He had suffered altitude sickness on Mt. McKinley and the Everest base camp at 17,200' on the Khumbu Glacier was just 3000' lower than McKinley's summit. For several reasons Karstens stayed home. On June 8, 1924, the British expedition's climbing leader, George Mallory, and his partner, Andrew "Sandy" Irvine, disappeared near Everest's summit. 75 years later, Mallory's frozen body was found at the 27,000' level on Everest's north face.

HENRY P. KARSTENS COLLECTION, #2292, KARSTENS LIBRARY

*Harry Karstens worked extremely hard to build and maintain the park headquarters on Riley Creek. Finding and keeping good help seemed at times a much more difficult, almost hopeless, task.*

tion nor with the idea of casting any reflection upon the ability of the present incumbent." Rather, Sterling submitted his application on the belief that the job was open or soon to be vacated.[4]

Late the previous year, Sutherland also had recommended A.F. "Judge" Stowe for superintendent, citing his "excellent education." In his letter, Sutherland called Stowe a student of wildlife and "a naturalist of considerable attainment." In response to a request for additional information, Stowe replied that his interest in the position "was predicated entirely upon the hypothesis of a vacancy . . . I would not for one moment interfere with Mr. Karstens retention of his position . . . He has an estimable wife and a sturdy brilliant young son, I am on friendly terms with them." This 60-year-old Klondike veteran praised Karstens, attributing his possible demise to conflicts with his rangers.[5]

In January, Karstens received a coded message from assistant director Cammerer, asking if the rumors of his resignation were true. Karstens immediately telegraphed back: "No Foundation for Rumor."[6]

About this time, Olaus Murie sent Karstens a long letter of counsel. He expressed his opinion that Karstens was "in the right and had done nothing that you had no right to do." However he went on to warn that in his opinion "considerable diplomacy is required [in carrying out policy.] I know it is hard to endure insults and put up with all kinds of criticism, but it is necessary to disregard them, to forget personal feelings and try to conciliate people."[7]

Murie acknowledged the strong local opposition to the park, and conservation in general, and cited the need for education. "Your work is pioneer work and of course is bound to be difficult. I told Mr. Cammerer you were accustomed to direct and vigorous dealings with people, which is characteristic of frontier life." He counseled Karstens to pay no attention to petty gossip and rumors around McKinley Station and reiterated that "winning the public good-will is very important."[8]

In his response, Karstens candidly admitted that some of the local criticism "is due to my errors in tact on occasions," then explained his difficulties in enforcing park laws. "You should know the temper of these people regarding their general lack of desire to co-operate when hunting and trapping is involved," he said. "I know too well what happens when you try to take something away from an Alaskan which he thinks he has had or still has a prior right to."[9]

The beleaguered superintendent allowed himself a bit of speculation. "I wonder sometimes how much of this . . . animosity against me comes from some of my former friends who think I am trying to ignore them," he said, and "who think I have a 'swelled head,' because on the few occasions when I do get to town I cannot take the time to visit them." Karstens, while tacitly admitting the serious nature of the oversight, also described his understanding of his role. "The real reason for my being here at all is dependent largely on securing and holding the good-will and co-operation of those living in the immediate vicinity of the park: the old-timers, prospectors, trappers." He went on to say that he wished he could travel to other communities to educate the public about the park but lacked the time and money.[10]

After reading a copy of Murie's long, thoughtful letter, Cammerer wrote Karstens that ". . . we are strong for you, and all we want you to do is to keep on sawing wood as best you know how."[11]

From the very outset, Cammerer had favorably impressed Karstens, and vice versa. "Mr. Cammerer has been the best ever," Karstens informed Sheldon. "He sure has a way of making one loyal to him." Cammerer deserved such praise. "Over the years Associate Director Arno Cammerer had grown into one of the best administrators in Washington," wrote Horace Albright, the second National Park Service Director, "and in his quiet, unassuming way saw to it that things got done."[12]

Even the most capable Washington bureaucrat, however, never could begin to fathom the challenge of life in an isolated Alaskan village or town. "Small things seem big in small towns," Nyberg explained. Without question Karstens lived, worked, and supported a family in an unusually volatile community. "The park seemed more prone to rumors, intrigues, and feuds than anywhere else I ever lived," said road foreman Pete Bagoy, "probably because so many disliked the government coming in and they wanted to cause trouble."[13]

Long before their hiring as rangers, both Nyberg and Robert Degen sent letters of support to Arno Cammerer. Degen described the attacks on Karstens as "unfair and unjust . . . prompted by jealous motives." Significantly, Degen, at the time he wrote that letter, was palling around with Harry Lucke and others at odds with Karstens. Cammerer responded that he was aware that anyone in Karstens' position would make enemies and said he was pleased with his accomplishments. "I know

HENRY P. KARSTENS COLLECTION, #292, KARSTENS LIBRARY

*Fritz Nyberg, left, stands in front of the Superintendent's Office with one of the rangers who found the isolation, low pay, and hard work, not to his liking and soon moved on.*

HENRY P. KARSTENS COLLECTION, #4195, KARSTENS LIBRARY

*Eugene, Harry, and Louise Karstens at Savage Camp. Among his myriad duties, Superintendent Karstens also entertained visitors with stories of wildlife and his 1913 Mt. McKinley climb.*

that his heart is in the right place and that he has only the best interests of Mount McKinley and the surrounding communities at heart."[14]

During the investigation, additional applications arrived in Washington. U.S. Army Lieutenant Richard Bassett, an experienced forester applied, as did Grant Courtney, a storekeeper at Glacier City during the peak of the 1905 Kantishna stampede. Courtney's application, also endorsed by Sutherland, included a petition signed by nearly 60 prominent Fairbanksans, including at least one shocker, R.C. "Dick" Wood, Karstens' long-time friend and former business partner. The petition was, for Karstens, a bitter public repudiation of everything he'd worked so hard to achieve.

Former candidates for the job also resurfaced. George A. Parks, soon to become governor, and Sutherland, both endorsed Hawley Sterling. Parks assured Director Mather that Sterling, unlike others, would not apply for the job unless it was vacant, and "would not do anything that might result in the discharge of Mr. Karstens." Parks was confident however that if the position was vacated, Sterling would accept it.[15]

"Mr. Karstens had a difficult position to fill . . . as would any other man occupying such position, in assuming the administration and control over a newly created park in Alaska," Mather agreed. "His honesty, loyalty and efficiency have been unimpeached." Nonetheless he held on to Sterling's application for further review.[16]

Mather also received similar support for Sterling from George Sexton, Republican Committeeman from Alaska, who also freely admitted that there had been a lot of "irritation forced on Mr. Carstens [sic] by certain people that only wanted to get his post for commercial exploitation of the Park."[17]

Cammerer replied to Sexton that "we would like to promote from inside the National Park Service the men who have made good in our ranks." In fact, Cammerer already had a possible successor in mind, James P. Brooks, then assistant superintendent and chief ranger at Montana's Glacier Park. Brooks, brother of famed geologist, Alfred Hulse Brooks, appeared willing to assume the position once a decision was rendered. Of all the government agents ever to serve in Alaska, geologist Brooks was the most revered, and his brother's candidacy whiffed of politics.[18]

As the investigation continued, Stowe wrote a remarkably candid letter to Cammerer detailing his observations based on a recent visit to McKinley Station. He said he knew the ex-rangers and would-be rangers making the accusations against Karstens and flatly rejected their claims against him. Powless, he said, had sought Karstens' job from the very beginning. He said that Powless, whom he described as "indolent," had already approached Judge Cecil Clegg and Matt Carlson, deputy clerk in the U.S. Marshal's Office, for letters of recommendation. Stowe also had little good to say about another ex-ranger. "Colonel McFarland is very quick-tempered and always having had others to command is loath to receive orders from another." He clearly stated that Karstens had fired McFarland because "the Colonel" would not follow orders. Another complainant, "would-be ranger" Rufus Nichols, Stowe dismissed as "always having trouble with the whole population" and his dispute with Karstens had no merit. Stowe said that a fair-minded individual armed with all the information would conclude that the charges against Karstens "have been prompted by spite, revenge or envy."[19]

Similar comments made by Governor Parks supported some of what Stowe alleged. Parks also dismissed McFarland's complaints saying that McFarland himself admitted disobeying orders. He also told the investigators that he personally knew Jon Way and did "not place much credence in an uncorroborated statement from him." Parks also believed that a solution to the controversy would be to move headquarters away from the railroad which would eliminate much of the day-to-day squabbles.[20]

Former Governor Bone, who knew Karstens and "esteemed him highly," said that "petty feuds are not rare, but [are] the rule . . . in remote communities in this Northland." He gave little weight to the charges leveled at Karstens, but suggested that a transfer to Yellowstone or some other park might be a fair solution.[21]

The testimony of prominent Alaskans like Governors Parks and Bone lent credibility to Stowe's letter, which was colored by his long friendship with Karstens. In a startling development, someone in Washington sent a copy of Stowe's letter to Edward McFarland. McFarland fired off a biting rebuttal to Stowe, with copies to the Director, Powless, Kennedy, Sterling, and Nichols. Both Kennedy and Powless confronted Stowe and "in a fit of rage" demanded redress. Stowe refused but did alter, in writing, his comments about Sterling, explaining to Cammerer that he had him confused with another man.

O.A. Waechter also stepped forward in support of Karstens. "We have known [him] for the past fifteen years . . . we believe him to be a fair, honest and capable man . . . we have always found his conduct to be above reproach . . . We believe he will do everything in his power while Superintendent of the Park to further the interests of the National Park . . ."[22]

Investigators learned that Karstens' critics out-numbered his supporters, with some of the harshest criticism coming from the road commission's Colonel Steese. "Karstens is undoubtedly temperamentally unfit to be a National Park Superintendent, or to have responsible and independent charge of any work of any importance. [Karstens has quarreled with all] that he has come in contact with the exception of George Parks and myself . . . and fired everyone who has ever worked for him." He attributed Karstens' trouble to "simple ignorance, or practical illiteracy." Steese clearly exaggerated parts of his testimony. Because Karstens had run away from home at 17 his education was incomplete, but he was not illiterate. He was a man who loved to read and who spent spare moments in bookstores instead of saloons. While he had in fact fired some of his rangers, many left for better pay, prospects, or marriage. Obviously some road workers despised Karstens for his "meddling" in their work, thus perhaps prejudicing Steese's opinion.[23]

In a show of fairness, Steese also rejected some of the charges made by former rangers, pointing out that McFarland, "now a candidate for Karstens' job," had prior difficulty with railroad management when he worked there. Despite some mitigating circumstances Steese believed that Karstens should be replaced, or at the least demoted. "His willingness to work under all sorts of disagreeable living conditions would make him a valuable man, under proper supervision," he concluded. The only solution, a he saw it, was the appointment of an "experienced man from Outside."[24]

The railroad's Noel W. Smith reluctantly agreed that Karstens should be removed. "I have a great deal of sympathy for Mr. Karstens because of the character of the people with whom he has to transact business," Smith wrote. He labeled McFarland, who he had once supervised, as "a complainer and a malcontent." He also castigated Nichols as "an agitator and an admitted defaulter and liar . . . I would not accept anything he says as evidence." Smith also suggested demoting Karstens to ranger and appointing an entirely new person to run the park.[25]

Judge Bunnell agreed with Smith's appraisal of McFarland and that Karstens bore no fault in that affair. Bunnell believed that McFarland's attacks on Karstens were being orchestrated by Duke E. Stubbs, a person Bunnell termed "contemptible."[26]

As the investigation wrapped up, E.W. Nelson, of the Biological Survey, received an anonymous letter, which he passed on to Mather. The letter protested any change in park administration. "Well it looks like they are going to give Karstens the worst of it," the writer said. "After three years of continually dirty work the political pot has stirred things up . . . You know Dr. I hate to see this done if they are going to put Karstens out they may as well close up the park, and open it for hunting . . . "[27]

The majority of those interviewed, while complimentary of Karstens physical prowess, outdoor skills, and knowledge, professed the opinion that Karstens sorely lacked the supervisory or administrative skills necessary to the job. Even a few of Karstens' old friends, interviewed at his request, reiterated some of his negative points. Karstens' personal enemies, however, stopped at nothing, tarnishing him with anonymous, vicious slanders duly recorded by the investigators.[28]

On June 25, the postal inspectors arrived at the park. The investigation was not yet complete but already they had formed their recommendation. "[Inspector] Neil told me there would be a change here," Karstens wrote in his personal journal, "but they would recommend my being transferred to Yellowstone Park. Steese, Bone & Smith recommend it. I am everything—a good, and honest loyal worker. But I don't know politics, which satisfies me, I don't want to."[29]

The final report, authored by Riddiford and Neil, was damning. The aggregate of the testimony repeatedly used terms like "undiplomatic," "aggressive," "pugnacious," and "unfit." Karstens lack of "executive" skills was cited repeatedly. The attack on Jon E. Way was a critical, irrefutable event tarnishing Karstens' defense. "Our personal impression of [Karstens] is that he is a man of little education whose life has been spent almost entirely out of doors and that in a country where he has had to rely upon his own physical ability and resources," wrote the inspectors. "This fact has probably accentuated his fundamentally pugnacious . . . disposition. He impressed us as a man inclined to meet trouble more than half way rather than to avoid it." The final report recommended that Karstens be "placed in some other park under proper supervision [because] . . . he is entitled to some consideration by reason of the fact that he has not had the training which would fit him for the position he is now holding."[30]

With the report in hand, Director Mather now had to make a decision. While pondering his move, Mather received a report from his friend, nature author and novelist Hal G. Evarts, who had made his own inquiries while traveling in Alaska. Evarts said the stories were flat wrong, largely political, and that Karstens "was really a good one." He said that "the sooner Karstens' ideas are put into effect the better for the park." He later sent a follow-up, praising Karstens as an "exceptionally good man." Evarts was highly esteemed in the fledgling conservation movement, with his writing compared to John Muir, Ambrose Briece, and Joaquin Miller. As a result, his opinion carried significant weight.[31]

Charles Sheldon, as expected, forcefully backed Karstens. He wholeheartedly believed that the fearless Karstens was the sole man best suited to protect the park's wildlife. Throughout his life Sheldon never wavered in the defense of his old friend.

Director Mather was simultaneously dealing with a similar, but more public, controversy surrounding Yellowstone Park Superintendent Horace Albright, one of his most trusted confidants. The Senate Committee on the National Park Service had authorized a thorough investigation of Albright based on continuing charges of favoritism and "dictatorial" park management.

Here, too, opponents stopped at nothing to undo the superintendent. Prior to a committee hearing held in Gardiner, Montana, committee counsel George K. Bowden illegally rifled Albright's desk and files looking for damaging documents. "When I arrived [for the hearing] I found that the dozen witnesses the committee counsel had lined up to testify on the management of Yellowstone National Park were all people who had reasons of one sort or another for disliking me personally," Albright said. "They included several bootleggers I had thrown out of the park . . . a disgruntled concessioner, and several former employees," including a doctor that Albright characterized as his "bitterest personal enemy."[32]

After all the committee's witnesses had been heard, Albright took his turn. A lawyer by training, Albright called his own witnesses to rebut the charges.

JAMES GORDON STEESE COLLECTION, #3028351518, DICKINSON COLLEGE

*The Alaska Road Commission was ordered to build a year-around road, over the shortest distance possible, from the railroad to the Kantishna mining district. Major John W. Gotwals, road commission engineer, explored several alternatives for the mountain route through the park.*

In his defense, he spoke to the senators for an hour without interruption. "I have been on trial all morning," he thundered, "with convicted bootleggers, an unreliable doctor, a discharged road foreman, an ex-ranger with a bad record, and other men with personal grievances testifying against me through the convenient method of leading questions from a man who assembled this group of malcontents . . ." Albright ultimately prevailed and a piqued Bowden lamented that he had thought we "had the goods on [Albright], but that nobody had told him that [he] had a legal background and was capable of a quick and clever defense."*[33]

Albright's situation closely paralleled the one at McKinley Park, with one major exception—Karstens never had the opportunity to confront his accusers face to face. In sharp contrast, Albright had "given the committee to understand that if convicted, he wanted it to be on the testimony of men who could themselves stand investigation." Lacking Albright's legal training and gift of oratory, Karstens could only "keep sawing wood" and await his fate. He had long before learned that real trouble could not be erased; only endured.[34]

Director Mather made his decision; both Karstens and Albright would retain their positions. From this decision, it is possible to assume that Mather had decided to keep in place the two men who were doing exactly what he wanted done. Today, we operate on a presumption of the value of the national parks. In the early 20th Century, no such value judgment prevailed; conservation was seen by many as a fad. Mather knew that his staff would be under constant fire from those who saw the parks only as an impediment to personal profit. Conflict went with the job. When Mather ultimately endorsed Harry Karstens, however, he also cautioned him to use restraint in all matters and maintain an unimpeachable conduct.

Decades removed from the controversy, we are left pondering one significant question.

Could any of the other original candidates for superintendent have accomplished as much, with so little, while avoiding similar trouble? Finding the right people to manage the pioneer national parks was never easy. "Superintendents and rangers would have to possess a love of the outdoors that would make them willing to live under rugged, somewhat primitive, and often isolated conditions," Albright explained, "and do it at very low salaries. And they would have to be able to deal effectively with visitors, get along with the concessionaire and the

*Albright, served as the National Park Service's acting director from 1917 to 1919, and director from 1929 to 1933.

owners of private land within park boundaries, and keep peace with political leaders in nearby localities. Training programs would help, but to develop them would take time and funds we did not have."[35]

Critics used terms like "aggressive" and "pugnacious" to describe Karstens. These are accurate terms but such traits were absolutely necessary given the character of the citizenry. A person of mild, retiring disposition would have been steamrolled by the likes of McFarland, Donnelly, and Stubbs. A wildly popular superintendent would have been someone who was not doing his job. As far as Karstens' alleged deficiency of "administrative and executive skills" how critical was that really, given a staff of two and a budget of $11,000? Karstens was fearless, resourceful, and absolutely honest, but also a man of volcanic temper, easily rankled by personal attacks. While he definitely lacked polite skills, he had the toughness and courage to persevere in the face of numerous tribulations, including this withering investigation.

Following Mather's decision, Karstens resumed work on the new headquarters above Rock Creek. Karstens hired Stowe as a temporary ranger, his age preventing a permanent appointment, and put him to work constructing the new facility. The move to Rock Creek was made in late September. "Strenuous activities constructing buildings at the new headquarters . . . carried on late into the night to beat the winter," Karstens informed Mather. "Conveniences we have none. Water has to be carried in, slops carried out, toilets are in the open, bathing has to be done in a wash-tub, etc. These inconveniences are taken with good grace by all . . ." In another letter, he said, "The loyalty and effectiveness of the present Park personnel is [sic] also very gratifying."[36]

Subsequent communiqués from Karstens to Mather emphasized improved community and staff relations. He advised Mather that in the community "no contention of any kind . . . Mr. Rufus Nichols, the trouble maker, has moved away . . . McKinley Park is now a normal community." That winter Governor Parks stopped in Washington to see Mather, and gave Karstens a "splendid endorsement." Mather informed Karstens that he was "particularly pleased with the reports coming in regarding your fine work." He then informed some key Karstens supporters that "it would seem that Mr. Karstens difficulties have been fairly well ironed out."[37]

Despite their heavy workload, rangers found time to conduct poaching patrols along the eastern and northern boundaries. Happily, Karstens could point to increased protection of park wildlife as one of his greatest achievements. "Some seventeen years ago two men visited [the region] and put out poison balls made from sheep fat," he said, and when he passed over their trail a year later, their work "could be traced by bones and decayed carcasses." With protection, the fur-bearing animals had made a comeback from near annihilation. In the winter of 1925–26, one legal trapper secured $4,000 worth of furs outside of the park, owing to the increased animal populations within park boundaries.[38]

Life in the new headquarters was not plush by any means, and still a pioneer endeavor. "We moved into our new home at the new headquarters, and I had my own [small] room," Eugene Karstens recalled. "We had a big stove in the center of the house and our light in the evening came from Aladdin kerosene lamps that used a mantle and gave a nice white light. We had a kitchen, a living room and dining room . . . and a room with a tub and washbowl . . . Mother heated water for these facilities on the stove, so we only took baths as necessary and not each day. Once or twice a week was the norm. We also had a big new two-holer toilet about 39 feet from the house."[39]

In June 1924, the McKinley Park grammar school had graduated its first two students, Denise Abbey and Frances Nichols, but in the autumn of 1925, the school closed for good due to insufficient enrollment. From then on, Eugene Karstens was home-schooled using the Calvert School program. "We got a big box at the beginning of the school year with all the equipment needed for the whole year broken down into daily classes by the calendar," he said. "Each week I would mail my lessons in and sometimes the following month I would get the corrected papers back all graded with an attached paper of comments on my work."[40]

Despite the primitive living conditions, Harry Karstens always had one ranger he could count on, his wife Louise. As Grant Pearson explained, "the park office was first housed in a tent . . . the water system consisted of a pair of husky water buckets . . . Baths were taken in a wash tub, the water being heated on a stove." Few people were willing to live like this, yet Louise seemed to cope.[41]

The Rock Creek site was warmer and sunnier than Riley Creek and controlled vehicle access into the park. Starting over was not easy, but the headquarters move eventually improved everyone's quality of life. Next, Karstens needed to find quality rangers to carry out his mandate to protect the park's wildlife.

In Nyberg, Karstens had found an ideal field ranger, but finding others seemed a daunting quest. "Men who can stand the isolation and the hardships of the trail," he later wrote, "are very hard to find and after a few weeks trial do not always show up as well as might be and their resignations are then requested." Nyberg agreed with him, saying that "when rangers quit it was because of their dislike for the solitude."[42]

HENRY P. KARSTENS COLLECTION, #4092, KARSTENS LIBRARY

*Colonel James Gordon Steese, head of the road commission, was, for a time, the most powerful government man in Alaska. He and Karstens skirmished over construction details of the park road, with Steese complaining to Washington about Karstens "meddling." His testimony during a government investigation nearly ended Karstens tenure as Superintendent.*

Karstens thought that many Alaskans had a "peculiar disposition . . . They are of a transient nature—deciding to accumulate a few hundred dollars and turn prospector or travel to other parts of the country," he wrote. "The older men, who know this country well, in few cases desire to settle down to a job for the year round. They would rather work in the summer and hibernate into their cabins in the winter. This latter type of man is by far the more preferable in the capacity of rangers, it takes too much time to be continually breaking in young men to mush dogs, to keep warm in the open spaces and familiarize them with the use of a saw and square and the caring of stock. The older man understands these things."[43]

The hiring of a new ranger in 1926 would finally give Karstens his team of ideal rangers, men up to the challenges of extending the rule of law throughout the park, all the way to, and beyond, the Kantishna.

# 15

# THE RANGER IDEAL

ON A CLEAR, BITTERLY COLD DAY in late December 1924, ranger Fritz Nyberg drove his dogteam out onto what appeared to be the solid ice of Savage River. Halfway across the river, his sled broke through plunging him and his dogs into numbing, thigh-deep overflow. His moccasins skidded on the underlying ice and he plunged to the waist in the freezing water. At -30°F he had just minutes to act before his limbs began to freeze.

Weighted down by his sodden clothing, he struggled to his feet and pushed with all his strength. He yanked the sled side-to-side trying to break it free. He found his whip and cracked it over the dogs, yelling in a ragged voice, "Hike! Hike! Or we all are gonna die."

Time and again the dogs lurched forward but the sled remained stuck in the rapidly refreezing water. Nyberg knew that if he didn't act fast the sled would be locked irretrievably in place. Desperate now, he slogged to the side of the sled and tore at the lashings. With numbing hands and feet he carried load after load to solid ice. Finally, he yelled a last frantic "*Hike!*" and the sled lurched free.

Once back on the trail, and leaving the gear behind, he drove the dogs hard for the nearby patrol cabin. He slung open the door and mushed the team right inside, unhooking the sled at the door. He slammed the door shut and soon had a hot fire crackling in the stove. As the cabin warmed, Nyberg tore off his clothing and was soon as bare as his dogs, the cabin filling with steam and the smell of wet dog hair. It took him two full hours to warm up and recover from his near miss. He had escaped frostbite, or even death, still had all his fingers and toes, his dogs were safe, and he had a warm sheltering cabin to huddle in. It was a close call, and Nyberg was lucky to have survived.[1]

Working as a ranger in Alaska's wilderness park demanded finely-honed skill and courage. Some of McKinley Park's pioneer rangers were without peer in America's fledgling ranger corps. It took Harry Karstens years to assemble the right men and develop them into a formidable force.

Following the creation of the National Park Service in 1916, Director Stephen Mather wrote and distributed regulations that set qualifications and standards, and mandated a unique uniform, including the military's distinctive campaign hat. Ranger applicants had to be between 21 and 40 years of age, possess a grade school education, be of good character, have sound health, and possess outdoor experience. They, like their cavalry predecessors, had to be proficient with horses and firearms. Some knowledge of trail construction and fighting forest fires was also essential.

Horace Albright sent out a form letter to all rangers that read: "The duties are exacting and require the utmost patience and tact at all times. A ranger's job is no place for a nervous, quick-tempered man, or for the laggard, or for one who is unaccustomed to hard work." In 1926, Karstens, drawing on his own hard-learned lessons, added to the basic directives. He told his rangers to "always be courteous but fearless in the execution of their duty and never to lose their temper or bring in a personal element into such matters as come within their duties." He offered one caveat to Albright's comment about patience and tact. "When a man drives dogs he is not held accountable for his language."[2]

Most applicants did not seek the job for the money. In 1923, starting pay began at $1000 per year, with the possibility of working up to $1,320. (When rangers came under the purview of the Civil Service Commission in 1926, their salaries increased to $2,400 per year.) Rangers also had to buy their own uniforms and food. In short, rangers endured hard work, long hours, and high risk, all for low pay. Albright, the service's second director, called park rangers " . . . one of the most romantic figures in life."[3]

In McKinley Park, mastery of outdoor skills meant the difference not just in successful law enforcement, but for survival itself. "Mushing and traveling on snowshoes is an accomplishment which is not possessed by all applicants," Karstens explained. "Care must be taken before a man is employed to be sure that he is able to handle dogs on the trail and can thoroughly take care of himself in the hills . . . but a man also must have the stamina to stand up under the strain of mushing long distances, for as it has been expressed by those who know, a man driving a dogteam is sometimes the biggest dog himself."[4]

In 1924, Karstens sent temporary (i.e., "probationary") ranger Nyberg on extended patrol. When Nyberg returned three months later, he was promptly sent out for another three months. When he came back from the second trip, Karstens offered him a permanent position with a raise of $50 a month. "Harry simply said 'you can't leave now!'" Nyberg recalled.[5]

Two years after his "temporary" appointment, Fritz Nyberg was promoted to Chief Ranger, upon which he promptly moved into the new chief ranger's cabin. "Regarding Ranger Nyberg, I cannot say too much . . . he has energy and spirit and his whole heart is in his work," Karstens reported. "Time, weather, or distance has no reckoning with Fritz."[6]

Despite the isolation and long cold winters, Nyberg seemed to thrive. Daily, he displayed incredible stamina. "Ranger Nyberg arrived at headquarters from Toklat River, making the trip in one day, a distance of 53 miles," said Karstens. While on patrol, Nyberg delighted in watching wildlife, especially sheep and wolves. "Ranger Nyberg reported that a male wolf became affectionately attached to himself and his team of dogs on December 3, and was in his company continually until December 24. On one trip the grayish-yellow wolf followed him from Sanctuary River to the western part of the park. Ranger Nyberg became so attached to it, that he stated he did not feel justified in killing it.

FRITZ NYBERG COLLECTION, #B75-134-36, ALASKA MUSEUM AT RASMUSON CENTER

*Bo'sun begs for a snack from Fritz Nyberg. The park's first Chief Ranger was indefatigable on patrol and annually covered more backcountry miles than any other ranger. In 1926 he patrolled a total of 3198 miles—2365 by dogteam, 833 miles on foot.*

"This incident proves conclusively that though there may be a few wolves in the park, they are not of a ferocious nature and consequently not dangerous to travelers," Karstens wrote. Nyberg's wolf would sometimes bed down within six feet of his dogteam which ignored it. That winter, Nyberg's "pet" followed him down the Toklat and out of the park. Barking dogs lured the wolf to Jim Burrows' camp where it was shot. "I missed him . . . really did miss him." Nyberg recalled.[7]

Nyberg counted and studied the sheep that he saw, including a herd he estimated at over a thousand. Unlike his contemporaries, Nyberg did not blame wolves for exaggerated sheep and caribou depredations. "Wolves done no damage in the park," he said years later.[8]

At Windy Creek on October 2, 1926, Nyberg recorded the first sighting ever of a bald eagle in the park A year earlier, he and Ranger Armstrong had seen two coyotes in the park, also a first, which triggered alarm in Karstens. "It is hoped that these animals do not get a hold on this country," he said.[9]

Nyberg counted very few moose in the eastern part of the park, but found many more on the flats bordering the Kantishna River. He said that moose began

## REINDEER, WOLVES, AND PORCUPINES

IN THE PARK'S EARLY YEARS, rangers and other area residents targeted certain species for elimination or reduction. The large reindeer herd that was grazed through the park in 1922 left strays behind. After conferring with biologist Olaus Murie, Harry Karstens ordered that these animals be shot on sight. "The white reindeer will be eradicated whenever found [within the park limits], for these animals will greatly depreciate the numbers and deteriorate the quality of our woodland caribou." Over the years, rangers killed several reindeer and at least two caribou by mistake. Government herders rounded up small bands of reindeer and led them out of the park.

Beginning in 1922, porcupines were designated "nuisance animals." "Porcupine are very thick throughout the park and are destroying trees, they should be exterminated . . . as they are chewing the bark off large numbers of trees and thereby killing them." Karstens reported "a great deal of damage done to the spruce trees in the vicinity of Mile 3 by these destructive pests . . . As the timber is somewhat scarce in this park and reforestation is very slow in germinating, it is thought that some action will have to be taken to rid certain localities of porcupine." By 1927, porcupines had "ruined acres of spruce trees . . . porcupine have now been declared outlaws and open season exists on them," with a policy of killing them on sight. The damage to trees in the so-called "porcupine forest" near the Toklat River was first noted in the 1920s.

to increase in the eastern part of the park only after railroad completion and the start of park road construction. "The Alaska Road Commission camps, first thing they did was set fire to woods to get rid of the mosquitoes," he explained. Plant growth in the wake of these wild fires created excellent forage for moose.[10]

Like his boss, Nyberg proved indefatigable, over his career annually logging the most patrol miles of any ranger. In 1926, when he became chief ranger, he covered 2,911 total miles. The next year, he traveled 3,198 miles—2,365 by dogteam, 833 miles on foot. "The patrol mileage figures prove conclusively what occurs when good and trustworthy rangers are on patrol," Karstens wrote. "Uncomplaining trips are the result of having qualified men on the personnel."[11]

One of Nyberg's biggest "adventures" occurred in 1925, when Karstens sent him and Ranger Armstrong, a former railroad surveyor, to bring back the park dogs from a summer fish camp on the Tanana River. Fishwheels, a type of fish trap invented by Alaska Natives, were used to catch large numbers of migrating king and chum salmon. Fresh fish were sold in town but many more were split, dried, and bundled for sale as dog food. A few of these fishermen summered sled dogs and fed them fish directly from the river.

A bark beetle infestation may have killed off the trees that were damaged and weakened by gnawing porcupines.

Wolves and coyotes were also deemed detrimental and killed when encountered. Rangers saw the first two coyotes in the park in 1925. Later, Karstens wrote that "numbers of wolves have been seen and heard . . . for the first time since protection was established in the park . . . If they are found to be increasing too fast, means will be found to get rid of them." Just after Christmas that year, Karstens shot and killed a wolf near headquarters.

"From 1921 to 1927, the wolves in the park were not many but are becoming alarmingly plentiful and causing considerable havoc among our game. The coyote has introduced himself in the past three years and is multiplying fast." Karstens said in 1928. After he resigned, concession staff killed three wolves near Savage Camp. In 1929, Superintendent Liek reported that "there are a few wolves and coyotes but we are doing everything possible to exterminate them. I have classed the wolverine as a predatory animal from what I could observe last winter, as they took a larger toll from the sheep than the wolves and coyotes did."

In June 1931, Rangers Wallace Anderson and Lee Swisher were sent into the hills to kill wolves and coyotes in their dens. They found one wolf den and dug out five pups, three of which were spared, and taken to the kennels to be bred later with the park's sled dogs. "It is doubtful if a satisfactory result can be attained, owing to the wildness and ferocity of the breed." Predator control in the park lasted through the early 1950s.

On November 3, two days after leaving headquarters, Nyberg wired Karstens from Fairbanks telling him that the Tanana River was still running with ice, rendering the fish camp twenty-four miles downstream inaccessible. In response, Karstens told him to wait it out but to send Armstrong back to McKinley Station. A few days later an ice jam flooded the land around the fish camp, further complicating things.

Anxious to retrieve the dogs and begin winter patrols, Nyberg sought suggestions from steamer captains and river pilots but they all advised him to wait. They told him that the running ice, combined with high water, made a river crossing too dangerous, perhaps even suicidal, to attempt. Nyberg then consulted by phone with his boss, who, in great detail, described a possible, but risky way to the fish camp.

Nyberg set out early the next morning, and after wading through flooded timber and river channels sluggish with ice, found an ice bridge across the main channel. In dim twilight, he gingerly stepped out onto the clear ice, dark swirling water visible beneath his feet. At each step, the ice flexed and undulated—if it broke, he'd be plunged into the frigid water with little way out. Tense moments later he reached the far shore, and staggered into the fish camp long after dark.

"On his trip downriver he managed to cross the river on a very flimsy ice jam," Karstens reported, "and then worked his way downstream mostly through the willows to the fish camp." The next day, Nyberg hooked 12 dogs to a sled and headed upriver, cutting a trail through the willows for several miles. Far upstream, he re-crossed the newly frozen river. "Crossing the ice with them was a dangerous business," Karstens said, "as he could shove a pole through the ice most anywhere."[12]

Fully two weeks after leaving headquarters, Nyberg returned with the dogs. In his usual fashion, Nyberg went right to work repairing sleds and harnesses, and assembling clothing for his winter assignment, a two-to-three month patrol. With over a ton of supplies to move over an unbroken trail, Nyberg did not tarry but left headquarters on Thanksgiving Day.

Besides stalking poachers, Nyberg also studied the feasibility of various park development schemes. One year, he mushed through Anderson Pass onto the West Fork Glacier, pioneering what Karstens hoped would be a route which summer tourists could take with dog teams to view the "hidden beauties of the Alaska Range from an altitude of many thousands of feet."[13]

While the robust Chief Ranger made his rounds, new employees were hired to do office work and camp chores. Ralph P. Mackie, a former World War I aviator, was hired in 1925 as the park's first clerk, "bringing to the Park Service a fund of constructive ideas that will add greatly to the service . . ."[14]

Mackie worked well with Louise Karstens, tackling mountains of routine paperwork and correspondence. Mackie wrote budgets and drafted the elevations and floor plans for new buildings. He assisted Karstens with carpentry, logging, and animal care. Mackie and his pregnant wife lived in a tent until the clerk's cabin was finished in late September.

"On March 25, 1926, a son was born to Mr. and Mrs. Ralph P. Mackie," Karstens noted in his log. "Mrs. Mackie had gone to the hospital in Fairbanks for the event but the honor is conceded to her for having the first baby born to an employee in Mt. McKinley National Park during their actual service here."[15]

The following Christmas, with the Karstens family Outside, and all the rangers on patrol, acting superintendent Mackie and his family celebrated the holiday alone. "It seemed very befitting to the Christmas season and yuletide spirits that lots of snow should fall during the month and cold, crisp weather prevail," Mackie wrote. "It was nearly complete—snow, cold weather, reindeer (or rather caribou!) but not Santa Claus. [The absence of everyone] made the headquarters camp a very much isolated and quiet place."[16]

A ranger's wilderness life was not for everyone; the turnover rate high. Beginning in 1925, six rangers came and went in little more than a year's time. Albert L. Winn's short stay was typical. "Ranger Winn is proving up fine and I believe he will run Nyberg a close second, though not having the experience Nyberg has or the knowledge of the park," Karstens said. "He is always ready to go, uses his head well and I am sure he is using Nyberg's work as an example. Such friendly rivalry gives interest and high hopes for ranger Winn." On one memorable occasion, Nyberg and Winn teamed up to apprehend miner Frank Giles at Copper Mountain with eight caribou in his possession. Winn, however, soon disappointed Karstens by resigning after spending just half a winter at the park. "This isn't the life I want," he explained. "I'm going back to California."[17]

Winn's short stay, however, resulted in a fortuitous connection. In Fairbanks, in the autumn of 1925, Winn and Ranger Lee Swisher met a *Cheechako* named Grant Pearson. Pearson, who had grown up in Michigan, had come north that spring on the *S.S. Alaska*. He found immediate employment with the road commission, which was then widening a section of the Richardson Trail. Pearson, influenced by the writings of Jack London, Rex Beach, and Robert Service, aspired to a life described by Ernest Gruening: "In Alaska a man or a woman is judged not by family, means or previous stateside condition, but by what he is and can do in Alaska."[18]

HENRY P. KARSTENS COLLECTION, #735, KARSTENS LIBRARY

*Ranger Grant Pearson quickly proved himself on a solo winter patrol. He flourished in isolation and built several ranger patrol cabins, including this one, the Kantishna Ranger Station at Big Timber. He and Nyberg expanded law enforcement west to include the Kantishna region, providing the first real protection for wildlife in that area.*

In February 1926, Pearson received a letter from Winn urging him to apply for the position of temporary ranger. "The pay isn't great—$140 a month, and you buy your own provisions—but the way I've heard you talk this is the life for you . . ." Following the successful relocation of park headquarters, Karstens intended to step up poaching patrols to protect the two most vulnerable sections of the park, the Kantishna and the Windy Creek area, and he needed another ranger.[19]

Pearson promptly applied for the job and reported for duty on February 4, 1926. Karstens greeted Pearson when he stepped down from the train at McKinley Station. "You're hired as a temporary ranger," Karstens said, "and what . . . 'temporary' means is, you're on trial."[20]

Winn became Pearson's mentor and taught him about sled dogs and what was expected of him. "In winter the boss figures our job is to . . . patrol . . . keeping a mean eye out for poachers," Winn told Pearson. "He does a lot of it himself. I think that's what he likes most, prowling around out in the wild country . . . but he demands a lot of a fellow . . . You have to keep humping, and you have to be smart."[21]

Pearson bunked with Ranger Swisher, an experienced musher and trapper, and natural history expert. Swisher excelled as a ranger and enjoyed a friendly rivalry with Nyberg, vying to see who could travel the most miles in the fiercest weather. Although it was not yet obvious to Karstens, in Swisher, Pearson, and Nyberg, he had found three extraordinarily capable rangers.

After only one training patrol, Pearson was assigned the Windy Creek and Riley Creek sector. "Grant, this will be a trial trip, a real test for you," he quoted Karstens as saying. "But don't worry about it. You'll make it if you use your head." Pearson, burdened by a 50-pound backpack, slogged thirty miles through deep snow and reached the safety of the Windy Creek cabin long after dark. That trip forever banished all of his romantic notions of a ranger's life. "It was dark. I was lost. I was up to my knees in wet snow," Pearson said. "My feet were wet, and the thermometer was well on the lower side of zero."[22]

Karstens was pleased with Pearson's initial efforts. "His first day he left headquarters with his bedding and 10 days of food on his back and snow-shoed through to Windy Creek Ranger Station in one day. His reports show exceedingly good travel and I feel confident of the best patrol in that section while Pearson is stationed there; though he is only temporary for a few months, I have let him know that in all probability there is a permanent job waiting for him after July 1st, providing he makes good and I believe he is doing it."[23]

"He will hike all of his patrols on snowshoes," Karstens announced. By the end of the first month, Pearson had covered 214 miles. "Pearson has started out with a bang," Karstens wrote, "and with a determination to make good." Pearson's April log reflected his unflagging energy, covering 20 miles by dogteam, 40 miles by snowshoes and 96 miles on foot, all during spring breakup conditions.[24]

Like most outdoorsmen of the era, Pearson found the idea of total land and wildlife protection a new concept to grapple with. "I'd always figured that animals grew to be killed and used for food," he wrote. "It wasn't until a considerable time later that I came to actually believe" in total protection.[25]

When Winn resigned, Karstens hired Pearson to fill the vacated permanent slot, a decision that pleased the chief ranger. "Grant was twice as good as any of us on the trail. He could walk five miles an hour, on a trot," Nyberg said.[26]

More than once Pearson demonstrated Nyberg's view of an ideal ranger. "When overtaken by blizzards and storms, there is nothing to do but keep pushing ahead and trusting to luck to reach the next cabin safely," Nyberg wrote. "This month, Ranger Pearson was overtaken by a blizzard while traveling from Toklat to Copper Mountain. There is no shelter and no firewood there and Pearson had to return 17 miles to Toklat in the dark and storm, feeling his way back over the [out-going] tracks, before the storm had covered them up."[27]

"Rangers must travel alone," he added, "and must stop where night overtakes them. A spruce tree is the best shelter to be found, while in some barren sections it is difficult to find enough willow for firewood. Mushing through overflows on the creeks and getting wet and then being forced to spend the night in the open in 20 to 30 below weather [is all part of the job.]" Pearson was quickly mastering the job.[28]

"Pearson was a bull of a man and his physical prowess incalculable," said one friend. "Where others might fear to tread, Grant plunged ahead. There was no holding him back when getting into trouble." More than once Pearson's formidable strength got him out of a jam. Conversely, it also got him into predicaments that more prudent men might have avoided.[29]

Once while en route from the upper Toklat patrol cabin to the lower cabin, Pearson plunged into overflow, soaking his legs to the knees. "This is the one danger that all Alaskans dread on the trail in winter—that of becoming wet with a possibility of freezing before they reach a cabin," he explained. Pearson cut the dogs loose and on foot raced madly for the cabin still several miles away. He made it to safety, the temperature -24°F.[30]

Even when rangers traveled together, danger lurked at every turn of the trail. One winter while attempting to cross the Alaska Range a mile east of Anderson Pass, Nyberg and Pearson were suddenly enveloped in dense clouds that obscured the way ahead. While descending from a high ridge, Nyberg's lead dog stopped abruptly in the gray mist and refused to move. Nyberg tipped his sled on its side and warily edged ahead of the team. What he saw through a brief break in the clouds sent a flash of fear up his spine. "My leader had stopped on the edge of a drop of about 1,000 feet," Nyberg said.[31]

By mid-1926, the park staff had grown to six, including a temporary ranger and "special ranger" Louise Karstens. Karstens received $3,600 per year, Mackie $2,400, Nyberg $2,400, and Grant Pearson $1,800. Mrs. Karstens received $1.00 a month, a total of $12 a year.[32]

Eugene Karstens recalled his mother's social contribution to park affairs.

"Mother, on the other hand, provided another aspect to our life at the Park Headquarters," he wrote. "She had to—at times—be prepared to feed in our house, small groups of dignitaries from cabinet officers to National Park Service Headquarters officials from Washington D.C. They all came to see Father's miracle—a national park in the wilds of Alaska.

"But they never expected to get the kind of meal that Mother prepared for them in the wilderness, served on good china and fine crystal in a log house on a homebuilt table. Mother would serve fresh vegetables from our garden, either wild or domestic meat, usually a big piece of apple pie with homemade ice cream. The whole meal was topped off with homemade sourdough bread or wild cranberry jelly, or blueberry pie or garden-grown strawberries or raspberries."[33]

Despite the growth in staff, and a full ten years after the park was established, market hunting remained an on-going threat to park wildlife. During the winter of 1926, Nyberg reported "wholesale breaking of rules" with extensive trapping and hunting in the park, with some animals killed solely for dog food. He witnessed the aftermath of large sheep slaughters on Stony Creek and the Toklat River. After one patrol, Nyberg reported that Natives from Nenana were trapping and hunting well up the Toklat River both for subsistence and for meat to sell in Fairbanks. The U.S. Commissioner singled out ex-warden Jim Burrows and miner Ed Jern as two men to make examples of "for they have killed for the market and dog feed . . ."[34]

Because of the size and physical character of the park, poachers easily eluded Karstens and his rangers. Acting on hunches and rare complaints, they found carcasses but made few arrests. "People living here deem it a crime to give evidence against illegal hunting," Karstens explained. "They admit it should be stopped, but are reluctant to give evidence." A few prospectors despised market hunting but exempted themselves from regulation.[35]

Karstens felt the only way to stop the illegal hunting was to close the loophole that allowed prospectors to hunt in the park. Separating genuine prospectors from those who used the special exemption as a cover for illegal activities had frustrated him from the beginning. NPS Director Stephen Mather agreed: "This privilege has been abused, and unless the residents of that section can be appealed to for a fuller observance of the law there is no satisfactory solution [except complete game protection]." According to Karstens, the honest miners "are very eager to comply in every way with the laws governing this park." On the other hand, he mentioned a prospector's camp where "there are numbers of caribou and sheep horns around the camp. [Yet] there is no prospecting around this camp . . . his mining ground is 20 to 30 miles westward."[36]

Karstens singled out Joe Quigley and John Anderson as "the type of prospectors who abide by all the park rules and regulations. It is only wished that the other prospectors in and around the park were of the same caliber. Their sympathy is with the park service in the preservation of the wild animal life."[37]

The proliferation of so-called "prospecting cabins," really nothing more than trapping and hunting camps, also alarmed Karstens. He suggested that burning the "numerous cabins located on numerous creeks" would be one way to eliminate much of the poaching. He said, however, that enforcement of any park regulations had to be done "very careful . . . as [locals] have an exalted idea of a bone-fide prospector's rights."[38]

Director Mather consulted with Governor Parks, who recommended a permit system for cabin building and logging. "I believe it would be a mistake to destroy any of the cabins," he said. "In a country of that kind it is never wise . . . because the location of most of the cabins are so widely known that men will sometimes travel miles in the hopes of finding shelter and it may mean the loss of life to remove one." Instead he suggested limits on green timber cutting but "there should be no objection to cutting and removing the dead and down timber . . ."[39]

In the late 1920s, with fox pelts selling for fabulous sums, trapping pressure in and near the park increased dramatically. In 1927, Nyberg reported "three times as many trappers on the park boundaries as usual . . . 35 to 40 trappers on the east and north boundary." Each of these trappers used small dog teams which were fed game meat. "Seven dogs will eat a sheep in one day and a caribou will only last two days," Karstens said. "It would be a conservative estimate that 30 sheep or 15 caribou are consumed each day by those trappers and their dogs."[40]

In addition, Nyberg reported that "the majority of trappers will remain near the boundary this summer and will keep their dogs, which will put more inroads on moose, sheep and caribou. In the wintertime they can get 40 to 50 caribou on a single hunt and freeze the carcasses, but in the summer time each trapper with seven dogs will shoot a caribou every other day."[41]

In 1927, territorial game wardens caught Slim Carlson illegally trapping north of the park and also cited him for killing a cow moose out of season. He was indicted for two violations of the Alaska Game Law. "Upon his trial he was found guilty on six counts and fined with costs aggregating $1,000 and his pelts confiscated. He had also been in the habit of using from 9 to 12 dogs in his team and was ordered by the game commission to use only 5 hereafter. The reason for this was the commission concluded that a man of his caliber did not require that many dogs and that such a large team was a bad drain on the wild animal life which he no doubt killed for dog-food," Karstens reported.[42]

"This type of 'prospector' is not wanted in this country as his operations are detrimental to the wildlife and also to the morale of others (though remunerative to the territorial treasury!). It is to be hoped that restrictions may be placed on such individuals while prospecting within the park. It may also be said in this case, that [I] had visited this man's 'prospecting' camp in the park about two years ago and therein found stretching boards [for fur], moose horns and other evidence of illegal hunting and trapping. Chief Ranger Nyberg also picked up a trapline, which it was conclusively found to belong to the same Mr. Carlson," Karstens said.[43]

Violators who used poison baits were even harder to catch than poachers using snares and traps. "[One problem] is the use of poison to procure fur-bearing animals in the park. It is a well known fact that trappers, in the central and western portion of this park, are resorting to this means of obtaining their catch," Karstens said. "A solution to this problem must be found in the near future."[44]

The Alaska Game Commission, created by the comprehensive Alaska Game Law of 1925, promulgated a regulation closing the prospectors' loophole: "Nothing in these regulations shall be construed to permit the taking at any time of any game animal, game bird, or fur-bearing animal in Mount McKinley National Park . . ." The new rule was soon voided, however, because the "miner's exemption" could be repealed only by congressional action. Three more years would pass before the loophole was finally eliminated.[45]

Undaunted, Karstens' three rangers carried out a vigorous schedule of patrols. By the end of February 1926, the rangers had covered 5,161 trail miles. For these strenuous, extended forays into the wilderness, rangers picked their dogs for strength rather than speed. Nyberg's team averaged 100 pounds and subsisted on dried salmon, rice and corn meal mush. Sled loads sometimes topped 1,000 pounds.

At first, rangers camped out in pre-positioned wall tents, but as the years rolled by they built strategically-placed patrol cabins. Elevated caches at Savage, Igloo, Toklat, Stony Creek, and Kantishna Gateway protected gear and food from weather, bears, and other hungry wildlife.

Karstens habitually lamented the necessity of using rangers as laborers, which cut into their patrol schedules. Despite having patrolled a combined 11,637 miles over the winter of 1926–27, his rangers filled their "spare" time with construction projects. Both Nyberg and Pearson helped build several

DENA #4-55, DENALI NATIONAL PARK & PRESERVE, MUSEUM COLLECTION

*Before construction of patrol cabins, rangers relied on wall tents for shelter. When sudden storms caught them in the open, they bundled up in their sleds or dug snow caves for protection. In the winter of 1924-5, Fritz Nyberg patrolled from the Toklat River ranger camp.*

headquarters structures. Although Nyberg said it was "fun to build cabins," he added that building them "really wasn't ranger work." Disputes over manual labor often fractured the relationship between the rangers and their boss. "Both supers [Karstens and, later, Harry Liek] wanted rangers to build things and they felt it really wasn't there job," recalled Bill Myers.[46]

Grant Pearson seemed to thrive in isolation. While Nyberg and Karstens guided Director Mather into the park in 1926, Pearson was at Big Timber building the 10'x12' Kantishna Gateway patrol cabin. He also helped build another on the McKinley River near Copper Mountain, cutting and hauling 150 logs by dogteam from the closest timber, 20 miles away. "Freighting the logs, roof poles, and firewood [took the] men nearly a month," Karstens explained. This cabin was built as both a patrol shelter and a base to monitor the nearby mining activity.[47]

The patrol cabins were few and widely scattered, and help was non-existent. "Patrolling the park is a man's job," Mather wrote, "the wilderness no place for the incompetent or incapable." The exploits of pioneer rangers engendered a unique ethos. "By tracking poachers and hunting varmints through the winter cold," wrote historian Theodore Catton, "the park ranger would seem to have made a suitable reincarnation of the fabled hunter-tracker of the frontier myth." In short, legions of youthful admirers saw park rangers as the embodiment of Daniel Boone and Kit Carson, fearless and tenacious in the protection of national treasures.[48]

In reality, not all rangers were expert outdoorsmen. For example, Karstens once assigned Eugene "Dinty" Moore to deliver the mail to the patrol camps. Moore chose his team from the unwanted dogs left in the kennel. "Huffy, though just a young dog, had as nasty a temper as I've ever seen," Moore said. "On this trip he ran true to form, causing more trouble than a porcupine in a sleeping bag . . . I trusted to my leader to pick the right trail . . . He thought that 'Whoa' meant an extra burst of speed. When I said 'Haw' he would look over his right shoulder and grin . . . when I said 'Gee' he would look over his left shoulder and keep moving straight ahead. When I said 'All right, mush, you blankety blank' he would come running back to the sled."[49]

"The dogs saw sheep on the (Sable Pass) ridges and tore down the [ice-covered] creek at a mad gallop. The brake was useless . . . I crashed into willows at every turn . . . If my eye had not connected with a stump, my momentum [when thrown off the sled] would have carried me through the snow drift." When Moore finally caught up with the rangers, they kidded him about his shiner and the "caribou stampede" that had destroyed all the willows along the trail.[50]

With an almost endless work load, rangers eagerly welcomed volunteers. Bill Myers was the 17-year-old son of Michigan newspaper publisher Harry Myers, a confidante of Stephen Mather's. The young Myers spent 13 months helping the rangers. Karstens first met Bill and Harry in 1926, and offered Bill a job when he graduated from high school. Consequently young Myers, just 5'1" and 105-pounds, was sent north for a year to "build up" before university. While at the park, Myers grew six inches and gained weight. He learned quickly and assisted rangers in all their duties. Karstens described him as pleasant, likeable, and "a natural for the job."[51]

In addition to law enforcement, animal care, and construction, rangers also occasionally escorted visitors into the park. Nyberg guided author Hal Evarts on an extended trip. Evarts' glowing account of this trip, which appeared in the *Saturday Evening Post*, included an insightful observation: "All national parks, in their infancy, were viewed as white elephants by the surrounding communities. The millions that now visit them annually shed such a crop of tourist dollars . . . that they are viewed as commercial assets of the tremendous value; to such an extent, in fact, that instead of their former struggle for existence, there is now a veritable deluge of bids for new national and state parks from all communities that are desirous of reaping a share of the tourist expenditures."[52]

Both Karstens and Nyberg guided Director Mather on his August 1926 park inspection trip, with logistical support provided by the staff of the McKinley Park Tourist and Transportation Company. Karstens and Nyberg led the group by horseback to Igloo, Sable, Polychrome, East Fork, Thorofare and Copper Mountain, where they turned around. The party traveled down the Toklat to Sheldon's old cabin. They then crossed a low pass to Stony Creek, ascended its right fork to the head of Moose Creek, and looped back to Copper Mountain.

Just as he had done in his other stints as a guide, Karstens provided a remarkable, first-class adventure. He knew what needed to be done and did it. "Harry had a few tricks of his own . . . but his were mostly a complete and flowing efficiency in the routine of outdoor living," Pearson said.[53]

The excursion gave Mather not only a chance to see the park but also time to confer with Karstens and concessionaire James Galen, an old acquaintance. Later, Mather spoke of the "wonderful cooperation" existing between the two men.[54]

Afterward, at the Tanana Valley Fair in Fairbanks, Mather gave a speech "quite enthusiastic in praise of the park." In interviews, he said that in time the park would attract numerous people willing to "rough it, especially the tourist who will be attracted to McKinley Park because of its wilderness appeal."[55]

At the end of the 1927 tourist season, which saw 651 visitors to the park, Karstens went into the field for a month, ostensibly to locate the site for a permanent hotel near Copper Mountain. He visited Pearson and Swisher who were working on patrol cabins. He inspected the newly built McLeod Creek cabin and helped build log kennels at Toklat, Stony Creek, and Kantishna Gateway.

In May 1928, the U.S. Congress finally repealed the miner's hunting provision. Poachers could no longer claim bogus prospector rights—without exception, hunting and trapping were prohibited throughout the park. Now Karstens had the legal authority, and staff, to fully protect the park. "The personnel of the present ranger force are fine specimen of outdoor men," Karstens wrote. "They are all loyal, trustworthy, efficient, and use their initiative to a good advantage and deserve high commendation for their lonely and hazardous life in the 'farthest north' national park."[56]

COURTESY OF CANDY WAUGAMAN

*Rangers relied on a good dog team and a well-trained lead dog to transport them safely through the wilderness. Thin ice, fierce winds, and sub-zero temperatures were constant hazards of the trail.*

HARPER'S FERRY COLLECTION, #0200, NATIONAL PARK SERVICE

*In 1926, Harry Karstens (l), guided Stephen T. Mather, Director of the National Park Service, through the park, with an important stop at Charles Sheldon's 1907–08 Toklat River cabin.*

By spring, rangers had patrolled over 10,000 miles on foot and by dogteam. May was beautiful with little snow. "There were no great extremes of cold [this winter]," Karstens wrote, "and to the people here at headquarters, it meant a new lease of life to observe the days grow longer and patches of bare ground emerge from under the white mantle of snow. The long winter was at last making way for the birth of a new spring." Thanks to men of purpose, courage, and character, the park was beginning to live up to its full potential, complete protection of its wildlife resources a growing reality.[57]

# 16

# Building the Highline

"Here was this old Ford flatbed, over-loaded with barrels of gasoline and equipment of various kinds, heading up one of the steepest sections leading to Polychrome summit," recalled road worker Pete Bagoy, "when for some reason—probably over-heating—the driver stopped, set the hand brake and got out. The next thing you knew the truck started rolling backward and before long picked up enough speed to be fairly flying—and at the first curve flying it did, right off that 800′ cliff!

"When it struck the lower rocks a glancing blow, it somersaulted and came down in splinters. Oh, the foreman was mad! Fired the kid on the spot. I think he was angrier over the incineration of our mail which was in the truck rather than the loss of the truck itself."[1]

By fits and starts, by human error and effort, each year the park road inched westward. A lack of a clear vision as to what the road would become and where it would go, coupled with inadequate funding hampered both construction and park tourism. Climate, soils, topography, unpredictable weather, and shortages of money and material, conspired to slow construction. The project, however brought an influx of people to McKinley Station, supported local businesses, spurred some new mining, and opened new areas for visitor exploration. The physical challenges involved in the actual building of the road also complicated Superintendent Harry Karstens' already difficult task.

From the very beginning, Karstens had pushed for a road into the heart of the park, calling it the "most urgent need" in the park's development. Early on, he proposed a road from McKinley Station that would wend west along Maurice Creek and Jenny Creek, then cross the Savage River to the Sanctuary River. In his plan, the road would then continue west across the Teklanika, lead through Sable Pass, bridge the East Fork, traverse Polychrome Pass,

ALASKA ROAD COMMISSION COLLECTION, #PCA 61-2-163, ALASKA STATE LIBRARY

*Building the Mt. McKinley National Park Road required endless pick and shovel work. Many road workers were former miners used to harsh weather and hard work. Laborers worked 10 to 12 hours a day, seven days a week, and were paid $6 per day plus board.*

ford the Toklat River, and continue through the mountain passes to Copper Mountain. From the terminus of the Muldrow Glacier the road would bridge the McKinley River and end at timberline on the Muddy River a few miles from the base of the mountain. He called his vision "a natural and interesting route for a purely park road."[2]

In 1922, Karstens had seized the initiative and forged a rugged wagon trail up Maurice Creek to the pass above Jenny Creek. It was clear, however, that actual road building was beyond his mandate and would necessarily fall under the purview of the Alaska Road Commission (ARC). Early reconnaissance by the road commission had identified two possible routes to the Kantishna Mining District with a so-called mountain route, roughly analogous to Karstens' proposal. According to Major John Gotwals, the road commission was ordered to build a year-around road, over the shortest distance possible, from the railroad to the mining district. Consequently the concept of a road built purely for summer tourism, and thus offering limited seasonal use for Kantishna miners, met local and national opposition.

National Park Service (NPS) Director Stephen Mather began work on a

DENA #6-50, DENALI NATIONAL PARK & PRESERVE, MUSEUM COLLECTION

*As road construction advanced westward, the road commission established work camps at convenient locations. This cabin, located at about Mile 14, served meals to crews working on the road and the Savage River bridge. Workers lived in wall tents, with wooden floors, and slept on straw mattresses atop World War I Army surplus cots.*

cooperative agreement with the road commission in 1921 and an informal agreement was forged the following spring. Under the terms of the agreement ARC assumed responsibility for engineering and construction of the 90-mile-long park road ending at Eureka, with NPS providing funding, design, and location input. The agreement benefited all three agencies with a stake in the park: the NPS would have a road necessary for development of tourism; the ARC would honor its mandate to develop the mineral resources of the Kantishna; and the railroad would have a destination that would attract visitors who would add to its revenues.[3]

Mather lobbied for immediate funding. Although congressional inaction delayed road start-up, in 1923, the road commission built two miles of crude road and bridged Rock Creek with felled timber. A year later the Interior Department announced an appropriation of $360,000 for a three-year road building program. The news sparked avid interest. "More men are seeking work at the park than the [ARC] can possibly place," said assistant chief engineer

Ike P. Taylor, "and it is estimated that hundreds of men are out of employment in Anchorage and are seeking work to the north." Taylor quickly hired 50 men and placed 200 more on a waiting list. He vigorously discouraged job-seekers from heading to the park for work.[4]

Undaunted by the cooperative agreement, in early 1924, Karstens traced out a possible road from Copper Mountain over Muldrow Glacier to the mountain's base, a route he considered to be "shorter and of more scenic value than [ARC's] proposed route from Copper Mountain to Wonder Lake." Differences of opinion about the road's location and quality would spark numerous turf battles between the "cooperating" government agencies.[5]

By mid-May, two crews of 85 to 90 men were actively clearing and improving the road sections built the previous year. "The location of the road is very good except the first half mile," reported Karstens, "but a portion has about a 10% grade."[6]

The initial work progressed well, with three miles of road finished by early July. Due to a bureaucratic snafu, a money shortage in mid-summer halted further construction and most of the men hired that spring were laid-off. By the end of 1924, two miles of road had been partially surfaced, 10 miles partially graded, 14 miles brushed out, and another 36.5 miles located. To that point, including private donations, the total cash outlay for road building amounted to less than $7,000.[7]

By autumn, automobiles could jolt their way west over the first nine miles of road, with horses or wagons needed to complete the journey to Savage Camp. Out of the 200 tourists who stopped at the depot in 1924, only 50 went into the park. "This number, while not large, was delighted with the trip," Karstens told reporters. He also expressed his disappointment that only nine miles of road had been constructed, which limited visitation.[8]

For the hardy few who ventured west of Savage River, the trail was still a matter of finding individual routes. Either road workers or rangers had placed inaccurate, or at best highly optimistic, mileage signboards along the right of way. "After seeing several of these signs we came to the conclusion that the mileage had been determined by the temperament and condition of the man that had put them down," observed William N. Beach. "At one time I walked four miles by the board in twenty minutes, and another two miles took us some four hours."[9]

Kantishna miners, already incensed by the choice of the mountain route, exploded when plans were drawn for the road to traverse the slab-sided mountain overlooking Polychrome Pass, rather than cross through the pass as common sense dictated. Even Karstens had championed the lower route but was over-ruled. The choice of "the highline" offered a more scenic route favorable to summer's admiring tourists, but that would be entirely unusable in winter or bad weather. Most of the outraged comments were unprintable but one miner called it the "ultimate folly of this entire worthless park."[10]

The concept of the park road as a dual–purpose tourism/Kantishna-access route varied from individual-to-individual, agency to agency. Road commission chief Colonel James G. Steese wanted not only to reach the Kantishna but push the road on to McGrath, Iditarod, and eventually to the shores of the Bering Sea. A few people saw the park road as only one of a network of roads connecting with the railroad. In 1924, the railroad proposed building a trail from its Curry Hotel on the Susitna River through the mountains, via Anderson Pass, to Copper Mountain where it would connect to the park road. Karstens supported this idea "because it will give travelers an opportunity to see a great portion of the more interesting parts of the park . . . the traveler will not be obliged to cover the same territory twice."[11]

Hawley Sterling, assisted by packer Bert Wilson, left McKinley Station in August to blaze a horse trail from the route of the park road, around the head of the Muldrow Glacier, and then to the suspension bridge at Curry. "If [he] does not get lost, or eaten by glacier blue bears, or get cold feet, and successfully reaches Curry, he will have gone through a part of Alaska never before traveled by white men and will open a region so rich in scenic beauty that nothing in reach of tourists can compare with it," opined a reporter.[12]

A little less than two weeks later, the men were back, Sterling reporting the "route would be impossible to travel mounted and almost out of the question on foot." The horses had picked their way precariously across two-foot wide crevasses with "no bottom in sight." The project was abandoned "on account of not being feasible."[13]

The idea of a route through the serrated backbone of the Alaska Range did not die easily. Three years later rangers Fritz Nyberg and Grant Pearson took dog teams on a trip through Anderson Pass to the West Fork Glacier as a demonstration of the proposed trail's viability. They succeeded in crossing the mountain range, but their journey was not without mishap and clearly beyond the capabilities of all but the most experienced and capable travelers.

Even after the right-of-way was surveyed, alterations and variations blossomed like spring wild flowers. As late as 1928, when the route should have been firmly fixed, Karstens accompanied a road commission party to examine the route from Mile 34 to Copper Mountain, Mile 73. Remaining loyal to Charles

Sheldon's original vision of a hotel near the base of Mount McKinley, Karstens again pushed for a road to the base of the mountain. In his plan, once that road was built, a side road would lead to Wonder Lake and on to Eureka. The park concessioner argued for a road tracing the "old horse trail" on the bluffs on the north side of McKinley River, citing it as more scenic. The latter choice won out and became the route used today. * [14]

Given the personalities involved, and the loose structure of the "cooperative agreements" hammered out between the two agencies, conflict was inevitable. Karstens wanted the road to be built with a certain aesthetic, not with the road commission's usual pioneer heavy-handedness. He did not want park visitors to see debris piles and open gravel pits. " . . . Those in charge of construction are following out the wishes of the service as they see it, but being used to pioneer work which is crude—their method shows up in their lack of extreme painstaking," he wrote. "The men remark they have never built such a road in the country before where everything is being cleaned up."[15]

Colonel Steese chastised Karstens for his rangers "meddling and interference" in construction activities, essentially saying "we will do our best, but as we see fit, not you, live with it." The once–friendly relationship between the two men rapidly deteriorated.[16]

Karstens had a difficult relationship with the road commission. He was sometimes stubborn, undiplomatic, and combative, a man who demanded of others the complete commitment and hard work that he himself put into the park. His legendary volcanic temper was a hallmark of the stress load that he carried, and dealt with poorly. The Army brass in charge of both the railroad and road commissions carried a share of the blame for the conflicts.

ARC was headed by three commissioners, usually career military officers, with an annual budget of about $500,000, 40% from territorial taxes, and 60% from Congress. Military officers of that era hailed from privileged backgrounds, were usually classically educated and well-connected, an integral part of a uniquely American aristocracy. Neither Colonel Frederick Mears, the overseer of construction of the Alaska Railroad, nor his successor, Colonel Steese, accepted the self-educated Karstens as an equal. Field-grade officers did not discuss, compromise, or seek consensus with underlings; they issued orders. In the six months after Mears was forced out as AEC chief in 1923,

*A spur road to Copper Mountain (Mount Eielson) branched off the main road about a mile and a half east of today's Eielson Visitor Center.

Steese headed the railroad, road commission, territorial public works, and the lighthouse service, wielding more real authority than the territorial governor. Karstens' insistence that the park road be built to unique standards, even though costing more money, time, and effort, did not sit well with Steese and his staff. When a news article appeared in the Anchorage paper that described wanton killing of wildlife by the park road builders, and cited Karstens as the source, tempers flared in a manner all too reminiscent of the earlier Mears flap. In this case, Karstens was *not* the complainant, but the damage on the local level was done. Ranger Edward McFarland, himself a reserve officer, took a high-handed manner with the road workers, further alienating them. It appears that Steese, who savaged Karstens' reputation during the 1925 investigation, came to view the park superintendent as someone challenging his supreme authority, and an irritant to neutralize.

Karstens seldom stepped away from a fight, especially when he thought he was in the right. He may not have known the technical aspects of road engineering, but he was determined that the park road would not be a primitive eyesore.

ALASKA ROAD COMMISSION COLLECTION, #61-002-240, ALASKA STATE LIBRARY

*Compressor crews positioned their equipment and drilling rigs at the edge of the Polychrome cliff and drilled six-to-eight-foot deep holes into the rock. A powder man then shoved a half-stick of dynamite to the back of the hole and detonated it. Laborers then cleared the rubble, forming a pocket in the hillside. Once they had 20, or more, of these pockets blasted into the outcropping, the men drilled multiple holes between them. They then jammed the holes full of 40 to 50 cases of dynamite, all wired together for a single blast.*

Even without bureaucratic in-fighting and funding glitches, road building across muskeg, tundra, and over high mountain passes, was incredibly challenging. Workers experienced seasonal delays caused by early or late break-up, heavy rain or unseasonable snows. The summer sun thawed the permafrost beneath the newly-built road, causing sections to slump or turn to mush, destroying what may have taken days to build. Bridges built one week washed out the next. Over the winter, ice, sometimes several feet thick, built up over stretches of completed road and had to be cleared away—often with dynamite—before new work could begin. The building season was short and each year precious days were lost repairing spring and winter damage.

"We began the season at Six Mile," Walter Teeland recalled, "and 20 men would clean the road and ditches as we moved west toward Sanctuary. It'd take us about a month to get into where we were going to work. We'd spend a week here, a week there, on the way in."[17]

Primitive wooden bridges regularly washed out in spring floods and had to be replaced. Others were destroyed by overflow ice. In bad storms, soil, gravel, and cobbles washed downstream to cover spans with as much as four to five feet of debris. Bridges were built upon bridges upon bridges.

The commission's buildings on the east side of the tracks opposite the depot served as base of operations. The complex included a large, well-equipped, shop/garage, with a mess hall in the north addition and a coal-fired furnace in the south. A heated warehouse, which in winter stored perishables brought up from Anchorage, sat north of the shop. Next door was the office and sleeping rooms.

The road commission established construction camps at intervals along the right-of-way, the first one just one and a half miles from the depot. Workers lived in wall tents, with wooden floors, and heated with coal or wood stoves. The men slept on World War I Army-issue cots, with straw mattresses, some of which were inhabited by red-backed voles. A large tent served as a cook shack and mess hall, with skilled cooks preparing the meals. The camp shower was a 50-gallon drum heated with a steam boiler.

Each camp housed a total of 15 to 20 workers, including equipment operators, drivers, wranglers, surveyors, laborers, and a cook and cook's helper. The supply department issued each worker a towel, bedding, matches and soap. Trucks delivered supplies once a week, and also brought the mail. Crews worked 10-to-12 hours a day, seven days a week, with the work season extending from early spring until mid-September. During one memorable season, the workers were given a half-day off on Sunday. Most workers spent the summer in camp, leaving only when autumn weather ended the work season.[18]

ALASKA ROAD COMMISSION COLLECTION, #61-361, ALASKA STATE LIBRARY

*With Stony Hill in the background, the work camp west of Fish Creek housed workers building the segment of road leading to a tourist camp, and the future site of Eielson Visitor Center.*

Foremen expected their men to be self-sufficient and prepared for all weather extremes. On some trips the freighters could be gone a week or more without communication of any kind. "No one got excited about it," Teeland said. "Oh, well, they'll get back some day, was the attitude."[19] Most communication was by written message or word-of-mouth and did not change until the installation of a temporary phone line.*

"Due to the isolation it was not easy to get men to work at the park in the early years," Teeland explained, "but summer wages, room and board, lured some." That changed as the 1920s matured. Alaska, presaging national woes, grappled with economic depression, tied to the slide in gold production. There was no such thing as welfare then and most people had only one choice, work or starve. Following the 1929 stock market crash, competition for scarce jobs

*In 1930, A.W. Kendall of Anchorage, formerly chief of the telegraph and telephone service for the Alaska Railroad, submitted the winning bid of $14,000 to construct a 73-mile-long phone line from the railroad to the base of Muldrow Glacier. Work began in September and was completed on November 27, despite encountering "temperatures in excess of 50 below . . ." The wire was supported on tripods in open country, and poles in timbered areas, some of which are still standing today.

ALASKA ROAD COMMISSION COLLECTION, #PCA 61-13-207, ALASKA STATE LIBRARY

*The Alaska Road Commission built their headquarters across the tracks from the railroad depot. The large, barn-like building provided warm storage and shop space complete with forge, machine tools, parts loft, and a vehicle lift.*

was fierce. Both Bagoy and Teeland felt fortunate to have their road jobs. "With frugal living, we could even come out ahead a little, a real feat in the 1920s and 30s," Teeland said.[20]

According to Teeland, most of the workers took great pride in their work. Camps boasted a cordial atmosphere, although some foremen could be officious and unpleasant. "Jack McDonald, at East Fork, was one foreman who was a mean son-of-a-gun," Bagoy said. "Much respect had to be shown him. Exactly at six a.m. he'd wake everybody up, yelling '*Daylight in the swamp.*' If you didn't get up immediately, a few minutes later he'd begin yelling, '*All out.*' Exactly at eight a.m., done eating or not, he'd yell, '*Roll out, or roll up.*' And you'd better be underway."[21]

A bad foreman could ruin morale, but good cooks and meals could improve it. "We always had great cooks," Bagoy remembered, "or they couldn't have kept a crew. Joe McMahon, a one-armed man, was an outstanding cook who prepared great meals. Like most cooks he kept fresh meat in a pail sunk in the creek. It kept cold but often by the end of a week it spoiled anyway." Workers also praised another cook, "Happy Jack," "who could turn out a meal in a tent as fast as the crews could unload the supply trailer."[22]

A few cooks were truculent and not to be trifled with. On Martin Cole's first day in camp he started for the cook shack "when suddenly there burst from the tent two workers, red-faced and eyes rolling, who scattered like quail before a shotgun blast . . . close on their heels . . . was the cook . . . brandishing a meat cleaver." Camp foreman Carl Johnson interceded and restored order. He gave the cook, "Deafy" Jones, a good "tongue lashing." The foreman told the men to bring their comments to him next time, but to be on the safe side, transferred Jones to another camp. In the new camp, Jones, resentful of jokes about his cooking, again chased a worker with his butcher knife. This time, road foreman Ben Cleary, courageously stepped between the two, and fired Jones.[23]

At least one other cook turned violent, although without creating a tragedy. With Karstens' help, John Fredson, a participant in the 1913 Mt. McKinley expedition, and then a college student, obtained a summer job as an assistant cook. One day there was a bizarre incident in which a drunken cook's helper chased Fredson with a butcher knife. Other than that, the summer passed well and Fredson returned to college with his earnings. "Carstens [sic] was very enthusiastic about Johnny [and] thinks his place is at Mt. McKinley Park," explained Fredson's biographer.[24]

Much of the work of bridge building, clearing, and filling, was done by hand. Slackers and the weak did not last long. "Nowadays they have these jobs out there where they have rest and recreation," Teeland said. "In those days . . . there was quite a bit of manual labor. We had a couple of power shovels, but most of the time all of the ditches were dug by hand and a lot of fill gravel was being spread by hand. It was a job for quite a few relatively older men in a way. They'd been miners used to a proportion of hard work."[25]

One of these older men, a resident of McKinley Station, died in a road camp. Teeland and another man loaded the body in a truck and took it to the depot. "We had lunch at Maurice Morino's and went back to our camp and that was our recreation for the year," Teeland said. "It was the only time we left the interior of the Park. We spent a couple of hours at the station, had lunch, and got back into the truck and went back out . . ."[26]

Pete Bagoy, originally hired as a laborer, became a skilled heavy equipment operator. The early tractor-crawlers that he ran, were not bulldozer-type with the blade on the front, but were used to pull graders, wagons, and sleds. The commission's workhorse was the Caterpillar Sixty tractor–crawler of 1919, the world's first successful bulldozer. The "60" as it was called, was powered by a 65–horsepower, 4–cylinder engine, famous for its simple design—individually mounted cylinders, overhanging radiator, lever controls, open clutch, straight exhaust, rough seat, and exposed fuel tank. Most importantly it was easy to work on and a vast improvement over the 1909 model, Cat 45, a steam tractor.

Bagoy, though expert with his "60," nonetheless wielded hand tools like everyone else. "We fought mosquitoes and bad weather while building the road," Bagoy explained. "When it got too wet to work with equipment, I was given a pick and shovel and told to go to work."[27]

The Alaska-born Teeland knew what to expect from the weather and the work. His father, John, took part in the 1898 Klondike stampede, and the 1903 Fairbanks rush. He moved from region to region, strike to strike, seeking his ever-elusive fortune. Walter, born in Cleary City, was just 16 when he came to McKinley Station in 1923, to assist with repairs to the Riley Creek bridge. The work required experience but also "a man young, strong and agile enough to climb around on the trestle and dodge trains." He then took a job with the road commission driving Model T and Model A trucks.[28]

The pioneer road meandered around obstacles, the route selected through simple criteria. H.E.D. Wallace ran one of the survey parties that worked ahead of the road crews. He admonished his crew to always remember two over-riding principles: "The first is not to exceed a six percent grade," he said, "and secondly—this is important—lay out the road where it will get the greatest sun exposure." The amount of fill needed to traverse a road segment, along with the location of culverts and bridges, also dictated routing. In places, the road snaked back and forth to the heads of little draws and the narrow points of water courses.[29]

Simple principles sometimes fell victim to expediency. "When Major Gillette, the road engineer, saw the ten percent grade by the park headquarters," Bagoy recalled, "he exploded, demanding a change. However, relocation would have been expensive and extensive, so it stayed as is." Even today, the incline challenges bus drivers hauling visitors into the park.[30]

In 1925, Hawley Sterling gave Karstens permission to advertise automobile tourism. By then the road was finished to the park's principle tourist destination, Savage Camp, at Mile 12. Park visitation that year climbed to 206, more than triple the previous year's total, largely due to improved access.

Road construction beyond Savage River inched along, reaching Mile 22 near Sanctuary River in 1926. The following spring, Sterling supervised road maintenance but informed Karstens that there would be "no new construction past Mile 22—no funds."[31]

Instead of prioritizing standardization of the uncompleted road section to Sanctuary, which would have enhanced visitor access, fully half of the funds allotted for 1927 went to maintenance of the existing road, an upgrade of the tour road to the head of Savage River, and clearing the right of way to Igloo Creek.[32]

Adequate funding remained a chronic problem. "Mt McKinley National Park where cement cost $4 per sack compared to 75 cents a bag ... construction costs were the highest of any park," explained one historian. Hawley Sterling's original construction estimate of $4,000 a mile turned out to be $15,000 per mile, nearly double the cost of similar interior Alaskan roads.[33]

During his 1927 visit to Washington, D.C., Karstens testified before the appropriations sub-committee. "My most urgent plea was for more road development," he recalled. "I eliminated all thought of other necessary and important development for the greater need of more roads, which means the very life of the park." Karstens preached the message to universities and town halls in New York, Illinois, Massachusetts, and Pennsylvania, and bent the ear of the editor of the *Saturday Evening Post*.[34]

Newspaperman Harry Myers also testified on the park's behalf. "The park should be opened up by a continuation of a motor road at least as far as Copper Mountain," he said. Even though Myers knew the sub-committee chairman, increased funding did not develop.[35]

In 1928, only 40 men, in two camps, were at work on the road. By the end of the season, despite a debilitating appropriation cut from $100,000 to $65,000, workers finished grading the road to the top of Sable Pass, allowing, in dry weather, vehicle traffic to the foot of the pass. Work there "progressing steadily [though] difficult and slow, lack of funds is a serious handicap," Karstens said. "The ARC deserves a great deal of credit ..."[36]

The next year, the road commission built a cabin at the East Fork River, to serve as the headquarters for the arduous and dangerous work of cutting the "skyline" or "highline" route over Polychrome summit. Prior to the bridge being built, road workers forded the river just upstream from the bridge site and drove the gravel bars below the bluffs to the southwest end of Polychrome. Construction proceeded from both sides of the summit at once. The access road beneath the cliffs was precisely the route Karstens, and Kantishna miners, had championed for the permanent road.

Upstream of the small creek that ran by the East Fork cabin, laborers mined high–quality coal for use in the commission's stoves. A string of trucks moved the coal to the camps or into McKinley Station for use in the shop heaters and forges. Mining coal here had unique dangers. Once when two laborers did not return to the cabin as expected, several men, fearing a cave-in, formed a rescue party. En route along the quarter-mile of tracks laid from the cabin to the mine, they scared off a grizzly bear that had pinned the men inside the shaft.[37]

Both Bagoy and Teeland worked on the highline. Laborers excavated the initial approaches with hand tools but stopped when they came to solid rock. At that point Teeland and his co-workers on the compressor crew positioned their equipment and drilling rigs at the edge of the cliff. They then drilled six-to-eight-foot deep holes into the rock. In a procedure called "springing the hole" a powder man would shove a half-stick of dynamite to the back of the hole and detonate it. Laborers then cleared the rubble, forming a pocket in the hillside. Once they had 20 or more of these pockets blasted into the rock outcropping, the men drilled twenty to thirty more holes in and between them. They then jammed the holes full of 40 to 50 cases of dynamite, all wired together for a single blast. Before the charges were wired, the equipment was pulled back at least a quarter-mile and everyone took cover in a shelter built of bridge timbers. The powder man attached the leads to a battery-powered detonator, and with a cry of "Fire in the hole!" triggered a thunderous explosion. Once the dust settled, the power shovels moved up to clear the debris. Some of the loose rock was used for fill but the majority was simply dumped over the cliff edge by power shovels. The "overcasting" along Polychrome bluffs took two years.[38]

Because of the powder men's expertise, few, if any, accidents occurred. The crews were nonchalant with their explosives. "The powder men kept the dynamite under their beds in the tent," Teeland said. "Sometimes we [the compressor men] would be sitting around on a case of dynamite, or having lunch at a campfire . . . sometime we'd get careless about smoking and they [the powder men] would have to warn us."[39]

The potential for accidents was ever present. Once a power shovel excavating rubble on Polychrome uncovered and hoisted a box of dynamite with six sticks hanging out of it. The blasting crew had cached the crate but had forgotten it when they moved on. Such incidents were uncommon.

Red foxes and ground squirrels sought handouts at the work camps. At one camp a cross fox named "Mickey" learned to sleep on the cook shack floor. Bears caused few problems in camps and were infrequently seen. Rarely did workers see a coyote or wolf. Dall sheep lambing seemed unaffected by the clattering vehicles and blasting.[40]

Taking full advantage of winter's rock-hard, frozen ground, workers hauled and pre-positioned heavy bridging materials. One November, a crew set up camp 35 miles downstream from the Toklat River bridge site and cut logs and hewed timbers for its construction. The two-man freight crew, Ben Cleary, a Canadian, and Bagoy, camped at the then–abandoned and partially–collapsed

Knight's Roadhouse. One night the temperature bottomed out at -50°F, and the wood stove, despite constant stoking, barely kept the cold at bay. In the extreme cold, they left their tractors running all night, with the big freight sleds pulled up on green poles to prevent the runners from freezing to the ground. During that logging operation the men only shut down their rigs four times in two weeks, for brief maintenance.

It took eight hours for the tractors to pull their heavily-loaded sleds from the old roadhouse to the bridge site, called the Toklat Crossing. On one trip Bagoy and Cleary pulled a Michigan sled loaded with 100 logs to the crossing in 10 hours. Tractors in those days had no protective cabs, so drivers sat in the open fully exposed to the brutal wind and cold. The two men repeatedly exchanged places, one driving, and the other running behind the sled to keep warm.

Freighting heavy loads on river ice was not without risk. On one trip, Bagoy heard a shouted warning just as their tractor broke through the ice nose first. The Cat plunged downward to a hard stop, pitching Cleary head–long across the ice. Cleary was uninjured but the "60" was trapped. Apparently when the Toklat had first frozen over that year, a solid layer of ice had formed, and when the water level dropped later in the winter, it again froze over leaving a tunnel between the two layers of ice. Luckily, the 20,500-pound tractor had broken through the first layer, but not the second.

The two men worked feverishly in sub-zero cold trying to free the Cat but by nightfall they only had managed to remove the pin binding the sled to the tractor. In the nearby timber they built a roaring fire and pitched a crude camp by its golden light. Early the next morning, after a fitful rest, they attacked the ice with picks and axes and "fought it for God knows how long, all the while hoping like hell the lower ice layer didn't break." Just as night was again settling in, the men succeeded in hacking out a ramp and walked the tractor out of the hole and back onto solid ice.[41]

Cleary had had a premonition that the journey would not go well. "Old Ben was very superstitious," Bagoy recalled. "On the very first morning when we left Knight's, I cut a green pole to use as a twister on the log chains. Old Ben said 'That's the kind of wood Christ was crucified on and that's bad luck and we'll never get there with the load.' I laughed at him then but after we fell through the ice he looked at me and said 'I told you, Pete. Now do you believe me?'"[42]

While Cleary and Bagoy worked downstream on the Toklat, Bill Sypher's crew trucked 350 to 400 tons of additional bridge building materials to the head of Igloo Creek. From there, Tom Finnegan relayed the loads with a tractor and sled over Sable Pass to the East Fork camp.

Until 1931, when summer trucking became feasible, heavy construction supplies moved only over frozen ground. For safety, the freighters always worked in pairs. One spring, Bagoy and another man, each driving a Caterpillar 30 pulling two sleds loaded with cribbing, coal, and gasoline, got stuck in a snow drift at Mile 5 where they stayed from eight o'clock one morning until five the next afternoon. Two miles down the road they found easy going where the road had been scoured to bare gravel by the wind.

Staying warm on the tractor was nearly impossible. Bagoy once bought a pair of flannel-lined, caribou fur pants from Fritz Nyberg. On his next trip from the depot to the Sanctuary cabin, with the temperature -30°F, he stayed fairly warm but when he arrived at the Sanctuary cabin he couldn't stand up because the untanned caribou skin had stiffened into a sitting position. Bagoy hobbled around in a crouch until the cabin warmed up enough for the pants to thaw out. "Well, at least I was warm anyway," he recalled with a laugh.[43]

Road segments were finished well before bridges were built over the major rivers, with crossings made at shallow fords. As late as 1930, travel was possible to the Toklat River, but not "on location," meaning some sections had to be by-passed. The Polychrome summit section did not open until late-August 1931. NPS Director Horace Albright, then on an inspection trip, described it as "one of the great sections of the national park highways. Built to all modern standards, except in width, this stretch of road offers a spectacular outlook over [the pass] and the Alaska Range." While right about the view, the rest of his statement was hyperbole.[44]

The Mt. McKinley National Park road did not reach Wonder Lake, 85 miles from the depot, until 1937. The next year it was extended to Eureka in the Kantishna and did not reach Friday Creek until 1940. Ironically, slightly over a year later, in the aftermath of Pearl Harbor, all gold mining in Alaska ceased. In all, the road to Wonder Lake took better than 15 years to build, for a total cost of about $1,400,000.[45]

In 1929, on the north side of the park, an independently-financed pioneer road was pushed west into the Kantishna hills. Billy Taylor cut the 50-mile-long winter road from Lignite to his Stampede mine, which he'd optioned to a wealthy Englishman. Rendered unusable in summer by thawing, innumerable stream crossings, floods, and unstable soils, this seldom–used road was re-worked in the 1950s, but quickly abandoned. It is still used by a small number of off–road–vehicles and remains a contentious part of various park commercial development schemes.[46]

Even after construction of the park road, the park itself remained unpopular with some Alaskans. "Monotonous" and "uninspiring" were frequent descriptions of the landscape. One writer suggested that even Indians would commit suicide if they were forced to go near those "bleak and barren hills . . . being fed to tourists as scenery." He reported that the effort to fasten "thrilling names to road locations—Inspiration Point, Look–Out Leap, Coolidge Dome—was hollow and doomed."[47] And, he seemed to imply, tourism was also doomed since the park service had nixed plans for a hotel at Copper Mountain.*

"I have heard some Alaskans say that the scenery at McKinley is monotonous," Karstens responded, "but if they could hear the tourists rave over it, they would have a different idea of the value of the park." As park amenities continued to develop, visitor numbers continued to climb, peaking in 1929 at 1,038. Alaska tourism dropped off sharply the next year due to the Great Depression.[48]

Road construction greatly facilitated efforts of park rangers to crack down on poaching. The partially completed road allowed rangers to travel in break-up conditions that had previously stymied them. In late April 1926, Karstens and Ranger Al Winn mushed dogs over the thawing right-of-way from Toklat to their tent camp in "Government Draw" near Copper Mountain. There they rendezvoused with Nyberg, just in from Big Timber. "After lunch we three went over to Copper Mt. to see Giles regarding the killing of 9 caribou," Karstens reported. "Mr. Giles did not deny killing 9 caribou but said he killed them outside of the park & just recently hauled them in. As to the offal and blood rangers had seen along the trail in Muldrow canyon he stated he knew nothing about it . . . we have no ruling as to a prospector hauling <u>in</u> game meat or having it in his possession, therefore it seems to me it is a case for the territory. One of the caribou found on the bars was not claimed by Giles who said some one else killed it, but would not tell us who. In all, Giles had 22 quarters at his cabin & two whole animals on the bar when the rangers first caught him. He did not deny killing them . . . and admitted killing the 9 some or most of which were cows & yearlings." Giles was neither arrested nor prosecuted, but the presence of the rangers deterred similar wanton killing.[49]

The construction of the park road forever changed the wilderness of Mt. McKinley and altered the lifestyles of the region's human population, eventually opening the country for visitors of a different stripe.

---

*"Inspiration Point" is today's Primrose pullout, and Coolidge Dome is Stony Hill. Except at the depot, no hotels were ever built inside the park.

DENA #25-0-8, DENALI NATIONAL PARK & PRESERVE, MUSEUM COLLECTION

*A small power shovel "overcasts" rubble left from a dynamite blast needed to cut out the roadway on the bluff above the McKinley River. Construction of the park road was slow and arduous. The road did not reach Wonder Lake, 85-miles from the depot, until 1937*

# 17

# Pioneering Science

One day early in the spring of 1926, two men stepped down from the train and shook hands with Harry Karstens. In their dark, woolen suits and ties, they didn't look much different than the average tourist who stopped at McKinley Station, but as their mountain of baggage was unloaded, onlookers quickly realized these two were different. Instead of suitcases they had rolled, canvas tents, sleeping bags, assorted camp gear, gun cases, and a few boxes marked "Scientific Supplies. Do Not Drop." These weren't hunters, one eavesdropper said, but "those eggheads coming to count birds and rocks and such." The village jokesters offered bets on how long the two *Cheechakos* would last before the bears or mosquitoes got them.

These two men were anything but green. They were competent outdoorsmen and trained naturalists, there to conduct the first detailed inventory of the park's wildlife. The leader of the project was Joseph S. Dixon of the University of California, Berkeley, assistant to Dr. Joseph Grinnell, the first director of Berkeley's Museum of Vertebrate Zoology and a major figure in his field. Dixon's assistant, George Melendez Wright, was an independently wealthy forestry student at Berkeley, who, upon graduation the following year, would finance the first comprehensive wildlife survey of the nation's parks.

During six trips to Alaska, Dixon had worked in the harshest weather conditions imaginable. He spent the winter of 1913–14 on the arctic slope at the eastern end of the Endicott Mountains, one of Alaska's most inaccessible regions. A McKinley Park project, though challenging, would not stretch his abilities.[1]

Dixon's protégé, Wright, would eventually profoundly influence wildlife science, advocating science-based wildlife management as critical to the perpetuation of the nation's wildlife. During an epic, three-year faunal tour of the national parks, he found that arbitrary park boundaries often excluded areas, especially winter ranges, essential to wildlife survival. He believed that park boundaries needed to conform to the needs of wildlife, rather than to neat lines drawn on maps.[2]

Era biologists viewed Yellowstone and Mt. McKinley as "the two greatest animal national parks in America." Despite that, Olaus Murie, the only trained biologist to have worked in the park, had not been able to conduct anything other than a few rudimentary observations of local wildlife due to the demands of his caribou capture project. Dixon was captivated by Mt. McKinley Park's remoteness and its relatively intact animal populations. Recognizing the unique opportunity to study predator and prey relationships, the National Park Service and the University of California, Berkeley, cooperatively funded Dixon's expeditions.[3]

Dixon and Wright left Berkeley on May 3, and arrived at McKinley Station in mid-month. Karstens trucked them and their supplies to the Savage River ranger cabin where they spent the next several weeks collecting specimens and counting wildlife.

One of their first sightings was of a group of caribou, which apparently included one reindeer. "One small reddish one had large white spots on it," Dixon wrote, "and was only about half the size of the others." Karstens had told them that several reindeer had been seen running with the caribou and his policy was to shoot them on sight, "to keep the caribou stock pure and undefiled." Later that summer the American Society of Mammalogists urged that all free-roaming reindeer in the park be killed.[4]

On May 28, Wright made a major discovery, the first surfbird nest known to science. Wright found the nest on a rocky ledge near a Dall sheep trail, 1,000' above timberline, and a minimum of 150 air miles from the nearest salt water. Although the surfbird had been identified over 150 years earlier, its nesting location had eluded searchers. Because it is a shorebird—its scientific name *Aphriza virgata* approximates "*I live in sea-foam* —ornithologists had hunted coastal areas for its nest. After making careful observations of the surfbird's nesting habits, Wright collected the adults, eggs, and nest, and added it to a growing collection of specimens.[5]

Somewhat surprisingly the discovery made local news. "Only recently, Prof. Joseph Dixon, was made the proud possessor of four eggs belonging to the surf bird, which were discovered by his assistant, Mr. Wright," a Fairbanks newspaper noted. "The eggs of this bird have been diligently searched for, but without results, for the last 200 years."[6]

Another unusual bird eluded the determined scientists. "Several of the park

RAY DAME PHOTOGRAPH, #B1793-1857, ANCHORAGE MUSEUM AT RASMUSON CENTER

*In 1922, government herders pushed 1,600 reindeer through McKinley Park, crossing the Toklat, Teklanika, Sanctuary, and Savage Rivers. The herd reached the Nenana River on August 7, having taken 280 days to move nearly 600 miles from Goodnews Bay on the Bering Sea to Broad Pass.*

rangers and officials reported seeing a male redstart [a warbler] in the willows at the caribou camp at the head of Savage River," Dixon wrote, "and at close range there seems to be little doubt of its identity." To this day, no further sightings of this species have been made.[7]

Dixon's collecting efforts veered from triumph to comedy. While attempting to run down a willow ptarmigan chick, Wright was attacked by the male bird which "slapped me with his beating wings...knocking my glasses askew." The chick escaped, its chastened pursuer slinking from the field of combat.[8]

On a bluff by the Sanctuary River, near the original park boundary, Dixon found the bleached bones of two bull caribou that had died with their antlers locked together " . . . so that they were unable to pull them apart and both had died victims of their own folly."[9]

On June 24, Karstens helped the scientists relocate to Murie's abandoned camp at the head of the river. "This is the place where Mr. Murie and crew . . . tried to capture some of the large 'woodland caribou' which Mr. Karstens says are more or less local here and do not move about much," Dixon wrote. "They caught two small animals but did not get the large bulls that they wanted to cross with and breed up the reindeer stock." Dixon thought the site to be a poor area for the capture project, but Wright found "a well beaten game trail leading over the divide from the Savage to Sanctuary River."[10]

Early on July 9, Wright and Dixon loaded their supplies on a pack string and headed west for the interior of the park. They walked downstream ahead of the horses and turned west up Caribou Creek. They crossed the Sanctuary River near Double Mountain, quizzing everyone they met about the local wildlife. "A Mr. Gilers [likely Giles] who is prospecting here and who has been in the region since 1909, said that the caribou begin to rut during the last of September and that by September 25 and always by September 29 the bulls begin to get strong [tasting and smelling]," Dixon wrote. "Gilers also provided accurate information about seasonal migrations, perhaps more reliable information than provided by park rangers and staff."[11]

Dixon and Wright found that sheep in the central part of the park were difficult to approach and wary of people. Hunting and poaching was common there, with "Mr. Gilers" a gleeful participant.

"We found the sheep tamer around Double Mountain than over by

## WILD OR TAME?

PARK ANIMALS SEEM not to fear people, seldom running from, or avoiding, humans. Have the animals been tamed, or trained, not to fear us? Is their lack of caution a learned, unnatural behavior? A look at the anecdotal evidence from early in the 20th Century indicates that these animals, when not hunted, display no inherent fear of people.

- In 1902, Alfred Hulse Brooks, leading a party that hunted sheep and caribou for food, wrote: "There was no sport in hunting such innocently tame creatures, and we never molested them except when we needed meat."
- In 1903, Dr Frederick Cook's party encountered a docile wolf that regularly came into their camp and "left unmolested."
- In 1921, Harry Karstens wrote: "Caribou are very curious, and at times a man can ride a horse among them, but more often they are wild and keep off at a distance. Their timidity is no doubt caused by their being hunted as is the case with the sheep. There is no doubt but with proper protection these animals will become very tame."
- In 1922, Woodbury Abbey wrote: "We saw our first sheep, two big ones on a little promontory above the trail. They never moved while we filed past, even when we stopped and made a fire for soup."
- In 1925, Fritz Nyberg enjoyed the continual company of a wolf for almost three weeks before the animal wandered out of the park and was shot. That

Muldrow Glacier," Dixon later wrote Charles Sheldon. "Sheep are being shot right along by prospectors at Copper Mountain. In the east end of the park they are well protected and are doing well."[12]

Dixon studied the impact of illegal trapping. Fritz Nyberg told him that he had seen numerous beaver in the Big Creek drainage in 1923, with marten abundant in forested areas. "[Nyberg] says that [both species] are now becoming scarce even in the park due to poaching trappers," Dixon wrote. Confirming the report, Dixon saw numerous empty beaver lodges and minimal marten sign.[13]

In mid-July, the men reached Wonder Lake and stopped at John and Paula Anderson's homestead. The Andersons shared an interest in birds and showed Dixon the skins of a downy woodpecker and a snowy owl. Polly led him to a nearby golden eagle nest and then to a gyrfalcon on Moose Creek, and gave him the five eggs that she'd taken from it. The Andersons promised Wright they would record the migration dates for all the birds.

Dixon inspected the skull of a wolf that John Anderson had shot the previous winter, and called it "the largest female wolf I have ever seen." He also

same year a wolf shadowed Ranger Charles Armstrong on several occasions, apparently exhibiting simple curiosity.

• In 1926, "Ranger Nyberg reports innumerable bands on all the hills in the western and northwestern section of the park. In all instances the mountain sheep were very tame and did not seem to mind the presence of dogs nor man in their presence."

• One tour driver complained in 1926 that "if they [Dall sheep] get any tamer, they will be butting our cars off the road."

• In 1927, "Sheep in the vicinity of Stony Creek are getting quite tame paying no attention to dog team or man," reported ranger Lee Swisher.

• Also in 1927, on the Polychrome cliffs Dall sheep presented a hazard—to themselves. Prior to rock blasting, workers chased the sheep away, but they came right back as soon as the dust settled. "The great amount of blasting and noise along the Park Road has not affected [the sheep]," Karstens reported. "If anything, they are more tame than ever, for a very large band of sheep ranges all the summer close to where the road crews were working."

• Finally, an example from outside the park boundaries. In the 1920s Olaus Murie hunted sheep on the Robertson River in the eastern Alaska Range. "I shot the ram, most of the flock arose, and some ran off. But I was amazed to see that the other yearling, lying there beside the dead one, did not even get up. I walked up to within a few yards...and we stood there looking at each other. Apparently these animals were not familiar with gunshot either. Surely here was nature's unspoiled domain."

JOHN E. ANDERSON COLLECTION, COURTESY OF JAY HATHAWAY

*Joseph W. Dixon, and George M. Wright, from the University of California, Berkeley, visited the park in 1926 to conduct wildlife research. On a mountain slope they discovered the nest of a surfbird, the first ever found. Dixon would complete the work in the early 1930s when he took this portrait of a red fox.*

COURTESY OF CANDY WAUGAMAN

*In the early 1930s, a grizzly bear wandered along the edge of the park road and passed by a bus filled with camera-toting tourists. Once hunting and poisoning were curtailed, the park bear population began a slow increase.*

examined the skull of a coyote killed the previous winter by miner Ed Jern, "it was typical . . . though not at all common to the area."[14]

On their way back to McKinley Station, Dixon again stopped to observe caribou at Copper Mountain. "There is also a larger woodland caribou here," he wrote, "that does not wander much but remains in local but small bands of 20 to 50 all the year. These are much larger than the barren ground caribou. All the photos that I have taken on the trip are of woodland." The belief that two different sub-species of caribou lived in the park was an apparent error.[15]

On July 20, Dixon and Wright encountered a "large female brown bear and her two cubs" in Sable Pass. In all, they saw very few bears, a small number of moose, two wolves, and plentiful caribou and sheep.

After walking 75 miles in four days of heavy rain, the men found the Savage River cabin a welcome haven. They spent the next two days preparing and drying their specimens for the journey home. From May 19 to July 30, Dixon and Wright covered 500 miles on foot, identifying 86 kinds of birds and 25 mammals. They collected 168 bird specimens, including a snowy owl, a short-eared owl, two surfbirds, a golden eagle, a gyrfalcon, a sharp-tailed grouse, and

83 mammals including one black bear, one "brown bear," one wolverine, and a variety of rodents.

Dixon would return in 1932 to complete his work. On that return visit Dixon trained the park's first ranger-naturalists, David Kaye, a medical student, and ranger Lee Swisher, whom he selected to continue the work throughout the winter. Dixon's book, *Birds and Mammals of Mount McKinley National Park,* was the first comprehensive volume of its kind.

Pioneer research at McKinley Park focused on large mammals, but a remarkable woman was the first to examine the region's flora. In 1928, Ynez Mexia conducted the park's first detailed botanical investigation, collecting plants for the University of California, Berkeley. Beginning in early June, Mexia, 57, worked her way west from McKinley Station to Mt. Eielson, amazing old-timers with her dedication and stamina. Chief Ranger Nyberg respectfully called her "Madam Mexia" and said that "she had a lot of [courage] coming up there like she did."[16]

By mid-summer, road workers had pushed west, up Igloo Creek, to the summit of Sable Pass, but by then Mexia was far beyond them, collecting plants near O.M. Grant's cabin at Copper Mountain. Alone, she ambled west to Wonder Lake where she spent the first three weeks of August, caching her pressed plants at the Big Timber ranger cabin.

For her era, Ynez Mexia's life and career were especially remarkable. This daughter of General Enrique Mexia and Mrs. Sarah Wilmer Mexia, was born in the Georgetown neighborhood of Washington, D.C. on May 24, 1870. Ynez's father, a representative of the Mexican government, owned an enormous land grant ranch in Limestone County, Texas. Ynez spent her formative years on the ranch, and in Mexico, along with attending private schools in Philadelphia and Ontario, Canada. She continued her education at St. Joseph's College in Maryland, and then the University of California, Berkeley. She was 52 years old when she began her botanical career as a member of a 1922 expedition led by E.L. Furlong, Curator of Paleontology at Berkeley. Three years later, she teamed with Roxana S. Ferris, of Stanford's Dudley Herbarium, for a collecting trip to Mexico. Subsequently she made three additional trips to Mexico, two to South America, and one to Alaska, amassing 145,000 specimens. "I suffer from a common affliction," she said, "wanderlust." Colleagues admired her carefully preserved specimens and richly detailed field notes. In all she found over 500 new species, of which 50 bear her Latinized name. She is widely regarded as the greatest botanical collector in American history.

On her expedition to McKinley Park, Mexia collected 365 plant types and

COURTESY OF DR. KATHRYN DAVIS

*The remarkable botanist, Ynez Mexia, was 52 years old when she began her botanical career. She visited McKinley Park in 1928 and collected 6,100 plant specimens. In her career, she found over 500 new species, of which 50 bear her Latinized name. She is widely regarded as the greatest botanical collector in American history.*

6,100 specimens in all.* When she departed she left "two or three enormous stacks [of pressed plants] between corrugated cardboard, three feet high . . ." for the rangers to bring out with their dog teams.[17]

These pioneer rangers found the worldly Mexia beyond their ken. When she departed Copper Mountain she "left some food . . . that nobody could eat, including an awful lot of curry sauce. We'd never used curry sauce before and put it in flour or something," Myers recalled, "and Lord, it burned your hat off . . ." At one point, Mexia became the target of a practical joke. Rangers Nyberg and Myers slipped one plant into her shipment that she'd never collected, a sample of the "native sourdough plant." The two jokesters took a branch off a willow and tied a couple hotcakes to it and pressed it between cardboard. Mexia never mentioned their plant, which they called "Slopover slopius."[18]

While the development of the park road made the work of rangers and pioneer scientists somewhat easier, its progress was critical to the future of the park visitor concession, the struggling Mt. McKinley Tourist and Transportation Company.

* Two plant varieties in the park carry her name: Erigeron mexiae (now subsumed by E. pallens) and Salix brachycarpa var. mexiae (now treated within S. niphoclada).

# 18

# Managing the Wild West

Dan T. Kennedy, the intrepid "Gold Rush Packer" could transport tons of gold bullion through lawless wilderness, stave off armed bandits, and cut trails through thickets that would thwart a grizzly bear. But in little more than two years, Kennedy had had his fill of wrangling tourists. In 1925, he sold his park permit to James L. Galen, with Tom Marquam retaining his stake in the company. As a term of the sale, Kennedy agreed to refrain from guiding hunters or tourists for two years, unless for the newly incorporated Mt. McKinley Tourist and Transportation Company (T'n'T.)

Even with the financial backing of lawyer Marquam, Kennedy's attempt to develop park tourism had failed completely. In March 1924, the Kennedy-Marquam partnership had lowered its rates for a round trip from the railroad depot to Savage Camp from $18 to $16, with lodging $1.50 per night and meals $2.00 each. Trips beyond Savage were extra. The reductions were an attempt to attract additional clientele by making the park more affordable, a move Harry Karstens lauded. Nonetheless, Karstens feared that the "trip to Savage alone was going to be a disappointment to many, as visitors wished to see the game and mountain up close."[1]

Kennedy had bought 16 gentle, "first class" saddle horses, and refurbished Savage Camp with new tents and amenities. The first seven tourists arrived on June 24. A few days later, under a dense pall of wildfire smoke, six more visitors arrived and were taken to camp. Despite the smoke, these visitors expressed their enjoyment of the trip and their accommodations.

Just 62 tourists visited the park that summer and the season ended in financial disarray for Kennedy and Marquam. Forest fires and the lack of a predictable train schedule inhibited tourism. The fledgling concession was also victimized by its own poor management. The last tent was not taken down until December and by then the "wind and snow had torn it up considerable."

COURTESY OF CANDY WAUGAMAN

*In 1925, the railroad moved the Curry depot building to McKinley Station and relocated the Healy agent to run it. A plan to move the shuttered Curry Hotel to the park entrance failed.*

Marquam blamed the failure to attract customers on the "steamship companies only selling roundtrip tickets along the coast without time to go inland." He said he thought the company had lost $3,000 in 1924.[2]

Karstens agreed that the railroad schedule prevented people from getting off the train, let alone into the park. In 1924, southbound trains stopped at McKinley Station at 1:15 a.m., and northbound trains at 2:40 a.m. The schedule, dictated by distance, track conditions, and the aging steam engines in use, could not have been more inconvenient. Because of the slowness of train travel, the railroad had built a hotel at Mile 248.5 on the bank of the Susitna River north of Talkeetna. The Curry Hotel, named for "Alaska's Friend," Congressman Charles Forrest Curry, an active supporter of railroad construction, was not lavish but still first class. The two-story hotel contained a lobby big enough for evening dances by the gramophone, a "Trainman's Reading Room," kitchen, pantry, storeroom, bakery, laundry, main dining room, "Men's Grill," and forty-seven guest rooms. Rooms were $4, "sumptuous" dinners cost $1.50, and breakfast available for $1. A clean cot in the dormitory behind the hotel cost $1 per night. In comparison, railroad buffet cars offered a variety of entrees, priced not much higher than town prices. A breakfast of ham and eggs was a dollar, shredded wheat was 25 cents, donuts were 20 cents, and coffee was 10 cents. Behind the hotel, workers built a bridge over the river and a three-mile-long trail to the top of a hill where the mountain could be viewed "from a totally new angle." As many as 150 guests fell asleep each night to the murmur of the nearby river.[3]

The railroad touted Curry, more than the park, as a major tourist destination. "It is not generally known, but one of the finest views of majestic Mt. McKinley is obtained from an advantageous point close to the Curry Hotel," read a typical promotion.[4] Although the railroad assigned special trains and "small gas cars" to make excursions between McKinley Station and Curry, few travelers stayed more than one night. The attempt to turn the railroad stop into a major destination failed when modern locomotives were introduced, eliminating the need for a layover and the hotel closed in 1925.*

New train schedules in 1925, delivered tourists to McKinley Station in daylight hours for the first time, a promising development for the new T'n'T. The re-organized concession now had a more reliable and convenient schedule to work with as well as the financial backing and management skills to make the enterprise work. Management of the company consisted of Thomas A. Marquam, President; James L. Galen, Vice President; John H. Kelly, Secretary; Guy E. Jenkins, Treasurer; and Robert Sheldon, General Manager. Stock holders eventually included Austin E. "Cap" Lathrop, and James E. Barrack, owner of Fairbanks' Samson Hardware.

Marquam hailed from Portland Oregon, where his father, Judge Philip A. Marquam, owned large tracts of land in Multnomah County. A Klondike veteran and graduate of the University of Oregon, and Stanford, Marquam moved to Fairbanks in 1906 where he opened a law office. He soon became "the most popular criminal lawyer in the territory."[5]

More than once, "Fighting Tom" made news for physically assaulting his opponents, and on one occasion, a prosecution witness. Two years after his arrival in town, he became editor of the *Fairbanks Times*, which he used to further bully his opponents. A running battle between defense attorney Marquam and District Attorney James Crossley led to Marquam's prosecution for adultery. After a well-attended trial and lengthy deliberations, the jury found Marquam not guilty, the case highlighting the contradictory nature of the territory's laws and mores.[6]

*When the hotel closed in 1925, the railroad moved the small Curry depot building to McKinley Station and relocated the Healy agent to run it. Next to the depot, the railroad built an exhibit booth and staffed an information desk. A plan to move the shuttered Curry Hotel to the park entrance failed. In May 1926, an Anchorage carpenter, on contract with the railroad, erected an iconic log archway over the park road 500' due south of the depot.

Marquam was elected Fairbanks mayor and served on the College Board of Regents. A well-connected Republican, he escorted President Warren Harding on the 1923 presidential visit to Alaska. Marquam ran for Congress in 1925, but lost to Dan Sutherland.[7]

Galen, who had bought out Kennedy, was also a seasoned Alaskan. A Notre Dame graduate, he stampeded to Nome in 1901 and a year later was sworn in as a Deputy U.S. Marshal. The corrupt Judge Arthur Noyes then appointed Galen U.S. Commissioner for Teller and Kougaruk. Judge James Wickersham, who replaced Noyes, removed Galen from office, largely for political reasons. Wickersham quickly came under fire from Galen's politically powerful family.

Galen's Irish parents, Hugh and Matilda, were honored as founders of Montana Territory. Hugh stampeded to California in 1849 but failed to strike it rich. He moved north to Montana where he ran a stagecoach line between Helena, Bozeman, and Virginia City. Hugh Galen's empire expanded to include power generation, banking, and ranching. James, one of seven children, was born in Helena on March 28, 1871. His brother, Judge Albert J. Galen, served on the Montana Supreme Court. Galen's brother-in-law was Thomas Henry Carter, a Republican Senator for Montana. Carter had been instrumental in legislating reform of Alaska's criminal code and dividing the Alaska Territory into judicial districts in 1900. After James Galen's removal as U.S. Commissioner in Teller, Carter bedeviled Wickersham every chance he got.

After his foray to Nome, Galen returned to Montana in 1912, to assume the position of Superintendent of Glacier National Park. President Taft had buckled in to political pressure when he appointed Galen superintendent. In one letter he acknowledged that he thought Galen was not qualified for the post but likely wouldn't do much damage before another administration came in and replaced him. After a year and a half in Glacier, Galen resigned his post and returned to Alaska as a scout for the Anaconda Mining Company.[8]

Galen secured for himself one of the first leases and options on the fabulous Kennecott copper deposit. In Cordova, he managed all steamship freight arriving from the States for the Kennecott Mine, and, in 1919, took over the Cordova Transfer Company. Galen, like his future partner, also ran for U.S. Congress against the incumbent Dan Sutherland but lost the Republican primary by a wide margin. Ever the entrepreneur, Galen next established the Richardson Highway Transportation Company.[9]

Besides being a competent and well-connected businessman, Jim Galen also possessed good people skills, a must in any tourism endeavor. Friends called the sweet-natured Galen "Alaska's idol, known and respected by all, from sourdoughs to fishing kings."[10]

Robert "Bobby" Sheldon was already somewhat of a legend when he assumed the position of general manager of Galen's Richardson Highway Transportation Company. Born in Snohomish, Washington, he was just 15 when he got off the boat in Skagway in 1898. Yukon trader Jack McQuesten had invited his father, an old friend from the California gold fields, to the Klondike but like many other stampeders, the Sheldons lacked the money to buy the supplies required to enter Canada. After earning a grubstake, the Sheldons started on the arduous trip over White Pass, but the elder Sheldon's failing heart forced them to retreat. When his father left for Seattle, young Bobby stayed in Skagway, hawking newspapers to survive. His father, Robert Sheldon Sr., died within a year.

On the night of July 8, Sheldon witnessed the shoot-out between surveyor Frank Reid and the notorious outlaw Soapy Smith. "Reid grabbed the muzzle of Smith's rifle," he said. "Smith jerked and jerked and finally got the muzzle pointed around enough to try to hit him in the middle and he pulled the trigger. That was the first shot . . . Then Reid fell to his knees and hung onto the rifle. Reid was big enough to prevent Soapy from shooting again . . . Reid finally got his revolver out of his pocket . . . He fired three shots . . . the third shot went right through Soapy's heart. His hat went one way and his rifle went the other way. Reid was rushed to a doctor for treatment but died a hero 10 days later."[11]

A mechanical genius, Sheldon found employment on steamers working between Skagway, Dyea, and Juneau, and eventually became engineer in the Skagway power plant. In 1905, he built the first automobile in Alaska out of salvaged buggy wheels, a homemade chassis, and a three-and-one-half horsepower marine engine. Sheldon built the car to win the affections of a beautiful Skagway girl. When asked if he won the girl's hand, he replied, "No, but three other fellows have married her since then." Because of his often self-deprecating humor, people referred to the good-humored Sheldon as the local "comedian" who "possessed a rare gift of speech, a keen sense of humor and charm of personality."[12]

Sheldon moved to Fairbanks in 1908, to manage the Northern Commercial Co.'s power plant. Five years later he spent $1,297 on a mail-order, four-passenger, Model T Ford convertible, and soon drew a lot of attention clattering around town in his new car, then one of only five in the Interior. Some friends asked him to drive them to Donnelly Roadhouse a hundred and twenty miles down the Richardson Trail. The trip, normally five days by horse and wagon, took seven hours in the Model-T. Embracing commercial transportation, Sheldon quit his job at the power plant and on July 29, 1913, with three passengers, started

SKINNER COLLECTION, # 44-05-081, ALASKA STATE LIBRARY

*In May 1926, an Anchorage carpenter, on contract with the railroad, erected a log archway over the park road 500' due south of the depot. Park visitors were met at the depot and driven to Savage Camp in cars and buses. In the background are Morino's hotel and out buildings.*

the "impossible" 370-mile trip to Valdez via the Richardson.

A young journalist, Lowell J. Thomas, who was to make the real-life "Lawrence of Arabia" famous, offered to be Sheldon's first paying customer. "When Bobby bragged that his Model T could cut the time to Valdez in half . . . I saw the chance for a good story . . . so I offered to be passenger No. 1 on the Sheldon Stage Line to Valdez," Thomas wrote. "There were only two bridges and two ferries in the entire 371 miles . . . we forded the rest of the streams or winched ourselves across with block and tackle. I held up the Ford on the downstream side so it would not wash away." After three and one-half days, and 59 hours of driving time, they arrived in Valdez. Sheldon was the first person to drive a car over the trail. "I never believed I would pay anyone $150 to push an automobile 371 miles across Alaska," Thomas said.[13]

Sheldon sold his sedan to a Valdez politician and returned to Fairbanks by horseback and bicycle, where he immediately ordered two more Model-T's.[14]

Galen hired the affable Sheldon to run his transportation company. While managing both Galen's company and Sheldon's Stage Line, Sheldon served a term as territorial commissioner of roads from which position he pushed for construction of a Kantishna road. He married Annie Bergman and had one

COURTESY OF CANDY WAUGAMAN

*Located about 13 miles west of the railroad depot, Savage Camp, on the east bluff of the Savage River was the park's main tourist destination and facility. In its heyday it included two barns, garage, storehouse, "tent-cabins," and a social hall and dining room, complete with a dance floor.*

daughter, Frances. Sheldon dropped his various enterprises to become the T'n'T's general manager.[15]

After buying out Kennedy, Galen liquidated his transportation company and transferred some of the rolling stock to the park. With the park road now passable to Savage Camp, he replaced horses and wagons for transport from the depot, with automobiles. He saw a golden opportunity at McKinley Park; with strong financial support, coupled with his experience at Glacier Park, he thought he could succeed where Kennedy had failed. He also had Sheldon to rely on.

"Bobby Sheldon, was a great guy," Fritz Nyberg said, "good to everybody, nobody said anything bad about him." Sheldon lived at Savage Camp, overseeing daily operations. No job was too big or too small for Sheldon. He cooked, cleaned, mended tents, repaired vehicles, ran the office, and entertained guests with a light, good-humored quality unmatched even by Galen. His animated, eyewitness account of the shooting of Soapy Smith delighted innumerable park visitors. Over time, Sheldon proved to be the heart and soul of the concession.[16]

The T'n'T management seemed destined to develop an outstanding

COURTESY OF CANDY WAUGAMAN

*The Mt. McKinley Tourist and Transportation Company's general manager, Robert "Bobby" Sheldon, was the heart and soul of the park's tourist concession. No job was too small, or too big, for the affable Sheldon, equally adept at repairing a tent with a treadle sowing machine, or soothing the nerves of a ruffled guest.*

operation, but they faced an uphill battle. Not only was train scheduling still a nuisance but the railroad itself faced an uncertain future. Because of spiraling operational deficits, Congress in 1925, debated total abandonment of the Alaska Railroad. A prominent Congressman flatly rejected further funding and convinced many colleagues to tear up the rails and turn the rail bed into a highway. Interior Secretary Hubert Work also supported abandonment of the line. Somehow, the railroad survived, and in 1926, its management began vigorously pursuing tourist traffic, promoting Mt McKinley National Park and package tours combining the Inside Passage cruises with rail tours to the Interior. Developing the park's tourism potential seemed one solid way to stem the railroad's red ink. Park tourism began a slow annual rise before tumbling in the wake of the 1929 Stock Market crash.[17]

The park's location also was a liability. Visiting it meant a considerable investment in time and money. "When [the park] officially opened in 1923, only twelve [tourists] registered during the summer," Sheldon explained. "In 1924 there were 42; in 1925 the number rose to 208; and this summer [of 1926] there were 502, and there is a possibility of 25 or 30 more before Savage Camp closes for the season." Sheldon's numbers varied from Karstens' but both agreed that only one visitor entered the park in September.[18]

Very few Alaskans toured the park. "Residents of Interior are inclined to think of the Park merely as a scenic attraction for tourists," Sheldon said. To spark local interest, special excursions were offered from Fairbanks, Healy, Suntrana, and sometimes Anchorage. One year, the railroad offered Fairbanksans a weekend special for $25, inclusive of one night at Savage Camp, meals, and round-trip train fare. Residents were treated as "tourists" and given the red-carpet treatment. Sheldon called the *Fairbanks Daily News-Miner* and guaranteed that fall colors would be perfect on Labor Day and encouraged people to sign up for the day-long rail excursion. "Bobby

COURTESY OF CANDY WAUGAMAN

*Bobby Sheldon points out a park attraction to a group of visitors. Almost everyone wanted to see a bear.*

COURTESY OF CANDY WAUGAMAN

*George Lingo unloads a pack horse carrying a Dall sheep that was killed outside the park. Sheep and caribou meat was occasionally served to Savage Camp guests. When Bobby Sheldon resigned as the concession's general manager, to become the Fairbanks postmaster in 1931, Lingo took his place.*

promises that the Park will be more beautiful than at any other season. He has had his crew out for the last week applying fall colors to the trees and bushes."[19]

In an effort to improve access to the park, the railroad in 1926 purchased a two-car train, powered by a 250-horsepower gasoline engine, from J.G. Brill & Company, the nation's largest manufacturer of trolley cars. The "Brill Car," which had a capacity of 90 passengers with room for baggage and food preparation, became the mainstay of park transportation.[20]

The Alaska Railroad provided crucial and substantial support to T'n'T. By special arrangement the railroad transported and stored the company's freight at discount, often—and illegally—for free. Even though railroad management tweaked the schedule to better serve the concession's needs, they could not eliminate costly derailments, rock slides and washouts which stranded and delayed passengers.[21]

Critics cited the slow development of the park road and the lack of a quality hotel as the major issues that hampered expansion of park tourism. Despite Maurice Morino's vigorous effort to spruce up his hotel in 1925, the place

#B88-52-50, ANCHORAGE MUSEUM AT RASMUSON CENTER

*The "wild west" ambiance of Savage Camp was a sharp contrast to the gold rush heritage of frontier Alaska. The Montana roots of Concessionaire James L.Galen influenced the camp's activities and entertainment, which included "bucking bronchos" and mock gunfights.*

remained crude and inadequate. Throughout the 1920s and 30s, there was a general assumption that one or more hotels would be constructed inside the park. At various times, hotels were proposed for McKinley Station, Inspiration Point, Sanctuary River, Copper Mountain, Peters Glacier, and Wonder Lake. Galen's brother, Judge Albert Galen, visited the park in 1926 in order to locate a hotel site at Copper Mountain. None of the proposed hotels were ever built, and it wasn't until 1937 that Congress appropriated $350,000 for construction of a depot hotel, a far more utilitarian design than the grand railroad-style hotel envisioned by Galen.[22]

Savage Camp, and its satellite camps, were all tent camps. After Marquam fell ill and moved to New York in 1928, a reorganization of the company resulted in improved tent camps at Igloo Creek, Polychrome Pass, Toklat River, and Copper Mountain.*

*In 1929, Copper Mountain was renamed Mount Eielson in honor of pilot Carl Ben Eielson who lost his life in a flight in a winter crash off the Siberian coast. In the summer of 1924, Eielson had flown a World War I Jenny biplane to Copper Mountain and landed on a gravel bar of the Thorofare River, the first landing in the park.

Savage Camp, located a short distance south of the park road, remained the main focus of visitor activity until the late 1930s. Instead of an appropriate gold rush, dog mushing, or mining motif, the camp offered an incongruous 1880s Wild West ambiance. Cowboys spun ropes, gallivanted in 10-gallon hats and sheepskin chaps, twirled pistols, and performed horse tricks. Mock stage holdups and hokey gun fight skits enlivened summer evenings. Vintage western stagecoaches transported guests upriver to a tent camp at the head of the river.

Kennedy's horses and wagons may have generated the initial Wild West air, but Galen definitely promoted the cowboy atmosphere. He told tall tales of his father's stage coaches and of outlaws like the Plummer Gang that threatened them. To him, horses and wagons were an accepted, and expected, part of the visitor experience in western national parks. Many of Galen's employees were Montana cowboys and ranch hands, further entrenching this bizarre subversion of early park and Alaska history. Nonetheless, beguiled visitors seemed to love Savage Camp and a taste of this contrived "wild" frontier.

# 19

# Savage Camp

Mt. McKinley will always be unique and a class by itself. It will never be over-run with the hordes of automobiles . . . that are beginning to detract from the enjoyment of many of the other national parks," wrote George Lingo, a Mt. McKinley Tourist and Transportation Company (T'n'T) employee. Its isolation "will always preserve it for the true lovers of nature and those who appreciate the primitive."[1]

Just getting to McKinley Park in the 1920s was an expedition, usually including a continental rail trip, a steamer voyage from Seattle to Seward, and a long, rattling train ride to the park. Travelers needed plenty of money and almost a half-summer to make the trip. The park itself seemed a thrilling, almost exotic destination, offering a trip back in time to America's frontier.

A few determined adventurers made the journey on the cheap. "I came [to Alaska] steerage on the *SS Yukon* of the old Alaska Steamship Line," one traveler wrote, "I bummed on the Alaska Railroad freight train from Anchorage, then a town of a few thousand, to McKinley Park. The trip . . . took two full days, with an overnight at Curry. McKinley Park wasn't connected to any other part of the territory by road, but there was a road in the park. The few cars [there] had been shipped from Anchorage on railroad flatcars."[2]

A few took the gold rush route from Yukon Territory. On his 1924 trip, Robert H. Mainzer, a wealthy New York banker, took a steamship from Vancouver to Skagway, caught the White Pass railroad to Whitehorse, then rode down the Yukon River on a sternwheeler to the mouth of the Tanana River, where he transferred to another paddle-wheeler going upstream to Fairbanks. From there he took the train to the park. He described the scenery as "unsurpassed in the world," and praised the park's sure-footed horses. "Nothing compared to leading a horse over Muldrow glacier next to the crevasses," he exulted.[3]

COURTESY OF CANDY WAUGAMAN.

*Two Concord stagecoaches acquired from Yellowstone Park and two Royal Mail stages purchased from the White Pass and Yukon Railroad, carried tourists on the "Big Game Drive" to the head of the Savage River.*

The Alaska Railroad began promoting the park in 1924, hailing the rail line as the "Mt. McKinley Route," but their publicity effort was sporadic. After prospecting in the Kantishna, geologist Stephen R. Capps spread the word that the "park would be a great Mecca for tourists." He believed that once the road and facilities were completed thousands would visit. His report of seeing "thousands of mountain sheep . . . and caribou, one herd . . . numbering about 15,000 head" circulated widely. The railroad's promotional efforts began to bear fruit the following year, just in time to help the new corporation.[4]

Park visitors were mostly well-traveled elderly people, many from New York and California. Beginning in 1925, automobiles and buses met the train and ferried guests to Savage Camp in the best cars T'n'T could afford, including Fords, Dodges, Pierce Arrows, and one Cadillac. Their buses also included a 14-passenger Graham Brothers bus, four used 18-passenger Studebakers, and a 20-passenger Fageol bus purchased from Yellowstone that proved too long and low for the park road.

Savage Camp, on the east bluff of the Savage River, was the park's main tourist destination and facility. In its heyday, it included two barns, a feed and harness cache, garage, storehouse, combination social hall and dining room, a large framed-in kitchen, and 26 10'x12' "tent-cabins" with wood frames and wooden floors. In 1926, the company built a dance floor in the dining and social hall, with an "orthophonic Victrola" providing the music. For winter storage, the concession built a large warehouse at the depot. A 1,500' airfield was added in the early 1930s for on-demand flight-seeing. Joe Crosson flew Governor George A. Parks on the first flight to the mountain and in 1935, took Wiley Post and Will Rogers on a similar flight the day before the two were killed in a crash near Point Barrow.[5]

Savage Camp was decorated to heighten the Wild West feel. An "antler tree"—a stack of intertwined moose and caribou antlers—dominated the arrival area. Antlers and sheep horns hung from poles in front of the cabins, with mounted caribou and bear heads, Indian handiwork, a "war bonnet," furs, paintings of Mt. McKinley, and "chief ranger Nyberg's red storm pants," in the social hall. For special occasions, like summer solstice or the Fourth of July, Ann Bergman Sheldon and Louise Karstens strung the interior with garlands of wild flowers and spruce boughs.

Starched white linen, cloth napkins, and genuine silverware graced the dining room's four long tables. Guests sat not on benches but on individual chairs.

COURTESY OF CANDY WAUGAMAN

*"Cowboys" greeted guests to Savage Camp. For the entertainment of camp guests, the concessionaire's nephew, J.A. Galen, rode bucking horses and twirled his pistols better than any Hollywood cowboy.*

Each sleeping tent contained a small wood stove, two iron cots, a washstand, and a chair. "While the camp life is not pretentious, it is comfortable and permits one to enjoy being close to nature's own without enduring hardships," read a company brochure. Superintendent Harry Karstens boasted of the company's effort. "They have done splendid work. The accommodations they offer the tourists are far better than is really expected."[6]

Savage Camp operated from June 1 to September 15. Since few travelers arrived that early, the opening date often was pushed back to mid-June. In a pinch, Savage Camp could accommodate 100 overnight guests, but the staff had to move out of their tents to provide room. In time, as many as fifteen or twenty tour companies—primarily the Criswell Company of Los Angeles, Haslick Tour, Tauck Tours, and the American Express Company—booked guests to camp. In 1926, 180 people visited in July, another 190 in August, with the year's total of 533, a 152% increase over the previous year.

For the first time, the concession possessed enough financial backing to develop its assets. Handyman Ray Sharpe established and refurbished forward camps: a five-tent complex and cache at Igloo Creek, a 14'x16' tent at Polychrome Pass; two tents and an 8'x8' cache at the Toklat River, and three tents and an elevated 8'x10' cache at Copper Mountain. "New sleeping tents and a cook tent together with a cache full of supplies constitute the camps," he explained.[7]

In an effort to get visitors out into the park and away from the main road, T'n'T built a 2.5-mile-long horse trail down the Savage River canyon. To provide better upriver access, the road commission spent parts of two summers improving the coach road.* Sharpe built and maintained a tent camp called Caribou Camp at the head of Savage River for both day use and overnight accommodations. In 1926, T'n'T bought two Concord stagecoaches from Yellowstone Park to replace the packhorses and buckboards then used for the "Big Game Drive" to the head of the river. Two years later, they obtained two additional stages from the White Pass and Yukon Railroad, which had been previously used to haul the Royal Mail through the Klondike gold fields. Tourists "greatly enjoyed [these wagons and four-horse teams] as reminiscent of the days of the wild west . . ."[8]

Through most of the 1920s, T'n'T offered park visitors four basic trips. The first, the 14-mile run from McKinley Station to Savage Camp, cost $14 round-trip. The $15 Big Game Drive to the head of the Savage River was integral to the basic overnight package. Two longer trips went west from Savage Camp, one to

*The Savage River road was last used in 1941.

COURTESY OF CANDY WAUGAMAN

*Entertainment at Savage Camp ran the gamut from wildlife talks to live music. John Fern entertained with his banjo and guitar. Dancers whirled to the music played on a Victrola.*

Igloo Creek Camp, and another to the Toklat River Camp. Before the road was built, cross–country travel beyond Savage was by horseback, with 20 pounds of personal baggage carried free. Custom excursions cost $20 per day per person, plus $8 per day for pack horses and $10 per day for saddle horses. Horseback trips from Savage to the foot of Mt. McKinley took about ten days.[9]

In 1926, T'n'T dropped their rates. A roundtrip from McKinley Station to Savage cost $10; a one night stay $25; a trip to Caribou Camp, $10; and Savage River to Copper Mountain, via saddle and pack horses, dropped to $106. Meal prices stayed at $6 per day.

Two trains a day stopped at McKinley Station. Beginning in 1925, travelers coming from the south arrived at noon, while the southbound train from Fairbanks arrived at about 2:00 p.m. Sometimes a "fleet of five autos made three trips to get all the tourists into the park," Karstens reported.[10]

Camp staff referred to guests as "24-hour people, 48-hour people, and campers," based on the visitors' length of stay. Noon arrivals took the afternoon Big Game Drive and nearly always saw sheep, caribou, and foxes. Late afternoon arrivals took the drive the following morning. If there were more people than the stage coaches could handle, the groups went by car. At Caribou Camp, guests were served a late lunch or breakfast. When the cooks saw the stages

Sheldon worked amicably together to resolve infrequent visitor complaints of "inefficiency, dirtiness, poor [and limited] food," but Galen and Karstens butted heads over sundry issues.[17]

"One year we had a lady, she was a food fadist," Howard said, "and . . . when she came to the table, this was wrong, that was wrong, something else was wrong . . . she told me that . . . we served too much starch . . . we were always serving beans . . . and she said, 'You had beans and you had potatoes and you had bread' and she said it was too much starch. Well, we said that . . . anybody can eat what they want to and . . . if they don't want beans, they don't have to eat them or if they don't want potatoes, they don't have to eat them or they can eat all of them. Well, she says, 'It isn't what the public wants, it's what they should eat' . . . after they got back to the states, she wrote me a letter . . . suggesting ways to . . . feed the public. [We met] all kinds of characters."[18]

One camp feature remained a constant source of annoyance—mosquitoes. Some summers the bugs were tolerable, other summers they were hellish. "People coming down river from Dawson would have all kinds of head nets and mosquito lotions, usually oil of citronella, which was quite popular at that time," Howard recalled. "People used to bring this oil of citronella and put that on their pillows. You can never get that smell out, just ruined the pillows."[19]

Even brief mid-summer nights could be cold. Each morning Johnny Howard, or another staffer, would go around to all the guest tents, build a fire in the stove, and fill the teakettles. The guests would arise to a warm tent and hot wash water. When asked, Sheldon would tell people, "Sure we've got running water, just tilt the kettle up, and there, now you have running, water."

Sheldon greeted everyone with a smile and story, a natural at public relations and expert at smoothing ruffled feathers. In the late fall, after the tourist rush slackened, Sheldon always did the cooking. At the sound of the breakfast gong, guests and staff alike hurried to his breakfast table. "He was not above pulling a practical joke on clients, whipping up an occasional iron-tough hotcake just to get a reaction," Lena Howard recalled.[20]

Savage Camp offered its own peculiar entertainment, often with Sheldon the star. "He had a knack of keeping people happy, telling them stories," Howard said. Karstens regaled visitors with his story of climbing Mt. McKinley and also supplied a small electric generator to show park movies. Rangers, who only wore their uniforms when at camp, demonstrated dog mushing techniques, their dogs pulling sleds over bare ground. Guests doted on the dogs. Half-day horseback trips and old-fashioned hay rides also were popular.[21]

A wide variety of races were always popular, and employees George Lingo

COURTESY OF CANDY WAUGAMAN

*Teddy Gentry (r), wrapped his arm around fellow employee, Count Ilia Tolstoy (l), the grandson of the famed Russian novelist. Tolstoy spent two summers at Savage Camp working as man-of-all-trades. Later in life, he pushed for the conservation and protection of the birds of the Caribbean.*

and Ann Elliott enjoyed a particular rivalry in horse racing. Everyone wagered sums on races staged with captive porcupines. During the annual Fourth of July celebration, Grant Pearson beat all the runners in the "cracker and whistle race...in nothing flat."[22]

Ranger Grant Pearson's physical prowess amazed visitors. On one trip to Copper Mountain he hiked while everyone else rode horses. He out-distanced the group and by the time the riders got to the Copper Mountain camp, he had the fires going and the coffee ready.[23]

Savage Camp never had trouble with bears. "It's strange, too," Howard explained, "because we had . . . the garbage pile, but they never seemed to bother that [but] we had foxes that would come to be fed." The lack of bear trouble is anecdotal evidence of the low number of bears then inhabiting the park. George Flood, who guided two summers for Dan Kennedy, never saw a wolf or grizzly. Guns were legally kept in camp for bear protection and once a staffer shot a prowling wolf. Moose were also hard to find.[24]

Almost every guest wanted to see a grizzly. One year two captive bears, named "Jim" and "Bob" in honor of Galen and Sheldon, entertained camp visitors. "The tourists were especially delighted with the two cub bears which were captured on the Richardson Highway and taken to the park by R.E. Sheldon," a reporter explained. Galen's ability with a lariat was put to the test when one of the grizzly cubs, named "September Morn" [aka Jim] escaped and eluded capture. "One dexterous twist of . . . the arm . . . brought the cub again under control." At the end of the season, Sheldon looked for someone who would "protect, love and zealously guard the bears" through the winter and release them the next spring. The bears were given to National Park Service Director Stephen Mather during his 1926 visit and he transferred them to Washington's National Zoo. The following winter, while attending a superintendents' conference in D.C., Karstens visited the bears and reported that, "they seemed to know me, and although they had grown to be quite large, I had quite a tussle with them."[25]

Extended horseback trips offered guests a chance to rough it. Usually one guide and seven horses were enough to support a party of three people. Each guest had a responsibility, either as cook, dish washer, or wood splitter and fire builder. All stayed busy while the guide cared for the horses and tack. The trips were costly but everyone seemed to enjoy the hands-on experience.

Horses were a huge drain on profits. Wintering the remuda entailed extensive logistics and mountains of expensive hay and grain. Wintering the animals in the Interior was impractical. One year Dan Kennedy wintered his horses on Kodiak Island, and the next near Palmer. Later, Louis Corbley tried wintering the company's horses on the Healy River but the animals suffered from the cold and powerful winds. After 1934, they over-wintered at a corral and barn built on a homestead near Lignite.

No matter how inspiring the taiga, tundra, and mountains of the Alaska Range, the vast majority of guests felt cheated if they didn't see *the* mountain. Camp guests "always enjoyed McKinley Park and," Howard remembered, "the main thing was to see . . . Mt. McKinley . . . sometimes they would blame us for the mountain not being out!

"Well it's a temperamental mountain, you never know," she said. "Sometimes the mountain would be clear and by the time they . . . brought the tourists out to camp, the mountain would be shrouded . . . then after they were gone, the next day the mountain would come out and before the next group got in it'd be clouded up again."[26]

On cloudy days, someone would stay up late to alert the guests if the mountain cleared. On one occasion, the sky stayed clear but the mountain remained under wraps. The next day, just as the buses were being loaded for the trip to the depot, "the clouds parted, Mt. McKinley stood out there just like a million. And, oh, the people were so excited, they said they wished they didn't have to go, didn't have to leave, wished they could stay longer. Well, it just folded up and the clouds closed in again."[27]

Guests could sometimes see wildlife right from the camp. Guides easily pointed out the park's numerous Dall sheep, caribou, ground squirrels, and ptarmigan. Foxes were common; wolves and lynx rarely seen.

As the road progressed westward, motor vehicles replaced wagons. The "48-hour people" were driven as far as construction would allow. The single lane road, with few turnouts, was a problem for passing vehicles especially on the mountain passes. "Sable Pass was . . . a sinner," Howard said. "When it rained, it'd be slippery, and people held their breath going down . . . "[*28]

Drivers provided commentary, spotted wildlife, and, almost daily, stopped to repair their vehicles. Passengers commonly got out and waded the river crossings, or helped push their trapped vehicle out of the mud. When the road opened to the Toklat River in 1932, many guests found the narrow, windy, cliff-edged road frightening. One visitor described Johnny Howard, who favored the reliable Studebaker coach for travel over Polychrome summit, as without

---

*According to Fritz Nyberg, Sable Pass was named in 1912 by geologist Stephen Capps because "it was yellow on one side, black on the other," which are the colors of a pine marten, or sable.

COURTESY OF CANDY WAUGAMAN

*As the 1920s progressed, motor vehicles replaced wagons and horses for guest transportation. Camp guests asked for frequent breaks in the jolting, cross-country travel.*

equal as a driver and game spotter. Some guests were too frightened to drive over Polychrome and chose to walk it. Concession staff called the steepest point on Polychrome, "Poison Point...One drop will kill you."[29]

Throughout much of the 1920s, T'n'T employed between 25 and 30 people. Nonetheless Savage Camp was always short-staffed. With a big crowd in camp, everyone pitched in. Even the horse wranglers washed dishes and cleaned tents. "Mr. Kelly, our auditor . . . was very meticulous about bookkeeping and everything . . . wanted to know [how much work everyone did] . . . for the kitchen, so much for the tents, and so much for the horses." The men wanted to know if they were "supposed to carry a notebook around . . . and write down so many hours washing dishes and so many hours taking care of the horses and so many hours in the tent." Kelly approved and paid for only eight hours per person per work day, which did not begin to compensate for actual duty time. Usually the help ate breakfast at 7:00 a.m. and worked until very late. Lena Howard once told time-keeper Teddy Gentry to "give me fifteen hours today." Gentry, constrained by the auditor, could not.[30]

During their precious free time the staff went horseback riding, berry picking, hiking, or simply relaxed. Other than rare trips to town for the dentist or doctor " . . . nobody ever asked for time off . . . or went to town unless they had

COURTESY OF CANDY WAUGAMAN

*With the unfinished Teklanika River Bridge in the background, road workers used a team and wagon to pull a stranded touring car across the river ford.*

... an emergency. We were all happy to stay right there," Howard said.[31]

The concession employed many talented, hard-working people. Camp cook Lena Howard, whose home was in California's Imperial Valley, spent the summer of 1922 touring Alaska with a friend. Her hobby was visiting America's national parks and Mt. McKinley National Park was on her list. As it turned out she "made a life job of" McKinley Park. Howard had heard so much about the winters that she wanted to experience it herself and so she moved to Fairbanks in September. "The next summer [I] took trips around to see what I had missed and ... [get] Alaska out of my system," but she was hooked. Because of the seemingly endless, un-paid hours of work at Savage Camp, Howard swore that she would not come back for another year, yet she always did. In 1927, her husband, Johnny Howard, got work with the T'n'T.[32]

Ms. Howard enjoyed the park, "especially as it was then ... So many people would say. 'Oh, when you got the hotel built, we'll be back,' and others would say, 'Don't ever build a hotel, that'll spoil it all ... They loved the tent camps, and ... they enjoyed the frontier life, while others didn't, just like today.'"[33]

Galen customarily hired people he knew personally. Louis Corbley, formerly of Galen's Cordova Transfer, had driven stages over the Richardson Highway, and before that managed roadhouses at Copper Center and Circle Hot Springs.

Galen hired him to supervise the horses and stage coaches.

In 1926, Corbley met an adventurous woman at the park named Sadie. "Billie," as she was called, had been in Alaska two years, living in Circle City, Rainbow, and Fairbanks. Billie had been one of the few people, and perhaps the only woman, to take a horse pack trip from Cantwell to Eureka Camp. Her route led up Windy Creek, through the Sanctuary headwaters, then past Cathedral and Sable Mountains, and on out to Kantishna. (Lou became a ranger and served as Chief Ranger for ten years.)[34]

One of Savage Camp's most colorful characters was Galen's nephew, J.A. Galen of Hollywood, an expert horseman. "The Western effect is carried out by Galen, and for the entertainment of camp visitors he has two 'bucking bronchos' [sic] which he rides." J.A. could spin a rope and twirl pistols better than any Hollywood cowboy.[35]

Scotty MacKeen, a Montana cowboy from Galen's hometown, wrangled horses and guided guests on day trips. Scotty wore a 10-gallon hat and sheepskin chaps, gallivanting about in classic Montana cow-puncher style.

Another Montanan, George Lingo, went on to a long, fruitful career with the T'n'T. Born April 30, 1901, in Anaconda, Montana, Lingo came to Alaska in 1918 with his parents who operated roadhouses along the Inside Passage and then in Prince William Sound. He finished high school in Seattle, and in 1927 graduated from the Alaska Agricultural College and School of Mines with a degree in mining. After graduation, he went to work with the T'n'T.

Lingo, an excellent hunter and naturalist, excelled at guiding guests keen on viewing wildlife. Once while leading a group on the Savage River he witnessed the aftermath of the battle of two large Dall rams. One was dead at the base of a 200' cliff and the other was struggling upward. Finally the sheep lost its footing and "dropped to his death beside the body of the ram it had killed."[36]

Like Sheldon, no task was too small for Lingo. He "wrangled horses and wrangled tourists," washed dishes, cleaned tents, and chopped firewood for the voracious tent stoves. Lingo wrote newspaper stories, gave interviews, and often traveled Outside to promote business. Lingo took over as General Manager when Bobby Sheldon left in the mid–1930s to become the Fairbanks Postmaster.

For two summers, the handsome and mysterious Count Ilia A. Tolstoy, grandson of the famed Russian novelist, worked in the camp, often doing dishes like anyone else. "He was a great attraction," said a guest. "I came to see your two chief attractions Mt. McKinley and Count Tolstoy."[37]

Galen hired another acquaintance from Cordova, Martin Ellingson, as chief packer. He also hired Frank Glaser and Harry Lucke as fill-in guides, both of whom knew the park intimately and could "gab" with the best of them.[38]

"Harry Lucky [sic] once was out with two photographers with a moving picture camera. A bear was sighted in the distance and the camera was set up," Olaus Murie recounted. "Presently the grizzly spied the camera and came for it. The photographer turned the crank until the bear came uncomfortably near. Then he turned and ran. When the bear came near enough to smell the tracks, he ran off, apparently much frightened." Needless to say, Glaser and Lucke repeated this story endlessly.[39]

Agnes Schlosser first came to Alaska in 1924 and taught in remote camps from Chicken to Akiak. In summers she supervised the "culinary department" at Savage Camp and prepared meals for camp, day trips, and hunting excursions. A one-time summer fling as a camp cook turned into a seasonal career lasting 13 years.[40]

Another teacher, Norma Jordet, worked as a camp housekeeper. She was born in North Dakota to Norwegian immigrant parents. She began teaching in 1921 and through friends got to know pilot Carl Ben Eielson, who enthralled and excited her with stories of Alaska's "glaciers, icebergs, mountains, and forests." Seeing Alaska as "exotic," she took a teaching job in Fairbanks and for four summers she "did dishes, made beds, everything." In 1932, she met Harry Hoyt, the road commission's lead mechanic, and a romance developed following a first kiss at Horseshoe Lake.

Partners John Fern (formerly Fernstrom) and Joe Gagnon, a Quebec Francophone, were also seasonal employees. In winter, they worked in area mines or trapped on the Healy River. Ernest Patty visited their camp while investigating the Healy River coal fields. "Joe, a good cook, had a fine dinner ready for us," Patty said, "and on New Year's Eve brought out several bottles of homemade beer for a New Year toast."[41]

Expert horseman and hunting guide Carl Anderson took charge of the stagecoach operation. His guiding skills were invaluable to T'n'T which derived important revenue from fall hunting trips. After one particularly dismal tour season, a full slate of hunters kept the business afloat.

Anderson arrived in Valdez on a steamer in 1903, and started out on foot for Fairbanks, arriving one month later. On a nearby creek he staked his first claim. With pick and shovel he sank an almost 200'–deep shaft but quit when he failed to reach bedrock. Later he heard that another prospector had hit bedrock and struck it rich.

After a stint as a mine laborer, Anderson and two partners began hauling freight

COURTESY OF CANDY WAUGAMAN

*Until sometime after World War II, most of the park road was a single lane with few pullouts. Whenever buses stopped at Igloo Creek, and other viewing sites, they completely blocked the road.*

to Valdez using horses in summer and dogs in winter. A decade later, Anderson contracted to haul freight for AEC and eventually homesteaded 160 acres at Lignite. From there, he ran a trapline and took hunters into the Wood River.

He went to work for the T'n'T' in the mid-1920s and from the outset proved his worth. "He was extremely good with horses, better than anyone else I was ever around," said one co-worker. "He handled them with kid gloves and was very gentle. He was more of a pioneer than Daniel Boone. The best guide by far."[42]

Anderson, "a gentleman by far," was honest and fair in his dealing and could captivate clients for hours with his stories. He recited poetry, told jokes, and was a good diplomat (the latter being very important for dealing with tired or petulant guests.)[43]

In autumn when park visitation slackened, guides gathered gear and prepared saddle and pack stock for hunts east of the Nenana River, or in the west near Mt. Dall. A two-week trip from Savage Camp to the Cody Creek Camp in Wood River cost $750 each for a party of four, including the services of 15 horses, three guides, a wrangler, and a cook. T'n'T used both cabins and wall tents. The company had contracted Theodore Van Bibber, a long-time Wood

River resident and trapper, to build two hunting "lodges," actually one-room cabins, on Cody Creek and Kansas Creek.

Jim Galen outfitted three hunting parties in 1927, the largest of which was the William Osgood Field party of Lennox, Massachusetts. George Lingo led the expedition of 11 men and 28 horses west toward Mt. Dall and the Tonzona River. After 41 days, the party returned to Savage Camp, their packhorses laden with hunting trophies and hides. (The wealthy Field later gained fame as a glaciologist and alpinist.) At the same time, two other groups led hunters into the Wood River, one guided by Galen, the other by Corbley.[44]

Hunters unanimously praised Galen as a "delightful and attentive host," with John Fern earning high marks as guide, horseman and packer. Frequent mention was made of the beauty of this drainage, an area that Olaus Murie, after hunting sheep there, informally recommended for inclusion in the park.[45]

When T'n'T's interest in hunting waned during the Great Depression, Anderson bought the horses and tack for his own guiding business.

Anderson's expertise with animals would one day involve him in one of the more odd wildlife endeavors in park history. Anderson and Lew Campbell were hired to capture Dall sheep for newspaper tycoon William Randolph Hearst's private zoo at San Simeon, California. The men, under the authority of a special permit issued to Hearst, caught the sheep in Riley Creek using wolf snares, fitted with a "keeper" to prevent strangulation. Nonetheless, they accidentally killed two sheep. Anderson shipped south nine sheep including "one exceptionally fine six-year-old ram . . . close to the 200-pound mark." In time, Hearst assembled the world's largest private zoo, with some 100 species, on his San Simeon estate. Some of the animals lived in cages, others, like the Dall sheep and Himalayan Thar, roamed free in fenced enclosures totaling 2,000 acres. In the wake of financial collapse, Hearst dispersed the collection in 1937. The fate of the Dall sheep is unknown.[46]

Word of the park's improved amenities and varied activities began to spread. Bookings for 1928 increased 26% over the previous year, with one quarter of that total from California. Again the company reduced rates—a roundtrip from the depot to Savage now costing $7.50, and the trip up Savage River was down from $10 to $7.50. Karstens' goal of affordable tourism was nearing realization.

In late 1927, the always rocky relationship between Galen and Karstens went aground on volatile shoals. In late autumn, Galen complained to Washington that rangers were killing caribou illegally at the Toklat ranger camp. Chief Ranger Fritz Nyberg claimed ignorance of the Toklat incident and in mid-October Karstens sent Nyberg to investigate. At the Toklat cabin, Nyberg found meat and a hide, with a note from ranger Lee Swisher explaining the circumstances. "Early on the morning of the 28th [September] I saw not far from the Toklat relief cabin, what I believed to be a reindeer, so having orders to kill…I shot and killed it but examination proved to be a whiter than usual caribou." Despite Swisher's explanation, Galen went before the Alaska Game Commission in November demanding action on the caribou kill, calling Nyberg a "poacher." (Why Galen singled out Nyberg in this case instead of Swisher is unclear. Karstens said that Galen had previously displayed a special "enmity to Nyberg" because of another incident.)[47]

According to Karstens, the enmity between Galen and the chief ranger was not hard to trace. The contretemps flared in the wake of a trip through the park made by Dr. and Mrs. Frank Oastler, influential friends of Charles Sheldon's and widely-known lecturers. After the trip, the Oastlers complained to Nyberg that their female cook had been inefficient, morose, and dirty but that Galen had taken no action on their complaints. Because Frank Oastler was well-connected, scheduling his park film at the Explorers Club in New York, Karstens grew alarmed at possible negative publicity. Karstens dutifully passed on their complaint to park service headquarters along with associated reports that Galen was having an open affair with the cook, which culminated in a heated public shouting match at Savage Camp between Galen, his wife, and the cook.[48]

Karstens' report enraged Galen, who claimed the issue had nothing to do with park business, and therefore was none of his business. In retrospect, this is an instance where Karstens should have reacted more cautiously. Allegations like those leveled at Galen, and earlier, his partner Tom Marquam, are always thorny. The concept of the concession and park service as a partnership, though new and evolving, required unimpeachable standards of conduct, both public and private. While the Roaring 20s witnessed the unraveling of morality laws, arrests and attempted prosecutions of such laws were still common, even in Alaska. The animosity engendered by the report seriously undermined Karstens relationship with Galen and would lead to bitter enmity.

The Wild West show that was often Savage Camp faded slowly. Judging by the writings and reminiscences of early camp guests, many thoroughly enjoyed the spectacle, while at the same time asking about "sourdoughs, dog mushing, and the gold rush era." By the late 1930s the ambiance had changed, replaced by more authentic Alaskan themes. By then, Karstens, the pioneer superintendent, was himself a storied part of the park's history.

# 20

# CHANGING OF THE GUARD

ALASKANS MARKED 1928 as a year of change. Residents nominated Admiralty Island for National Park status; Native children won the right to attend public school; Carl Ben Eielson became the first to fly the Arctic Ocean; giant gold dredges displaced independent miners; and the U.S. Congress finally rescinded the "miners' exemption," outlawing all hunting in Mt. McKinley National Park. Other news from Outside and around the world, excited and dismayed Alaskans. The New York Yankees of Babe Ruth and Lou Gehrig won the World Series; Amelia Earhart became the first woman to fly the Atlantic; and the Stock Market careened up and down. More ominously, Adolph Hitler's party won a majority in Bavaria and Japan sent troops to Manchuria.

The year started off well for Harry Karstens. In late winter a young and upcoming photographer from California wrote seeking assistance for a summer trip. Always eager to help anyone who might spotlight the park, Karstens promptly agreed to help but the young man, Ansel Adams, decided to postpone his trip for a year. In the spring the park service announced that Karstens would again climb Mt. McKinley "in the interest of science," with a stated goal of retrieving the recording thermometer that he and Hudson Stuck had left there in 1913, which would determine "whether the peak is the coldest spot on earth." Once again, however, Karstens' plans for a second ascent would be thwarted due to heavy work demands.[1]

Karstens praised the road commission's progress under the supervision of M.C. Edmunds. "By fall the road will reach Sable Pass, 40 miles from the railroad . . . " he enthused. Under Edmunds' guidance, the road commission again upgraded the road to the head of the Savage River, so that the round trip could be made by automobile in as little as one hour. The new trail down the Savage River opened new "game and fishing country and makes patrol work much easier by enabling rangers to go through the canyon instead of over the mountains."[2]

Good publicity, which made the park a touchstone for any trip to Alaska, resulted in a "heavy" increase in tourism. In mid-summer, Karstens reported a 33% increase over the previous year's total. (In all, 802 people visited the park in 1928.) To Karstens it appeared that park visitation finally had turned the corner, allowing the concession to make a consistent profit. In early summer rangers Fritz Nyberg and Grant Pearson accompanied cinematographer and lecturer Gene Miller on a one month filming foray. They climbed to 8,000' on the mountain and filmed the summit and glaciers. Altogether, the men covered 300 miles on horseback and afoot and saw "10,000 mountain sheep, and 7,000 to 8,000 caribou," Nyberg reported. "Miller obtained pictures never before taken." For Karstens, the film represented a public relations coup that would draw even more visitors.[3]

Recognizing that many Alaskans could not "afford an extended stay in the Park," Karstens and the T'n'T collaborated on plans to establish public camping sites, with well-equipped tents available at a minimal charge. Nyberg said that Karstens had numerous plans for the future and was very good to park visitors, always seeking ways to improve their experience.

Park wildlife also seemed to be doing well. Grizzlies, once uncommon, appeared to be steadily increasing while sheep and caribou remained numerous. An increase of wolves and coyotes, however, worried Karstens. "So serious is the situation becoming that an expert predatory animal hunter will be brought in and a campaign of extermination . . . inaugurated," he told the press.[4]

Development of the new park headquarters at Rock Creek continued. Work began in the spring on a water system and three new buildings, a barn, ranger dormitory, and warehouse. The accelerated pace of park activities increased everyone's work load. "The present personnel barely able to meet all demands placed upon it," Karstens said, "the Park employees have little spare time."[5]

There was literally no end to the work. With constant labor the living conditions had improved dramatically since the 1925 move. "Fritz's cabin would be the envy of any woman, no matter how good a housekeeper she thought she was," Bill Myers said. "He is a bachelor . . . but has a mahogany-finished dining room set in his cabin, together with a leather couch, a writing desk, and dresser. All the logs on the inside of the cabin are peeled and shellacked. The walls are decorated with caribou horns, a mountain sheep's head, a bear skin, and several pictures of mountain sheep and dogs. There are curtains and over-hangings on the windows. To top it off there is an Orthophonic Victrola

COURTESY OF CANDY WAUGAMAN

*In 1925, Harry Karstens began the relocation of McKinley Park headquarters to a site on a sunny bench above Rock Creek. The new location was warmer than Riley Creek and removed from the day-to-day squabbles of McKinley Station.*

and scads of records. This doesn't look much like the picture of the bleak and barren cabins that we usually think of as being typical of Alaska. I tell you, there's solid comfort in Fritz's cabin."[6]

The move to Rock Creek, and away from the depot, had defused some of the early antagonisms that had vexed Karstens. Morino and Karstens, although still wary of one another, had developed a mutual respect. Now, instead of the old bluster and bellow, they talked things out. Duke Stubbs remained provocative but Rufus Nichols, another malcontent, had moved on. However, the concessionaire, Jim Galen, would not let the alleged caribou poaching incident die. In early 1928, he again wrote Director Mather about Nyberg's "caribou poaching." On February 24, Director Mather, Arno Cammerer, Karstens, and Galen convened at Yosemite's Ahwahnee Hotel to discuss the matter. "This conference was called because of differences between Mr. Galen and Mr. Karstens . . . that each was interfering unnecessarily in the other's bailiwick."[7]

Galen asserted that what he called "the caribou poaching incident" had been covered-up and accused Karstens of interfering in personnel matters, specifically the employment of his cook, Agnes Schlosser. Karstens denied a cover-up and recounted the numerous complaints about Galen and Schlosser. Mather made it clear "that in his opinion [Karstens] had overstepped his authority by making more of a personal matter out of his objection to the young lady in question." Mather warned Galen not to spread criticism and false charges, and told both men to make an "earnest effort to get along amicably in the future." Both Karstens and Galen took their lumps in the meeting, but neither man let go of their resentment.[8]

Back at the park, the endless workload had created a deep fissure between the superintendent and his rangers. Major conflict swirled around the construction work. On several cold, autumn days, Nyberg and Myers had to work waist deep in the icy waters of Riley Creek to help workmen float building logs downstream for use in various projects. The logs "floated" from one rock pile to another or crashed onto the banks, requiring super-human labor to re-float them. Nyberg seemed to have temporarily lost his good humor and forgotten his personal ranger motto: "No matter how cold and wet it is, we're always warm and dry."[9]

Although Karstens pushed his rangers hard, he pushed himself harder. According to Myers, Karstens got in "over his head" because he bit off more than he could accomplish. A mere $10,000 had been appropriated for the construction of the three buildings. "Everybody, except the superintendent, could see that it wouldn't be near enough for all this work and accordingly [the rangers] tried to get Karstens to give up until he got more money," Myers wrote his father. He explained that, in his opinion, Karstens saw this as simple insurrection, so "he kept all the rangers home working on the buildings instead of letting them go out into the hills and get the work done out there which has to be done in the summer time or not at all."[10]

Karstens, a man of action by nature, fared poorly under the growing stress, his temper growing volcanic. "When we got him [Karstens] away from the office . . . he was one of the best you ever saw on the trail and in nature and you couldn't beat him," Nyberg said. "There wasn't a finer man to be on the trail with." But the paperwork and bureaucratic in-fighting drove the indomitable Karstens up the wall. Nyberg said that Karstens didn't understand office work and it got the best of him. It "really wasn't a problem with funds, or accounting, office work got him down completely," he said. "Karstens was quite irritated when around headquarters." Nyberg remembered an incident when out of total frustration Harry threw a coal oil lamp at Louise, missing her by inches. "I got away from the paperwork as fast as I could," Nyberg concluded. The new park clerk, Eugene G. "Dinty" Moore, seemed to operate on his own agenda and exacerbated some situations.[11]

Unlike some other area residents, alcohol was not a factor in Karstens' irascibility. "He was not a drinking man at all," Nyberg said. "Don't believe he had alcohol in the house." He said that Karstens was a likable man but flew off the handle a lot. "Anyone who crossed him," Nyberg recalled, "he lost his temper and that was it."[12]

In mid-September, Nyberg and Karstens clashed over yet another building project, a sub-text to a larger dispute. Fritz said that Karstens, in retaliation for the Galen dispute, had ordered him not to visit Savage Camp, or assist T'n'T in any way. In essence, he told Nyberg to stay out of Galen's way and to avoid further antagonizing the man. "Of course this was a little too much for Fritz," Myers wrote, "and figuratively speaking; he thumbed his nose at the Superintendent."[13] The opening of the fall hunting season necessitated intensive patrols along the east and north boundaries of the park. Nyberg and his protégé, Myers, trudged the hills looking for poachers. In mid-September, despite the need to patrol, "work on a ranger's cabin was behind so Fritz had to help with that . . ." Myers explained, and he carried out the patrols alone.[14]

HENRY P. KARSTENS COLLECTION, #630, KARSTENS LIBRARY

*As the park's staff and funding increased in the late 1920s, Harry Karstens found himself increasingly trapped at his desk, buried beneath never-ending paperwork. Infrequently, he escaped alone to patrol the park's backcountry by dogteam.*

HENRY P. KARSTENS COLLECTION, #0633, KARSTENS LIBRARY

*In 1928, Karstens traveled to San Francisco to attend a conference of National Park Superintendents, where he met Tom Boles, Superintendent of Carlsbad Caverns National Park. The two men briefly considered swapping positions, but within weeks Karstens resigned his position as Mt. McKinley National Park's first superintendent.*

In a volatile confrontation at headquarters, Nyberg insisted he needed to prepare for winter patrols and that laborers should do the cabin construction. Karstens exploded and fired him on the spot. Nyberg appealed to Washington citing the civil service regulation that a person could not be fired without just and due cause. He soon learned that no formal charges had been received and that only the Interior Secretary could suspend or dismiss him. Two days later, after receiving a wire from Washington, Karstens ordered Nyberg back to work.

Karstens then informed Nyberg that he would soon file charges against him. "I am interested in knowing what the charges are," Nyberg wrote Director Mather, "but so far he has not given me a copy of [them] . . . I would appreciate knowing as soon as possible whether or not his charges are sustained, for I do not feel like spending two hundred dollars for a winter outfit if . . . my services may no longer be required . . ." A portion of his letter devolved into a petty attack on Karstens' work ethic.[15]

In early October, Karstens wired Washington that he would resign "as he had had enough." With the Galen and Nyberg conflicts fresh in their minds, his superiors were ready to act. "I think we have been very considerate of Mr. Karstens and that he has rendered very good service taken as a whole," Arno Cammerer wrote Horace Albright. "We feel, however, that the time has come when for the good of the Service and the good of Mr. Karstens a change will have to be made . . . he has allowed park problems to thwart his judgment and wear on his mentality that . . . it is best for him to be relieved."[16]

Karstens' resignation was accepted, effective October 15, 1928. Until a replacement could be named, Moore would serve as acting superintendent. Nyberg retained his position as chief ranger for two more years.

"When [Karstens] quit he was more or less tired of the whole thing . . . Was fed up with it," Nyberg explained. "The trouble with Karstens, was, when he was appointed superintendent, he thought he was in charge of Alaska from Ketchikan to Point Barrow. He took in too much territory. If somebody would have started him off right, he would have been as good a superintendent of the park as you would want."[17]

At that time Bill Myers, then 19, the youngest ranger in the National Park Service, sided with his friend and mentor Nyberg. Concerning the resignation, he said "this is but the ending to a rather long story, in fact beginning when Mr. Karstens first went on the job. From what I've been able to find out he's been losing friends and becoming more unpopular with everyone who knows him or has worked for him. Maybe this sounds a bit prejudiced but the truth is I've never heard anybody say a good word for him since I've been here . . ."[18]

Years later, and no longer under Nyberg's influence, Myers had a slightly different view. Then he described Karstens as "an honest man" who did "nothing irregular" and was very sorry to see the circumstances that led to his resignation. He felt that Karstens removal was "not quite justified" and that E.G. Moore, who was sympathetic to Nyberg, became the "hatchet man" to oust Karstens. Local residents suspected that Nyberg wanted the superintendent's job for himself and had intentionally created some of the conflict.[19]

Others supported Myers' latter view. Nyberg was not well liked, they said. More than one person described him as haughty and pretentious. "Most of the boys liked Grant [Pearson] and Karstens," Pete Bagoy said. "Everyone liked Harry Karstens but not many people liked Nyberg." Bagoy remembers Karstens as a "nice guy, quiet and soft-spoken" but "Fritz was a meanie as far as I was concerned," and "the bossy type. Nyberg got a little authority and threw his weight around."[20]

Dan Wilder, speaking from his experience as a ranger and construction foreman, described Nyberg as a chief ranger who "preferred the comfort of his easy chair, warm fire and oranges in headquarters." In fairness, if the patrol logs

HENRY P. KARSTENS COLLECTION, #0855, KARSTENS LIBRARY

*Clerk Ralph Mackie (l), and Chief Ranger Fritz Nyberg (r), at a Savage Camp social gathering. After several years of faithful service, Nyberg got into a row with his boss, Harry Karstens, and was fired. Reinstated, Nyberg remained difficult, even after Harry Liek replaced Karstens as superintendent. Years later, Nyberg ruefully said, "I just should have kept my mouth shut."*

are accurate, Nyberg annually covered more territory than any other ranger. Wilder's comments probably reflected the natural resentment of an employee who was told what to do, rather than led by example. The fact that Nyberg referred to his ranger as "Wildman" demonstrated a lack of respect.[21]

Years later, Nyberg alluded to partial blame in the Karstens affair, as well as contrition for the behavior that led to his eventual firing by the second superintendent, Harry Liek. "It was the best job I ever had," he said, "I just should have kept my mouth shut with the two Harrys [Karstens and Liek.]"[22]

Karstens' replacement, Harry Liek, formerly of Yellowstone Park, was hand-picked by Horace M. Albright. Two years into his Mt. McKinley National Park assignment, Liek wrote Albright to explain his difficulties and conflicts with rangers. Lack of funds had forced him to use rangers as construction crew, necessary for the completion of park headquarters. "I found it impossible to construct some of the projects with the amount . . . appropriated," he said, and had no other alternative but to use rangers. "It has never been my intention to work rangers on construction only in case of emergency, and I considered this one. Otherwise I would have had to stop long before the buildings were completed."[23]

In the letter, Liek frankly charged that Nyberg and Moore had been less than cooperative and the source of much of his difficulties. "The trouble started very shortly after my arrival here," he wrote. "At that time I [blamed the problem] on Moore, who was the clerk and had been acting superintendent, however I found out after that Nyberg was implicated as much as Moore was. They seemed to take the attitude that they would continue to run the park, they had in a way compelled Karstens to resign . . ."[24]

Liek went on to describe Nyberg as "sullen," and said that he "did every thing he could in his underhanded way to give me trouble . . . He was having trouble with someone all the time, the prospectors and the road commission people, and a row over something that did not concern him or his work. Even outside the park he had trouble with the trappers." Moore resigned in late 1929, and Nyberg was fired in 1930.[25]

Liek also butted heads with local residents. Duke Stubbs badgered Liek and his patrol rangers constantly. The new superintendent faced the same difficulties that had bedeviled Karstens throughout his tenure.

After all the struggle, effort, and turmoil, why did Karstens quit when he did? The conflicts with Nyberg and Galen seemed rather minor in comparison to other challenges he'd faced. Maybe, as Nyberg said, he'd simply had "had enough." But perhaps another event shattered his determination.

On September 21, 1928, Western Union delivered the stunning news: Charles "Billie" Sheldon, 61, was dead. "Billie died very suddenly of heart failure this morning." The man most responsible for the creation of the park and for Karstens' role as its first superintendent was gone.[26]

There had been no warning signs. At the time of his death, Sheldon and his family were summering at his camp at Kedgemakooge, Nova Scotia. Friends reported that he'd never seemed better or happier. Puttering in the woods around the cabin with his children, especially his son Bill, brought him great joy. On "Friday morning, he seemed as well as ever and sat joking and talking with us apparently in exuberant spirits," one friend recounted. "Later he told Louisa that he was not feeling well. He suddenly had a bad pain and in a few minutes he was gone."[27]

From all over the country, heart-felt condolences flowed in to the Sheldon family. "His premature passing . . . leaves a profound void in the hearts of all the many friends and associates who had the privilege of knowing him," wrote his close friend Edward W. Nelson. "The great debt the public owes him for his forceful assistance in . . . the conservation of our wildlife resources, the National Forests and the National Parks, will never be fully known and appreciated. This is due largely to the fact that with all his masterly ability, Sheldon was one of the most self-effacing men I have ever known . . ."[28]

"He fell on sleep—as he would have wished to if he could have chosen—in the woods to which he had so long been devoted," wrote one grieving friend. "By his death the associations with which he was connected, the causes in behalf of which he worked, and his friends have suffered an irreparable loss."[29]

To Karstens, Sheldon was mentor, father figure, and friend who had unwaveringly supported him in his fight to develop the national park of Sheldon's vision, a wildlife preserve without peer. The loss, to a man like Karstens, who prized above all else, loyalty to a friend, and the honor and sanctity of a man's word, was incalculable.

Historians have not always been kind to the memory of Harry Karstens. At times he's been called "rough-hewn," "an un-polished frontiersman" and, harshly, "un-fit for the job." Yet none of his critics have questioned his remarkable achievement of creating a park in such hostile circumstances.

With pitiful funding, no political power, and limited personnel, Karstens possessed the commitment, energy, practical skills, and unflinching force of will needed to carry out his mandate. What he lacked in administrative ability, he more than made up for in his expertise with livestock, machinery, construction, and knowledge of the territory and its people. More than anything, however, he possessed the

COURTESY OF CANDY WAUGAMAN

*Harry Karstens was able to protect the park's Dall sheep from poachers but not from the cruelties of the sub-arctic winter. Following Karstens' resignation, two severe winter storms decimated the herds. The starving, emaciated animals were easily caught by hand and a few rescued. The herds never rebounded to their former abundance.*

resolute courage needed to stand up to the wrath of Alaskans who hated the federal government, as embodied by the new national park. He faced down his powerful neighbors and antagonists—the ex-Legionnaire, the former park superintendent, the one-time U.S. Commissioner, the unbending military men—and in the process, protected the wildlife and natural resources of Mt. McKinley National Park while at the same time building the necessary infrastructure.

Harry Karstens fares well when compared to his pioneer successors, none of whom left a legacy as compelling. Although Liek and Pearson summited Mt McKinley in 1932, only the second such success, their climb was primarily a public relations gambit to bolster respect for the park, and park service, among Alaskans. Even though Pearson was associated with the park for over 30 years, with lengthy stints as superintendent, he did not leave an indelible imprint on the park. He did, however, establish the position of full-time, year-around, park naturalist and assign the first ranger to Katmai National Monument, then a unit under his supervision. Under his tenure, winter patrols were sporadic and often conducted only after rangers badgered him for permission. He too faced personnel conflicts and controversies. In the late 1940s, Pearson butted heads with Adolph Murie over wolf control in the park. One ex-ranger described Pearson's role at McKinley Park as an "official greeter more than anything else."

Personnel squabbles and conflicts with area residents were not issues unique to Karstens' tenure, but simply part of the job.

Superintendents in the modern era faced a whole range of challenges unknown to the pre-World War II pioneers, especially two pivotal issues. In the 1970's, Superintendent Dan Kuehn, described as "efficient, trust-worthy, and supportive of his staff," helped implement the park's unique visitor transportation system. Frank Betts, in charge when the park was expanded by the Alaska National Interest Lands Conservation Act of 1980, was somewhat insulated from much of the public backlash, with President Jimmy Carter and Interior Secretary Stewart Udall drawing the ire of angry Alaskans. Both men, as well as their successors, enjoyed the expertise of a highly qualified, local staff, a well-developed and funded national agency, and broad public support. In contrast, Karstens' accomplishments were achieved without such backing, in an era when a supportive constituency did not exist, and at a time when public hostility was open and palpable.[30]

Karstens' grand achievement—the carving of a national park out of the wilderness—remains an enduring treasure. Perhaps a portion of a memorial poem written for Sheldon at the time of his death, says it best for these two men, the visionary and the man who gave life to the vision:[31]

"The grizzly bear and mountain sheep,
Can wander, feed, and calmly sleep,
The great-horned moose and caribou,
Are safe in wood and marsh below.

"His was the noble thought and plan,
to guard the game from ruthless man.
So let his name remembered be,
By all who love the wild and free."

# EPILOGUE

On March 19, 1932, President Herbert Hoover signed into law an act expanding the park to include an additional 246,693 acres. Boundaries extended on the east to the "natural boundary" of the Nenana River and in the west taking in Wonder Lake. With the expansion, McKinley Station as a viable community ceased to exist and its citizens scattered to the winds. Maurice Morino kept his hotel and patented land. Duke and Elizabeth Stubbs moved to New York, where they petitioned the government for loss of income and business. On December 7, 1932, they were awarded $50,000, the equivalent of an estimated $1 million during the Depression. John and Paula Andersons' 160-acre homestead on Wonder Lake became a source of contention, with the government eventually initiating condemnation proceedings to acquire it. Paula Anderson asked for $12,500 ($75 an acre) for her homestead. Government appraisers fixed the price at $800. On February 19, 1942, a federal jury in Fairbanks set the value of the homestead at $1,600. Perhaps the most valuable piece of property in the entire park was purchased by the Government for $10 an acre.

Although Harry Karstens and his rangers ultimately succeeded in protecting the park's Dall sheep from market hunters and poachers, no one could prevent two catastrophic winter die-offs. In the storms of 1928 and 1932, mountain sheep starved by the hundreds.

The winter of 1928-29 brought a disastrous six-foot deep snowfall followed by a Chinook that sealed the forage in thick ice. "The frantic sheep tried to paw their way through the ice, and cut their legs to the bone, often injuring themselves so they couldn't walk. Hundreds of the poor, gentle creatures died of starvation that winter," Grant Pearson said.

An Easter Sunday storm dumped three feet of snow. The hungry and weakened sheep bogged down in ravines and creek bottoms and could not climb out. In March, rangers saw sheep searching for feed on the flatlands nine miles from the mountains, an incredible distance from the peaks for these mountain-dwellers. Lethargic rams did not run away and a person could "go up to the rams and grab them by the horns they were so weak." April was a tough month, too, when "it is believed many sheep starved to death." A group of starving rams and ewes were picked up along the road and brought into headquarters where they were kept in a temporary shelter pen built at the end of the barn. The animals soon calmed down and began eating out of rangers' hands and rapidly gained weight.

The winter slaughter continued. On May 28, yet another storm dropped 20 inches of snow in 15 hours, devastating the new born lambs.One prospector called the storms "the worst he had witnessed in his 35 years here."

In early 1932, a heavy late season snowfall provided the killer blow. "All records for snow fall were broken during February, the amount recorded being 73 inches in six days . . . The winter of 1931–1932 will in years to come, be remembered as the year of the big snow," Harry Liek said, "30 inches in a few hours, and the losses to the wild game will be severe." Rangers found starving and dead sheep all along the East Fork and Toklat Rivers as far as ten miles outside the northern hills.

Rangers and road workers caught starving lambs and fed them. "Some people blamed wolves because they were seen eating sheep," Pete Bagoy said, "but we knew different. They starved. We collected starving lambs and trucked them into headquarters where they were fed until spring. The sheep were kept in the dog kennel area and released near capture sites. Sable Pass had always been a great place for sheep but after the big die off you could drive the road and not see a sheep."

Rangers Nyberg and Myers found a small band of sheep on the flats near Igloo Creek, floundering exhausted in the deep snow. They captured two rams and two ewes, and carried the weakened animals in their sleds to the Igloo cabin. Over the course of three days, the rangers caught other sheep and brought them to the cabin. In late May, two lambs were born in captivity, one of which died because its mother did not lactate as a result of her malnutrition.

How many sheep died during those two winters will never be known. Early estimates placed the park population as high as 15,000, or more, before the bad winters. "I sat at Toklat cabin with my binoculars and counted 3,000 Dall sheep grazing on the slopes," Nyberg once said, "and that was just one batch." He personally estimated 5,000 to 8,000 sheep prior to the winter kills.

"In August 1932, former ranger Lee Swisher told me that . . . he did not believe that there were more than 1,500 sheep in the entire park, as contrasted with a count between 10,000 and 15,000 that he had found . . . in the same area in 1929," said Joseph S. Dixon. "The . . . reduction is not clearly understood but it has been attributed variously to 1) starvation and death caused by heavy snowfall and prolonged winter weather; 2) failure of the surviving sheep to reproduce, due to their poor physical condition; 3) destruction of many sheep by coyotes and wolves. The problem needs careful investigation."

Biologist L.J. Palmer estimated that moose had suffered like the sheep. "Their legs from the knee down are worn to the bone, and each moose trail is covered with blood. It is possible to walk right up on a moose as they have not got the courage or strength to try and run away." In 1941, Adolph Murie counted 2,732 Dall sheep but after the war, he revised his estimate downward to 500. The public blamed wolves for the catastrophe. A 2008 aerial survey found slightly more than 1,500 sheep in the park.

In 1980, Federal action added nearly 4 million acres to Mt. McKinley National Park, tripling it in size. The additions included important wildlife habitat on both sides of the Alaska Range. The legislation also changed the park's name to Denali, the original Athabascan name for Mt. McKinley, and the name preferred by the park's original sponsors, Charles Sheldon and Belmore Browne.

Today, Denali National Park and Preserve annually hosts nearly a half million visitors, with its 6,075,029 acres, or nearly 9,500 square miles, presided over by a large, professionally-trained staff dedicated to "preserve unimpaired [Denali's] natural and cultural resources and values . . . for the enjoyment, education, and inspiration of this and future generations."

## APPENDIX

# THE LAST TRAIL

After graduating from Barnard College with a B.A. in English literature, **DENISE M. ABBEY** spent 27 years as a Foreign Service officer stationed mostly in Europe. During World War II she worked in intelligence and psychological warfare and went to Rome immediately after it fell to the Allies. In all, she visited 100 countries. Fifty years to the day that her father first took her to Wonder Lake, she again visited the Kantishna and other familiar locales. On February 17, 2007, she died at 96, in Des Moines, Washington. Her father, **WOODBURY ABBEY**, passed away in Seattle in 1963. He was 79.

**PETER J. BAGOY SR.**, 89, died December 27, 1997 at his home in Anchorage. At the time of his retirement in 1972, he was the maintenance superintendent for the Palmer district, Alaska Department of Transportation. The Alaska State Legislature passed a resolution commending Bagoy for his "47 years of faithful service to Alaska and its residents."

After his 1922 expedition, **WILLIAM N. BEACH** made at least two subsequent trips to the park. Beach visited Alaska 16 times, collecting hunting trophies for his personal collection as well as that of the Smithsonian Institution. For nearly three decades he was a power within the influential Camp Fire Club and battled the park service over wolf control. He died in his Long Island home in May 1955, at age 82.

On the evening of August 20, 1957, **JOHN BUSIA**, 66, died quietly in his cabin. Two long-time friends, ex-rangers Grant Pearson and John Rumohr, conducted the burial service. Locals covered his grave with river cobbles and planted a wooden cross with a marker that read: "Here Lies John Busia. Born Sept. 11, 1891, Died Aug. 10, 1957. Little Johnnie of the Kantishna, an Alaska Pioneer, 1891-1957." His obituary read: "So warm was his welcome, so steadfast his kindness, generosity and honesty, that Little Johnnie had become a living symbol of the spirit of Interior Alaska's pioneer days."

On a cold December 2, 1943, John Busia found **Joe Dalton**, 70, dead in his cabin. Fannie Quigley, and friend Walter Harris, had nursed Dalton during a month-long "stomach illness." After the ground thawed the following spring, Busia buried Dalton on Eureka Creek. "On April third, I wrapped him in a blanket and put him in a shallow hole with an old board to mark his grave," and so passed the discoverer of the richest placer claim in Kantishna history.

After a sudden, brief illness, **James Galen**, 68, died of cancer on January 15, 1939, at St. Vincent's Hospital in Portland, Oregon. The territorial governor wired this statement: "As long as the history of Alaska is written, the name of James L. Galen will be remembered."

Trappers worked in isolation without human contact. **Frank Giles** once went six months without seeing another person. Consequently, when he disappeared, no one thought to look for him until many weeks later. Locals believed that Giles had been murdered by an old trapping partner. An inquest ruled that Giles, whose remains were found on September 1, 1933, died by accident, likely drowning, on or about May 25, 1933. Rumors of his murder persist to this day.

**Frank Glaser**, 86, died May 16, 1974. In his lengthy career as a predator control agent with the U.S. Fish and Wildlife Service, he targeted wolves.

Former Deputy U.S. Marshal **James Hagan**, 68, died of cancer on October 11, 1938, in Everett, Washington, where he had served as sheriff. His "friends have lost a wonderful and true friend."

On August 2, 1923, two weeks after his Alaska visit, **President Warren G. Harding** died in San Francisco, just 29 months into his term. The official cause of death was listed as a stroke but other doctors in attendance cited a heart attack. Some said that the President had fallen ill after eating spoiled crab in Alaska.

**Eugene H. Karstens** passed away on April 10, 2001. Born in the AEC hospital at Nenana in 1917, he was only three when his mother brought him to Riley Creek. A graduate of the University of Alaska, with a BS in Civil Engineering, Eugene joined the military and eighteen years later was awarded the Legion of Merit for his work on the A-20 Havoc bomber. After 23 years of active duty in the U.S. Air Force, with service in two foreign wars, he retired with the rank of Lt. Colonel. He was survived by five children and nine grandchildren.

In 1906, **Frieda Louise Karstens'** first journey north was cut short by a nearly fatal bout of typhoid fever. After her husband passed away in 1955, Louise sold her home in Fairbanks and moved Outside. Years later she moved back to Fairbanks, where, at 91, she died on October 4, 1974.

After resigning from the park service, **HENRY P. "HARRY" KARSTENS** returned to Fairbanks and re-entered the transportation business. In 1944, Karstens, a Republican, ran unsuccessfully for the Fourth Division seat in the Territorial Legislature. As he aged, the powerful Karstens slowed down. "I have developed a bit of Asthma," he explained. On November 28, 1955, he died at home of congestive heart failure. During his internment at Birch Hill, the clouds parted and mourners glimpsed Mt. McKinley in the distance.

After his stint with the T'n'T, **GEORGE LINGO** was employed as registrar for the General Land Office. He was also a member of the college Board of Regents and won election to the Territorial Legislature. During World War II he served with the U.S. Navy. Lingo, a man ahead of his time, opened the first hamburger stand at McKinley Park in 1957, the same year the Denali Highway opened. Anticipating commercial air traffic he then cleared a large airfield at Milepost 229, Parks Highway. He moved to Palm Springs in 1961, where he died on May 21, 1976, at age 75.

**HARRY LUCKE**, 71, died on August 11, 1947, at St. Joseph's Hospital in Fairbanks, from respiratory failure and congestive heart failure due to advanced tuberculosis. He was buried at Birch Hill Cemetery.

While on a collecting trip to Oaxaca, Mexico, **YNES MEXIA** took ill. She died in San Francisco, on July 12, 1938. She was 68.

On November 23 1934, a passerby found **JERRY MCCARTHY**, aka "McClarty," frozen in his cabin on the Morino homestead. Maurice Morino and L.N. Sisley used a case of dynamite to blast out a grave in the rocky, frozen hillside above the roadhouse. They marked the grave of this ARC laborer with chain-linked posts and a cross which read simply: "Jerry McLarty, 1872-1932."

For two long years **MAURICE MORINO** battled esophageal cancer. Twice he made lengthy trips Outside for treatment and family visits. The second lasted from August 1935, to July 1936, during which time his nephew, Joe Morino, managed his McKinley Park property. Maurice died in Everett, Washington on March 6, 1937. Before he died, he made the arrangements for his own funeral, picking a steel casket and choosing the park as his burial site. Joe Dalton, his friend of 25 years, carried out his last wishes and accompanied his remains to McKinley Station. Lee Swisher, and others, helped carry Morino's remains to the burial site, blasted out of rock, on the hill overlooking his homestead and the Nenana River valley. In 1950, a transient started a fire that destroyed the hotel.

**ADOLPH MURIE** spent almost thirty-two years working for the National Park Service, undertaking pioneering studies that were published in three books: *The Wolves of Mount McKinley, The Ecology of the Coyote in the Yellowstone, and The Grizzlies of Mount McKinley.* The National Park Service awarded him the Distinguished Service Award. His approach to wildlife management ran contrary to prevailing opinion and took into account whole ecosystems, rather than focusing on single species. In 1945, his family settled in Jackson Hole, where he continued his work until his death at Moose, Wyoming on August 16, 1974. His long association with McKinley Park profoundly affected its management and development.

In 1927, **Olaus Murie**, with his wife Margaret, moved to Jackson Hole, Wyoming to study the largest elk herd in North America. His visionary approach to habitat preservation placed him at the forefront of wilderness conservation in America. In 1945, Olaus accepted the position of the first president of the Wilderness Society. In the final years of his life, he and "Mardy" worked to protect the Brooks Range, culminating in the establishment of the Arctic National Wildlife Refuge. He died in Jackson Hole, on October 21, 1963, shortly before passage of the landmark Wilderness Act.

**Fritz Nyberg**, a 65-year Alaska resident, died May 4, 1985, at the Anchorage Pioneers Home. Born April 11, 1894 in Sweden, he left home at 17 and wended his way to Alaska. In later life, he worked as a bank maintenance supervisor. "I loved the park and its wildlife and should never have left."

**Grant H. Pearson** became chief ranger in 1942, and seven years later, after a stint at Sitka National Monument, was appointed Superintendent of Mt. McKinley National Park, a position he held, minus two years, until 1956. His book, written with Philip Newill, *My Life of High Adventure*, is an Alaska classic. In 1958, he was elected to the First Alaska State Legislature. Friends remembered him as a great talker who recounted astounding tales of his life, some embellished, but many others all too true. He died on September 6, 1978, in Anchorage. He was 78.

Johnnie Busia found **Fannie Quigley**, 73, dead in her cabin on August 25, 1944, dressed in the same clothes that she had been wearing three days earlier when he last saw her. He deduced that she had laid down to rest after stacking wood and had died in her sleep. Following her last wishes, he took her remains to Fairbanks for burial. Although Fannie and Joe Quigley were often less than congenial during their latter years together, when Joe received the news of the death of his first wife, "his eyes filled with tears."

**Joe Quigley**, Alaska-Yukon pioneer and discoverer of Kantishna gold, died in Seattle in November 1958.

ROBERT E. "BOBBY" SHELDON died at 99, on January 4, 1983, at the Pioneers' Home in Fairbanks. After seven years as Fairbanks postmaster, he resigned and was elected to two terms in the Territorial Legislature. He "possessed a rare gift of speech, a keen sense of humor and charm of personality."

In May 1931, while at work on the park road, MICHAEL JOSEPH SULLIVAN, age 71, collapsed with severe abdominal pains and was rushed to Fairbanks, where he died on May 25th, 1931. He was buried in the Fairbanks City Cemetery.

Another ARC employee, OLIVER M. SMITH, died on September 9, 1930. Quiet and enigmatic, Oliver M. Smith and his brother, Frank, came to Alaska around the turn of the century. Not long after they left home, relatives in California received news that the brothers had drowned in the Yukon River. For nearly 30 years the family heard nothing from, or about, "Ollie," who in fact had survived the boating accident that had claimed his brother, until a year after his sudden death at McKinley Station. Maurice Morino used dynamite to blast out Smith's grave on the rocky hillside overlooking the station, built a coffin, and marked the grave with a lettered cross, posts and chains.

From 1927 to 1934, JAMES GORDON STEESE served with the U.S. Corps of Engineers in Africa, Mexico and South America. After his retirement he went into the oil business but rejoined the military at the outbreak of World War II. After a six-month stint as assistant governor of the Panama Canal Zone, the much decorated Steese returned to Pennsylvania. Steese, 75, was killed in an auto accident in January 11, 1958, in Banqui, French Equatorial Africa.

HAWLEY STERLING moved to South America in 1928, to work as chief engineer for South American Gulf Oil. He died in 1948.

D.E. "DUKE" STUBBS' health began to fail in 1937, suffering recurring bouts of what he believed to be malarial fever. He died in November 1938, just a few months after Congress appropriated the funds to pay his McKinley Park land compensation claim.

In 1934, GEORGE M. WRIGHT was appointed chief of the Wildlife Division of the National Park Service, a branch he helped establish and fund. Wright, 31, was killed in an auto accident near Deming, New Mexico on February 25, 1936. He was a passenger in a car en route from El Paso to Tucson, along with other members of the International Wildlife Refuge Commission, when an oncoming car served due to a blowout and slammed into their vehicle.

# BIBLIOGRAPHY


Interviews by Author

Abbey, Denise, November 1994, November 1996, April 8, 1998, August 1998.
Abbey, Woodbury "Bud", April 8, 1998.
Bagoy, Peter, November 23, 1995, March 21, 1996, March 30, 1996, February 20, 1996.
Coghill, Jack, March 25, 1998.
Horn, John, April 20, 1999.
Mercer, Berle, March 1995.
Morino, Joe Jr., October 1990.
Morino, Jim, July 1999.
McCutcheon, Steve, January 4, 1991.
Nancarrow, William, Numerous.
Nyberg, Fritz, October 1974.
Onka, Oliver, November 23, 1995.
Plumb, Earl, April 19, 1998.
Stroecker, William G., June 12, 1992.
Teeland, Walter, April 23, 1991.
Waugaman, William, Sr., Numerous.
Wear, Jean Simmons, November 2, 1992.
Wright, Jesse, February 9, 2002.

Periodicals

Alaska Gazetteer and Directory (1915–16)
Alaska Journal
Alaska Magazine
Alaska Railroad Record
Alaska Sportsman Magazine
Alaska-Yukon Magazine
Alaska Weekly
American Alpine Journal
American Forests and Forest Life
Backlog, Camp Fire Club
Campfire Girls Magazine
Cordova Daily Times
Farthest North Collegian
Forest and Stream Magazine
Greatlander

Helena Daily Independent
Hunter-Trapper-Trader Magazine
National Geographic Magazine
Outing Magazine
Pacific Monthly Magazine
Pathfinder of Alaska
Spirit of Missions

## NEWSPAPERS

Alaska Citizen
Alaska Daily Empire
Alaska Weekly
Anchorage Daily Times
Fairbanks Daily News-Miner
Fairbanks Daily Times
Fairbanks Evening News
Fairbanks Miner
Fairbanks Weekly News
Iditarod Pioneer
Jessen's Weekly
Nenana News
New York Times
Skagway Alaskan
Tanana Miners' Record
Tanana Semi-Weekly Miner
Tanana Weekly Miner
Valdez News

## ARCHIVAL SOURCES

Alaska State Archives, Juneau, Probate Records.
Alaska State Archives, Juneau, U.S. Commissioners Court of Alaska, Fourth Division, Criminal Court Case Files, 1903–1961.
Alaska State Library, Juneau, Alaska Engineering Commission Records.
Denali National Park and Preserve, Museum Collection.
Dickinson College Archives and Special Collections.
Karstens Library, Longmont, Colorado.
Jim Rearden Collection.
National Archives and Records Administration (NARA), Washington, D.C.
Shelburne Museum Archives.
Smithsonian Institution, Charles Sheldon Papers, Edward W. Nelson Collection.
State of Alaska, Nenana Recording District Mining Records, Fairbanks, Alaska.
University of Alaska, Fairbanks, Rasmuson Library, Archives, Alaska and Polar Regions Department.
University of Alaska, Anchorage, Consortium Library, Dianne Gudgel-Holmes Collection.

Books/Reports

Albright, Horace M. *The Birth of the National Park Service: The Founding Years, 1913-1932*, Howe Brothers, Salt Lake City, 1985.

Atwood, Evangeline, and DeArmond, R.N., *Who's Who in Alaskan Politics*. Alaska Historical Commission, 1977.

Crittenden, Katharine Carson, et al, *Get Mears! Frederick Mears, Builder of the Alaska Railroad*. Binford & Mort Publishing, Hillsboro, Oregon, 2001.

Beach, William N. *In the Shadow of Mt. McKinley*. Derrydale Press, New York, 1931.

Beeman, Marydith. *Lost and Found in Alaska and Yukon and Klondike*, Volume 1 and 2. Private Printing, Eagle River, 1995.

Bernhardt, J. The *Alaska Engineering Commission*. D. Appleton & Company, New York, 1922.

Brooks, Alfred H. *Blazing Alaska's Trails*. University of Alaska Press, Fairbanks, 1953.

Brooks, Alfred H. *An Exploration to Mt. McKinley America's Highest Mountain*. Journal of Geography, Washington, DC, 1903.

Brown, William E. *Denali, Symbol of the Alaskan Wild*. The Donning Company/Publishers, Virginia, 1993.

Burford, Virgil. *North to Danger*. Robert Hale Ltd, London, 1955.

Buzzell, Rolfe G. *Drainage Histories of the Kantishna Mining District. 1903-1968*. National Park Service, Alaska Region, Anchorage, 1989.

Capps, S. R. *The Kantishna Region Alaska*. USGS Bulletin #687, 1919.

Catton, Theodore, *Inhabited Wilderness: Indians and Eskimos in Alaska*. University of New Mexico Press, Albuquerque, 1997.

Close, Verna, et. al., *Snow on the Mountain*, Volume 2, Short Stories by Pioneer Home Residents. Palmer, Alaska, Undated.

Coates, Ken & Morrison, Bill. *The Sinking of the Princess Sophia, Taking the North Down With Her*. University of Alaska Press, Fairbanks 1991.

Cole, Martin, *Journey to Caribou Land*. Cole Revocable Trust #1, Whittier, CA, 1983.

Collins, Miki and Julie, *Lake Minchumina Past and Present*. Students and Teachers of Minchumina Community School, 2000.

Davis, Mary Lee. *We Are Alaskans*. W.A. Wilde Co., Boston, 1931.

Dixon, Joseph S. *Birds and Mammals of Mt. McKinley National Park*. Fauna Series No. 3, GPO, Washington, D.C. 1938.

Dodson, Peggy Rouch, *Girl in the Gold Camp*. Epicenter Press, Seattle, 1996.

Evarts, Hal Jr., *Skunk Ranch to Hollywood: The West of Hal Evarts*. Capra Press, Santa Barbara, 1989.

Fitch, Edwin M., *The Alaska Railroad*. Praeger Publishers, New York, 1967.

Gudgel-Holmes, Dianne. "Steven Foster of the Kantishna River," *Native Place Names of the Kantishna Drainage, Alaska*. Oral History Project, Department of the Interior, National Park Service, Alaska Region, 1991.

Gudgel-Holmes, Dianne. *Ethnohistory of Four Interior Alaska Waterbodies*. State of Alaska, Department of Natural Resources, 1979.

Haigh, Jane G., and Murphy, Claire Rudolf. *Gold Rush Women*. Alaska Northwest Books, Portland, 1999.

Haigh, Jane G., *Searching for Fannie Quigley*. Swallow Press/Ohio University Press, Athens, Ohio, 2007.

Hilscher, Herb and Miriam, *A Parade of Alaska History*. Alaska Mutual Savings Bank, 1976.

Kreps, Bonnie, and Craighead, Charles, *Arctic Dance: The Mardy Murie Story*. Graphic Arts Center Publishing, Portland, 2002.

Mackenzie, Clara Childs, *Wolf Smeller, A Biography of John Fredson, Native Alaskan*. Alaska Pacific University Press, Anchorage, 1985.

Marsh, Floyd R., "*20 Years a Soldier of Fortune*. Binford and Mort, Portland, 1976.

McClelland, Linda Flint, *Building the National Parks*. The Johns Hopkins University Press, Baltimore and London, 1998;

Morgan Lael, *The Good Time Girls*. Epicenter Press, Fairbanks and Seattle, 1998.

Murie, Adolph. *The Wolves of Mt. McKinley*. Fauna of the National Parks of the United States. Fauna Series #5, GPO Washington, 1944.

Murie, Olaus J., *Yukon Caribou*. Fauna Series, #54, Government Printing Office, June 1935.

Myers, Harry M., and William A., *Back Trails*. Private Printing, Lapeer County, 1932.

Norris, Frank, *Crown Jewel of the North: An Administrative History of the Denali National Park and Preserve*. National Park Service, Anchorage, 2006.

Patty, Ernest N. *North Country Challenge*. David McKay Co, New York, 1969.

Pearson, Grant. *A History of Mount McKinley National Park, Alaska*. National Park Service, 1953.

Pearson, Grant, and Newell, Philip. *My Life of High Adventure*. Ballantine Books, New York, 1962.

Postell, Alice, *Where did the reindeer come from?* Amaknak Press, Portland, Oregon, 1990

Prince, Bernadine, L., *The Alaska Railroad in Pictures, 1914–1964*. Ken Wray's Print Shop, Anchorage, 1964

Rand McNally and Company. *Rand McNally Guide to Alaska and Yukon*. New York, 1922.

Ricks, M.B. *Directory of Alaska Post Offices and Postmaster, 1867-1963*. Tongass Publishing, Ketchikan, 1965.

Saleeby, Becky M. *Quest for Gold*. C.R.I.M.M., National Park Service, Alaska Region, 2000.

Schneider, William; Gudgel Holmes, Dianne; Dalle-Molle, John. *Land Use in the North Additions of Denali National Park and Preserve: An Historical Perspective*. National Park Service, Anchorage, 1984.

Sheldon, Charles. *The Wilderness of Denali*. Charles Scribner's Sons, New York, 1930.

Sherwood, Morgan B. *Big Game in Alaska: A History of Wildlife and People*. Yale University Press, New Haven, 1961.

Slemmons, Mary Anne. *James Wickersham, U.S. District Judge of Alaska, Transcripts of Diaries 1-13, January 1, 1900-February 13, 1908*. Alaska State Library, Juneau 2000.

Stuck, Hudson, *20,000 Miles With A Dogteam*. Wolfe Publishing Inc., Prescott AZ, 1988.

Tremblay, Ray, *Trails of an Alaska Trapper*, Alaska Northwest Books, Anchorage, 1983.

Webb, Melody, *Yukon: The Last Frontier*. University of Nebraska Press, Lincoln, 1993.

Wickersham, James. *Old Yukon: Tales-Trails-and Trials*. Washington Law Book Co, Washington, DC. 1938.

Wright, George M., Dixon, Joseph S., and Thompson, Ben H., *Fauna of the National Parks of the United States: A Preliminary Survey of Faunal relations in National Parks*. Fauna Series #1, GPO, Washington, 1933.

# NOTES

Many of the records pertaining to the Mt. McKinley National Park in the National Archives and Records Administration (NARA) at College Park, have changed and are now found in Entry P9, Boxes 109-112. In this work I have cited the original Record Group 79, Records of the National Park Service, General Records, Central Files, 1907–1939. These are now part of Entry P9, specifically, Box 109. In the book I use the original citations.

Chapter One

1. Sheldon, Charles, "To the Committee on Appropriations of the House of Representatives, Appropriations File, Box 111, Mt. McKinley National Park, Entry 6, RG 79, (NARA), College Park, Maryland.

2. Letter, Sheldon, Charles, to Grinnell, G.B., March 5, 1917, Charles Sheldon Papers, Box 1, File 6, Archives, Alaska and Polar Regions Department, Rasmuson Library, University of Alaska, Fairbanks.

3. Letter, Karstens, Henry P., to Washburn, Bradford, February 7, 1951, "*Highlights of my existence in the north*," Dartmouth College Library.

4. Letter, Sheldon, Charles, to Karstens, Henry P., January 5, 1920, Karstens Library.

5. Diary entry, Stuck, Hudson, February 21, 1915, Hudson Stuck Collection, Archives, Alaska and Polar Regions Department, Rasmuson Library, University of Alaska, Fairbanks; Fairbanks Daily Times, July 11, 1914.

6 The Nenana News, January 26, 1918.

7. The Nenana News: December 8, 1917; June 12, 1919; November 14; 1919.

8. The Nenana News, May 1, 1919.

9. The Nenana News: April 10, 1919; September 22, 1919.

10. Fairbanks Sunday Times, June 21, 1914; Fairbanks Daily News-Miner, November 27, 1920; Berton, Pierre, *The Klondike Fever*, Alfred A. Knopf, Inc., New York, 1958.

11. Fairbanks Sunday Times, June 21, 1914.

12. Fairbanks Daily News-Miner, June 6, 1921.

13. Letter, Karstens, Henry P., to Sheldon, Charles, January 11, 1921, Box 2, Folder 2, Charles Sheldon Papers, Archives, Alaska and Polar Regions Department, Rasmuson Library, University of Alaska, Fairbanks.

14. Letter, Karstens, Henry P., to Sheldon, Charles, March 29, 1920, Box 2, Folder 2, Charles Sheldon Papers, Archives, Alaska and Polar Regions Department, Rasmuson Library, University of Alaska, Fairbanks.

15. Ibid.

16. Letter, Karstens, Henry P., to Sheldon, Charles, February 28, 1921, Box 2, File 2, Charles Sheldon Papers, Archives, Alaska and Polar Regions Department, Rasmuson Library, University of Alaska, Fairbanks.

17. Ibid.

18. Letter, Karstens, Henry P., to Sheldon, Charles, January 11, 1921, Box 2, File 2, Charles Sheldon Papers, Archives, Alaska and Polar Regions Department, Rasmuson Library, University of Alaska, Fairbanks.

19. Letter, Karstens, Henry P., to Sheldon, Charles, February 21, 1921, Box 2, Folder 2, Charles Sheldon Papers, Archives, Alaska and Polar Regions Department, Rasmuson Library, University of Alaska, Fairbanks.

20. Letter, Karstens, Henry P., to Sheldon, Charles, January 11, 1921, Box 2, Folder 2, Charles Sheldon Papers, Archives, Alaska and Polar Regions Department, Rasmuson Library, University of Alaska, Fairbanks.

21. Ibid.

22. Alaska Citizen, November 5, 1917; Letters: Karstens, Henry P., to Sheldon, Charles, March 29, 1920 and January 11, 1921, Box 2, Folder 2, Charles Sheldon Papers, Archives, Alaska and Polar Regions Department, Rasmuson Library, University of Alaska, Fairbanks.

23. Letter, Karstens, Henry P., to Sheldon, Charles, January 11, 1921, Box 2, Folder 2, Charles Sheldon Papers, Archives, Alaska and Polar Regions Department, Rasmuson Library, University of Alaska, Fairbanks.

24. Letter, Mather, S.T., to Riggs, Thomas, February 7, 1921, Box 2, Folder 2, Charles Sheldon Papers, Archives, Alaska and Polar Regions Department, Rasmuson Library, University of Alaska, Fairbanks; Fairbanks Daily News-Miner: October 13, 1920; November 4, 1920; October 25, 1923.

25. Letter, Karstens, Henry P., to Sheldon, Charles, January 11, 1921, Box 2, Folder 2, Charles Sheldon Papers, Archives, Alaska and Polar Regions Department, Rasmuson Library, University of Alaska, Fairbanks.

26. Letter, Mather, S.T., to Sheldon, Charles, January 27, 1921, and Letter, Mather S.T., to Riggs, T.A., February 7, 1921, Box 2, Folder 2, Charles Sheldon Papers, Archives, Alaska and Polar Regions Department, Rasmuson Library, University of Alaska, Fairbanks.

27. Letter, Nelson, Edward W., to Sheldon, Charles, February 14, 1921, E.W. Nelson Collection, R.U. 7364, Box 9, Folder 9, Smithsonian Institution.

28. Letter, Karstens, Henry P., to Sheldon, Charles, February 28, 1921, Box 2, Folder 2, Charles Sheldon Papers, Archives, Alaska and Polar Regions Department, Rasmuson Library, University of Alaska, Fairbanks.

29. Ibid.

30. Superintendent's Monthly Report, Mount McKinley National Park, June 1921, Denali National Park & Preserve Museum Collection; Letter Karstens, Henry P., to Mather, S.T., 17 June 1921, in "Reports-Superintendent," Entry q, Tray 383, RG 79, NARA, College Park, Maryland.

31. The Nenana Daily News: February 24, 1917, April 18, 1918; Fairbanks Daily-News Miner, July 12, 1922.

32. Fairbanks Daily News-Miner, April 6, 1917.

33. The Nenana Daily News: March 15, 1921; August 11, 1921.

34. See "Getting There," by Eugene G. Karstens, www.karstenslibrary.org.

35. The Nenana News: May 21, 1921; June 9, 1921; June 11, 1921.

36. The Nenana News, June 9, 1921.

37. Annual report, Alaska Engineering Commission, 1916, Senate Document 741, 69th Congress, GPO, 1917.

38. Interview, Jack Coghill, March 25, 1998.

39. The Nenana News: November 20, 1920; February 17, 1921; August 16, 1921.

40. Superintendent's Monthly Report, Mount McKinley National Park, October 1921, Denali National Park & Preserve Museum Collection.

41. Karstens, Eugene Henry, *My Life*, Denali National Park & Preserve Museum Collection; Superintendent's Reports, November, 1921, Denali National Park & Preserve Museum Collection.

42. Karstens, F.L., Memoirs of Mrs. H.P. Karstens, Dartmouth College Library.

## Chapter Two

1. Prince, Bernadine, L., *The Alaska Railroad in Pictures, 1914–1964*, Ken Wray's Print Shop, Anchorage, 1964.

2. Compton, Cleonne, *Railroad Report for Alaska State Legislature, Transportation Committee*, State of Alaska, December 1979.

3. *Alaska Railroad Record*, February 10, 1920, Volume IV. No. 4, and Volume IV, No. 18.

4. 1920 United States Census; Nabokov, Vladimir, *Speak, Memory*, Victor Gollancz Ltd., London 1951; Interview, Peter Bagoy, November 1995.

5. Records of the Alaska Engineering Commission, Volumes 8–10, MS 8, Roll 3, Alaska History Documents, Alaska State Library; The Nenana News, August 14, 1920.

6. The Nenana News: December 23, 1919; April 6, 1920; August 2, 1920; August 7, 1920; September 8, 1921.

7. Fitch, Edwin M., *The Alaska Railroad*, Praeger Publishers, New York, 1967; Brown, C.M., and Kennedy, Michael S., *The Alaska Railroad: Probing the Interior*, Office of Statewide Cultural Programs, Alaska Division of Parks, Anchorage, October 1975; Letter, Brooker, Edgar, Jr., February 25, 1984, RG-08, DENA 5462, Folder B-12, Denali National Park & Preserve Museum Collection.

8. The Nenana News: November 1, 1918; December 3, 1919; December 23, 1918.

9. The Nenana News: February 3, 1921; April 26, 1921; August 25, 1921; October 4, 1921; November 24, 1921.

10. The Nenana News, November 22, 1921.

11. The Nenana News: November 22, 1921; December 15, 1921; December 24, 1921; Fairbanks Daily News-Miner, November 22, 1921; November 29, 1921; December 1, 1921; December 3, 1921; and January 9, 1922.

12. Brown, C. M., and Kennedy, Michael S., *The Alaska Railroad: Probing the Interior*, Office of Statewide Cultural Programs, Alaska Division of Parks, Anchorage, October 1975; The Nenana News: December 1, 1921; February 2, 1922; February 4, 1922; February 7, 1922.

13. U.S. Commissioners Court of Alaska, Fourth Division, Criminal Court Case Files, 1903–1961, Case #114, RG 504, Boxes 18–19, Alaska State Archives, Juneau; Fairbanks Daily News-Miner, January 13, 1922.

14. U.S. Commissioners Court of Alaska, Fourth Division, Criminal Court Case Files, 1903–1961, Case #134, Case #137, RG 504, Boxes 18–19, Alaska State Archives, Juneau.

15. U.S. Commissioners Court of Alaska, Fourth Division, Criminal Court Case Files, 1903–1961, Case #79, RG 504, Boxes 18–19, Alaska State Archives, Juneau.

16. U.S. Commissioners Court of Alaska, Fourth Division, Criminal Court Case Files, 1903–1961, Case #99 and Case #118, RG 504, Boxes 18–19, Alaska State Archives, Juneau; The Nenana News: February 21, 1921; February 23, 1922; The Fairbanks Daily News-Miner, February 21, 1921.

17. Fairbanks Daily News-Miner, June 12, 1922.

18. U.S. District Court, Alaska Criminal Case Files, RG 21, Box 43, Case File #883, and #884, NARA, Washington, DC.

19. Lautaret, Ron, *Alaska Journal*, Alaska Northwest Publishing Company, 1981

20. The Nenana News: August 3, 1922; September 21, 1922.

21. Superintendent's Monthly Report, Mount McKinley National Park, January 1924, May 1924, December 1924, November 1925, and January 1925, Denali National Park & Preserve Museum Collection.

22. Superintendent's Monthly Report, Mount McKinley National Park, May 1924, Denali National Park & Preserve Museum Collection.

23. Letter, Karstens, Henry P., to Sheldon, Charles, Box 2, Folder 2, Charles Sheldon Papers, Archives, Alaska and Polar Regions Department, Rasmuson Library, University of Alaska, Fairbanks.

24. Atwood, Evangeline, and DeArmond, R.N., *Who's Who in Alaskan Politics*, Alaska Historical Commission, 1977.

25. Superintendent's Monthly Report, Mount McKinley National Park, October 26, 1921, Denali National Park & Preserve Museum Collection.

26. Crittenden, Katharine Carson, et al, *Get Mears! Frederick Mears, Builder of the Alaska Railroad*, Binford & Mort Publishing, Hillsboro, Oregon, 2001.

27. Alaska Engineering Commission Records, Volumes 8–10, MS 8, Roll 3, Alaska History Documents, Alaska State Library.

28. Letters, Karstens, Henry P., to Sheldon, Charles, January 12, 1922, and February 7, 1923, Box 2, Folder 2, Charles Sheldon Papers, Archives, Alaska and Polar Regions Department, Rasmuson Library, University of Alaska, Fairbanks.

29. Superintendent's Monthly Report, Mount McKinley National Park, December 1922, Denali National Park & Preserve Museum Collection.

30. Personal communication, Eugene G. Karstens, Karstens Library.

31. Superintendent's Monthly Report, Mount McKinley National Park, October 1922, Denali National Park & Preserve Museum Collection; Letter, Karstens, Henry P., to Sheldon, Charles, February 7, 1923. Box 2, Folder 2, Charles Sheldon Papers, Archives, Alaska and Polar Regions Department, Rasmuson Library, University of Alaska, Fairbanks.

32. Letter, Karstens, Henry P., to Sheldon, Charles, February 7, 1923, Box 2, Folder 2, Charles Sheldon Papers, Archives, Alaska and Polar Regions Department, Rasmuson Library, University of Alaska, Fairbanks.

33. Ibid.

34. Letter, Karstens, Henry P., to Sheldon, Charles, January 12, 1922, Box 2, Folder 2, Charles Sheldon Papers, Archives, Alaska and Polar Regions Department, Rasmuson Library, University of Alaska, Fairbanks.

35. Superintendent's Monthly Report, Mount McKinley National Park, October 26, 1921, Denali National Park & Preserve Museum Collection.

36. Fairbanks Daily News-Miner, August 28, 1923.

CHAPTER THREE

1. Interviews, Denise Abbey, November, 1992, and November 1996.

2. Skagway Daily Alaskan, October 21, 1918; Letter, McQueen, Auris, Alaska Daily Empire, October 30, 1918.

3. Fairbanks Daily News-Miner: February 26, 1921; March 5, 1921.

4. The Nenana News, June 9, 1921.

5. Fairbanks Daily News-Miner, May 19, 1921.

6. Fairbanks Daily News-Miner, May 19, 1921; The Nenana News, June 16, 1921.

7. Fairbanks Daily News-Miner, July 1, 1920.

8. For a fine overview of the survey see, The Nenana News: June 25, 1921; July 16, 1921; July 23, 1921.

9. The Nenana News, July 23, 1921.

10. The Nenana News, September 29, 1921.

11. Memorandum, Abbey, Woodbury, June 6, 1921, Denali National Park & Preserve Museum Collection.

12. Letter, Mears, Frederick, to Fall, Albert B., May 29, 1922, Denali National Park & Preserve Museum Collection.

13. Letter, Parks, George A., to Fall, Albert B., Secretary of the Interior, November 10, 1922, Denali National Park & Preserve Museum Collection; Letter, Fall, A.B., to Representative N. J. Sinnott, June 15, 1921, Report No. 326, December 6, 1921, Denali National Park & Preserve Museum Collection.

14. Fairbanks Daily News-Miner, January 24, 1922.

15. Fairbanks Daily News-Miner, January 24, 1922.

16. Fairbanks Daily News-Miner: July 3, 1922; August 23, 1922.

17. Fairbanks Daily News-Miner, March 25, 1927.

18. Ibid.

19. Fairbanks Daily News-Miner, March 25, 1927; Interviews, Denise Abbey, November 1992, and November 1996.

20. Fairbanks Daily News-Miner, March 25, 1927.

21. Davis, Mary Lee, *We Are Alaskans*, W.A. Wilde Company, Boston, 1931; Interviews, Denise Abbey, November, 1992 and November 1996.

22. Interviews, Denise Abbey, November 1992, and November 1996.

23. Interview, Denise Abbey, April 8, 1998.

24. Postell, Alice, *Where did the reindeer come from?* Amaknak Press, Portland, Oregon, 1990; Luick, Jack R. *The Cantwell Reindeer Industry*, 1921-1928, Alaska Journal, Volume 3, #2.

25. Interview, Denise Abbey, April 8, 1998; Sherwood, Morgan, *Big Game in Alaska, A history of Wildlife and People*, Yale University, New Haven, CT. 1982.

26. Fairbanks Daily News-Miner, August 17, 1925.

27. Beach, William N., In *the Shadow of Mount McKinley*, The Derrydale Press, New York, 1931.

28. Interview, Denise Abbey, November 1996.

29. Original manuscript, Denise Abbey, 1927, author's collection; Beach, William, N., *In the Shadow of Mt McKinley*, Derrydale Press, New York, 1931.

30. Interview, Denise Abbey, November 1996; Interview, Peter Bagoy, March 30, 1996; Fairbanks

Daily News-Miner: September 22, 1938; April 12, 1941.

31. Original manuscript, Denise Abbey, 1927, author's collection.

32. Interview, Denise Abbey, November, 1996.

33. The Nenana News, October 7, 1922.

34. The Nenana News, October 7, 1922.

35. Interview, Denise Abbey, November, 1996; Original manuscript, Denise Abbey, 1927, author's collection.

Chapter Four

1. Fairbanks Daily News-Miner, June 11, 1921.

2. Diary entry, Henry P. Karstens, June 23, 1922, Karstens Library.

3. Superintendent's Monthly Report, Mount McKinley National Park, July 1922, Denali National Park & Preserve Museum Collection; Diary entry, Henry P. Karstens, June 23, 1922, Karstens Library; Diary Entry, Olaus J. Murie, O.J. Murie Collection, Box 7, Folder 15, Archives, Alaska and Polar Regions Department, Rasmuson Library, University of Alaska, Fairbanks.

4. Diary Entry, Olaus J. Murie, O.J. Murie Collection, Box 7, Folder 15 & 17, Archives, Alaska and Polar Regions Department, Rasmuson Library, University of Alaska, Fairbanks.

5. Letter, Karstens, Henry P., to Sheldon, Charles, May 21, 1923, Charles Sheldon Papers, Box 2, Folder 2, Archives, Alaska and Polar Regions Department, Rasmuson Library, University of Alaska, Fairbanks.

6. Diary entry, Henry P. Karstens, July 16, 1922, Karstens Library.

7. Diary Entry, Olaus J. Murie, O.J. Murie Collection, Box 7, Folder 15, Archives, Alaska and Polar Regions Department, Rasmuson Library, University of Alaska, Fairbanks.

8. Superintendent's Monthly Report, Mount McKinley National Park, September 1922, Roads and Trails, Denali National Park & Preserve Museum Collection.

9. Letter, Karstens, Henry P., to Sheldon, Charles, February 29, 1921, Charles Sheldon Papers, Box 2, Folder 2, Archives, Alaska and Polar Regions Department, Rasmuson, Library University of Alaska, Fairbanks.

10. Fairbanks Daily News-Miner, November 1, 1922.

11. Fairbanks Daily News-Miner: August 7, 1920; October 19, 1920.

12. Letter, Karstens, Henry P., to Sheldon, Charles, May 21, 1923, Historical Letters file, Denali National Park & Preserve Museum Collection.

13. Superintendent's Monthly Report, Mount McKinley National Park, August 1922, Roads and Trails, Denali National Park & Preserve Museum Collection.

14. Diary Entry, Olaus J. Murie, O.J. Murie Collection, Box 7, Folder 15, Archives, Alaska and Polar Regions Department, Rasmuson Library, University of Alaska, Fairbanks.

15. Superintendent's Monthly Report, Mount McKinley National Park, August 1922, Roads and Trails, Denali National Park & Preserve Museum Collection; Telegram, Chandler, W.F., to Mather, S.T., July 24, 1922. RG 79, Entry 6, Box 369, NARA, College Park, Md.

16. Fairbanks Daily News-Miner, August 12, 1922; Letter, Chandler, W.F., to Karstens, Henry, P., August 10, 1922, Historical Letters File, Denali National Park & Preserve Museum Collection.

17. The Nenana News, October 26, 1922.

18. The Nenana News: September 26, 1922; September 30, 1922.

19. The Nenana News, October 5, 1922.

20. Letter, Karstens, Henry P., to Sheldon, Charles, March 29, 1920, Charles Sheldon Papers, Box 2, Folder 2, Archives, Alaska and Polar Regions Department, Rasmuson, Library University of Alaska, Fairbanks.

21. Fairbanks Daily News-Miner, June 11, 1921; Letter, Karstens, Henry P., to Beach, William N., June 19 1922; Letter, Karstens, Henry P., to Sheldon, Charles, February 7, 1923, Historical Letters Collection, Denali National Park & Preserve Museum Collection.

22. Letter, Cammerer, Arno, B., to Karstens, Henry P., July 14, 1922, Historical Letters Collection, Denali National Park & Preserve, Museum Collection.

23. Beach, William N., *In the Shadow of Mt. McKinley*, The Derrydale Press, New York, 1931; Letter, Karstens, Henry P., to Sheldon, Charles, February 7, 1923, Charles Sheldon Papers, Box 2, File 2, Archives, Alaska and Polar Regions Department, Rasmuson Library, University of Alaska, Fairbanks.

24. Fairbanks Daily News-Miner, August 23, 1923.

25. Beach, William N., *In the Shadow of Mt. McKinley*, The Derrydale Press, New York, 1931.

26. Ibid.

27. Letter, Karstens, Henry P., to Beach, William N., November 13, 1922, RG 79, CCF, Box 112, File: Wild Animals, NARA, College Park, Md.

28. Letter, Cammerer, A.B., to Albright, H.C., Acting Director, May 16, 1923, RG 79, CCF, Box 112, File: Wild Animals, NARA, College Park, Md.

29. Letter, Karstens, Henry P., to Bone, Scott C., Alaska Governor, February 5, 1924, RG 79, CCF, Box 112, File: Wild Animals, NARA, College Park, Md.

30. Letter, Karstens, Henry P., to Sheldon, Charles, May 21, 1923, Charles Sheldon Papers, Box 2, File 2, Archives, Alaska and Polar Regions Department, Rasmuson Library, University of Alaska, Fairbanks.

31. Letter, Karstens, Henry P., to Bone, Scott C., Alaska Governor, February 5, 1924, RG 79, CCF, Box 112, File: Wild Animals, NARA, College Park, Md.

32. *Big Game in Alaska*

33. *In the Shadow of Mt. McKinley*

34. Letter, Cammerer, A.B., to the Secretary of Interior, April 10, 1923, RG 79, CCF, Box 112, File: Wild Animals, NARA, College Park, Md.

35. Superintendent's Report, Mount McKinley National Park, September 1923, Denali National Park & Preserve Museum Collection; Judgment, Criminal Case #1237, William N. Beach Collection, Album #20, Page 20, Shelburne Museum Archives.

36. Interview, Peter Bagoy, November 23, 1995; The Nenana News: November 18, 1922; February 10, 1923; June 5, 1923.

37. The Nenana News: August 3, 1922; September 21, 1922.

38. Fairbanks Daily News-Miner, April 14, 1922.

39. Superintendent's Monthly Report, Mount McKinley National Park, October 1922, November 1922, Denali National Park & Preserve Museum Collection.

40. Nyberg, Fritz, Oral History Tape #509A, Denali National Park & Preserve Museum Collection.

## Chapter Five

1. Interview, Denise Abbey, November 1994; Letter, Wear, Jean Simmons, to Cunningham, R. Clay, July 18, 1986, Historical Letters Collection, Denali National Park & Preserve Museum Collection; Norma Hoyt Oral History Tape #513, February 9, 1982, Denali National Park & Preserve Museum Collection.

2. Interview, Denise Abbey, January1995; Letter, Wear, Jean Simmons, to Walker, Tom, October 29, 1992.

3. Interview, Walter Teeland, April 23, 1991.

4. Interview, Walter Teeland, April 23, 1991; Interview, Steve McCutcheon, January 4, 1991; Interview, Joe Morino Jr., April 1989.

5. Fritz Nyberg Oral History Tape #509B, Denali National Park & Preserve Museum Collection; Pearson, Grant, *My Life of High Adventure*, Prentice-Hall, New York, 1961.

6. Lena Howard Oral History Tape #506, August 4, 1972, Denali National Park & Preserve Museum Collection.

7. Fairbanks Daily News-Miner, September 18, 1908; Fairbanks Daily Times, January 31, 1907.

8. Fairbanks Daily News-Miner, March 12, 1910.

9. Fairbanks Daily News-Miner: March 10, 1925; May 21, 1927.

10. Fairbanks Daily News-Miner, July 10, 1908; Fairbanks Sunday Times: May 9, 1909,;May 10, 1909.

11. Maurice Morino, Territory of Alaska, Homestead Entry, Final Proof, Record Group #49, Serial Patent File #1071246, NARA, College Park, MD.

12. Fritz Nyberg, Oral History Tape #509B, Denali National Park & Preserve Museum Collection; Rhodes, Herb, *Tales of the Great Land*, The Greatlander, no date.

13. The Nenana News, December 19, 1918.

14. Fairbanks Daily News-Miner, December 1, 1921; Interview, William Nancarrow, October 23, 1995.

15. Fairbanks Daily News-Miner, December 1, 1921; The Nenana News, November 19, 1921; Letter, Wear, Jean Simmons, to Cunningham, R. Clay, July 18, 1986, Denali National Park & Preserve Museum Collection.

16. Superintendent's Monthly Report, Mount McKinley National Park, April 1924, Denali National Park & Preserve Museum Collection; Lena Howard Oral History Tape #506, August 4, 1972, Denali National Park & Preserve Museum Collection.

17. Letter, Wear, Jean Simmons, to Cunningham, R. Clay, July 18, 1986, Historical Letters File, Denali National Park & Preserve Museum Collection.

18. Interview, Peter Bagoy, November 23, 1995.

19. Maurice Morino, Territory of Alaska, Homestead Final Proof, Record Group 49, Serial Patent File #1071246, NARA, College Park, Maryland.

20. Interview, Walter Teeland, April 23, 1991.

21. Interview, Denise Abbey, November 1994.

22. Close, Verna, *Snow on the Mountain*, Volume 2, Short Stories by Pioneer Home Residents, Palmer, Undated.

23. Norman Bright, American Alpine Journal, 1939.

24. Norma Hoyt Oral History Tape #513, February 9, 1982, Denali National Park & Preserve Museum Collection.

25. Letter, Wear, Jean Simmons, to Cunningham, R. Clay, July 18, 1986, Historical Letters File, Denali National Park & Preserve Museum Collection.

26. Ibid.

27. Letter, Wear, Jean Simmons, to Cunningham, R. Clay, July 18, 1986, Historical Letters File, Denali National Park & Preserve Museum Collection; Fairbanks Daily News-Miner, April 20, 1931.

28. Pearson, Grant, *My Life of High Adventure*, Prentice-Hall, New York, 1961.

29. Fairbanks Daily News-Miner, April 25, 1924.

30. Fairbanks Daily News-Miner, July 31, 1924.

31. Superintendent's Monthly Report, Mount McKinley National Park, July 1924, Denali National Park & Preserve Museum Collection.

32. Superintendent's Monthly Report, Mount McKinley National Park, March 1924, Denali National Park & Preserve Museum Collection.

33. Letter, Karstens, Henry P., to Sheldon, Charles, Letter, May 21, 1923, Charles Sheldon Papers, Box 2, Folder 2, Archives, Alaska and Polar Regions Department, Rasmuson Library, University of Alaska, Fairbanks.

34. Superintendent's Monthly Report, Mount McKinley National Park, February 1922, Denali National Park & Preserve Museum Collection.

35. Ibid.

36. Interview, Peter Bagoy, November 23, 1995.

37. Superintendent's Monthly Report, Mount McKinley National Park, March 1922, Denali National Park & Preserve Museum Collection.

38. Ibid.

39. Ibid.

40. Letter, Karstens, Henry P., to Sheldon, Charles, May 21, 1923, Charles Sheldon Papers, Box 2, Folder 2, Archives, Alaska and Polar Regions Department, Rasmuson Library, University of Alaska, Fairbanks.

41. Letter, Karstens, Henry P., to Sheldon, Charles, July 16, 1921, Historical Letters File, Denali National Park & Preserve Museum Collection; Superintendent's Monthly Report, Mount McKinley National Park, Sept 7, 1924, Denali National Park & Preserve Museum Collection; Letter, Karstens, Henry P., to Parks, George, January 16, 1923, Historical Letters File, Denali National Park & Preserve Museum Collection; Executive Order 3617, January 13, 1922, GPO, Washington, DC.

42. Letter Cammerer, Arno B., to Karstens, Henry P., February 3, 1923, Records Group 79, Entry 6, Box 369, NARA, College Park, Md.

43. Letter, Karstens, Henry P, to Sheldon, Charles, May 21, 1923, Charles Sheldon Papers, Box 2, Folder 2, Archives, Alaska and Polar Regions Department, Rasmuson Library, University of Alaska, Fairbanks; Maurice Morino, Immigration and Naturalization Records, August 8, 1921, Michael Morino Collection.

44. Letters, Karstens, Henry P., to Sheldon, Charles, February 7, 1923, and May 21, 1923, Box 2, Folder 2, Charles Sheldon Papers, Archives, Alaska and Polar Regions Department, Rasmuson Library, University of Alaska, Fairbanks.

45. Ibid.

46. Superintendent's Monthly Report, Mount McKinley National Park, April 1924, Denali National Park & Preserve Museum Collection.

47. Letter, Karstens, Henry P., to Sheldon, Charles, Feb 7, 1923, Box 2, Folder 2, Charles Sheldon Papers, Archives, Alaska and Polar Regions Department, Rasmuson Library, University of Alaska, Fairbanks.

48. Letters, Murie, Olaus, to Nelson, Edward W., March 12, 1921, and January 7, 1922, Alaska Reports of Olaus Murie, RG 22, U.S. Fish and Wildlife Service Records, NARA, Washington, DC.

### Chapter Five Sidebar

1. R.L. Polk's Alaska-Yukon Gazetteers and Business Directory.

2. Probate Records, Box 17371, Alaska State Archives; Fairbanks Daily News-Miner, June 12, 1922.

3. Alaska Railroad Commission, House Document No 610, 64th Congress, Map VII, drawn from USGS Map, Talkeetna-Fairbanks Section, December 31, 1914, locating engineers T.H. Bacon, R.A. Gray, and F.H. Bailey.

4. Fairbanks Daily News-Miner: March 5, 1907; July 3, 1908.

5. Fairbanks Daily News, July 8, 1908.

6. Fairbanks Daily News-Miner: July 8, 1908; July 16, 1908.

7. Fairbanks Daily News-Miner, July 16, 1908.

8. Fairbanks Daily News-Miner, April 15, 1921.

9. Probate Records, Coroner's Inquest, Box 17371, Alaska State Archives.

10. Alaska Daily Empire, August 21, 1918.

11. Alaska Daily Empire: April 10, 1921; April 16, 1921; Fairbanks Daily News-Miner April 15, 1921.

### Chapter Six

1. The Pathfinder of Alaska, September 23, 1919.

2. Fairbanks Daily News Miner, January 3, 1927..

3. Fairbanks Daily-News Miner, February 9, 1928.

4. Fairbanks Daily News-Miner April 2, 1924.

5. The Nenana News, December 2, 1920; Alaska Weekly, July 3, 1923.

6. Marsh, Floyd R., *20 Years a Soldier of Fortune*, Binford and Mort, Portland, 1976.

7. The Nenana News, June 20, 1919.

8. The Nenana News: July 31, 1919; August 28, 1920.

9. The Nenana News, March 24, 1921.

10. The Pathfinder, June 12, 1919.

11. Alaska Daily Empire, September 12, 1916; Fairbanks Daily News-Miner, September 7, 1916.

12. The Nenana News, August 18, 1917; Fairbanks Daily News-Miner, September 29, 1916; Alaska Daily Empire, October 5, 1916.

13. Draft Registration Records, Nenana District; Letter, Wilson, C. Herbert, October 4, 1919, Denali National Park & Preserve Museum Collection; History Manuscript 1984, Brooker, Edgar Jr., RG-08, DENA 5462, Folder B-12, Denali National Park & Preserve Museum Collection; Fairbanks Daily News-Miner, March 26, 1920; The Nenana News, August 29, 1919.

14. Buzzell, Rolfe G., *Drainage Histories of the Kantishna Mining District, 1903-1968*, National Park Service Regional Office, Anchorage, 1989; Salisbury and Dietz, Inc., *1983 Minerals Resource Study: Kantishna.*

15. U.S. Commissioner's Records, Misc. Court Journal No."A", page 456, and Misc. Court Journal No."A", page 404, Alaska State Archives; Buzzell, Rolfe G., *Drainage Histories of the Kantishna Mining District, 1903-1968*, National Park Service Regional Office, Anchorage, 1989; History Manuscript 1984, Brooker, Edgar Jr., RG-08, DENA 5462, Folder B-12, Denali National Park & Preserve Museum Collection; The Nenana News, December 27, 1921; Fairbanks Daily News-Miner: January 6, 1923; February 10, 1923

16. Letter, Brooker, Edgar Sr. to U.S. Marshall, Fairbanks, April 20, 1922, Probate Records, Box 18028, Alaska State Archives; Stewart, B.D., Annual Report of the Territorial Mine Inspector to the Governor of Alaska, Alaska Territorial Mines, 1920.

17. Ibid.

18. Fairbanks Daily News-Miner July 21, 1920; Haigh, Jane, G., *Searching for Fannie Quigley: A Social, Prosperous Time of Life*, Heartland Magazine, June 20, 1999; The Pathfinder of Alaska, September 23, 1919.

19. The Nenana News, May 29, 1919.

20. Fairbanks Daily News-Miner: July 6; 1920; July 26, 1920; The Nenana News: September 1, 1917; March 17, 1921; March 22, 1921.

21. Kantishna Recording District Misc. Records, Volume 1 with Index, 1905-1920, Instrument #186-2870; Cordova Daily Times, December 24, 1919.

22. Cordova Daily Times, December 24, 1919.

23. The Nenana News, September 28, 1918.

24. Ibid.

25. The Nenana News: September 24, 1919; December 4, 1919; December 11, 1919.

26. Stewart, B.D. Annual Report of the Mine Inspector to the Governor of Alaska, Alaska Territorial Mines, 1922; Buzzell, Rolfe G., *Drainage Histories of the Kantishna Mining District, 1903-1968*, National Park Service Regional Office, Anchorage, 1989.

27. The Nenana News, December 30, 1920.

28. The Nenana News, January 29, 1920; Bundtzen, Thomas K., *A History of Mining in the Kantishna Hills*, The Alaska Journal, Spring 1978.

29. Fairbanks Daily News-Miner, August 4, 1922.

30. Brooks, Alfred H., and Martin, G.C., *"The Alaska Mining Industry in 1919,"* USGS Bulletin #714, G.P.O., Washington, D.C.; Fairbanks Daily News-Miner, January 29, 1923; Bundtzen, Thomas K., *A History of Mining in the Kantishna Hills*, The Alaska Journal, Spring 1978; The Pathfinder, August, 1921.

31. The Pathfinder, June 12, 1919; Letter, Karstens, Henry P., to Cammerer, Arno B., January 10, 1922, Charles Sheldon Papers, Box 2, Folder 2, Archives, Alaska and Polar Regions Department, Rasmuson Library, University of Alaska, Fairbanks.

32. Stewart, B.D., Annual Report of the Mine Inspector to the Governor of Alaska, Alaska Territorial Mines, 1922.)

33. Ibid.

34. Testimony of James A. Wickersham, in *A Bill to Establish the Mount McKinley National Park*, Government Printing Office, May 5, 1916.

35. See: Section 6, "An act to establish the Mount McKinley National Park in the Territory of Alaska," approved February 26, 1917.

36. The Nenana News, April 23, 1921

37. Probate Records, Box 10277, Alaska State Archives; Pathfinder, December, 1922.

38. Fairbanks Daily News-Miner August 8, 1922; Kantishna Recording District, Misc. Records, Volume I; Fairbanks Daily News-Miner, May 13, 1909.

39. The Nenana News, February 10, 1919.

40. Fairbanks Daily News-Miner: July 26, 1920; April 6, 1921; February 10, 1923: Murie, Olaus, *Physiography Toklat River Region*, December 11, 1920–January 8,1921, O.J. Murie Papers, Folder # 64, Box # 2, Archives, Alaska and Polar Regions Department, Rasmuson Library, University of Alaska, Fairbanks.

41. The Nenana News, December 14, 1920.

Chapter Seven

1. Interview, Denise Abbey, November 1994.

2. The Nenana News, December 27, 1921.

3. Interview, William Nancarrow, September 30, 2001; Saleeby, Becky M., *Quest for Gold. C.R.I.M.M.*, National Park Service, Alaska Region, 2000.

4. Pearson, Grant, *Little Johnnie of Kantishna*, Alaska Sportsman, July, 1948; Interview, William Nancarrow, September 30, 2001.

5. Buzzell, Rolfe G., *Drainage Histories of the Kantishna Mining District, 1903-1968*, National Park Service Regional Office, Anchorage; Kantishna Recording District, *Deed Record Book, 1905-1919*, State of Alaska.

6. Interview, William Nancarrow, September 30, 2001.

7. Pearson, Grant, *Little Johnnie of Kantishna,* Alaska Sportsman, July, 1948.

8. Alaska Weekly: December 21, 1934; September 30, 1938.

9. Alaska Weekly, October 20, 1933.

10. Alaska Weekly: December 21, 1934, September 30, 1938; Carson, Ruth, *Joe and Fannie Quigley*, Alaska Magazine, April 1970.

11. Gudgel-Holmes, Diane, *Ethnohistory of Four Interior Alaskan Waterbodies*, State of Alaska, Department of Natural Resources, Division of Research and Development, Anchorage, 1979.

12. Kammersgard, Ed., *Minchumina Trapper*, Fur-Fish-Game Magazine, January, 1963.

13. Fairbanks Daily News Miner, January 26, 1927.

14. Fairbanks Daily News Miner: January 31, 1924; February 3, 1924.

15. Pearson, Grant, *Little Johnnie of Kantishna*, Alaska Magazine, July 1948.

16. Collins, Florence, Firm, Jo Ann, and Thiede, Diane, *Slim Carlson,* Alaska Magazine, June 1970; Rearden, Jim, *Alone in Alaska*, Outdoor Life Magazine, June, 1956.

17. Patty, Ernest N, *North Country Challenge*, David McKay Co, Inc., New York, 1969.

18. Ibid.

19. Pearson, Grant, *Fannie Quigley, Frontierswoman*, Alaska Magazine, August 1947; Meyers, Bill Oral History Tape #508, Denali National Park and Preserve Museum Collection.

20. The Nenana News, January 13, 1921.

21. Fairbanks Daily News-Miner, January 25, 1938; Tremblay, Ray, *Trails of an Alaska Trapper*, Alaska Northwest Books, Anchorage, 1983.

22. Fairbanks Daily News-Miner, March 9, 1931; *Anchorage Daily News*, July 25, 1999.

23. Collins, Florence, Firm, Jo Ann, and Thiede, Diane, *Slim Carlson*, Alaska Magazine, June 1970; Rearden, Jim, *Alone in Alaska*, Outdoor Life Magazine, June, 1956.

24. Tremblay, Ray, *Trails of an Alaska Trapper*, Alaska Northwest Books, Anchorage, 1983.

25. The Nenana News: December 2, 1919; December 22, 1919; January 31, 1920.

26. Collins, Florence, Firm, Jo Ann, and Thiede, Diane, *Slim Carlson*, Alaska Magazine, June 1970.

27. The Nenana News, November 15, 1921.

28. Kammersgard, Ed., *Minchumina Trapper*, Fur-Fish-Game Magazine, January 1962.

29. Myers, Harry M. and Myers, William A, *Back Trails*, Lapeer County, 1932.

30. Fairbanks Daily News-Miner: July 8, 1922; August 23; 1922; Probate Records, Box 17371, Alaska State Archives.

31. Fairbanks Daily News-Miner, August 23, 1922.

32. Probate Records, Box 10277, Alaska State Archives

33. Kantishna Mining Records, Deed Record Book, 1905-1919, State of Alaska; Probate Court Records, Box 17371, Alaska State Archives.

34. Myers, Harry M. and Myers, William A, *Back Trails*, Lapeer County, 1932.

35. Ibid.

36. Ibid.

37. Patty, Ernest N., *North Country Challenge*, David McKay, Co, New York, 1969.

38. Ibid.

39. Letter, Karstens, Henry P., to Sheldon, Charles, undated, circa 1914, Charles Sheldon Collection, Box 2, File 2, Archives, Alaska and Polar Regions Department, Rasmuson Library, University of Alaska, Fairbanks.

40. Davis, Mary Lee, *We Are Alaskans,* W.A. Wide Company, Boston, 1931.

41. Ibid.

42. Fairbanks Daily News-Miner, March 14, 1938; Superintendent's Monthly Report, Mount McKinley National Park, March, 1938, Denali National Park & Preserve Museum Collection; Probate Records, Box 17370, Alaska State Archives.

43. Probate Records, Box 17370, Alaska State Archives.

44. Fairbanks Daily News-Miner, January 11, 1932; Pearson, Grant, *My life of High Adventure,* Prentice-Hall, New York, NY, 1962.

45. Fairbanks Daily News-Miner, January 11, 1932; Probate Records, RG 509, Box 17370, Alaska State Archives.

46. Ernest N. Patty, *North Country Challenge,* David McKay Co, New York, 1969.

47. Probate Records, Box 18000, Alaska State Archives.

48. Marsh, Floyd R., *20 Years a Soldier of Fortune,* Binford and Mort, Portland, 1976.

CHAPTER EIGHT

1. Webb, Melody, *Yukon: The Last Frontier*, University of Nebraska Press, Lincoln, 1993.

2. Gudgel-Holmes, Diane, *Kantishna Oral History Project,* Box 2/3, Archives, University of Alaska, Anchorage; Superintendent's Monthly Report, Mount McKinley National Park, January 1924, Denali National Park & Preserve Museum Collection.

3. Superintendent's Monthly Report, Mount McKinley National Park, January 1924, Denali National Park & Preserve Museum Collection.

4. Letter, Karstens, Henry, P., to Sheldon, Charles, April 25, 1921, Charles Sheldon Papers, Box 2, Folder 2, Archives, Alaska and Polar Regions Department, Rasmuson Library, University of Alaska, Fairbanks.

5. Fairbanks Daily News-Miner: March 15, 1930; March 21, 1930; U.S. Commissioners Court of Alaska, Fourth Division, Criminal Court Case Files, 1903-1961, RG 504, Boxes 18-19, Case #396.

6. Fairbanks Daily News-Miner, October 9, 1926.

7. Stuck, Hudson, *20,000 Miles With A Dogteam,* Wolfe Publishing Inc., Prescott AZ, 1988.

8. Fairbanks Daily News-Miner, February 9, 1928.

9. Kammersgard, Ed., *Minchumina Trapper,* Fur-Fish-Game Magazine, January 1962.

10. Beach, William N., *In the Shadow of Mt. McKinley,* The Derrydale Press, New York, 1931.

11. Tremblay, Ray, *Trails of an Alaska Trapper,* Alaska Northwest Books, Anchorage, 1983; Collins, Miki and Julie, Lake Minchumina Past and Present, Students and Teachers of Minchumina Community School, 2000.

12. Fairbanks Daily News-Miner: May 8, 1919; February 14, 1924.

13. The Pathfinder, June 12, 1919.

14. Loney, Bill, *The Caribou's Boo,* Vol VI, No 2, Farthest North Collegian, March, 1928.

15. U.S. Census Bureau, Housing and Household Economic Statistics Division.

16. Fairbanks Daily News-Miner: March 28, 1926; March 24, 1927; Troyer, Will, *Records of White Moose in the McKinley Park,* Alaska Interagency Moose Meeting, May 1, 1980.

17. Pearson, Grant, *My Life of High Adventure,* Prentice-Hall, New York, 1962.

18. Marchand, Leslie, *The Farthest North Collegian,* Volume 5, No. 1, 1927.

19. Beach, William N., *The Backlog,* Campfire Club of America, Volume XI, No. 6,Feb, 1938.

20. Personal Communication, Michael Carey.

21. Rearden, Jim, Frank Glaser Interview, 1953.

22. Letter, Karstens Henry P., to Mather, Stephen T., January 4, 1924, RG 79, CCF, Box 112, File Wild Animals, NARA College Park, Md.

23. Letter, Karstens, Henry P., to Sheldon, Charles, July 16, 1921, "Historical letters," Denali National Park and Preserve Museum Collection.

CHAPTER NINE

1. Murie, Olaus, *Caribou and Reindeer,* American Forests and Forest Life, January 1924.

2. Murie, Olaus, *Caribou and Reindeer,* American Forests and Forest Life, January 1924; Anchorage Daily Times, August 18, 1923; Fairbanks Daily News Miner, August 12, 1922.

3. Murie, Olaus J., *Yukon Caribou*, North American Fauna Series, No. 54, Government Printing Office, June 1935.

4. Murie, Olaus J., Box 2, Folder 64, Physiography Toklat River Region, Olaus J. Murie Papers, Archives, Alaska and Polar Regions Department, Rasmuson Library, University of Alaska, Fairbanks.

5. Ibid.

6. Karstens, Henry P., Journal entry, July 14, 1922, Karstens Library.

7. The Nenana News, August 12, 1922.

8. Rearden, Jim, *Alaska's Wolfman*, Pictorial Histories Publishing Co, Missoula, 1998.

9. Ibid.

10. Loftus, Jule, *Corralling Caribou—A Wilder West Sport*, Farthest North Collegian, Volume II, I, 1924.

11. *Fairbanks Daily News Miner*, August 12, 1922.

12. Rearden, Jim, *Alaska's Wolfman*, Pictorial Histories Publishing Co, Missoula, 1998.

13. Murie, Adolph, Box 5, File Folder 1G, Journal, 1922-23, October 21, 1922, Adolph Murie Collection, Archives, Alaska and Polar Regions Department, Rasmuson Library, University of Alaska, Fairbanks.

14. Murie, Olaus, *Caribou and Reindeer*, American Forests and Forest Life, January, 1924.

15. Loftus, Jule, *Corralling Caribou—A Wilder West Sport*, Farthest North Collegian, VOL II, I, 1924.

16. Murie, Adolph, Journal Entry, date unrecorded, Box 5, File Folder 1G, Journal, 1922-23, Adolph Murie Collection, Archives, Alaska and Polar Regions Department, Rasmuson Library, University of Alaska, Fairbanks.

17. Murie, Olaus, Journal entries, July and August, 1923, Box 6, file 7, Olaus J. Murie Papers, Archives, Alaska and Polar Regions Department, Rasmuson Library, University of Alaska, Fairbanks.

18. Ibid.

19. Rearden, Jim, *Alaska's Wolfman*, Pictorial Histories Publishing Co, Missoula, 1998.

20. Loftus, Jule, *Corralling Caribou—A Wilder West Sport*, Farthest North Collegian, VOL II, I, 1924.

21. Murie, Adolph, Journal 1922-23, Box 5, File Folder 1G, Adolph Murie Collection, Archives, Alaska and Polar Regions Department, Rasmuson Library, University of Alaska, Fairbanks.

22. Superintendent's Monthly Report, Mount McKinley National Park, August and September 1924, Denali National Park & Preserve Museum Collection.

23. Superintendent's Monthly Report, Mount McKinley National Park, March 1924, Denali National Park & Preserve Museum Collection.

24. Letter, Murie, Olaus J., to Karstens, Henry P., March 14, 1924, Box 6, Olaus J. Murie Papers, Archives, Alaska and Polar Regions Department, Rasmuson Library, University of Alaska, Fairbanks.

25. Murie, Olaus J., Nesting Records of the Wandering Tattler, Volume XLI, 1924, Box 7, Folders 15 & 17, Olaus J. Murie Collection, Archives, Alaska and Polar Regions Department, Rasmuson Library, University of Alaska, Fairbanks.

26. Kreps, Bonnie, and Craighead, Charles, *Arctic Dance: The Mardy Murie Story*, Graphic Arts Center Publishing, Portland, 2002.

## Chapter Ten

1. Karstens Diary Entries, March 13, and March 20, 1923, Eugene G. Karstens, Karstens Library.

2. The Pathfinder *of Alaska*, July 1923.

3. Superintendent's Monthly Report, Mount McKinley National Park, November 1922, Denali National Park & Preserve Museum Collection.

4. Superintendent's Monthly Report, Mount McKinley National Park, April and May 1923, Denali National Park & Preserve Museum Collection.

5. Superintendent's Monthly Report, Mount McKinley National Park, November 1921, Denali National Park & Preserve Museum Collection.

6. Superintendent's Monthly Report, Mount McKinley National Park, August 1921, and April 1923, Denali National Park & Preserve Museum Collection.

7. Fairbanks Daily News-Miner, January 29, 1923; Alaska Weekly, July 3, 1923.

8. The Pathfinder of Alaska, May 1923.

9. Fairbanks Daily News-Miner, April 29, 1909.

10. AEC Annual Report, 1914, Government Printing Office, 1916.

11. Fairbanks Daily News-Miner: October 3, 1925; Oct 3, 1925; Alaska-Yukon Magazine, April, 1917.

12. Superintendent's Monthly Report, Mount McKinley National Park, January and April 1923, Denali National Park & Preserve Museum Collection.

13. Superintendent's Monthly Report, Mount McKinley National Park, March 1923, Denali National Park & Preserve Museum Collection.

14. The Pathfinder of Alaska, July 1923.

15. Letter, Cammerer, Arno B., to Karstens, Henry P., February 3, 1923, RG 79, Entry 6, Box 369, NARA, College Park, Md.; Superintendent's Monthly Report, Mount McKinley National Park, March 1923, Denali National Park & Preserve Museum Collection.

16. Pearson, Grant, *History of Mount McKinley National Park*, NPS, 1953.

17. Fairbanks Daily News-Miner: January 20, 1923; January 29, 1923; The Pathfinder of Alaska, January 1924.

18. Karstens Diary entries, May 21-July 4, 1923, courtesy of Eugene G. Karstens, Karstens Library.

19. Stroud, George S., History of the Concession at Mount McKinley National Park, NPS, March, 1985.

20. Superintendent's Monthly Report, Mount McKinley National Park, July 1923, Denali National Park & Preserve Museum Collection; Olaus Murie Diary Entry, July 9, 1923, Olaus Murie Collection, Box 13, Archives, Alaska and Polar Regions Department, Rasmuson Library, University of Alaska, Fairbanks; Pearson, Grant, A History of Mount McKinley National Park, NPS, 1953.

21. George Flood, Oral History Tapes #504 A&B, Archives Denali National Park and Preserve Museum Collection.

22. Anchorage Daily Times, August 18, 1923.

23. Liek, Harry, "Denali," The High One, Alaska Sportsman, February 1935.

24. Interview tapes, Frank Glaser, Jim Rearden Collection, 1953; George Flood, Oral History Tape #504A&B, Denali National Park and Preserve Museum Collection

25. Interview tapes, Frank Glaser, Jim Rearden Collection, 1953.

26. Interview, Woodbury "Bud" Abbey, Jr. April 8, 1998.

27. Interview, Woodbury "Bud" Abbey, Jr., April 8, 1998; George Flood, Oral History Tape #504A&B, Denali National Park and Preserve Museum Collection.

28. Interview, Denise Abbey, November 1994.

29. Olaus Murie Diary Entry, July 9, 1923, Olaus Murie Collection, Box 13, Archives, Alaska and Polar Regions Department, Rasmuson Library, University of Alaska, Fairbanks.

30. Karstens Diary Entry, July 15, 1923, courtesy Eugene G. Karstens, Karstens Library.

31. The Pathfinder *of Alaska*, November 1919.

32. *Fairbanks Daily-News Miner*, September 7, 1923.

33. Superintendent's Monthly Report, Mount McKinley National Park, May and July 1923, Denali National Park & Preserve Museum Collection.

34. Superintendent's Monthly Report, Mount McKinley National Park, June 1923, Denali National Park & Preserve Museum Collection.

35. Superintendent's Monthly Report, Mount McKinley National Park, August 1923, Denali National Park & Preserve Museum Collection; Letter, Karstens, Henry P, to Kennedy, Dan T., July 12, 1923, RG 79, Box 111, CCF, folder Annual Reports, NARA, College Park, MD.

36. Letter Kennedy, Dan T., to Karstens, Henry P., July 20, 1923, RG 79, Box 111, CCF, folder Annual Reports, NARA, College Park, MD; Anchorage Daily Times, August 18, 1923.

37. George Flood Oral History, Tape #504A&B, Archives, Denali National Park & Preserve Museum Collection.

38. Ibid.

39. Anchorage Daily Times, August 18, 1923.

CHAPTER ELEVEN

1. Karstens, Eugene Henry, *My Life*, Denali National Park & Preserve Museum Collection.

2. Ibid.

3. Superintendent's Monthly Report, Mount McKinley National Park, April and March, 1924, Denali National Park & Preserve Museum Collection.

4. Superintendent's Monthly Report, Mount McKinley National Park, December, 1924, Denali National Park & Preserve Museum Collection.

5. Karstens, Eugene Henry, *My Life*, Denali National Park & Preserve Museum Collection.

6. Ibid.

7. Ibid.

8. Ibid.

9. Ibid.

10. Ibid.

11. Ibid.

12. Ibid.

13. Karstens, Eugene Henry, *My Life*, Denali National Park & Preserve Museum Collection; Superintendent's Monthly Report, Mount McKinley National Park, November 1921, Denali National Park & Preserve Museum Collection.

14. Interview, Denise Abbey, November 1994.

15. Karstens, Eugene Henry, *My Life*, Denali National Park & Preserve Museum Collection.

16. Interview, Denise Abbey, November 1994.

17. Karstens, Eugene Henry, *My Life*, Denali National Park & Preserve Museum Collection.

18. Fairbanks Daily News-Miner, April 5, 1924.

19. Fairbanks Daily News-Miner, January 29, 1923.

20. Letter, Karstens, Henry P., to Sheldon, Charles, February 7, 1923, Charles Sheldon Collection, Box 2, File 2, Archives, Alaska and Polar Regions Department, Rasmuson Library, University of Alaska, Fairbanks; Interview, Denise Abbey, November 1994.

21. Cole, Martin, *Journey to Caribou Land*, Cole Revocable Trust #1, Whittier, CA, 1983.

22. Fairbanks Daily News-Miner, July 23, 1924.

23. Interview tapes, Frank Glaser, 1953, Jim Rearden Collection.

24. Ibid.

25. Ibid.

26. Geburtsschein #50/1876, Bureau of Vital Statistics, German Democratic Republic, Frankfurt; RG 94, Unit Records, Enlistment Papers, Henry Lucke, 7W2 1894-1912, 7/1/F, Box 805, NARA, Washington, D.C.; Interview, William Stroecker, June 12, 1992.

27. Tanana Weekly Miner, November 23, 1906.

28. Fairbanks Daily News-Miner: March 25, 1914; June 29, 1914; September 9, 1914.

29. Beach, William N., *In the Shadow of Mt. McKinley*, Derrydale Press, New York, 1931; Fairbanks Daily News-Miner: May 29, 1922; April 14, 1923.

30. Interview, William Stroecker, June 12, 1992.

31. Superintendent's Monthly Report, Mount McKinley National Park, November 1924, Denali National Park & Preserve Museum Collection.

32. Interview, William Stroecker, June 12, 1992.

33. The Nenana News, May 19, 1917.

34. The Nenana News, July 12, 1918.

35. U.S. Commissioners Court of Alaska, Fourth Division, Criminal Court Case Files, 1903-1961, Case 44, 4/13/1918, RG 504, Boxes 18-19, Alaska State Archives, Juneau.

36. The Nenana News: April 4, 1918; April 17, 1918.

37. Interview, Denise Abbey, November 1994.

38. Interview, Peter Bagoy, November 23, 1995.

39. Ibid.

40. Superintendent's Monthly Report, Mount McKinley National Park, January 31, 1924, Denali National Park & Preserve Museum Collection; Fairbanks Daily News-Miner, April 19, 1924; Olaus

Murie Diary Entry, January 1920, Box 6, FF 7, Olaus Murie Collection, Box 13, Archives, Alaska and Polar Regions Department, Rasmuson Library, University of Alaska, Fairbanks.

41. Interview, Peter Bagoy, March 30, 1996.

42. Fisher, Churchill, *Healy Storekeeper*, Alaska Sportsman, November 1942.

43. Fairbanks Daily News-Miner August 4, 1934; Prince, Bernadine L., *The Alaska Railroad in Pictures*, 1914-1964, Ken Wray Print Shop, Anchorage, 1964; Interview, William Nancarrow, December, 2006.

44. Interview, Peter Bagoy, March 30, 1996; Letter, Carlisle, Harvey K, to Commissioner, General Land Office, May 4, 1933, Historical Letters File, Denali Park & Preserve Museum Collection.

45. Interview, Peter Bagoy, March 30, 1996.

46. Interview, William Nancarrow, January 16, 2001.

Chapter Twelve

1. Fairbanks Daily News-Miner: September 15, 1923; June 24, 1924; Nenana Recording District Probate Records, Box 17371, Alaska State Archives, Juneau.

2. Nenana Recording District Probate Records, Box 17371, Alaska State Archives, Juneau.

3. Polk Directories, 1901-12; Fairbanks Genealogical Society Databases; Fairbanks Daily News-Miner, July 14, 1908.

4. US District Court, Alaska Criminal Case Files, RG 21, Box 43, Case File 917, NARA, College Park, MD; Anchorage Times, May 28, 1931

5. Fairbanks Daily News-Miner: September 15, 1923; June 24, 1924; Nenana Recording District Probate Records, Box 17371, Alaska State Archives, Juneau.

6. Fairbanks Daily News-Miner: September 15, 1923; June 24, 1924; Dodson, Peggy Rouch, *Girl in the Gold Camp*. Epicenter Press, Seattle, 1996; Nenana Recording District Probate Records, Box 17371, Alaska State Archives, Juneau.

7. Fairbanks Daily News-Miner: September 15, 1923; June 24, 1924; Nenana Recording District Probate Records, Box 17371, Alaska State Archives.

8. Fairbanks Daily News-Miner: July 16, 1908; May 14, 1919.

9. Fairbanks Daily News-Miner: September 15, 1923; June 24, 1924; Nenana Recording District Probate Records, Box 17371, Alaska State Archives, Juneau.

10. Interview, Walter Teeland, April 24, 1991.

11. Superintendent's Monthly Report, Mount McKinley National Park, March 1932, Denali National Park & Preserve Museum Collection.

12. Interview, Peter Bagoy, November 1995; Superintendent's Monthly Report, Mount McKinley National Park, November 1934, Denali National Park & Preserve Museum Collection; Nenana District Probate Records, Box 18031, Alaska State Archives.

13. Fairbanks Daily News-Miner, February 14, 1923; The Nenana News, February 22, 1923; Denali National Park and Preserve Land Records, National Park Service Regional Office, Anchorage.

14. The Nenana News, August 1, 1922; Fairbanks Daily News-Miner, April 9, 1924.

15. Alaska Sportsman, December, 1949.

16. Interview, Berle Mercer, April, 1991; Interview, William Waugaman, Sr. October 25, 1998; Interview, Peter Bagoy, November 1995.

17. Interview, Peter Bagoy, November 1995; Fairbanks Daily Times, September 20, 1909.

18. Pearson, Grant, *A History of Mt. McKinley National Park*, National Park Service, 1953.

19. The Nenana News: January 7, 1922; January 10, 1922; Letter, Kennedy, Dan T., to Karstens, Henry P., July 20, 1923, RG 79, CCF, Box 111, Folder: Annual Reports, NARA, College Park, Md.; Fairbanks Daily News-Miner, January 19, 1931; Land Records, Denali National Park and Preserve, NPS Regional Office, Anchorage.

20. The Pathfinder of Alaska, April, 1923; Fairbanks Daily News-Miner, September 2, 1924; Nenana Recording District Records, Entry #3317, Box 2, Page 496; H.K. Carlisle Report, April 26, 1933, General Land Office, Washington, Denali National Park & Preserve Museum Collection.

21. Letter, Stubbs, D.E. to Black, Loring M., March 19,1934, Attachment to SB 2238, HR 6177, Payment of Damages, Government Printing Office, Washington, D.C.; Fairbanks Daily News-Miner,

May 25, 1926; Hoyt, Norma, Oral History tape #513, February 9, 1982, Denali National Park & Preserve Museum Collection.

22. Fairbanks Daily News-Miner: August 25, 1925; August 2, 1930.

23. Letter, Stubbs, D.E., to Mather, Stephen T., November 27, 1924, RG 79, CCF, Box 110, folder Lands General, NARA, College Park, MD.

24. Fairbanks Daily Times: August 22, 1911; September 9, 1911.

25. Fairbanks Daily News-Miner: May 20, 1921, July 22, 1921.

26. Fairbanks Daily News-Miner: March 10, 1922; October 12, 1922; January 19, 1931; Interview, Peter Bagoy, November 1995; Nyberg, Fritz, Oral History tape #509B, Denali National Park & Preserve Museum Collection.

27. Letter, Bunnell, Charles, to Cammerer, Arno B., November 6, 1924, Charles Bunnell Collection, Box 10, File 188, Archives, Alaska and Polar Regions Department, Rasmuson Library, University of Alaska, Fairbanks; The Pathfinder of Alaska, May 1922.

28. Letter, Stubbs, D.E., to Liek, Harry J., October 19, 1932, Historical Letters File, Denali National Park & Preserve Museum Collection.

29. Henry P. Karstens Journal Entry, Dec 29, 1924, courtesy of Ken Karstens, Karstens Library.

30. The Pathfinder of Alaska, May 1922; Interview, Peter Bagoy, November, 1995.

31. Superintendent's Monthly Report, Mount McKinley National Park, April 1922, Denali National Park & Preserve Museum Collection.

32. Superintendent's Monthly Report, Mount McKinley National Park, January 1924, Denali National Park & Preserve Museum Collection.

33. Ibid.

34. Superintendent's Monthly Report, Mount McKinley National Park, January 1924, and October 16, 1924, Denali National Park & Preserve Museum Collection; Letter, Karstens, Henry P., to Mather, Stephen T., January 4, 1924, RG 79, CCF, Box 112, File Wild Animals, NARA, College Park, Md.

35. Superintendent's Monthly Report, Mount McKinley National Park, January 1924, Denali National Park & Preserve Museum Collection.

36. Superintendent's Monthly Report, Mount McKinley National Park, February 1924, Denali National Park & Preserve Museum Collection.

37. Ibid.

38. Ibid.

39. Letter, Karstens, Henry P., to Sheldon, Charles, May 21, 1923, Box 2, File 2, Charles Sheldon papers, Archives, Alaska and Polar Regions Department, Rasmuson Library, University of Alaska, Fairbanks.

40. Superintendent's Monthly Report, Mount McKinley National Park, April 1924, Denali National Park & Preserve Museum Collection.

41. Ibid.

42. Work, Hubert, Annual report of the Secretary of the Interior, 1923, GPO, Washington, 1924; The Pathfinder of Alaska, January, 1923.

43. The Pathfinder of Alaska, January 1924.

Chapter Thirteen

1. Superintendent's Monthly Report, Mount McKinley National Park, July 1924, Denali National Park & Preserve Museum Collection.

2. Fairbanks Daily News-Miner, July 15, 1924..

3. Superintendent's Monthly Report, Mount McKinley National Park, July 1924, Denali National Park & Preserve Museum Collection.

4. Fairbanks Daily News-Miner, July 15, 1924.

5. Karstens, Eugene Henry, *My Life*, Denali National Park & Preserve Museum Collection.

6. Fairbanks Daily News-Miner, July 25, 1924.

7. Superintendent's Monthly Report, Mount McKinley National Park, July 1924, Denali National Park & Preserve Museum Collection.

8. Fairbanks Daily News-Miner, July 31, 1924.

9. Superintendent's Monthly Report, Mount McKinley National Park, June 1924, Denali National Park & Preserve Museum Collection.

10. Ibid.

11. Fairbanks Daily News-Miner, June 24, 1924.

12. Telegram, Letter, and Affidavit, Karstens, Henry P., to Pullman Company, November 5, 1923, RG 79, Entry 6, Box 369, NARA, College Park, MD.

13. Superintendent's Monthly Report, Mount McKinley National Park, December 1923, Denali National Park & Preserve Museum Collection.

14. Fairbanks Daily News-Miner: September 31, 1923; April 9, 1924; May 7, 1924; June 10, 1924.

15. Superintendent's Monthly Report, Mount McKinley National Park, June 1924, Denali National Park & Preserve Museum Collection.

16. Letter to the Editor, Jon Way, *Alaska Magazine*, May, 1966.

17. Superintendent's Monthly Report, Mount McKinley National Park, June 1924, Denali National Park & Preserve Museum Collection.

18. Superintendent's Monthly Report, Mount McKinley National Park, August 1924, Denali National Park & Preserve Museum Collection; Henry P. Karstens, Journal Entry, August 12, 1924, Karstens Library.

19. Ibid.

20. Henry P. Karstens, Journal Entries, August 12-16, 1924, Karstens Library.

21. Superintendent's Monthly Report, Mount McKinley National Park, August 1924, Denali National Park & Preserve Museum Collection.

22. Ibid.

23. Ibid.

24. Ibid.

25. Ibid.

26. Superintendent's Monthly Report, Mount McKinley National Park, September 1924, Denali National Park & Preserve Museum Collection.

27. Superintendent's Monthly Report, Mount McKinley National Park, August 1924, Denali National Park & Preserve Museum Collection.

28. Personal Communication, Eugene Gregory Karstens, December 2007.

29. Letter, Karstens, Henry P., to Sheldon, Charles, February 7, 1923, Box 2, Folder 2, Charles Sheldon Papers, Archives, Alaska and Polar Regions Department, Rasmuson Library, University of Alaska, Fairbanks; Letter, Karstens, Henry P., to Cammerer, Arno B., January 10, 1922, Historical Letters File, Denali National Park& Preserve Museum Collection.

30. Letter, Karstens, Henry P., to Cammerer, Arno B., January 10, 1922, Historical Letters File, Denali National Park & Preserve Museum Collection.

31. Letter, Karstens, Henry P., to Sheldon, Charles, February 7, 1923, Box 2, Folder 2, Charles Sheldon Papers, Archives, Alaska and Polar Regions Department, Rasmuson Library, University of Alaska, Fairbanks.

32. Fritz Nyberg, Oral History tape #509A, Denali National Park & Preserve Museum Collection.

33. Obituary, Anchorage Times, May 8, 1985; Rhodes, Herb, *Tales of the Great Land*, undated, Denali National Park & Preserve Museum Collection; Fritz Nyberg, Oral History Tape #509A, Denali National Park & Preserve Museum Collection.

34. Ranger Patrol Monthly Record, December 1924, Denali National Park & Preserve Museum Collection.

35. Interview, William Nancarrow, March 15, 1998.

36. Superintendent's Monthly Report, Mount McKinley National Park, October 1922, Denali National Park & Preserve Museum Collection.

37. Alaska Daily Empire, March 28, 1923; Fairbanks Daily News-Miner: February 14, 1923; February 25, 1924; March 5, 1924; June 20, 1924.

38. Fairbanks Daily News-Miner, July 23, 1924.

39. Superintendent's Monthly Reports, Mount McKinley National Park, April, May, June, and September 1924, Denali National Park & Preserve Museum Collection.

40. Fairbanks Daily News-Miner, June 24, 1924.

41. Superintendent's Monthly Report, Mount McKinley National Park, September 1924, Denali National Park & Preserve Museum Collection.

42. Superintendent's Monthly Report, Mount McKinley National Park, October 1924, Denali National Park & Preserve Museum Collection.

43. Ibid.

44. Ibid.

45. Ibid.

46. Ibid.

47. Ibid.

48. Superintendent's Monthly Report, Mount McKinley National Park, November 1924, Denali National Park & Preserve Museum Collection.

49. Superintendent's Monthly Report, Mount McKinley National Park, October 1924, Denali National Park & Preserve Museum Collection.

50. The Nenana News, Dec 31, 1921.

51. Superintendent's Monthly Report, Mount McKinley National Park, November 1924, Denali National Park & Preserve Museum Collection.

52. Letter, Karstens, Henry P. to the Director, Mather, Stephen T., November 18, 1924, RG 79, CCF, Box 112, File Wild Animals, NARA, College Park, MD.

53. Superintendent's Monthly Report, Mount McKinley National Park, November 1924, Denali National Park & Preserve Museum Collection; Letter, Karstens, Henry P. to the Director, Mather, Stephen T., November 18, 1924, RG 79, CCF, Box 112, File Wild Animals, NARA, College Park, MD.

54. Fairbanks Daily News-Miner: October 3, 1906; November 5, 1908; June 12, 1908; March 24, 1909; January 4, 1910; Fairbanks Sunday Times, December 25, 1910.

55. Superintendent's Monthly Report, Mount McKinley National Park, October 1924, Denali National Park & Preserve Museum Collection;

56. Letter, Cammerer, Arno B., to Karstens, Henry P., December 23, 1924, RG 79, CCF, Box 111, Wild Animals NARA, College Park, Md.

57. Superintendent's Monthly Report, Mount McKinley National Park, November 1924, Denali National Park & Preserve Museum Collection.

58. Superintendent's Monthly Report, Mount McKinley National Park, December 1924, Denali National Park & Preserve Museum Collection;

59. Ibid.

## Chapter Fourteen

1. Post Office Department, Office of Inspector, Case #2462H, June 29, 1925, RG 79, Records of the National Park Service, General Files, Central Files 1907-1939, Entry P9, Box 110, NARA, College Park, Md.

2. Letter, Burnham John B., to Sheldon, Charles, October 15, 1923, and Letter, Demaray, A. E. to Cammerer, Arno B., October 17, 1923, and Telegram, Demaray to Cammerer, October 22, 1923, RG 79, Entry 6, Box 369, NARA, College Park, Md.

3. Letter, Baker, John, to Mather, Stephen T., March 22, 1924, RG 79, Records of the National Park Service, Central Files, 1907-1939, Entry P9, Box 110, Employment Applications, NARA, College Park, Md.

4. Letter, Sterling, Hawley, to Mather, Stephen T., January 12, 1924, RG 79, Records of the National Park Service, Central Files, 1907-1939, Entry P9, Box 110, Employment Applications, NARA, College Park, Md.

5. Letter, Stowe, A.F., to Cammerer, Arno B., January 31, 1925, RG 79, Records of the National Park Service, Central Files, 1907-1939, Entry P9, Box 110, Employment Applications, NARA, College Park, Md.

6. Telegrams, Cammerer, Arno B., to Karstens, Henry P., January 23, 1924, and January 26, 1924, RG 79, Entry 6, Box 369, NARA, College Park, Md..

7. Letter, Murie, Olaus, to Karstens, Henry P., March 14, 1924, RG 79, Entry 6, Box 369, NARA, College Park, Md.

8. Ibid.

9. Letter, Karstens, Henry P., to Murie, Olaus, March 25, 1924, RG 79, Entry 6, Box 369, NARA, College Park, Md.

10. Ibid.

11. Letter, Cammerer, Arno B., to Karstens, Henry P., April 10, 1924, RG 79, Entry 6, Box 369, NARA, College Park, Md.

12. Letter, Karstens, Henry P., to Sheldon, Charles, January 12, 1922, Box 2, Folder 2, Charles Sheldon Papers, Archives, Alaska and Polar Regions Department, Rasmuson Library, University of Alaska, Fairbanks; Albright, Horace M., *The Birth of the National Park Service, The Founding Years, 1913-33*, Howe Brothers, Salt Lake City, 1985.

13. Fritz Nyberg and Bill Meyers, Oral History Tape #509B, Denali National Park & Preserve Museum Collection; Interview Peter J. Bagoy, February 20, 1997.

14. Letter, Degen, Robert H, to Cammerer, Arno B., January 20, 1924, and Letter, Cammerer Arno B., to Degen, Robert H., February 9, 1924, RG 79, Entry 6, Box 369 NARA, College Park, Md.

15. Letter, Parks, George A., to Mather, Stephen T., April 15, 1925, RG 79, Entry 6, Box 369, NARA, College Park, Md.

16. Letter, Mather, Stephen T., to Parks, George A., April 27, 1925, RG 79, Entry 6, Box 369, NARA, College Park, Md.

17. Telegram, Sexton, George, to Cammerer, Arno B., September 21, 1925, RG 79, Entry 6, Box 369, NARA, College Park, Md.

18. Telegram, Cammerer, Arno B., to Kraebel, July 28, 1925, and Letter, Cammerer, Arno B., to Sexton, George, September 21, 1925, RG 79, Entry 6, Box 369, NARA, College Park, Md.

19. Letter, Stowe, A.F., to Cammerer, A.B., March 23, 1925, RG 79, Records of the National Park Service, Central Files, 1907-1939, Entry P9, Box 110, Employment Applications, NARA, College Park, Md.

20. Post Office Department, Office of Inspector, Case #2462H, June 29, 1925, RG 79, Records of the National Park Service, General Files, Central Files 1907-1939, Entry P9, Box 110, NARA, College Park, Md.

21. Ibid.

22. Ibid.

23. Ibid.

24. Ibid.

25. Ibid.

26. Letter, Bunnell, Charles E., to Cammerer, Arno B., November 6, 1924, Charles E. Bunnell Collection, Box 10, File 188, Archives, Alaska and Polar Regions Department, Rasmuson Library, University of Alaska, Fairbanks

27. Letter, Anonymous to Nelson, E.W., July, 1925, RG 79, Entry 6, Box 369, NARA, College Park, Md.

28. Post Office Department, Office of Inspector, Case #2462H, June 29, 1925, RG 79, Records of the National Park Service, General Files, Central Files 1907-1939, Entry P9, Box 110, NARA, College Park, Md.

29. Diary Entry, Henry P. Karstens, June 25, 1925, courtesy of Eugene G. Karstens, Karstens Library.

30. Post Office Department, Office of Inspector, Case #2462H, June 29, 1925, RG 79, Records of the National Park Service, General Files, Central Files 1907-1939, Entry P9, Box 110, NARA, College Park, Md.

31. Letter, Evarts, Hal G., to Mather, Stephen T., undated, and Telegram, Evarts, Hal G., to Mather, Stephen T., August 25, 1925, RG 79, Entry 6, Box 369, NARA, College Park, Md.

32. Albright, Horace M., *The Birth of the National Park Service, the Founding Years, 1913-33*, Howe Brothers, Salt Lake City, 1985

33. Ibid.

34. New York Times, August 31, 1925.

35. Albright, Horace M., *The Birth of the National Park Service, the Founding Years,* 1913-33, Howe Brothers, Salt Lake City, 1985.

36. Letter, Karstens, Henry P., to Mather, Stephen T., November 5, 1925, RG 79, Entry 6, Box 369, NARA, College Park, Md.

37. Letter, Karstens, Henry P., to Mather, Stephen T., February 26, 1925, and Letter, Mather, Stephen T., to Karstens, Henry P., March 15, 1926, and Letter, Demaray, A.E., to Evarts, Hal G., February 13, 1926, RG 79, Entry 6, Box 369 NARA, College Park, Md.

38. Alaska Weekly, November 5, 1926.

39. Karstens, Eugene Henry, *My Life*, Denali National Park & Preserve Museum Collection.

40. Karstens, Eugene Henry, *My Life*, Denali National Park & Preserve Museum Collection; Fairbanks Daily News-Miner: June 10, 1924; September 19, 1924; July 29, 1925.

41. Pearson, Grant, with Newill, Philip, *My life of High Adventure*, Prentice Hall, New Jersey, 1962.

42. Superintendent's Monthly Report, Mount McKinley National Park, January 1926, Denali National Park & Preserve Museum Collection.

43. Superintendent's Monthly Report, Mount McKinley National Park, December 1925, Denali National Park & Preserve Museum Collection.

CHAPTER FIFTEEN

1. Mt. McKinley National Park, Ranger Patrol Report, December 1924, Denali National Park & Preserve Museum Collection; Mt. McKinley National Park, National Weather Service Cooperative Weather Station Records, Denali National Park and Preserve Museum Collection.

2. Letter, Karstens, Henry P., to Sheldon, Charles, May 21, 1923, Charles Sheldon Papers, Box 2, File 2, Archives, Alaska and Polar Regions Department, Rasmuson Library, University of Alaska, Fairbanks; Letter, Karstens, Henry P., to Mather, Stephen T., April 15, 1926, RG 79, Entry 6, Box 369, NARA, College Park, Md.

3. Albright, Horace M., *The Birth of the National Park Service, 1913-33*, Howe Brothers, Salt Lake, 1985; NPS 75th Anniversary Brochure, *National Park Rangers, Generations of Change*,1991.

4. Superintendent's Monthly Report, Mount McKinley National Park, September 1924, Denali National Park & Preserve Museum Collection.

5. Fritz Nyberg, Oral History Tape #509A, June 19, 1979, Denali National Park & Preserve Museum Collection.

6. Letter, Karstens, Henry P., to Mather, Stephen T., February 26, 1926, RG 79, Entry 6, Box 369, NARA, College Park. Md.

7. Letter, Karstens, Henry P., to Mather, Stephen T., February 4, 1926, RG 79, Entry 6, Box 369, NARA, College Park. Md.; Superintendent's Monthly Report, Mount McKinley National Park, January 1926, Denali National Park & Preserve Museum Collection; Fritz Nyberg, Oral History Tape #509A, June 19, 1979, Denali National Park & Preserve Museum Collection.

8. Fritz Nyberg, Oral History Tape #509A, June 19, 1979, Denali National Park & Preserve Museum Collection.

9. Superintendent's Monthly Report Mount McKinley National Park, September 1925, Denali National Park & Preserve Museum Collection.

10. Fritz Nyberg, Oral History Tape #509B, Denali National Park & Preserve Museum Collection.

11. Superintendent's Monthly Reports, Mount McKinley National Park, February 1926, May 1927, April 1928, Denali National Park & Preserve Museum Collection.

12. Superintendent's Monthly Report, Mount McKinley National Park, November 1925, Denali National Park & Preserve Museum Collection.

13. Superintendent's Monthly Report, Mount McKinley National Park, March 1927, Denali National Park & Preserve Museum Collection.

14. Fairbanks Daily News-Miner, September 10, 1925.

15. Superintendent's Monthly Report, Mount McKinley National Park, March 1926, Denali National Park & Preserve Museum Collection.

16. Ibid.

17. Fritz Nyberg, Oral History Tape #509A, Denali Park & Preserve Museum Collection; Letter, Karstens, Henry P., to Mather, Stephen T., February 26, 1926, RG 79, Entry 6, Box 369, NARA, College Park, Md.

18. Pearson, Grant, with Newill, Philip, *My Life of High Adventure*, Prentice Hall, New Jersey, 1962.

19. Ibid.

20. Ibid.

21. Ibid.

22. Ibid.

23. Letter, Karstens, Henry P., to Mather, Stephen T., February 26, 1926, RG 79, Entry 6, Box 369, NARA, College Park, Md.

24. Ibid.

25. Pearson, Grant, with Newill, Philip, *My Life Of High Adventure*, Prentice Hall, New Jersey, 1962.

26. Fritz Nyberg, Oral History Tape #509A, Denali Park & Preserve Museum Collection.

27. Mt. McKinley National Park, Ranger Patrol Report, December 1924, Denali National Park & Preserve Museum Collection.

28. Ibid.

29. Interview, William Nancarrow, March 15, 1998.

30. Pearson, Grant, with Newill, Philip, *My Life of High Adventure*, Prentice Hall, New Jersey, 1962.

31. Mt. McKinley National Park, Ranger Patrol Report, March 1927, Denali National Park & Preserve Museum Collection.

32. Organizational chart, Mt McKinley National Park., RG 79, Entry 7, Box 1404, NARA, College Park, Md.

33. Karstens, Eugene Henry, *My Life*, Denali National Park & Preserve Museum Collection.

34. Letters, Karstens, Henry P., to Mather, Stephen T., February 4, 1926, and Karstens, Henry P., to Mather, Stephen T., February 26, 1926, RG 79, Entry 6, Box 369, NARA, College Park, Md; Fritz Nyberg, Oral History Tape #509B, Denali National Park & Preserve Museum Collection.

35. Superintendent's Monthly Report, Mount McKinley National Park, January 1924, Denali National Park & Preserve Museum Collection; Fairbanks Daily News-Miner, November 22, 1913.

36. Letter, Karstens, Henry P., to Mather, Stephen T., April 15, 1926, RG 79, Entry 6, Box 369, NARA, College Park, Md.; Department of the Interior, Report of the Director of the National Park Service, 1924, Government Printing Office, Washington, DC.

37. Superintendent's Monthly Report, Mount McKinley National Park, March 1926, Denali National Park & Preserve Museum Collection.

38. Letters, Karstens, Henry P., to Mather, Stephen T., February 4, 1926, and Karstens, Henry P., to Mather, Stephen T., February 26, 1926, RG 79, Entry 6, Box 369, NARA, College Park, Md.

39. Letter, Parks, George, to Mather, Stephen T., March 12, 1926, RG 79, Entry 6, Box 369, NARA, College Park, Md.

40. Superintendent's Monthly Report, Mount McKinley National Park, December 1927, Denali National Park & Preserve Museum Collection.

41. Superintendent's Monthly Report, Mount McKinley National Park, October 1927, Denali National Park & Preserve Museum Collection.

42. Superintendent's Monthly Report, Mount McKinley National Park, April 1927, Denali National Park & Preserve Museum Collection.

43. Superintendent's Monthly Report, Mount McKinley National Park, May 1927, Denali National Park & Preserve Museum Collection.

44. Superintendent's Monthly Report, Mount McKinley National Park, January 1926, Denali National Park & Preserve Museum Collection.

45. See: The Alaska Game Law of 1925, Reg. 14, GPO, Washington, D.C.

46. Bill Meyers, Oral History Tape #508, Denali National Park & Preserve Museum Collection.

47. Superintendent's Monthly Reports, Mount McKinley National Park, August 1926 and February 1928, Denali National Park & Preserve Museum Collection.

48. Department of the Interior, Report of the Director of the National Park Service, 1922, Government Printing Office, Washington, DC; Catton, Theodore, *Inhabited Wilderness: Indians and Eskimos in Alaska*, University of New Mexico press, Albuquerque, 1997.

49. Moore, Eugene G., *Hounding Hounds About McKinley*, The Farthest North Collegian, Vol. 6, No.3, June 1928.

50. Ibid.

51. Fritz Nyberg, Oral History Tape #509A, Denali National Park & Preserve Museum Collection.

52. Mt. McKinley National Park, Ranger Patrol Report, December 1924, Denali National Park & Preserve Museum Collection; Evarts, Hal G., *Game in the Foreground*, The Saturday Evening Post, May 22, 1926.

53. Pearson, Grant, with Newill, Philip, *My Life Of High Adventure*, Prentice Hall, New Jersey, 1962.

54. Fairbanks Daily News-Miner, September 3, 1926.

55. Ibid.

56. Superintendent's Monthly Report, Mount McKinley National Park, February 1927, Denali National Park & Preserve Museum Collection.

57. Ibid.

CHAPTER SIXTEEN

1. Interview, Peter Bagoy, November, 1995.

2. Letter, Karstens, Henry P., October 3, 1921, RG 79, Entry 6, General Files, Mt. McKinley National Park, Box 379, NARA, College Park, Md.

3. Letters, Mather, Stephen T., to Steese, James Gordon, March through June, 1921, Central File 1907-33, Record Group 79, NARA, College Park, Md.

4. Fairbanks Daily News-Miner: August 7, 1920; May 24, 1923; October 25, 1923; January 12, 1924; January 24, 1924; May 21, 1924; May 26, 1924.

5. Superintendent's Monthly Report, Mt. McKinley National Park, February 1924, Denali National Park & Preserve Museum Collection.

6. Superintendent's Monthly Report, Mt. McKinley National Park, May 1924, Denali National Park & Preserve Museum Collection.

7. Fairbanks Daily News-Miner: May 26, 1924; July 12, 1924; July 23, 1924; September 4, 1924; Annual Reports of the Alaska Road Commission, FY 1923, Alaska Road Commission Collection, Alaska State Library, Juneau.

8. Fairbanks Daily News-Miner, September 4, 1924.

9. Beach, William N., *In the Shadow of Mt. McKinley*, Derrydale Press, New York, 1931.

10. Fairbanks Daily News-Miner, July 8, 1925.

11. Superintendent's Monthly Report, Mt. McKinley National Park, May 1924, Denali National Park & Preserve Museum Collection; Karstens, Henry P., *Mount McKinley National Park*, The Pathfinder of Alaska, Volume 5, No. 9, July, 1924.

12. Fairbanks Daily News-Miner, August 4, 1924.

13. Fairbanks Daily News-Miner: August 8, 1924; September 11, 1924.

14. Superintendent's Monthly Report, Mt. McKinley National Park, May 1928, Denali National Park & Preserve Museum Collection.

15. Henry P. Karstens, Journal Entry, Courtesy of Ken Karstens, Karstens Library.

16. Superintendent's Monthly Report, Mt. McKinley National Park, May 1924, Denali National Park & Preserve Museum Collection; see Henry P. Karstens, Journal Entries, May and June, 1924, Ken Karstens, Archivist, Karstens Library.

17. Interview, Walter Teeland, April 23, 1991.

18. Ibid.

19. Ibid.

20. Ibid.

21. Interview, Peter Bagoy, March 30, 1996.

22. Ibid.

23. Cole, Martin, *Journey to Caribou Land*, Cole Revocable Trust #1, Whittier, 1983.

24. Mackenzie, Clara Childs, *Wolf Smeller, A Biography of John Fredson, Native Alaskan*, Alaska Pacific University Press, Anchorage, 1985.

25. Interview, Walter Teeland, April 23, 1991.

26. Ibid.

27. Interview, Peter Bagoy, March 30, 1996.

28. Interview, Walter Teeland, April 23, 1991.

29. Cole, Martin, *Journey to Caribou Land*, Cole Revocable Trust #1, Whittier, 1983.

30. Interview, Peter Bagoy, November, 1995.

31. Superintendent's Monthly Report, Mt. McKinley National Park, May 1926, Denali National Park & Preserve Museum Collection.

32. Fairbanks Daily News-Miner, March 8, 1927.

33. McClelland, Linda Flint, *Building the National Parks*, The Johns Hopkins University Press, Baltimore and London, 1998; Superintendent's Monthly Report, Mt. McKinley National Park, May 1921, Denali National Park & Preserve Museum Collection; Alaska Road Commission Annual Report, FY 1939, Alaska Road Commission Collection, Alaska State Library, Juneau.

34. Fairbanks Daily News-Miner, February 15, 1927.

35. Fairbanks Daily News-Miner, November 29, 1926.

36. Fairbanks Daily News-Miner: May 19, 1927; August 27, 1928; Superintendent's Monthly Report, Mt. McKinley National Park, July 1928, Denali National Park & Preserve Museum Collection.

37. Interview, Oliver Onka, November 1995.

38. Interview, Walter Teeland, April 23, 1991.

39. Ibid.

40. Superintendent's Monthly Reports, Mt. McKinley National Park, May 1921, and November 1927, Denali National Park & Preserve Museum Collection.

41. Interview, Peter Bagoy, March 30, 1996; Fairbanks Daily News-Miner: January 6, 1930; October 21, 1930.

42. Interview, Peter Bagoy, March 30, 1996.

43. Ibid.

44. Fairbanks Daily News-Miner: January 6, 1930; June 4, 1930; July 21, 1931; July 23, 1931; January 14, 1932.

45. Fairbanks Daily News-Miner: June 18, 1931; August 18, 1931; Alaska Road Commission Annual Reports, FY 1923 to FY 1937, Alaska Road Commission Collection, Alaska State Library, Juneau.

46. Alaska Weekly, March 29, 1929.

47. Fairbanks Daily News-Miner, April 20, 1931.

48. Fairbanks Daily News-Miner, October 9, 1926.

49. Henry P. Karstens, Journal Entry, April 20, 1926, Courtesy of Ken Karstens, Karstens Library.

## Chapter Seventeen

1. Letter, Dixon, Joseph S., to Sheldon, Charles, March 22, 1927, Box 42, Folder 2, Record Unit 7364, Series 1, Edward W. Nelson Collection, Smithsonian Institution, Washington, D.C.

2. Letter, Dixon, Joseph S., to Sheldon, Charles, March 22, 1927, Box 42, Folder 2, Record Unit 7364, Series 1, Edward W. Nelson Collection, Smithsonian Institution, Washington, DC; Wright, George M., Dixon, Joseph S., and Thompson, Ben H., *Fauna of the National Parks of the United States: A Preliminary Survey of Faunal relations in National Parks*, Fauna Series No. 1, GPO, Washington, 1933.

3. Dixon, Joseph S., *Birds and Mammals of Mt. McKinley National Park*, Fauna #3, GPO Wash, 1938.

4. Palmer, L.J., *Raising Reindeer*, GPO, Washington, DC 1927.

5. Dixon, Joseph, *The Surf-Bird's Secret*, The Condor, Volume 29, Number 1, January-February, 1927.

6. Fairbanks Daily News-Miner, June 21, 1926.

7. From Field Notes, Joseph S. Dixon, Mt. McKinley District, Alaska, May 15 to July 29, 1926, pages 1933 to 2065, Special Collections, Bancroft Library, University of California, Berkeley.

8. Ibid.

9. Ibid.

10. Ibid.

11. Ibid.

12. Letter, Dixon Joseph S., to Sheldon, Charles, March 4, 1927, Box 42, Folder 2, Record Unit 7364, Series 1, Edward W. Nelson Collection, Smithsonian Institution, Washington, DC.

13. From Field Notes, Joseph S. Dixon, Mt. McKinley District, Alaska, May 15 to July 29, 1926, pages 1933 to 2065, Special Collections, Bancroft Library, University of California, Berkeley.

14. Ibid.

15. Ibid.

16. Fritz Nyberg/Bill Meyers Oral History Tape #510A&B, Denali National Park & Preserve Museum Collection; Personal Communication, Dr. Kathryn Davis.

17. Fritz Nyberg/Bill Meyers Oral History Tape #510A&B, Denali National Park & Preserve Museum Collection.

18. Ibid.

## Chapter Eighteen

1. Superintendent's Monthly Reports, Mt. McKinley National Park, June and July 1924, Denali National Park & Preserve, Museum Collection.

2. Superintendent's Monthly Report, Mt. McKinley National Park, December 1924, Denali National Park & Preserve, Museum Collection.

3. The Curry Hotel, *The Pathfinder of Alaska*, Volume 5, No 9, July, 1924, Valdez, Alaska: AEC Railroad Menu, 1920, Candy Waugaman Collection.

4. Fairbanks Daily News-Miner, October 1925; "Ketchikan to Barrow," *Alaska Sportsman*, May 1960.

5. Fairbanks Evening News, August 1906.

6. Morgan Lael, *The Good Time Girls*, Epicenter Press, Fairbanks and Seattle, 1998; Case #314, U.S. vs Thomas A. Marquam, RG 21, US District Court, 4th Division, Fairbanks Criminal Cases 1900-1920, Box 13, #314, NARA, Alaska Regional Office, Anchorage.

7. McKinley Tourist & Transportation Company Financial Records, Box 1, Archives, Alaska and Polar Regions Department, Rasmuson Library, University of Alaska, Fairbanks.

8. Personal Communication, historian Deidre Shaw, Glacier National Park, May 1, 2008; Fairbanks Daily News-Miner, September 2, 1929.

9. Alaska Sportsman, April 1965; The Alaska Weekly, January 27, 1939; Cordova Daily Times, August 29, 1908.

10. Helena Daily Independent, January 16, 1939.

11. Fairbanks Daily News-Miner, July 21, 1975.

12. Fairbanks Daily News-Miner: October 23, 1931; February 6, 1940; February 7, 1940; February 16, 1940.

13. Hilscher, Herb and Miriam, *A Parade of Alaska History*, Alaska Mutual Savings Bank, 1976.

14. From "Ketchikan to Barrow," Alaska Magazine, May 1958.

15. Fairbanks Daily News-Miner: May 21, 1920; May 24, 1920; July 18, 1923; December 27, 1923.

16. Fritz Nyberg Oral History Tapes #509 A&B, Denali National Park & Preserve Museum Collection.

17. Fitch, Edwin M., *The Alaska Railroad*, Frederick A. Praeger, Publishers, New York, 1967; Stroud, George S., *History of the Concession at Mount McKinley National Park*, National Park Service, March, 1985; Mt. McKinley Tourist & Transportation Company Financial Records, Box 1, Archives, Alaska and Polar Regions Department, Rasmuson Library, University of Alaska, Fairbanks.

18. Fairbanks Daily News-Miner, September 4, 1926; Superintendent's Monthly Report, Mt. McKinley National Park, September 1925, Denali National Park & Preserve Museum Collection.

19. Fairbanks Daily News-Miner: July 15, 1926; July 20, 1926; August 18, 1926; June 24, 1927; April 16,1928; August 28, 1928; May 17, 1930; August 20, 1930; August 21, 1930; July 9, 1931.

20. Fairbanks Daily News-Miner: August 14, 1926; June 24, 1927.

21. Stroud, George S., *History of the Concession at Mt McKinley National Park*, NPS, March 1985.

22. Fairbanks Daily News-Miner: April 14, 1922; August 31, 1929; September 2, 1929.

## Chapter Nineteen

1. Lingo, George, *Farthest North Collegian*, Vol. VII, 32, June 1929, University of Alaska, Fairbanks.

2. Wilson, George S, *McKinley Then and Now*, Alaska Magazine, January, 1976.

3. Fairbanks Daily News-Miner, July 23, 1928.

4. Fairbanks Daily News-Miner, October 8, 1925.

5. Fairbanks Daily News-Miner, May 26, 1926.

6. Alaska Railroad Brochure, 1924, *Alaska via the McKinley Park Route*; Fairbanks Daily News-Miner, July 13, 1926.

7. Fairbanks Daily News-Miner, August 11, 1926.

8. Cordova Daily Times, Alaska Review, 1928.

9. *The Pathfinder of Alaska*, Volume 5, No. 9, July 1924, Valdez.

10. Superintendent's Monthly Reports, Mt. McKinley National Park, July 1925, Denali National Park & Preserve Museum Collection.

11. Lena Howard Oral History Tape #506, August 4, 1972, Denali National Park & Preserve Museum Collection.

12. Ibid.

13. Ibid.

14. Earl Plumb Oral History Tape, November 8, 2006, Jane Bryant interviewer, Denali National Park & Preserve Cultural Resources Collection

15. Lena Howard Oral History Tape #506, August 4, 1972, Denali National Park & Preserve Museum Collection.

16. Ibid.

17. Superintendent's Monthly Report, Mt. McKinley National Park, October 1927, Denali National Park & Preserve Museum Collection.

18. Lena Howard Oral History Tape #506, August 4, 1972, Denali National Park & Preserve Museum Collection.

19. Ibid.

20. Ibid.

21. Bill Meyers Oral History Tape #508, Denali National Park & Preserve Museum Collection.

22. Fairbanks Daily News-Miner: July 13, 1926; April 1, 1931; July 9, 1931.

23. Fairbanks Daily News-Miner, July 13, 1926.

24. Lena Howard Oral History Tape #506, August 4, 1972, Denali National Park and Preserve Museum Collection.

25. Fairbanks Daily News-Miner: June 26, 1926; July 15, 1926; July 23, 1926; September 1, 1926; September 4, 1926; February 15, 1927; Alaska Weekly, September 24, 1926.

26. Lena Howard Oral History Tape #506, August 4, 1972, Denali National Park & Preserve Museum Collection.

27. Ibid.

28. Lena Howard Oral History Tape #506, August 4, 1972, Denali National Park and Preserve Museum Collection; Fritz Nyberg/Bill Meyers Oral History Tape #510A&B, Denali National Park & Preserve Museum Collection.

29. Ordway, Fred K., *Game Paradise*, Alaska Sportsman, March 1937; Lena Howard Oral History Tape #506, August 4, 1972, Denali National Park & Preserve Museum Collection.

30. Lena Howard Oral History Tape #506, August 4, 1972, Denali National Park & Preserve Museum Collection.

31. Ibid.

32. Ibid.

33. Ibid.

34. Fairbanks Daily News-Miner, January 15, 1929.

35. Fairbanks Daily News-Miner: July 15, 1926; July 23, 1926.

36. Fairbanks Daily News-Miner, September 18, 1928.

37. Fairbanks Daily News-Miner, September 23, 1931.

38. Fairbanks Daily News-Miner, May 25, 1926.

39. Olaus Murie Journal Entry, November. 16. 1920, Maurice Creek, Box 6, File 7, Olaus J Murie Collection, Archives, Alaska and Polar Regions Department, Rasmuson Library, University of Alaska, Fairbanks.

40. Fairbanks Daily News-Miner, June 25, 1927.

41. Patty, Ernest, *North Country Challenge*, David McKay, Co, New York, 1969.

42. Interview, Jesse Wright, February 9, 2002.

43. Ibid.

44. Fairbanks Daily News-Miner, November 3, 1927.

45. Morgan, William Gerry, MD, Pamphlet, June 1, 1928, Washington, DC.

46. Interview, William Nancarrow April 20, 1999; Fairbanks Daily News-Miner: October 27, 1930; February 20, 1931; Interview, John Horn, April 20, 1999, Historian, Hearst Castle, San Simeon.

47. Mount McKinley National Park, Ranger Patrol Records, Administrative Records, W-Box 43, Denali National Park & Preserve Museum Collection.

48. Superintendent's Monthly Report, Mt. McKinley National Park, September 1927, Denali National Park & Preserve, Museum Collection.

Chapter Twenty

1. Fairbanks Daily News-Miner, May 19, 1928.

2. Fairbanks Daily News-Miner, August 23, 1928.

3. Fairbanks Daily News-Miner, June 22, 1928.

4. Fairbanks Daily News-Miner, August 23, 1928.

5. Ibid.

6. Myers, Harry M., and Myers, William A., *Back Trails*, Lapeer Michigan, 1933, Denali National Park & Preserve Museum Collection.

7. Memorandum, Arno Cammerer, March 13, 1928, RG 79, Entry 6, Box 372, NARA, College Park, Md.

8. Ibid.

9. Myers, Harry M., and Myers, William A., *Back Trails*, Lapeer, Michigan, 1933.

10. Letter, Myers, Bill, to Myers, Harry, October 15, 1928, RG 79, Entry 6, Box 372, NARA, College Park, Md.

11. Fritz Nyberg Oral History Tape #509A&B, June 19, 1979, Denali National Park & Preserve Museum Collection.

12. Ibid.

13. Letter, Myers, Bill, to Myers, Harry, October 15, 1928, RG 79, Entry 6, Box 372, NARA, College Park, Md.

14. Myers, Harry M., and Myers, William A. Myers, *Back Trails*, Lapeer, Michigan, 1933.

15. Letter, Nyberg, Fritz, to Mather, Stephen T., October 3, 1928, RG 79, Entry 6, Box 372, NARA, College Park, Md.

16. Letter, Cammerer, Arno B., to Albright, Horace, October 9, 1928, RG 79, Entry 6, Box 372, NARA, College Park, Md.

17. Fritz Nyberg Oral History Tape #509A&B, June 19, 1979, Denali National Park & Preserve, Museum Collection.

18. Letter, Myers, Bill, to Myers, Harry, October 15, 1928, RG 79, Entry 6, Box 372, NARA, College Park, Md.

19. Bill Myers Oral History Tape #508, June 19, 1979, Denali National Park & Preserve Museum Collection; Interview, Peter Bagoy, March 30, 1996.

20. Interview, Peter Bagoy, March 30, 1996.

21. Letter, Wilder, Dan, to Family, February 8, 1931, Denali National Park & Preserve Museum Collection.

22. Interview, Fritz Nyberg, October, 1976.

23. Letter, Liek, Harry J., to Albright, Horace M., February 3, 1931, RG 79, Records of the National Park Service, General Classified Files, 1907–1949, National Parks (Entry 10), Box 373, Folder 201-006, Superintendents and Custodians (Mt. McKinley National Park), 1929-1932, NARA, College Park, Md.

24. Ibid.

25. Ibid.

26. Telegram, Louisa Sheldon, Charles Sheldon Papers, Box 9, Folder 12, R.U. 7364, E.W. Nelson Collection, Smithsonian Institution.

27. Letter, Ashbel to Nelson, Edward W., September 24, 1928, Charles Sheldon Papers, Box 9, Folder 11, R.U. 7364, E.W. Nelson Collection, Smithsonian Institution.

28. Nelson, Edward W., Memorial to Charles Sheldon, *American Forest and Forest Life Magazine*, Charles Sheldon Papers, Box 24, Folder 13, R.U. 7364, E.W. Nelson Collection, Smithsonian Institution.

29. Letter, Grinnell, George Bird, to Nelson, Edward W., November 22, 1828, Charles Sheldon Papers, Box 5, Folder 4, R.U. 7364, E.W. Nelson Collection, Smithsonian Institution.

30. Interview, William Nancarrow, September 18, 2008.

31. Poem, Dennis D. Lyell, Belmont, Moffat, Scotland, Charles Sheldon Papers, Box 24, Folder 13, R.U. 7364, E.W. Nelson Collection, Smithsonian Institution.

# INDEX